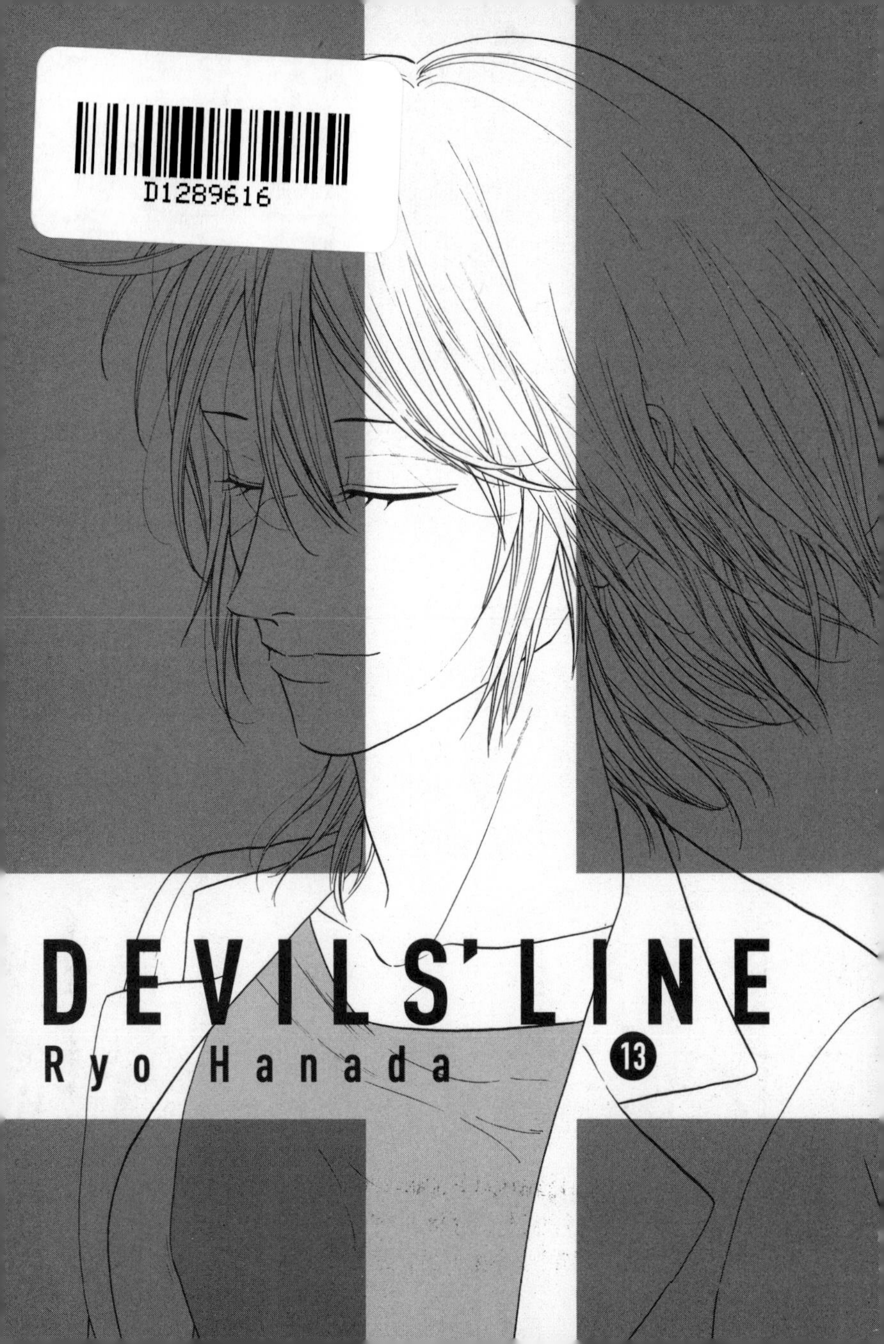
DEVILS' LINE
Ryo Hanada
13

Character and Relationship Diagram

(based on relationships up to the last volume)

TAKESHI MAKIMURA
(Zero Six)

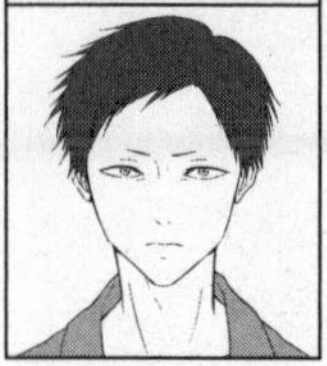

Came into contact with the CCC for an undercover investigation. Currently working with Mayu Sumimori.

NAOYA USHIO
(Zero Five)

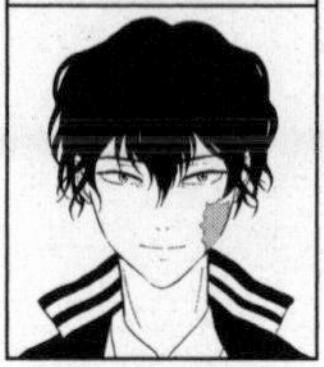

Former CCC member. He took the chance to escape police custody and is currently on the run.

KIRIO KIKUHARA
(Zero Two)

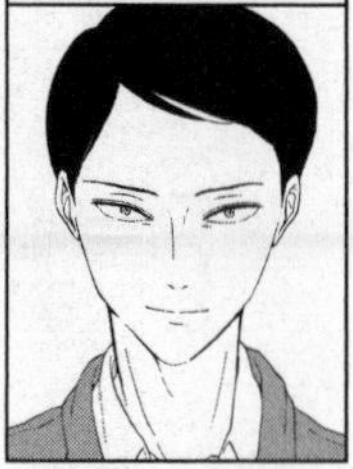

He was the leader of Public Safety Division 5's A Squad, but he was also secretly the commander of the CCC. Someone put a bomb in his car.

YUUKI ANZAI

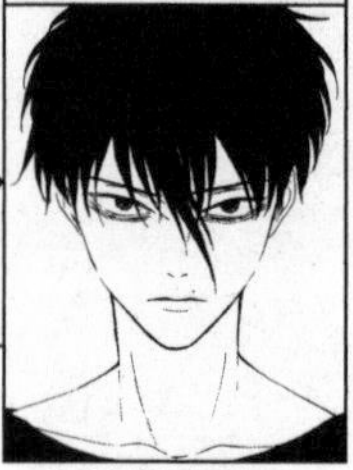

Half-devil, half-human. He was with the police's Public Safety Division 5, but now works for East Bay Security.

MEGUMI ISHIMARU
(Jason)

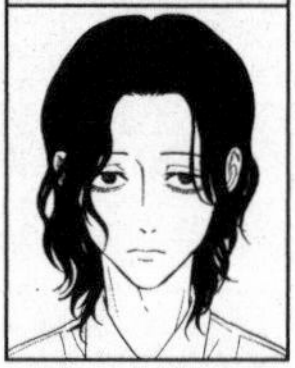

Came into contact with the CCC while working with Division 5 for an undercover investigation. Transferred back to Public Safety General Affairs.

AKIHITO KANZAKI
(Queen)

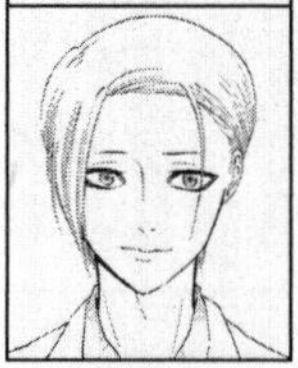

A doctor attached to the CCC. Runs an elite squad of armed guards.

KANAME SHIRASE
(Zero One)

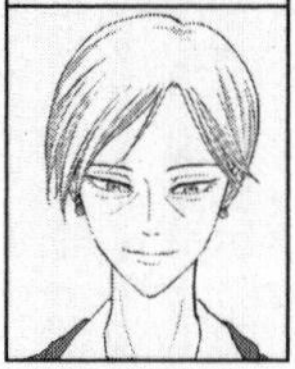

Parliamentary Secretary of Health, Labor and Welfare. Secretly a major player in the CCC.

YANG WEI SHEN

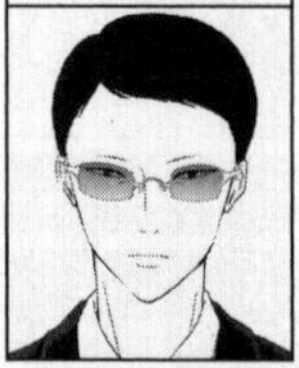

Anzai's boss at East Bay Security. Works in tandem with Anzai on patrols.

JULIANA LLOYD

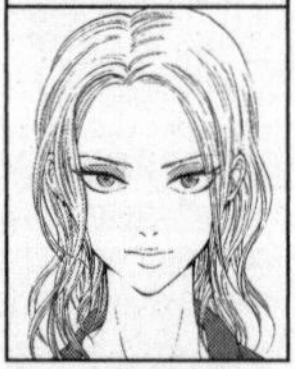

Former devil police officer. Currently employed by East Bay Security along with Anzai.

TAKASHI SAWAZAKI

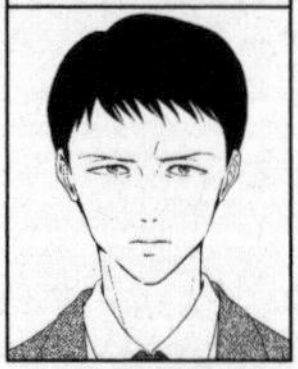

Senior police officer with Public Safety Division 5. Transferred to the General Admin department.

YOUSUKE ASAMI

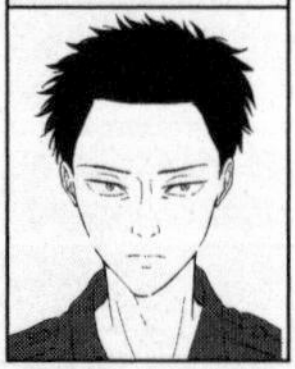

A member of Investigation Division 1, he was assigned to Public Safety Division 5 temporarily.

KEN'ICHI YOSHII
(Zero Nine)

A hacker for the CCC.
In love with Zero Seven.

NANAKO TENJO
(Zero Seven)

She was a CCC sniper, but
has deserted the group. Was
on the run alone, but is now
under Ishimaru's protection.

MAYU SUMIMORI
(Eleven)

She was responsible for
accounting and intel
gathering. Makimura's quick
thinking saved her life.

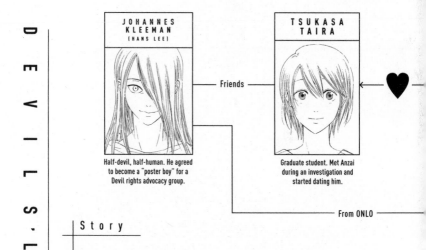

DEVILS'LINE

JOHANNES KLEEMAN
(HANS LEE)

Half-devil, half-human. He agreed
to become a "poster boy" for a
Devil rights advocacy group.

— Friends —

TSUKASA TAIRA

Graduate student. Met Anzai
during an investigation and
started dating him.

♥

— From ONLO —

Story

The existence of devils becomes known to the world at large, dramatically changing society.
In the midst of this upheaval, Anzai was fatally wounded in a fierce battle with the CCC, and
Tsukasa's blood saved his life. The weight of his actions heavy on his mind, Anzai decides to
take leave of the police force as well as break up with Tsukasa for the time being, in order to
confront his own devil self. Tsukasa accepts his decision and resolves to also move forward.
After many twists and turns, they are reunited in Obihiro, and they strengthen their bond by
undergoing intercourse training. Meanwhile, public opinion towards devils is growing more
antagonistic, and Queen's troops have taken over the Prime Minister's residence...!

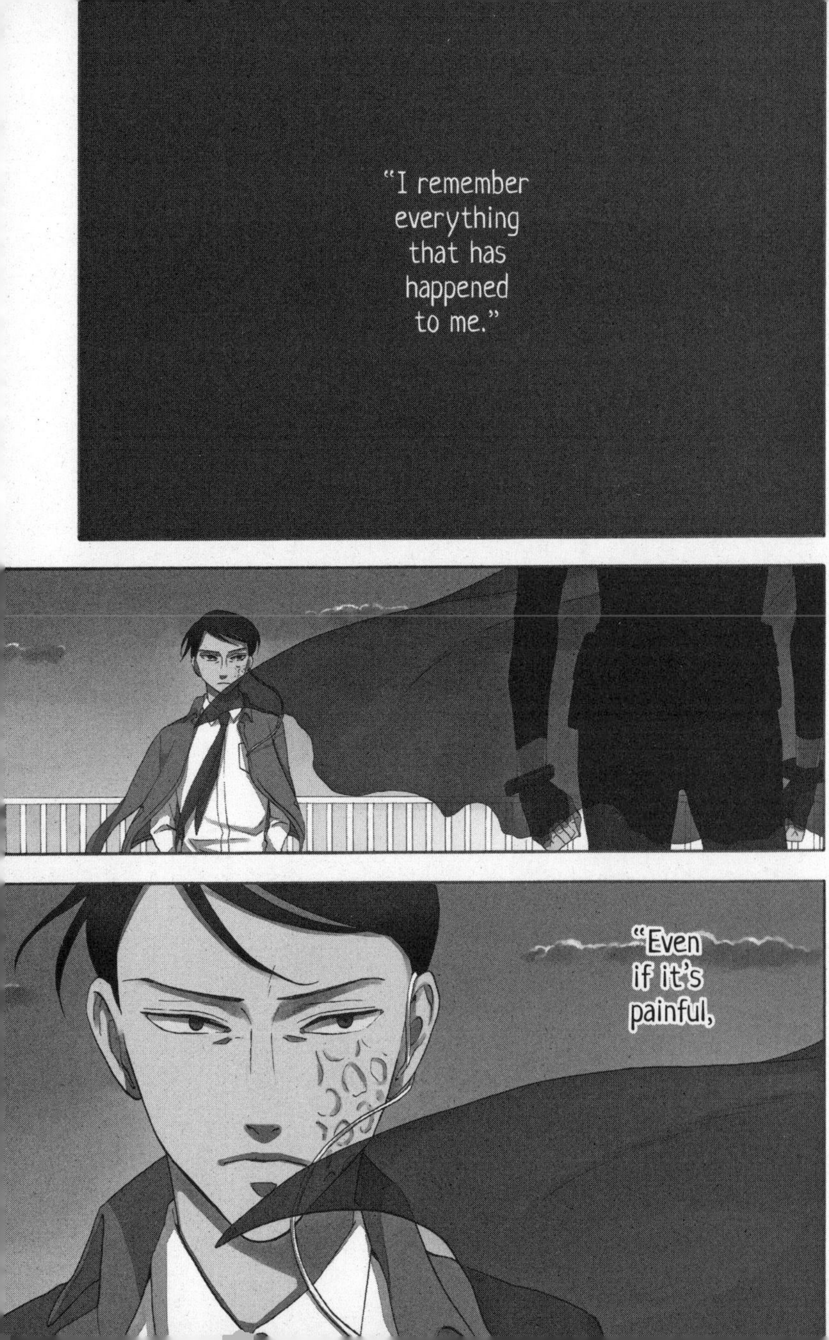
"I remember everything that has happened to me."
"Even if it's painful,

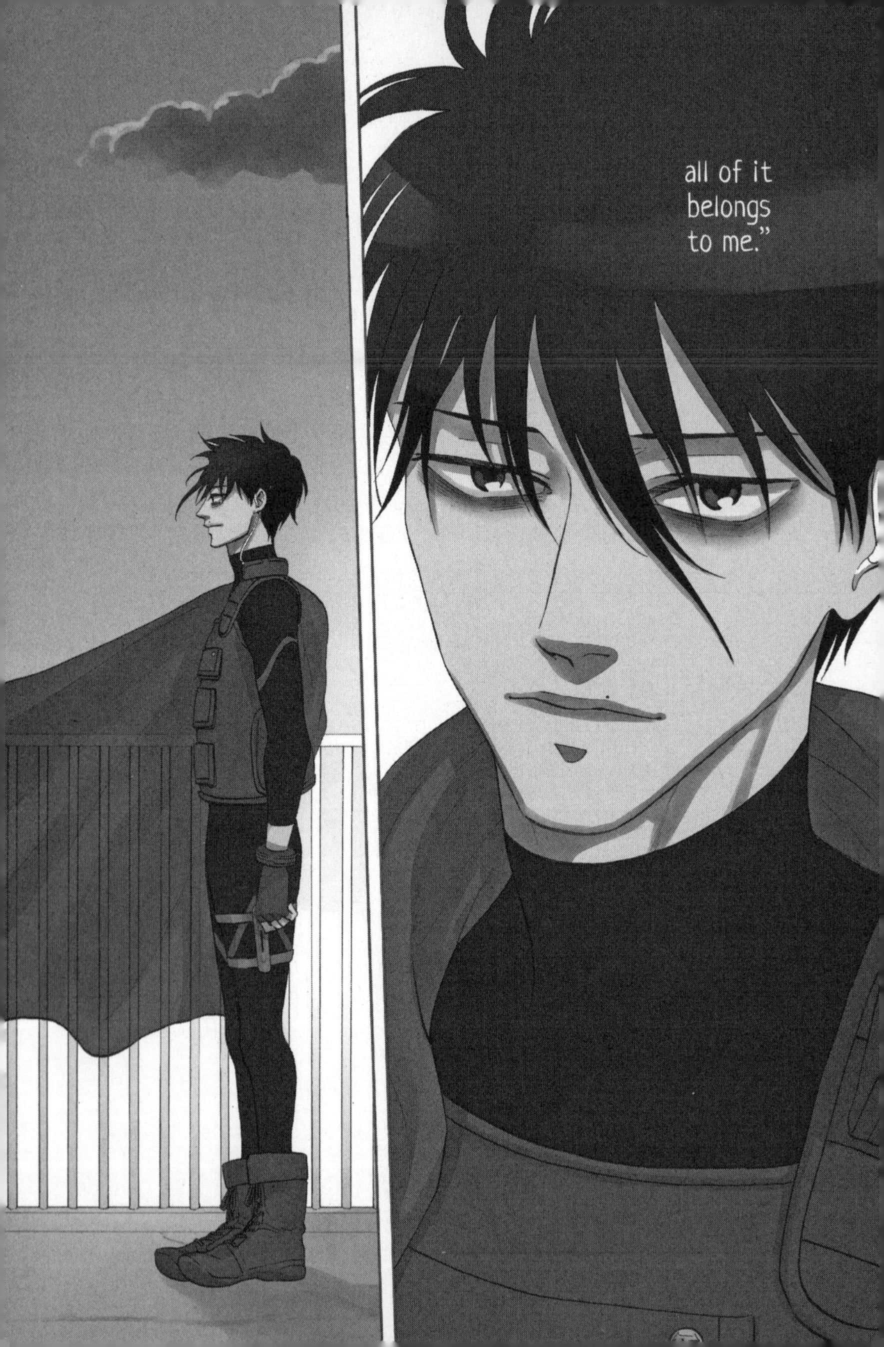
all of it belongs to me."

Line 63
Coup d'État

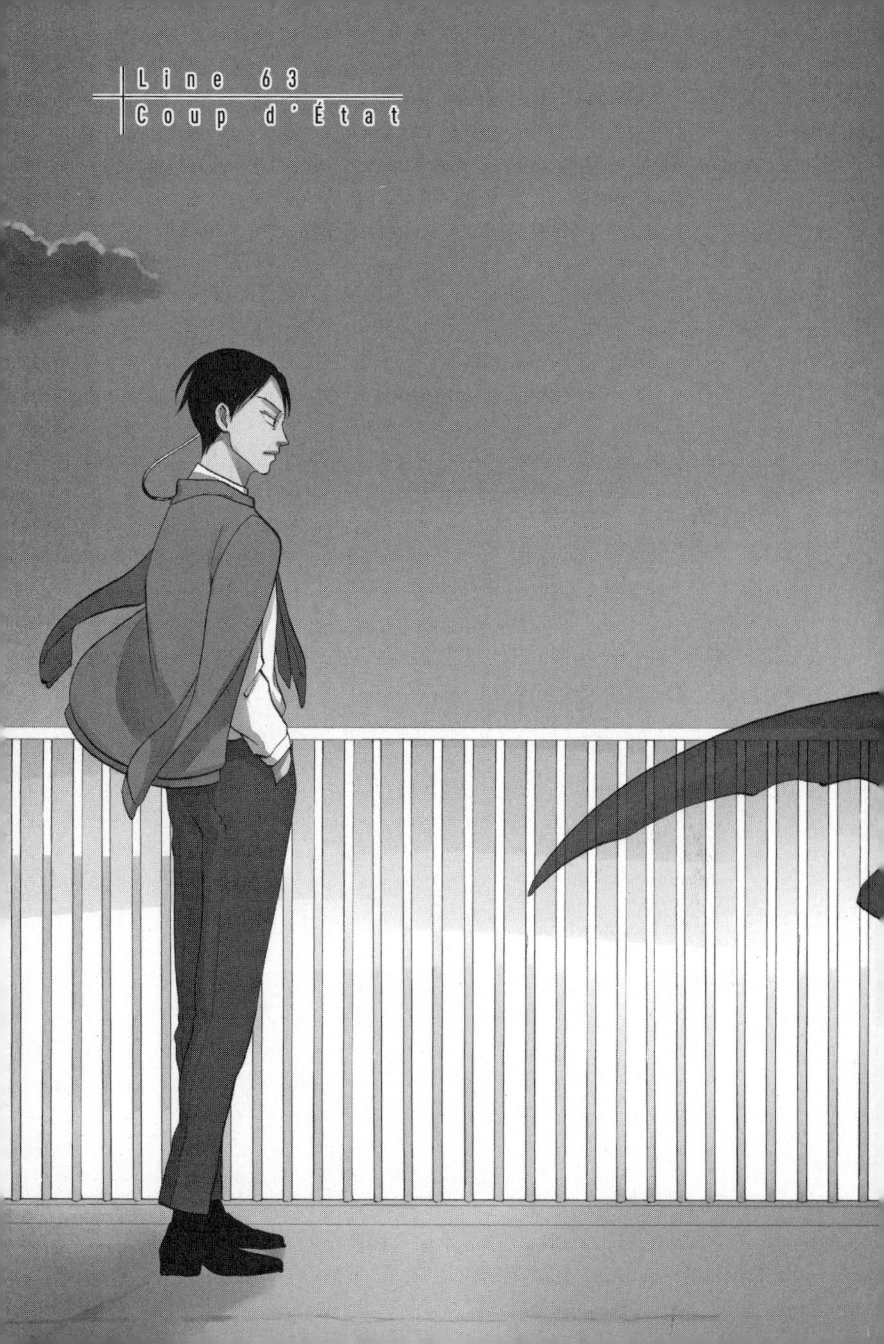

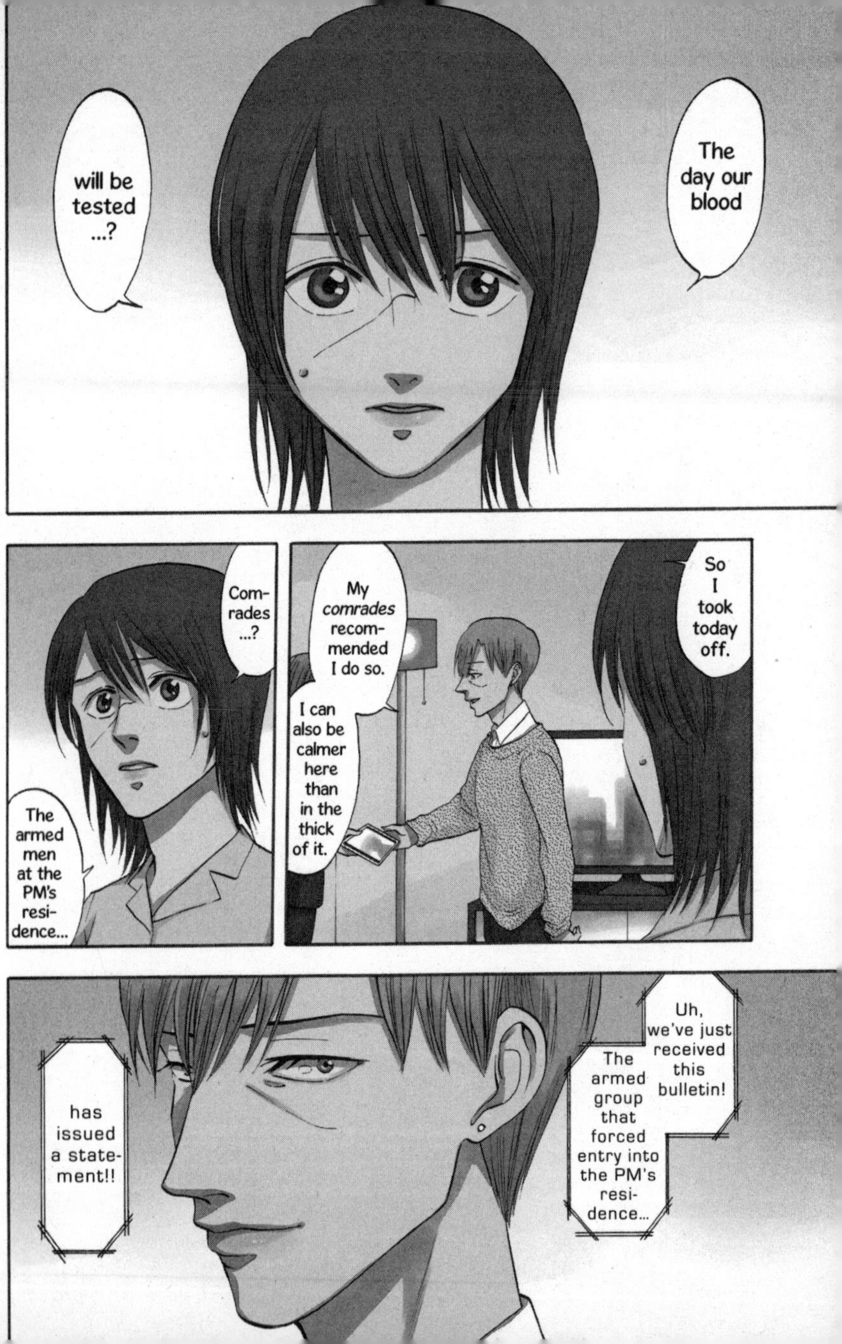
The day our blood
will be tested ...?
So I took today off.
My *comrades* recommended I do so.
I can also be calmer here than in the thick of it.
Comrades ...?
The armed men at the PM's residence...
Uh, we've just received this bulletin!
The armed group that forced entry into the PM's residence...
has issued a statement!!

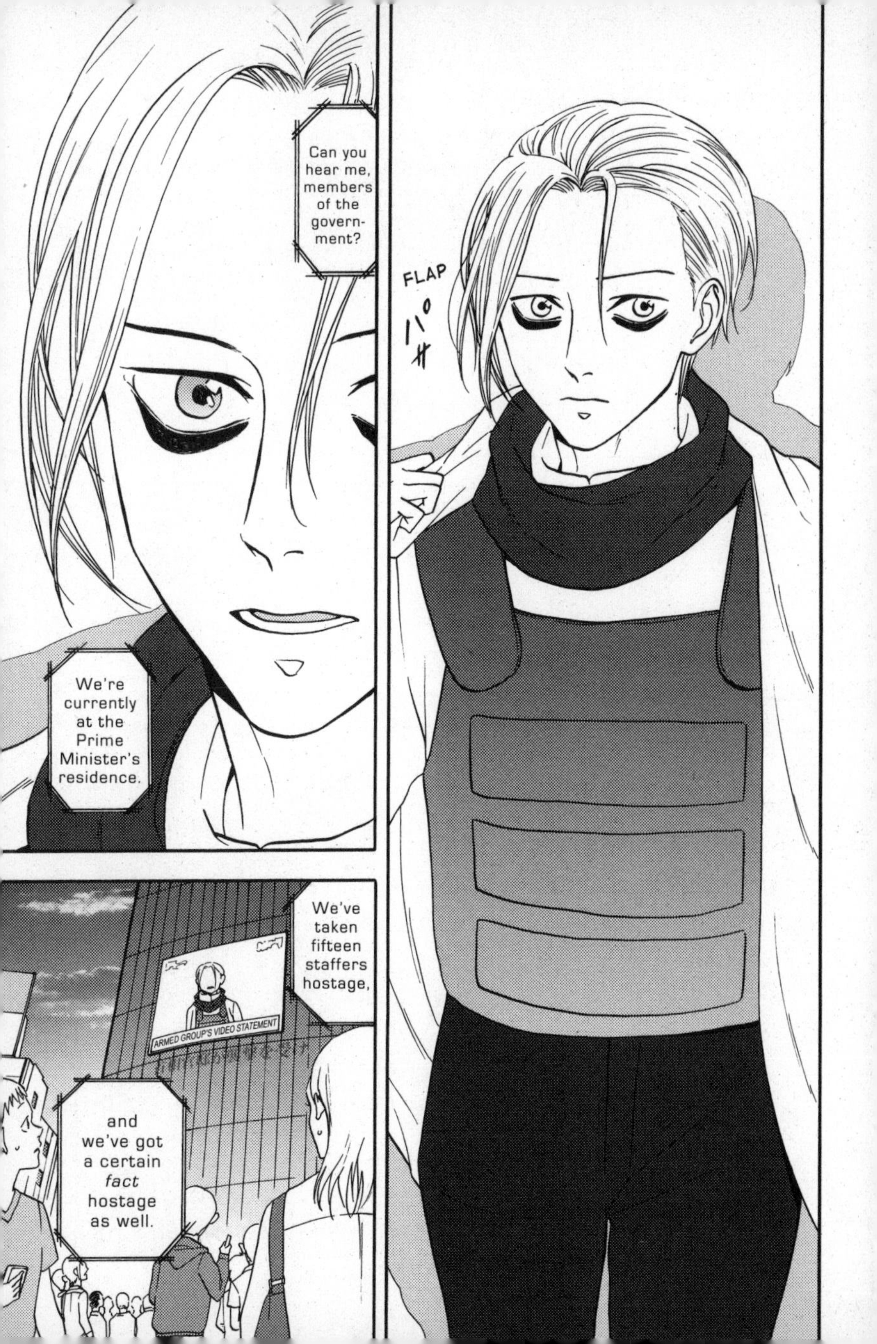
FLAP
パッ
Can you hear me, members of the govern-ment?
We're currently at the Prime Minister's residence.
We've taken fifteen staffers hostage,
ARMED GROUP'S VIDEO STATEMENT
and we've got a certain *fact* hostage as well.

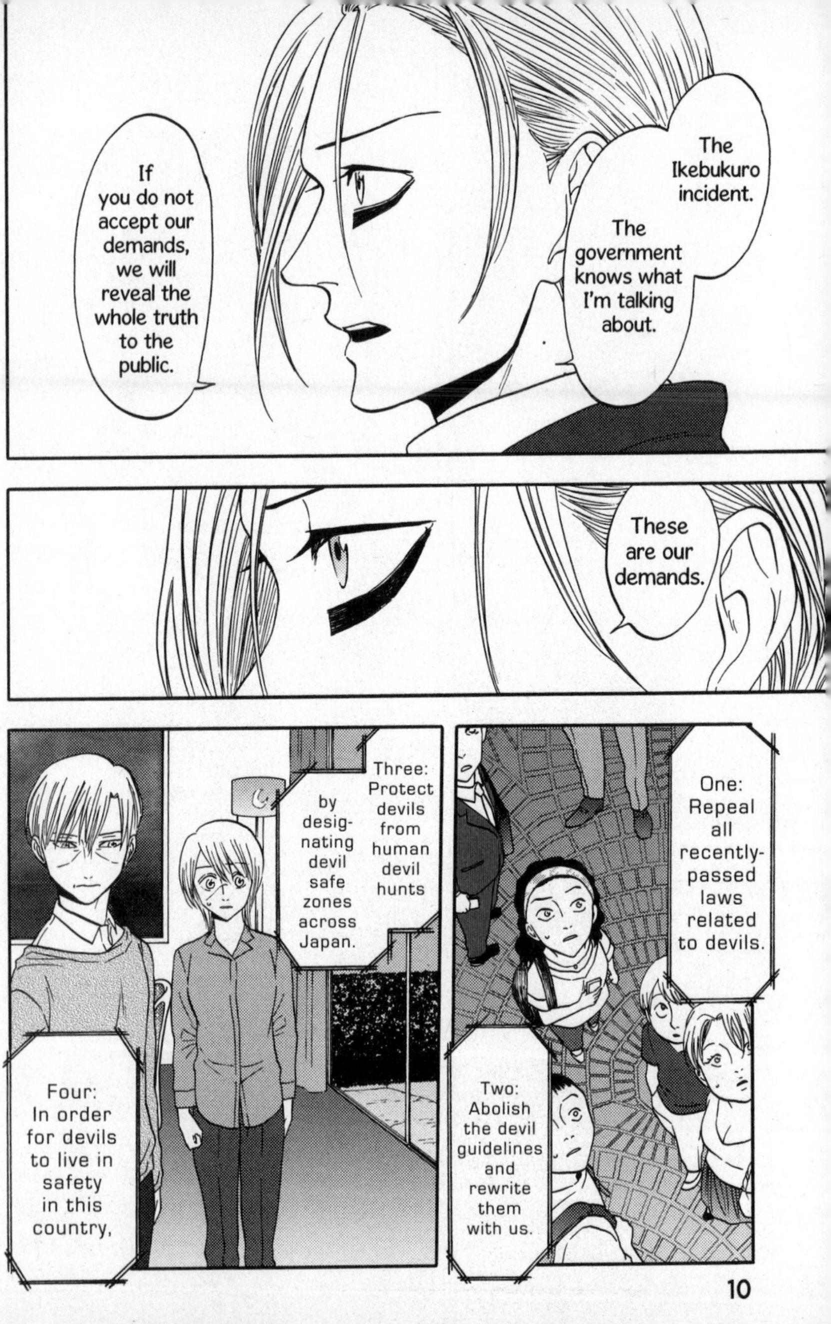
The Ikebukuro incident.
The government knows what I'm talking about.
If you do not accept our demands, we will reveal the whole truth to the public.
These are our demands.
One: Repeal all recently-passed laws related to devils.
Two: Abolish the devil guidelines and rewrite them with us.
Three: Protect devils from human devil hunts
by designating devil safe zones across Japan.
Four: In order for devils to live in safety in this country,

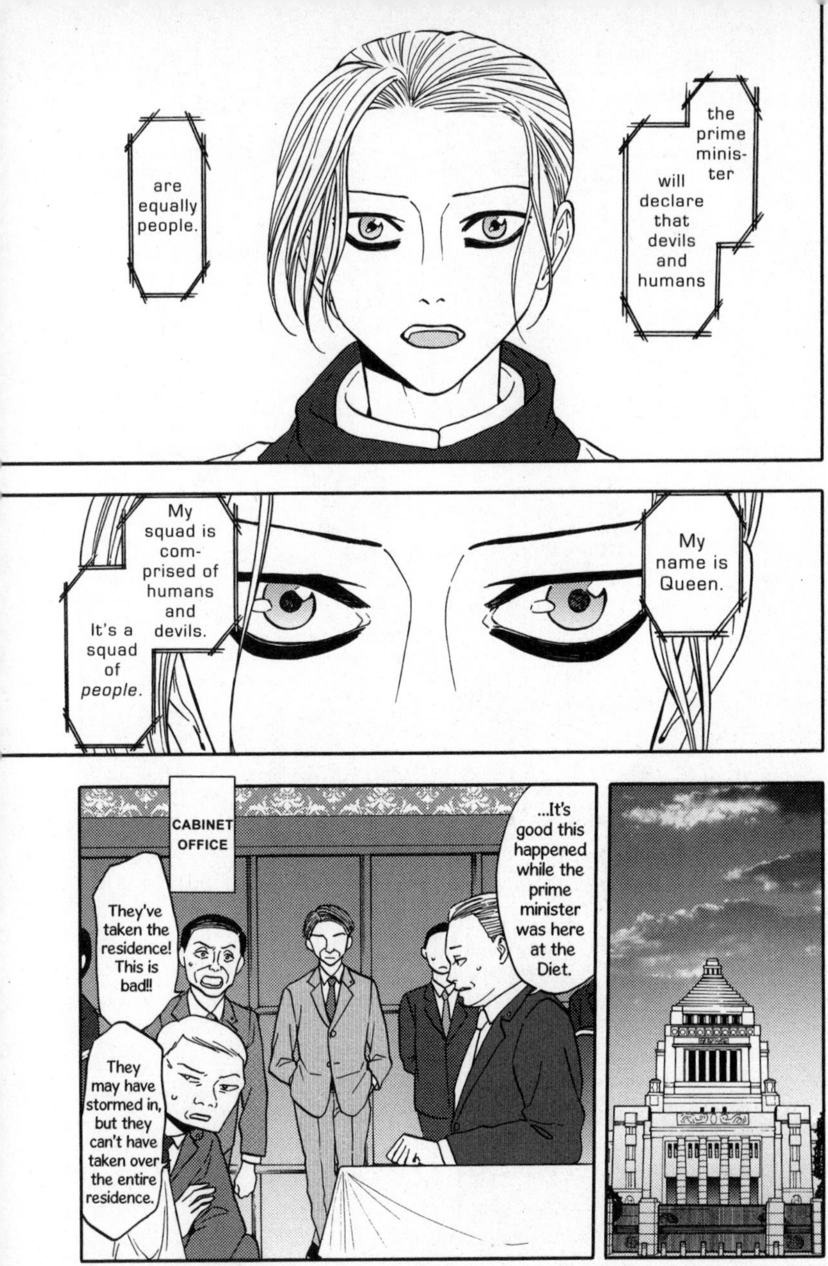

the prime minister will declare that devils and humans
are equally people.
My name is Queen.
My squad is comprised of humans and devils.
It's a squad of *people*.
...It's good this happened while the prime minister was here at the Diet.
CABINET OFFICE
They've taken the residence! This is bad!!
They may have stormed in, but they can't have taken over the entire residence.

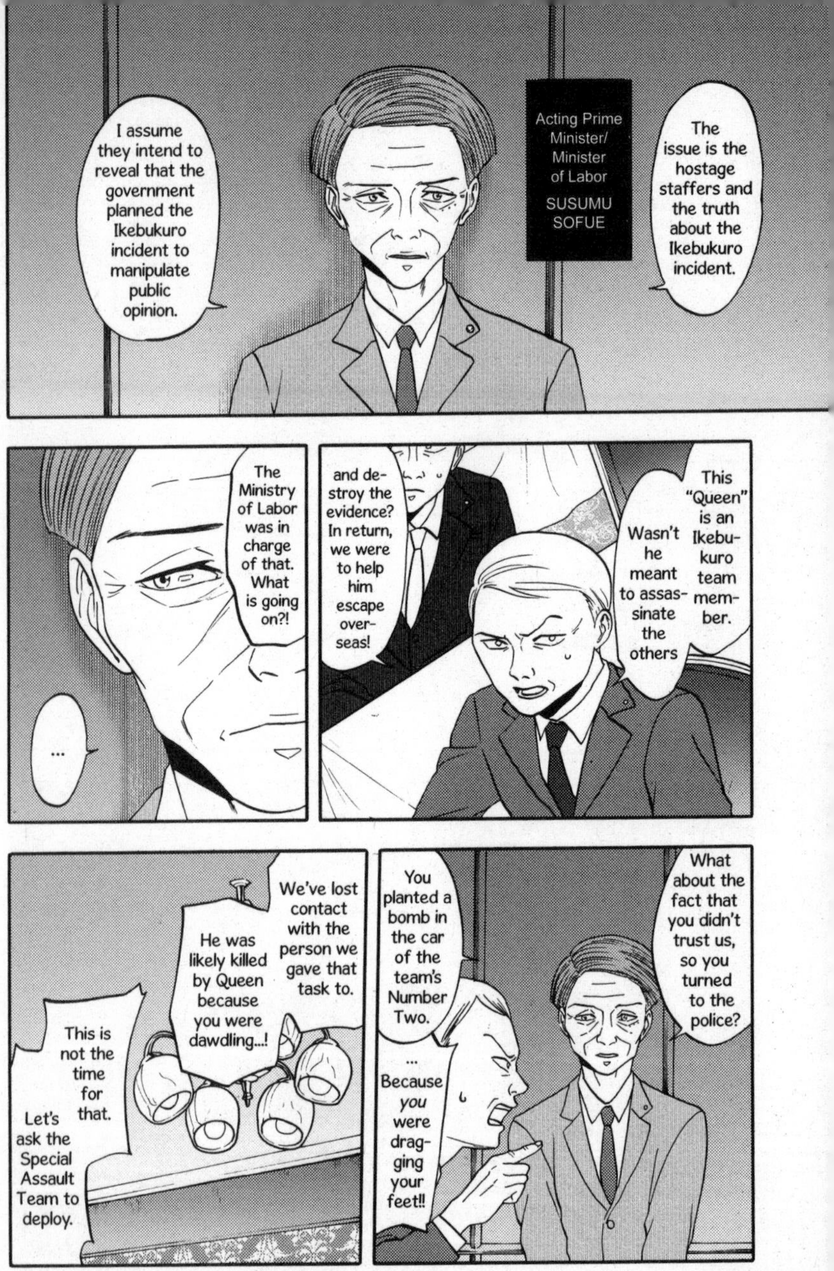
The issue is the hostage staffers and the truth about the Ikebukuro incident.
Acting Prime Minister/ Minister of Labor
SUSUMU SOFUE
I assume they intend to reveal that the government planned the Ikebukuro incident to manipulate public opinion.
This "Queen" is an Ikebukuro team member.
Wasn't he meant to assassinate the others
and destroy the evidence? In return, we were to help him escape overseas!
The Ministry of Labor was in charge of that. What is going on?!
...
What about the fact that you didn't trust us, so you turned to the police?
You planted a bomb in the car of the team's Number Two.
... Because *you* were dragging your feet!!
We've lost contact with the person we gave that task to.
He was likely killed by Queen because you were dawdling...!
This is not the time for that.
Let's ask the Special Assault Team to deploy.

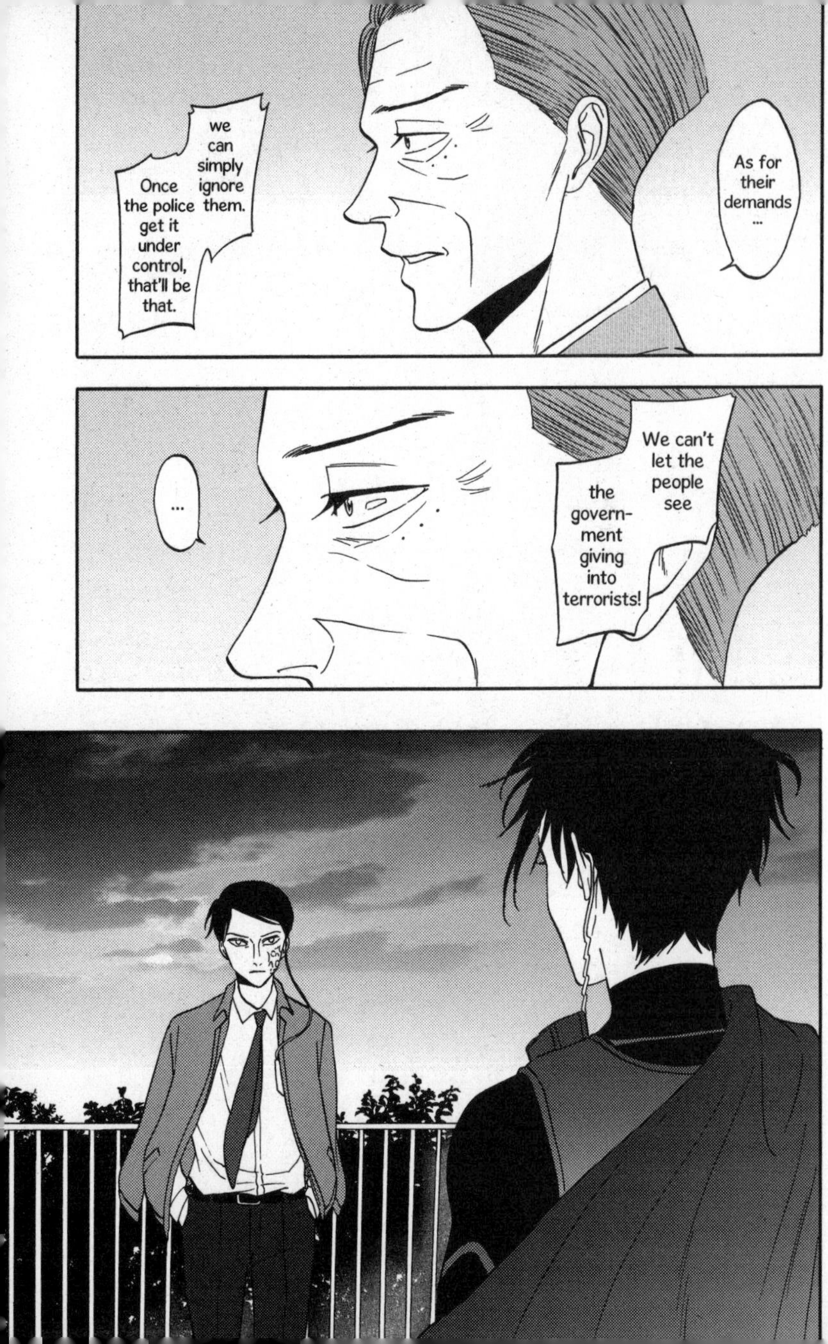
As for their demands ...
we can simply ignore them.
Once the police get it under control, that'll be that.
We can't let the people see the government giving into terrorists!
...

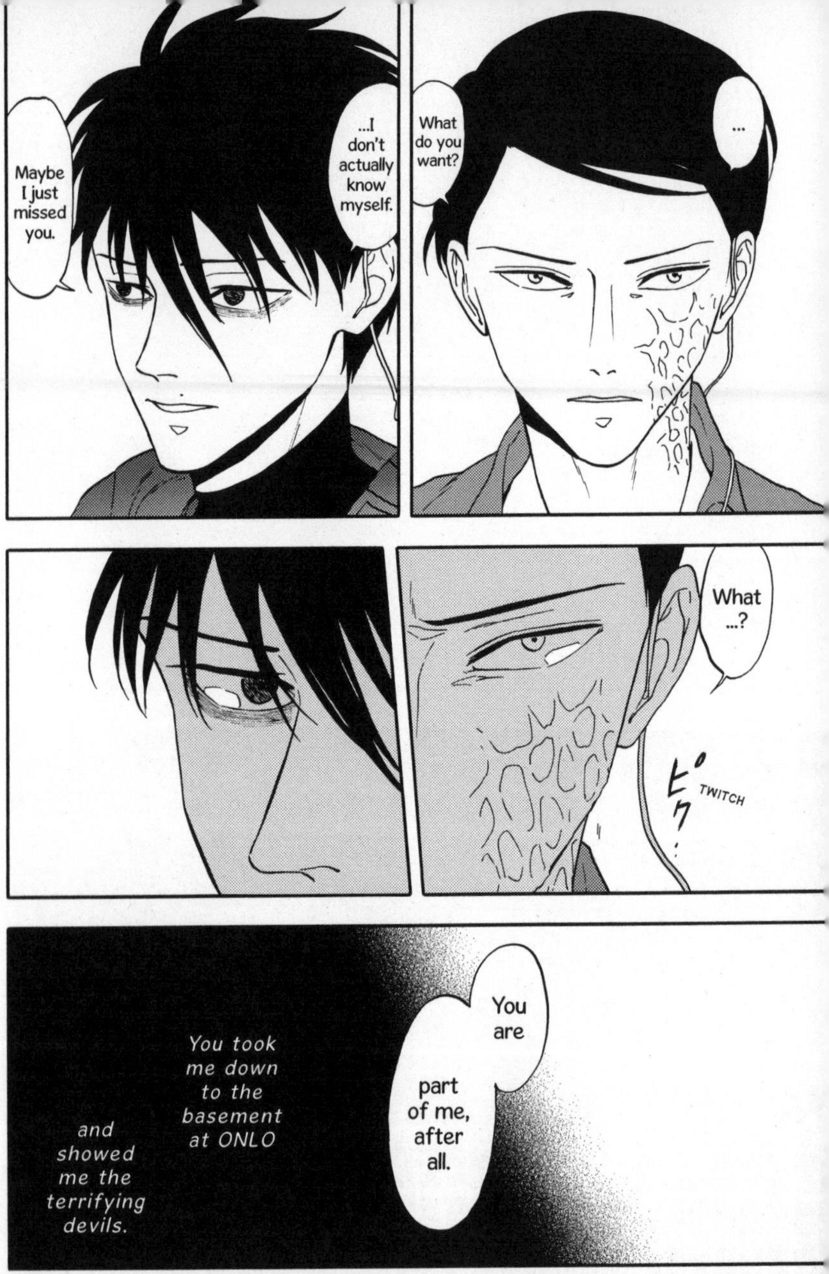
...
What do you want?
...I don't actually know myself.
Maybe I just missed you.
What ...?
TWITCH
You are part of me, after all.
You took me down to the basement at ONLO
and showed me the terrifying devils.

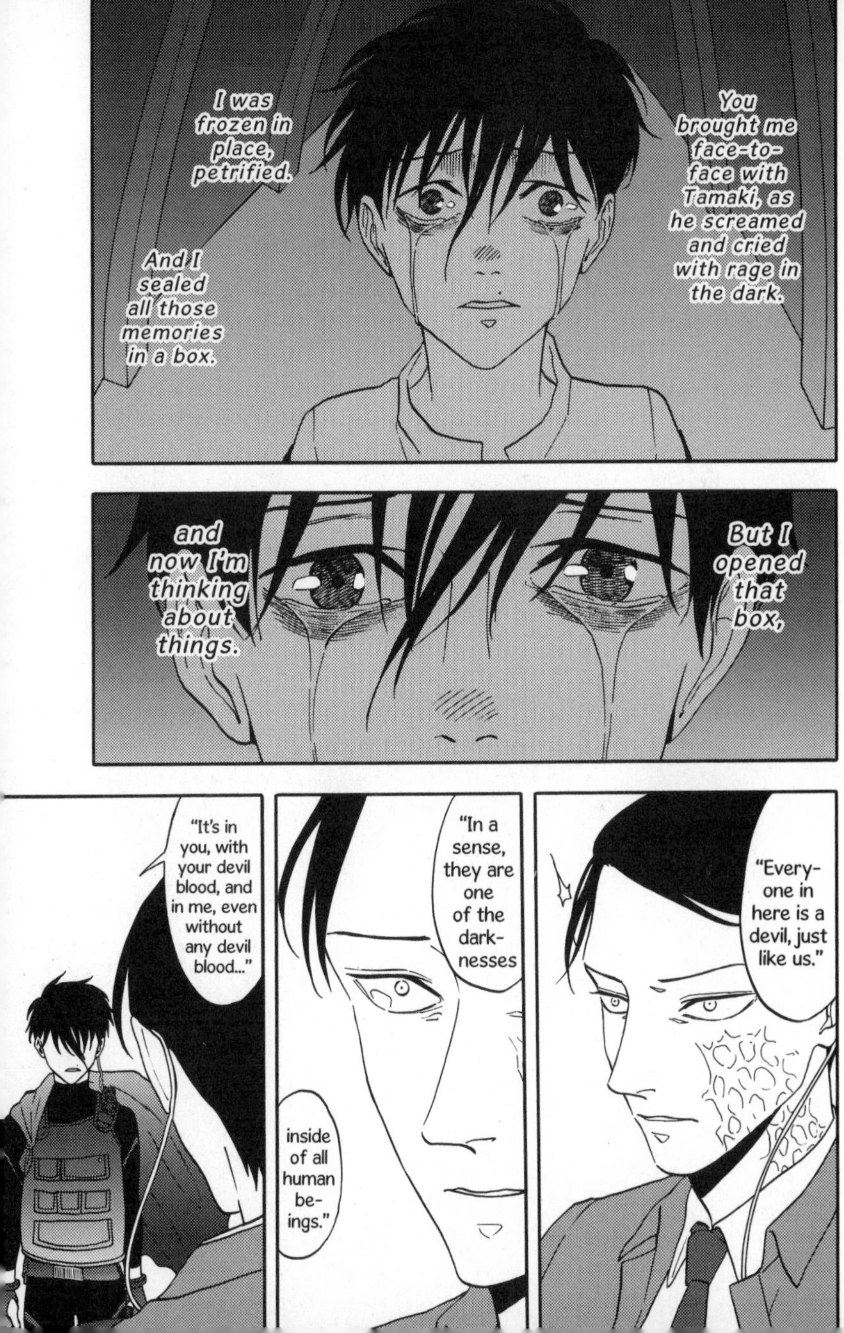
You brought me face-to-face with Tamaki, as he screamed and cried with rage in the dark.
I was frozen in place, petrified.
And I sealed all those memories in a box.
But I opened that box,
and now I'm thinking about things.
"Every-one in here is a devil, just like us."
"In a sense, they are one of the dark-nesses
inside of all human be-ings."
"It's in you, with your devil blood, and in me, even without any devil blood..."

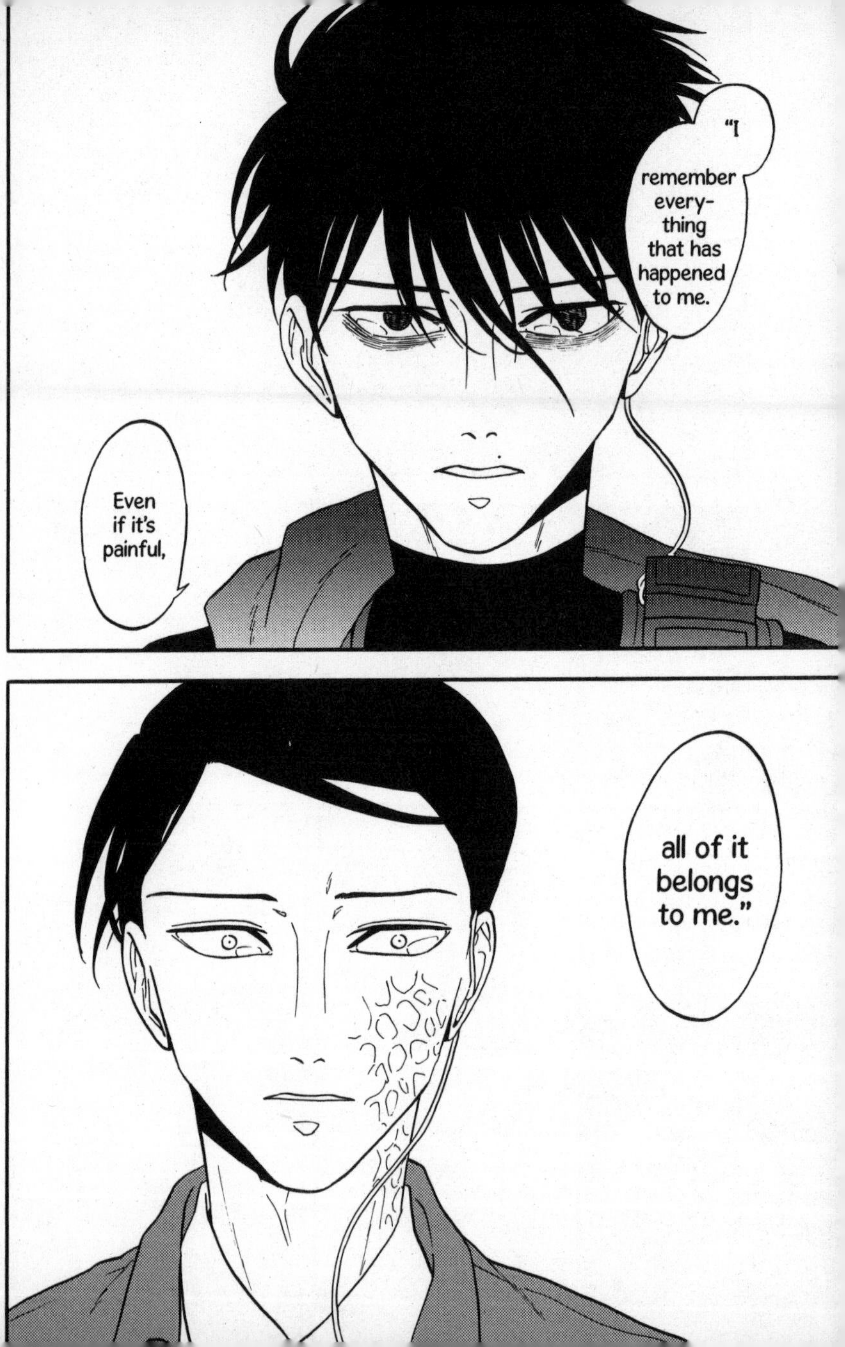
"I remember every-thing that has happened to me.
Even if it's painful,
all of it belongs to me."

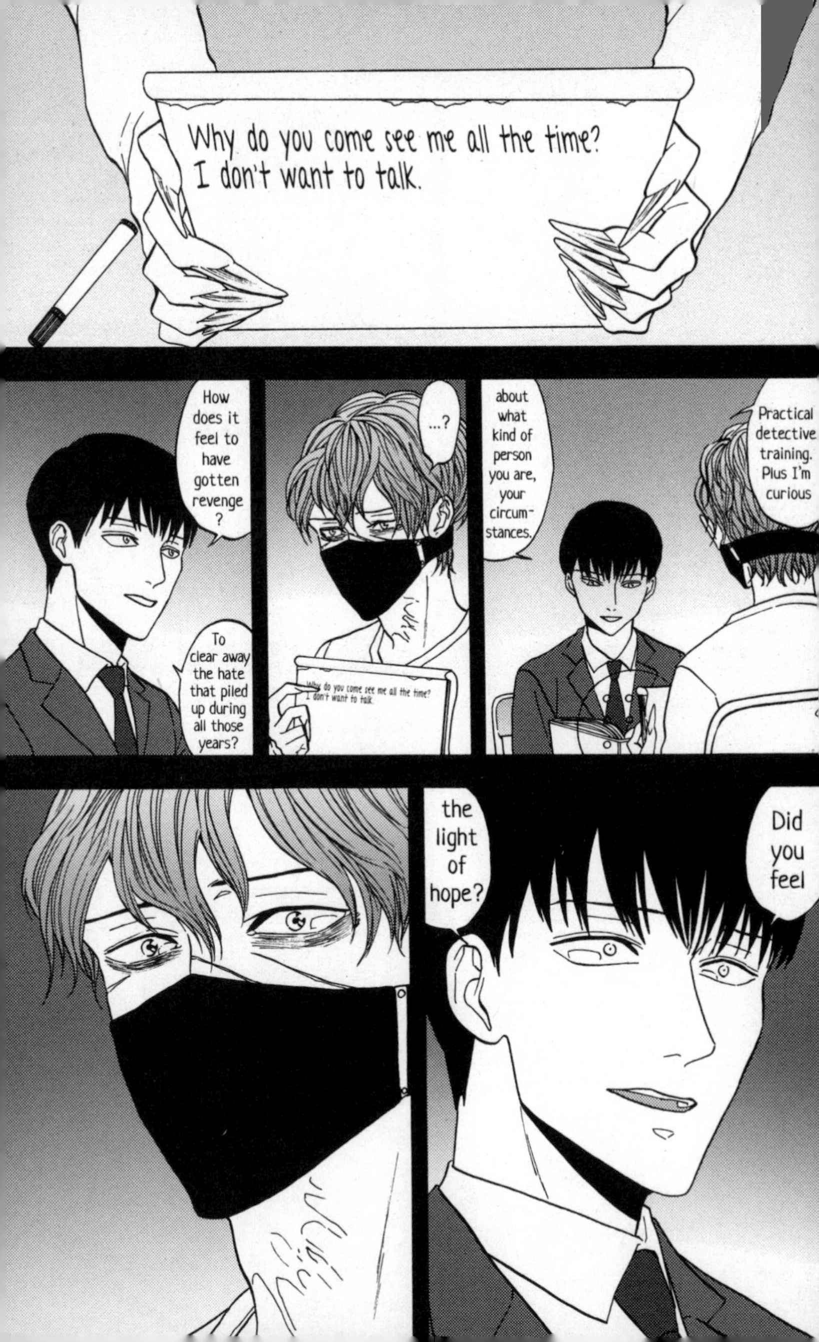
Why do you come see me all the time? I don't want to talk.
Practical detective training. Plus I'm curious
about what kind of person you are, your circum-stances.
...?
Why do you come see me all the time? I don't want to talk.
How does it feel to have gotten revenge?
To clear away the hate that piled up during all those years?
Did you feel
the light of hope?

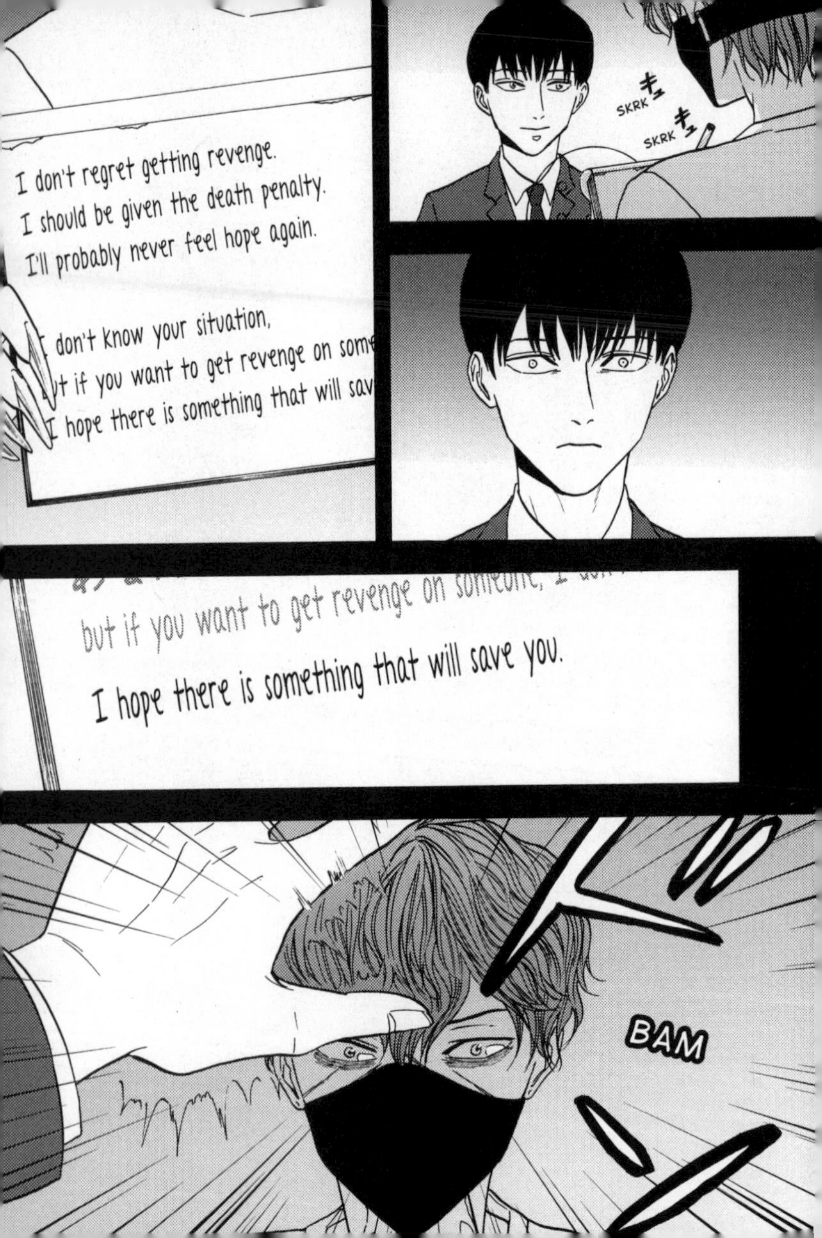
SKRK
SKRK
I don't regret getting revenge.
I should be given the death penalty.
I'll probably never feel hope again.
don't know your situation,
t if you want to get revenge on some
hope there is something that will sav
but if you want to get revenge on someone,
I hope there is something that will save you.
BAM

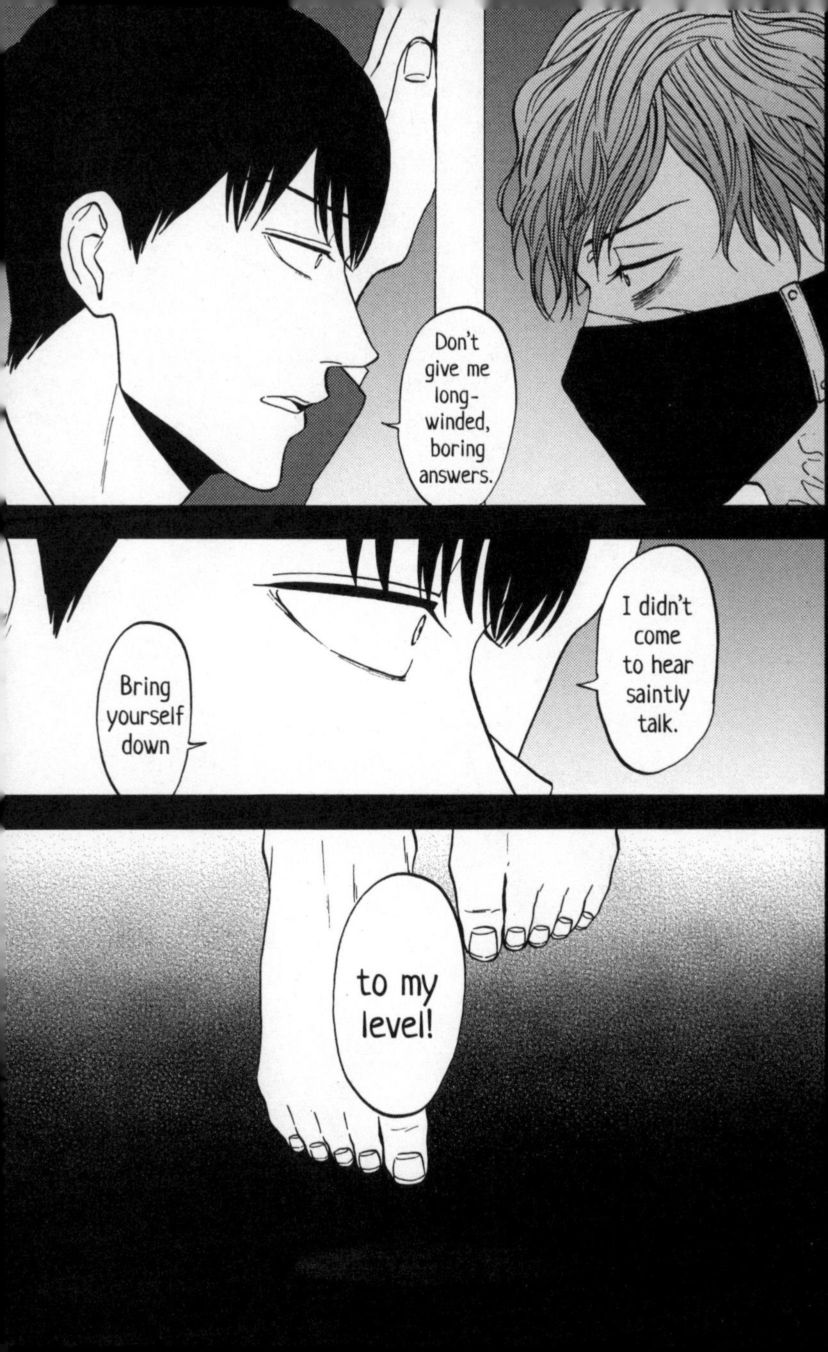
Don't give me long-winded, boring answers.
I didn't come to hear saintly talk.
Bring yourself down
to my level!

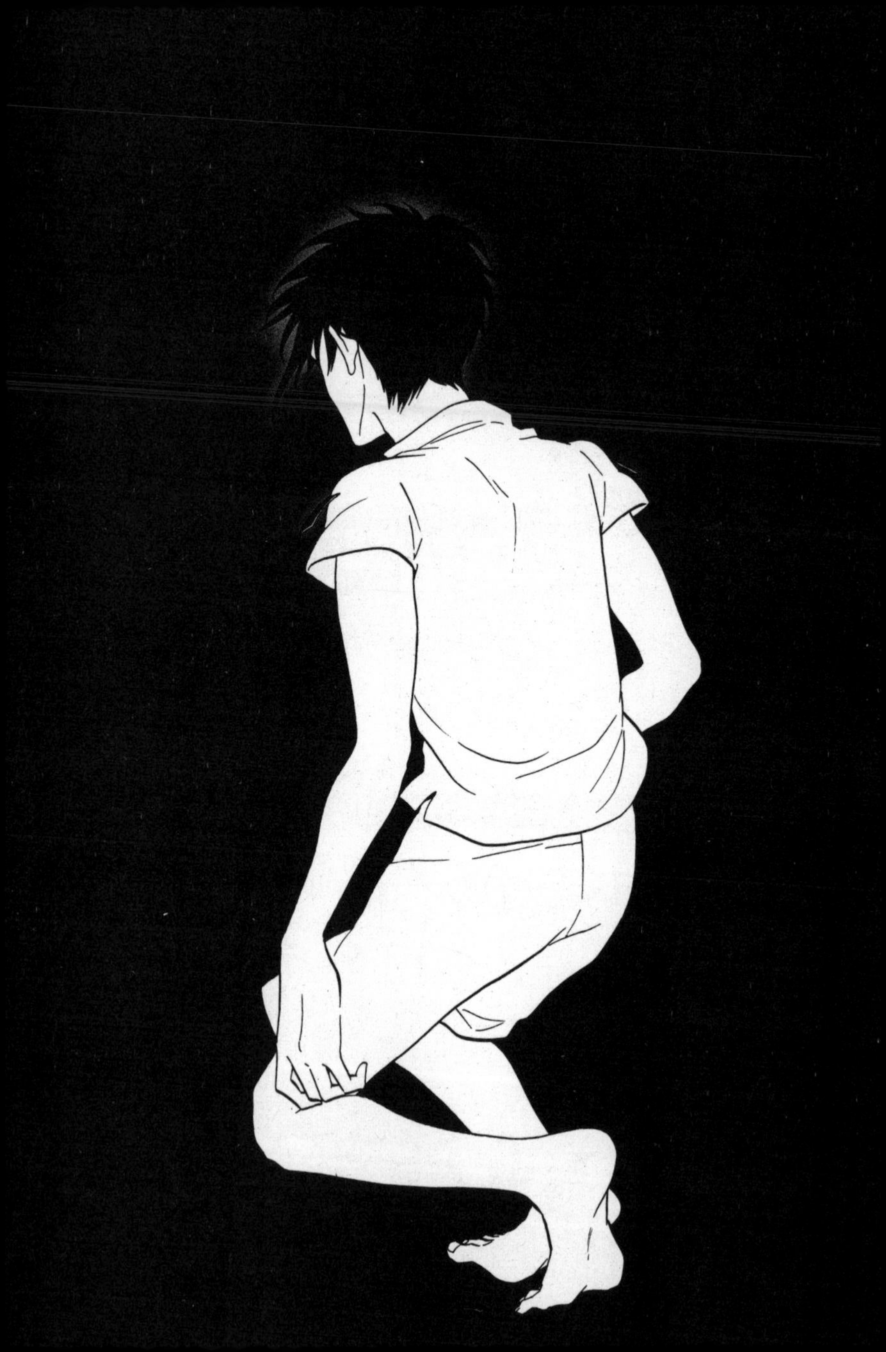

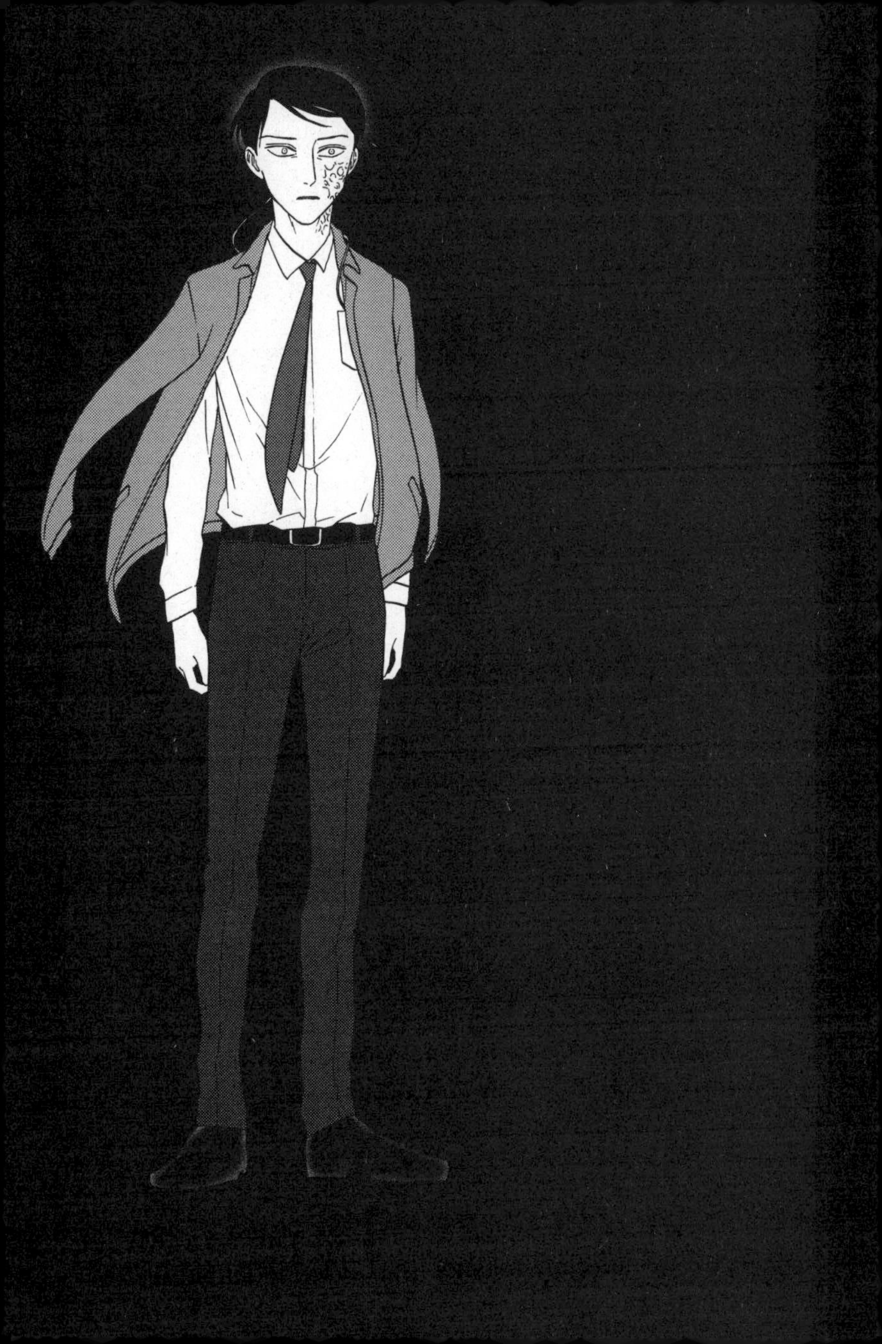

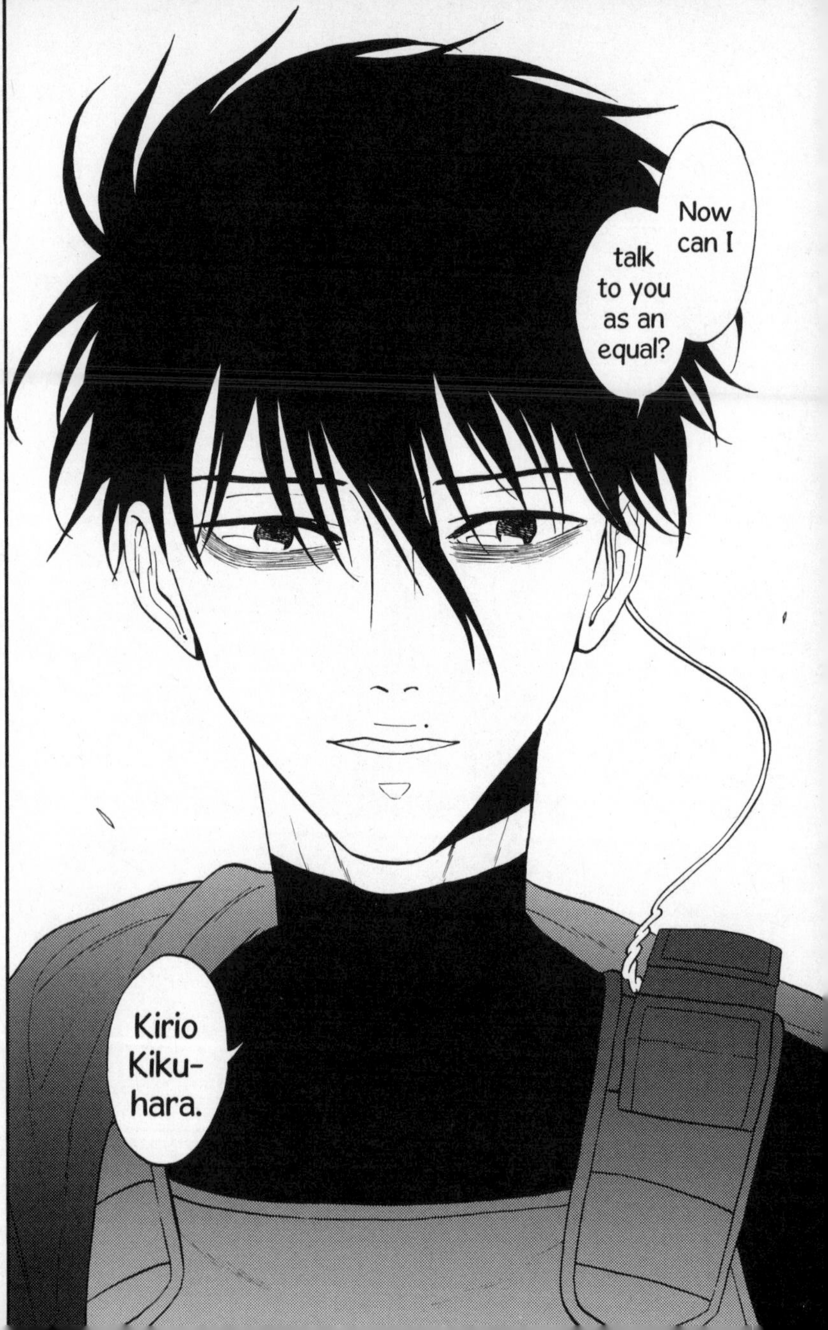
Now can I talk to you as an equal?
Kirio Kiku-hara.

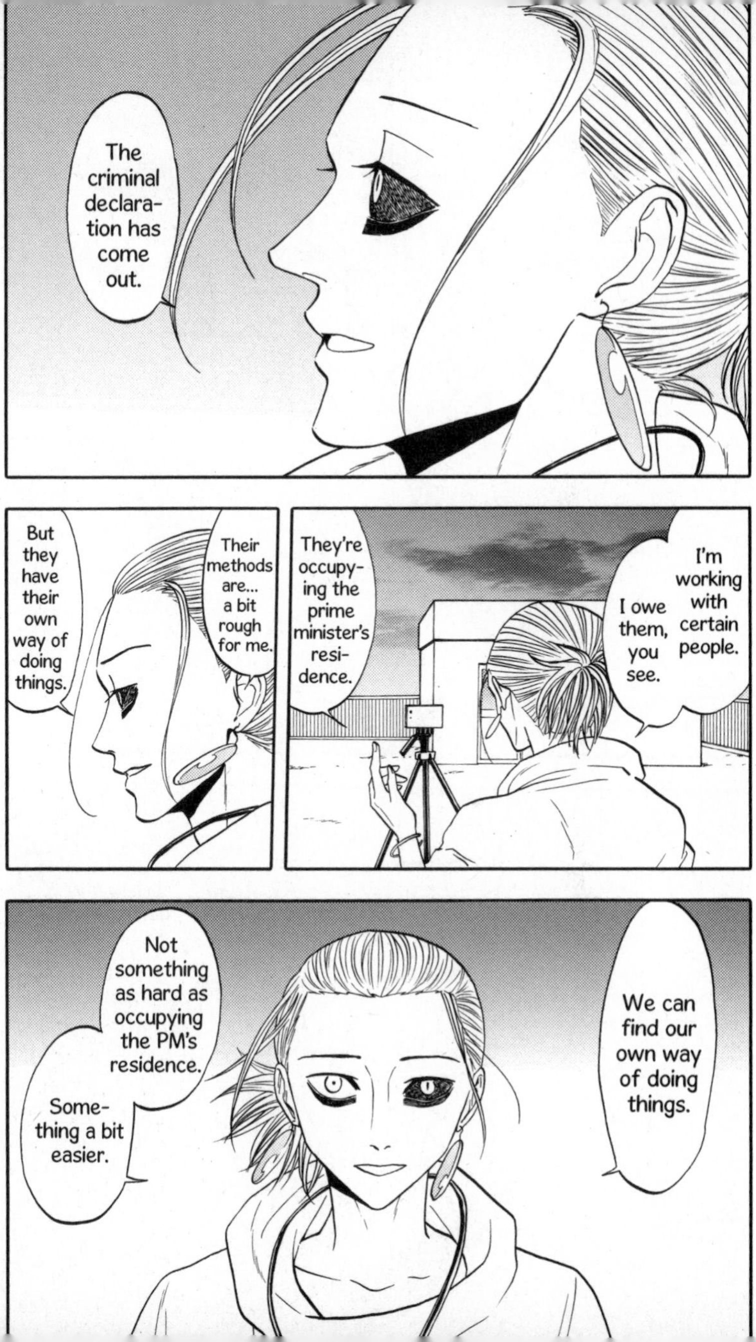
The criminal declaration has come out.
I'm working with certain people.
I owe them, you see.
They're occupying the prime minister's residence.
Their methods are... a bit rough for me.
But they have their own way of doing things.
We can find our own way of doing things.
Not something as hard as occupying the PM's residence.
Something a bit easier.

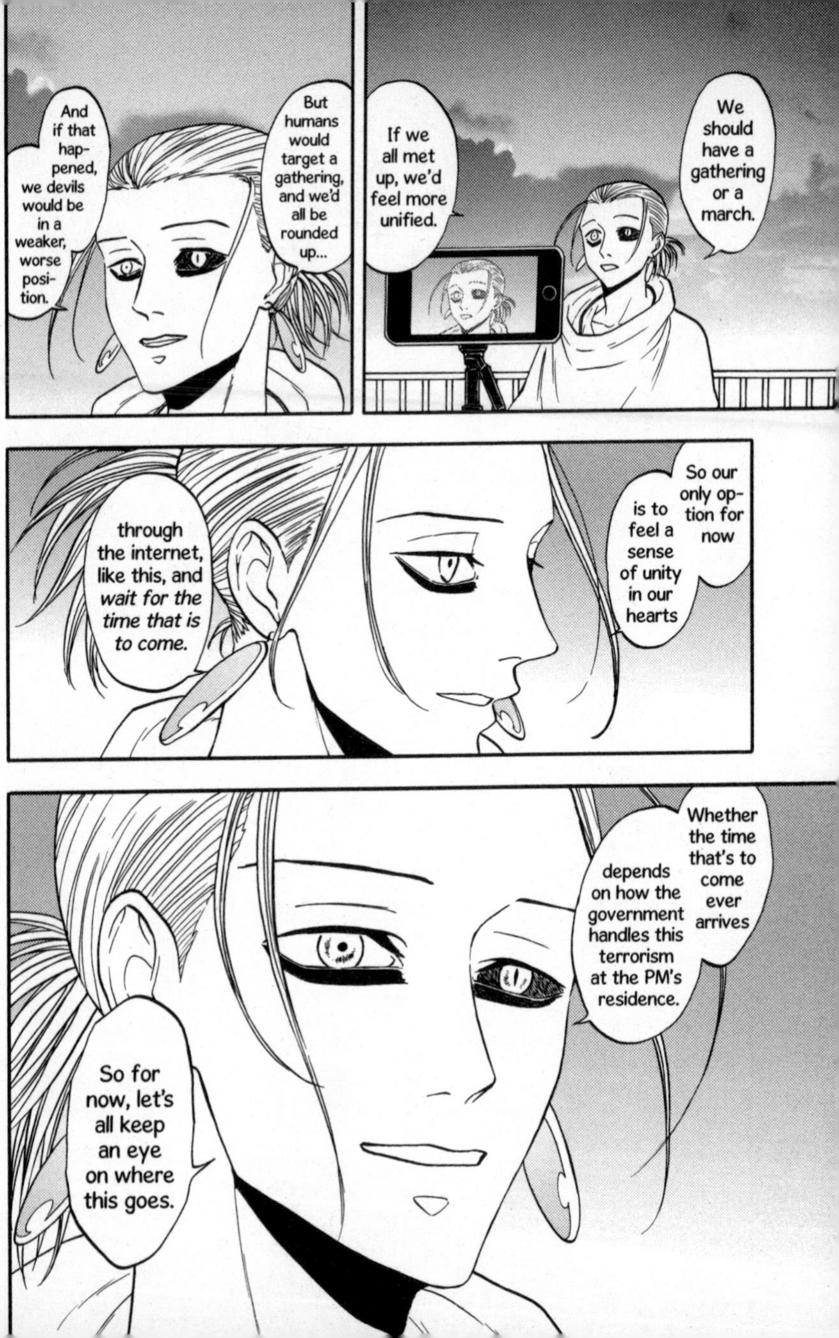
We should have a gathering or a march.
If we all met up, we'd feel more unified.
But humans would target a gathering, and we'd all be rounded up...
And if that hap-pened, we devils would be in a weaker, worse posi-tion.
So our only op-tion for now
is to feel a sense of unity in our hearts
through the internet, like this, and *wait for the time that is to come.*
Whether the time that's to come ever arrives
depends on how the government handles this terrorism at the PM's residence.
So for now, let's all keep an eye on where this goes.

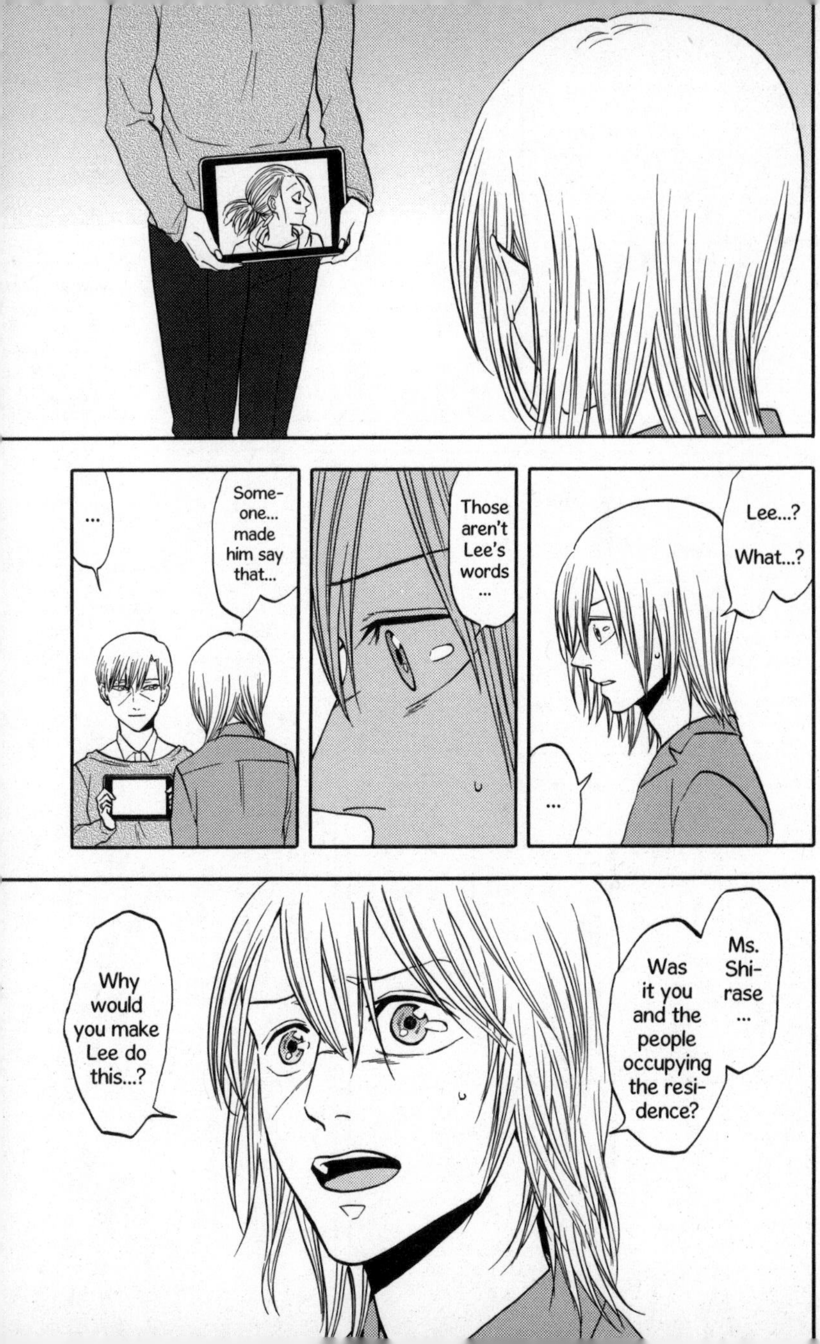
Lee...?
What...?
...
Those aren't Lee's words ...
Some-one... made him say that...
...
Ms. Shi-rase ...
Was it you and the people occupying the resi-dence?
Why would you make Lee do this...?

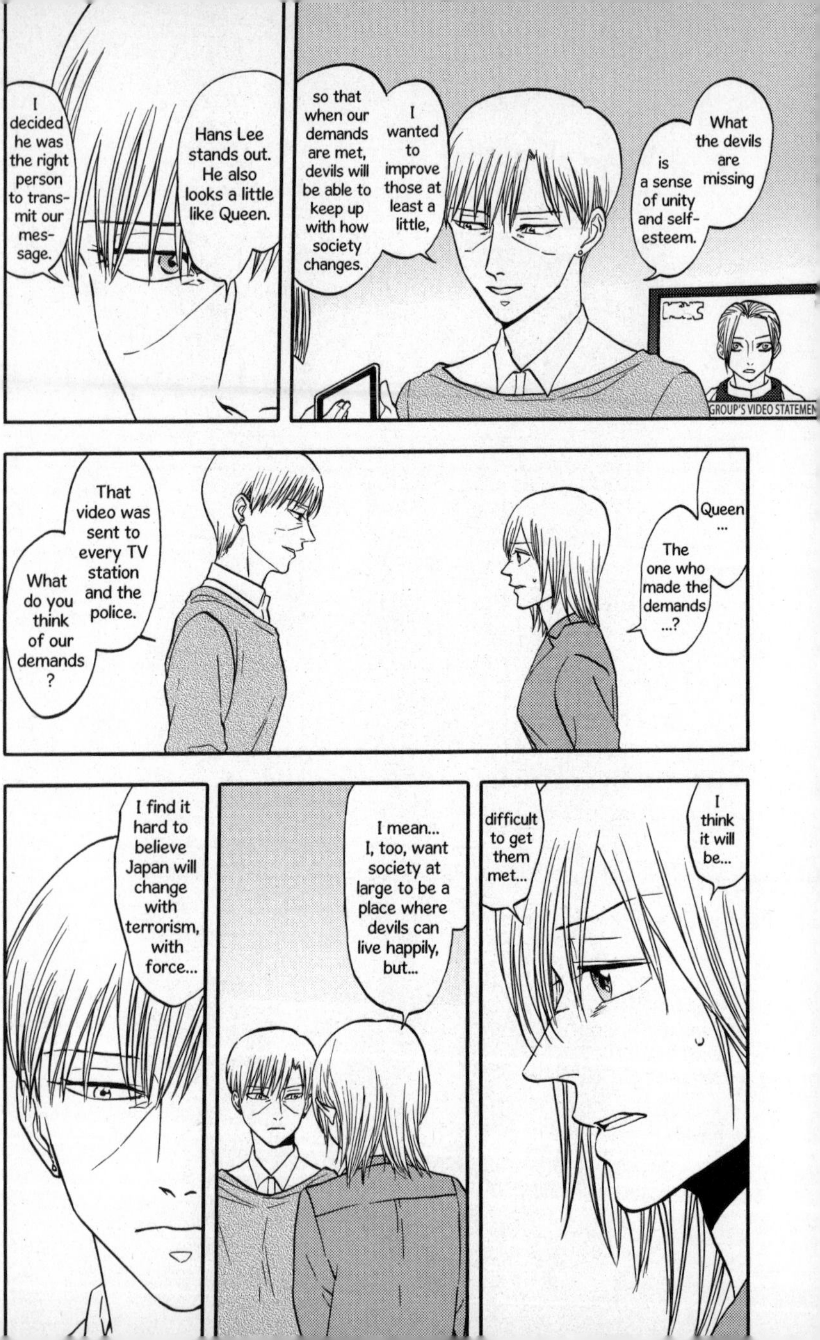
What the devils are missing is a sense of unity and self-esteem.
I wanted to improve those at least a little,
so that when our demands are met, devils will be able to keep up with how society changes.
GROUP'S VIDEO STATEMEN
Hans Lee stands out. He also looks a little like Queen.
I decided he was the right person to transmit our message.
Queen... The one who made the demands...?
That video was sent to every TV station and the police.
What do you think of our demands?
I think it will be...
difficult to get them met...
I mean... I, too, want society at large to be a place where devils can live happily, but...
I find it hard to believe Japan will change with terrorism, with force...

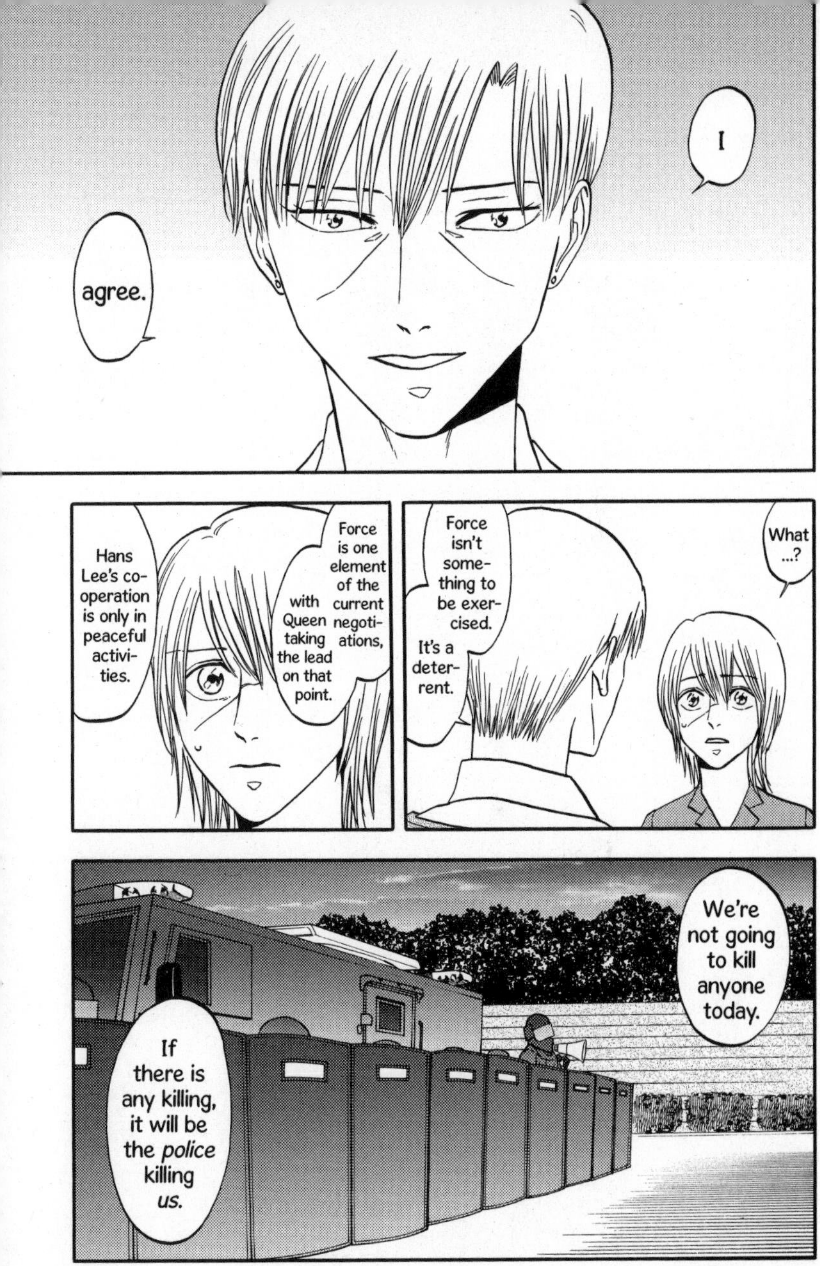
I
agree.
What ...?
Force isn't something to be exercised.
It's a deterrent.
Force is one element of the current negotiations,
with Queen taking the lead on that point.
Hans Lee's cooperation is only in peaceful activities.
We're not going to kill anyone today.
If there is any killing, it will be the *police* killing *us*.

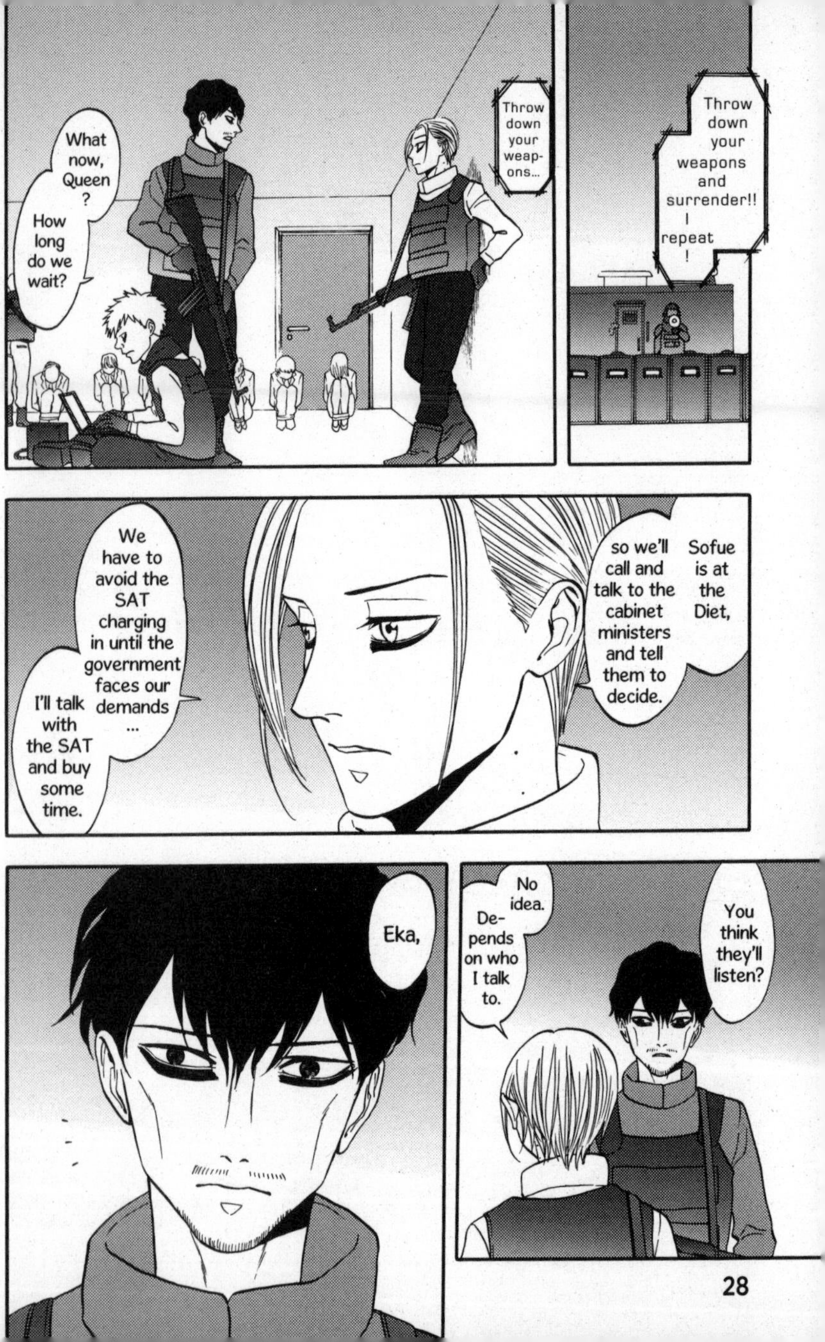
Throw down your weapons and surrender!! I repeat!
Throw down your weap-ons...
What now, Queen?
How long do we wait?
Sofue is at the Diet,
so we'll call and talk to the cabinet ministers and tell them to decide.
We have to avoid the SAT charging in until the government faces our demands...
I'll talk with the SAT and buy some time.
You think they'll listen?
No idea. Depends on who I talk to.
Eka,

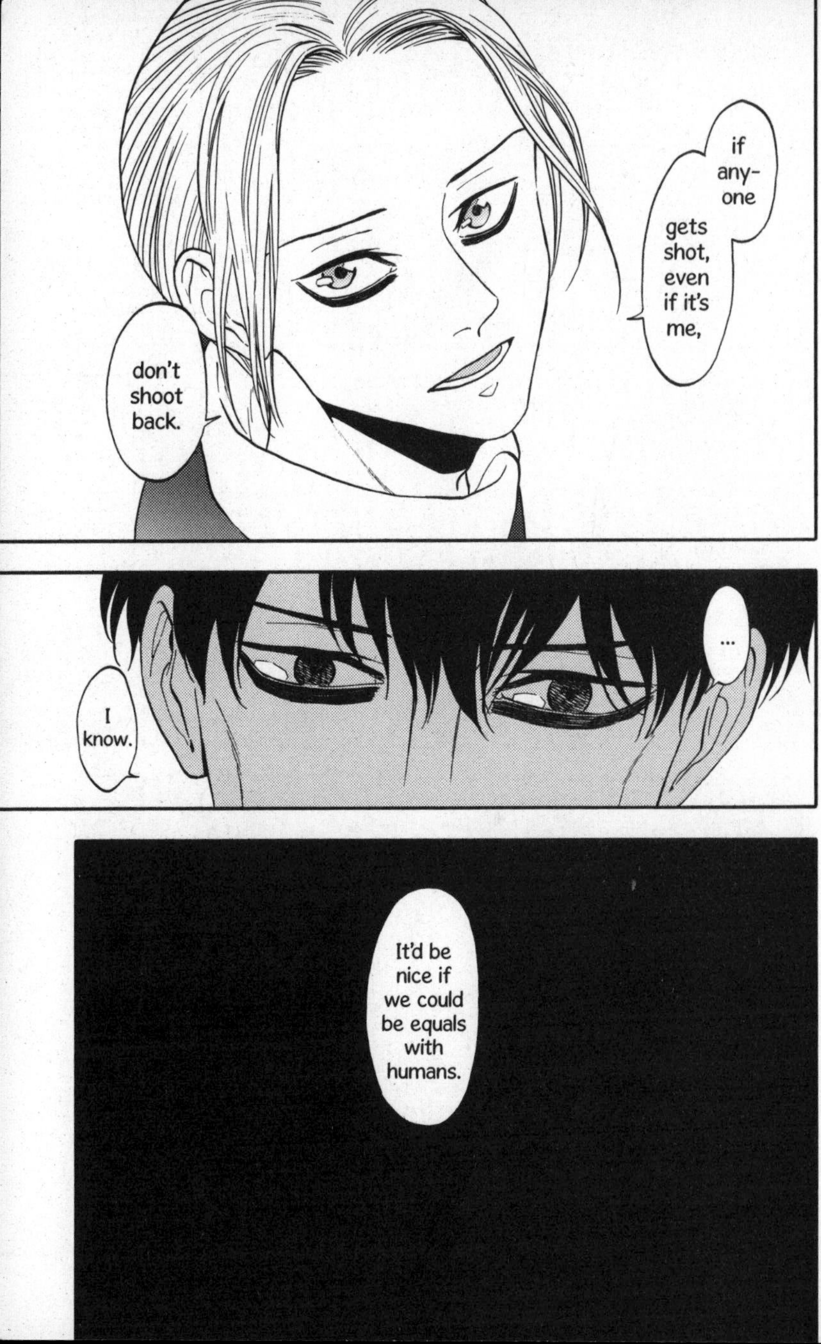
if any-one gets shot, even if it's me,
don't shoot back.
...
I know.
It'd be nice if we could be equals with humans.

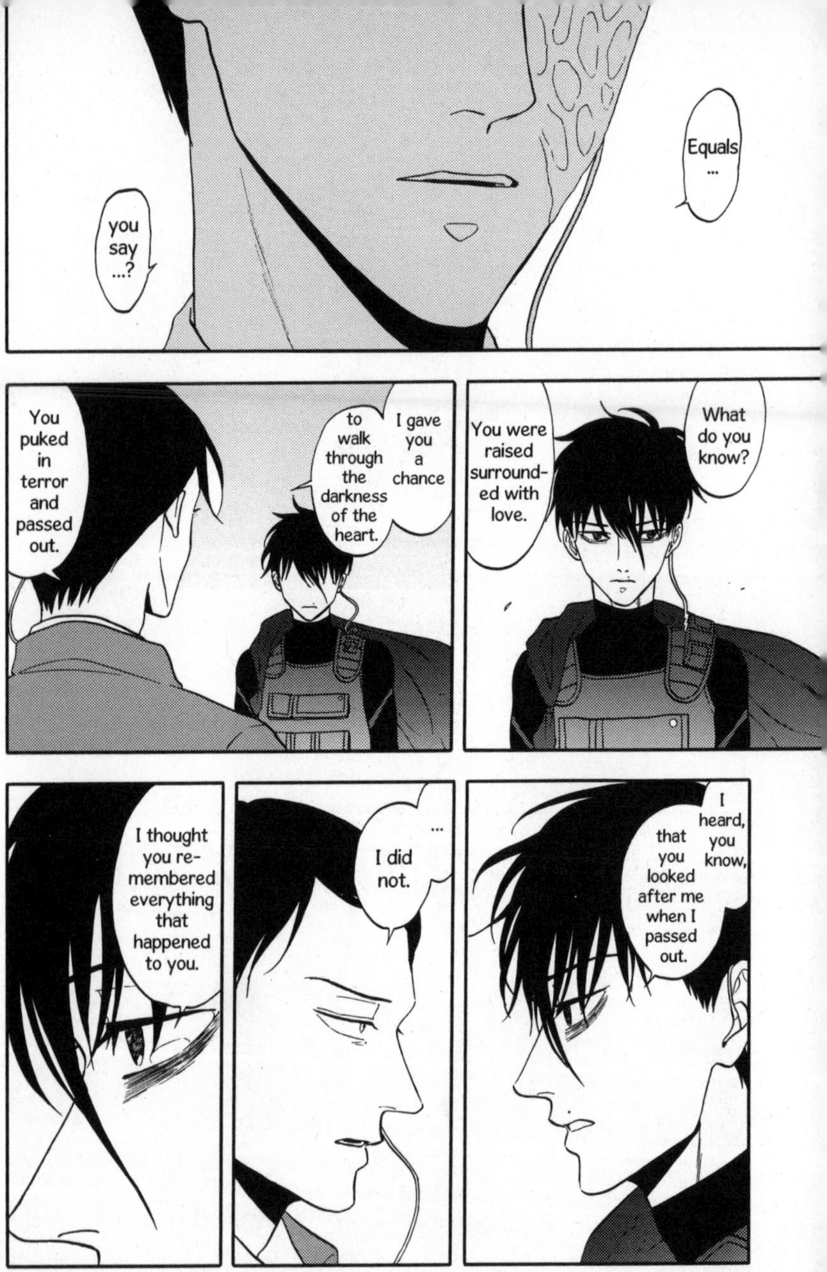
Equals ...
you say ...?
What do you know?
You were raised surround-ed with love.
I gave you a chance
to walk through the darkness of the heart.
You puked in terror and passed out.
I heard, you know,
that you looked after me when I passed out.
... I did not.
I thought you re-membered everything that happened to you.

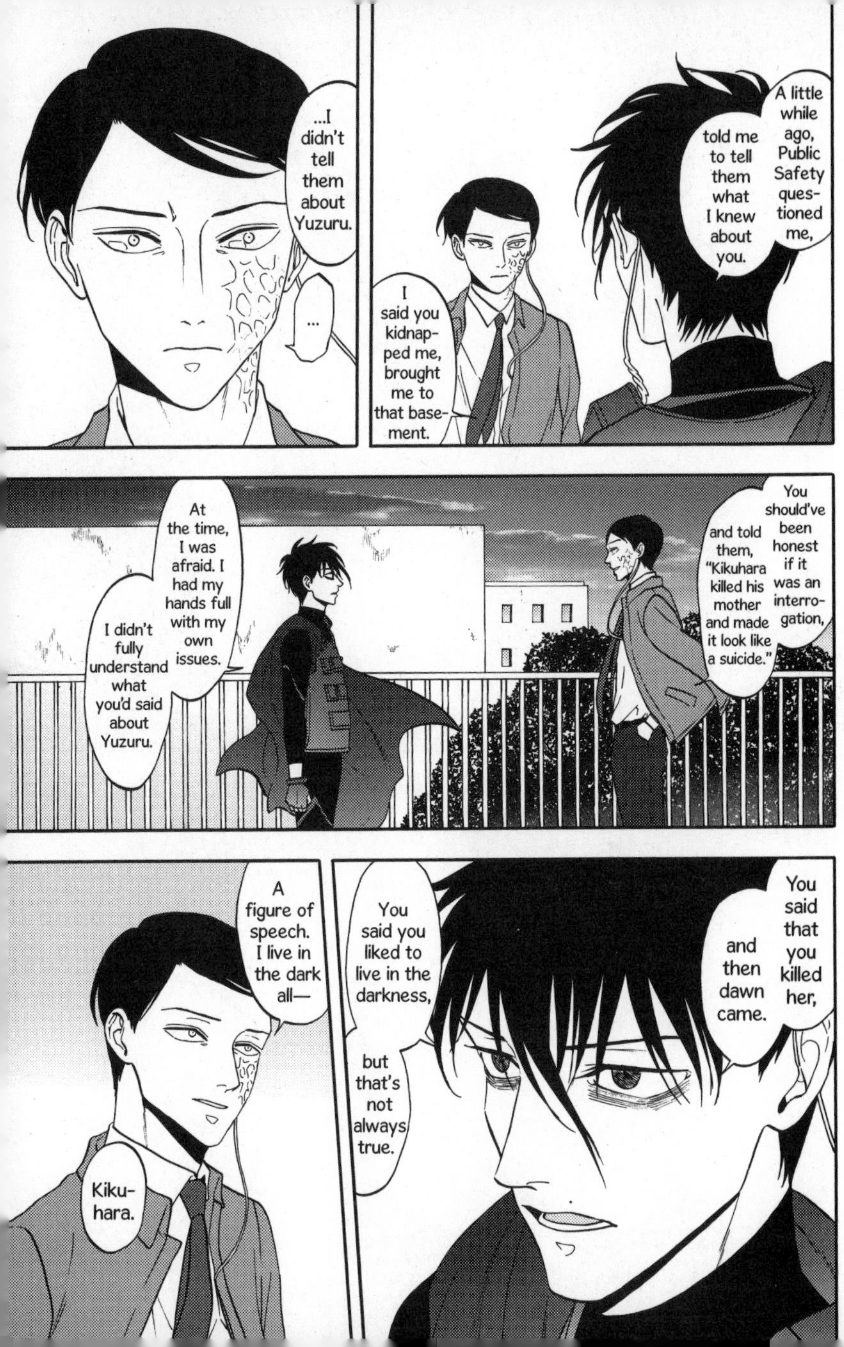
A little while ago, Public Safety questioned me,
told me to tell them what I knew about you.
I said you kidnapped me, brought me to that basement.
...I didn't tell them about Yuzuru.
...
You should've been honest if it was an interrogation,
and told them, "Kikuhara killed his mother and made it look like a suicide."
At the time, I was afraid. I had my hands full with my own issues.
I didn't fully understand what you'd said about Yuzuru.
You said that you killed her,
and then dawn came.
You said you liked to live in the darkness,
but that's not always true.
A figure of speech. I live in the dark all—
Kikuhara.

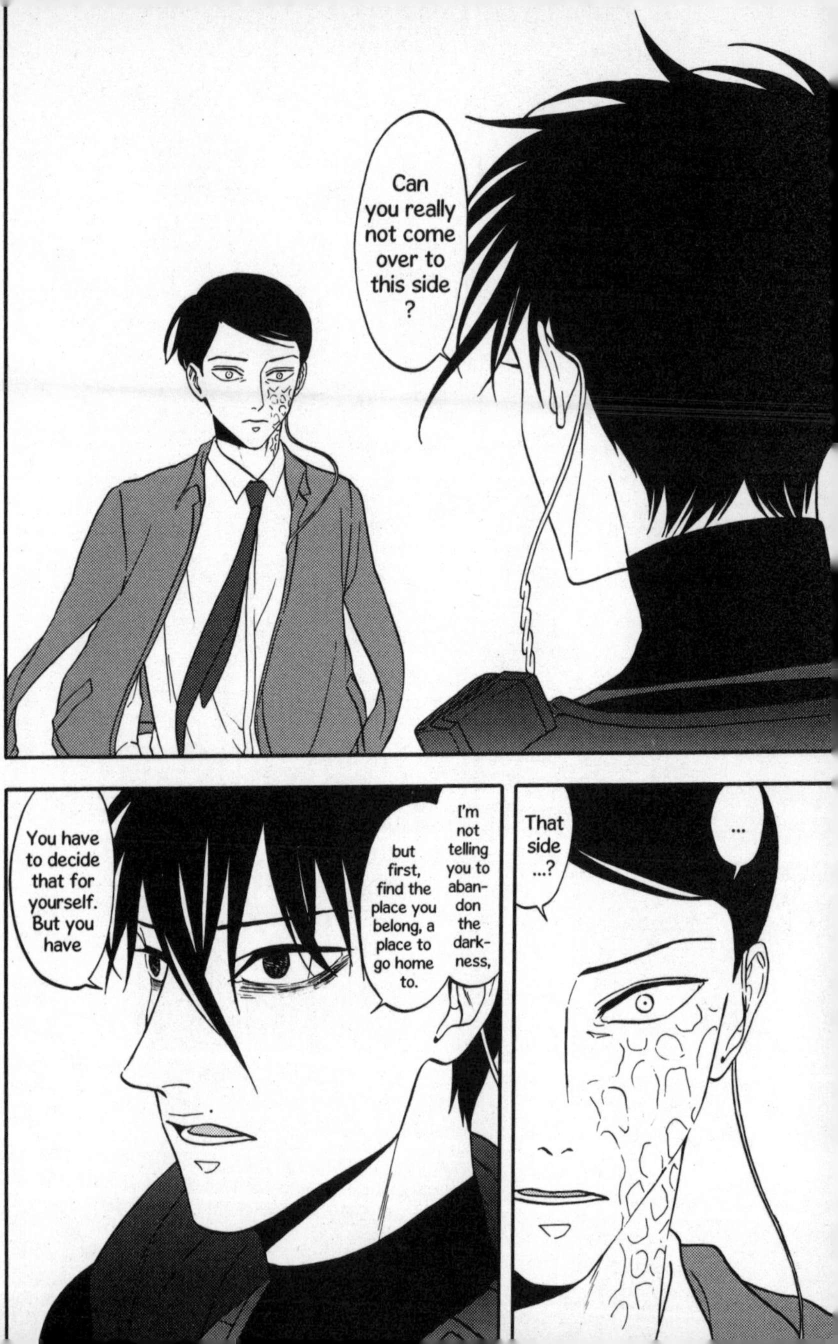
Can you really not come over to this side ?
...
That side ...?
I'm not telling you to abandon the darkness,
but first, find the place you belong, a place to go home to.
You have to decide that for yourself. But you have

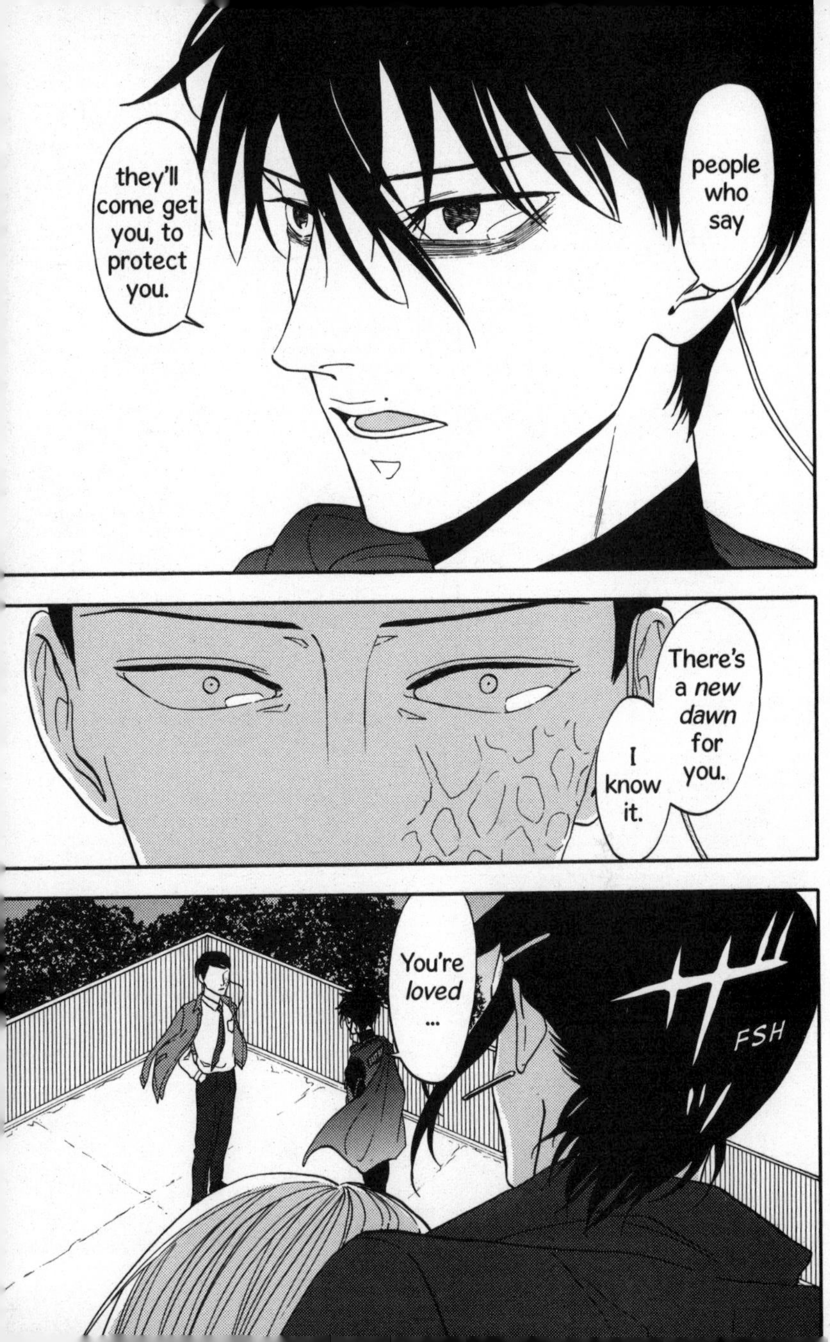
people who say
they'll come get you, to protect you.
There's a *new dawn* for you.
I know it.
FSH
You're *loved* ...

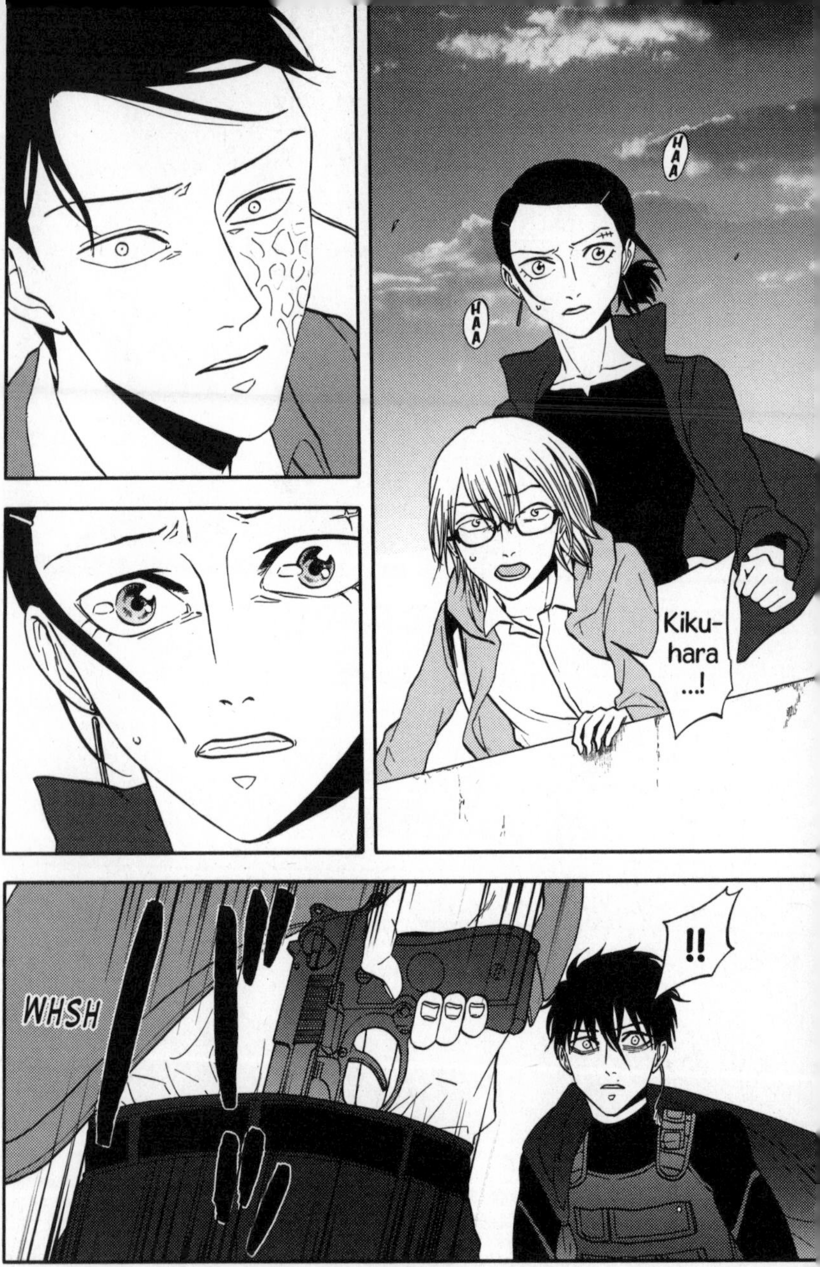
HAA
HAA
Kiku-hara ...!
!!
WHSH

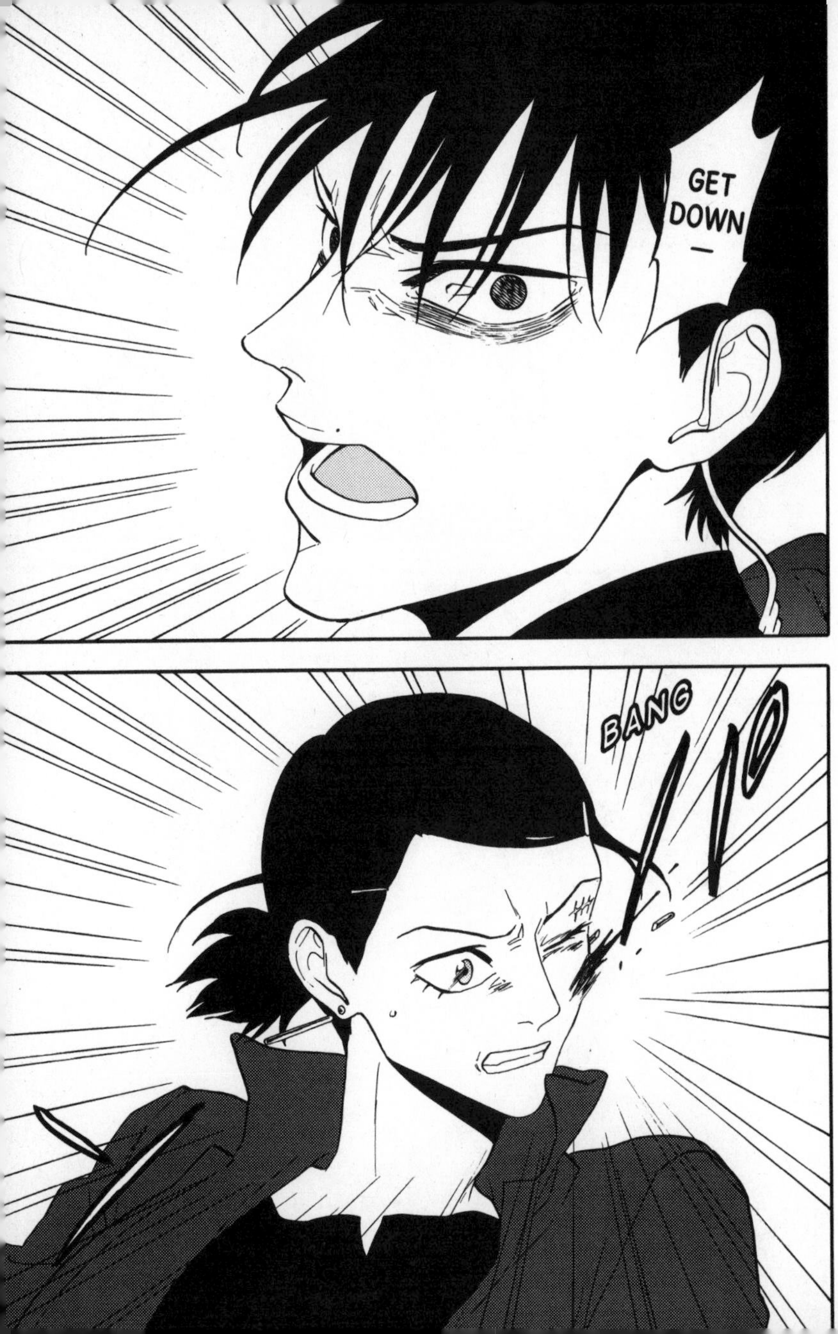
GET DOWN —
BANG

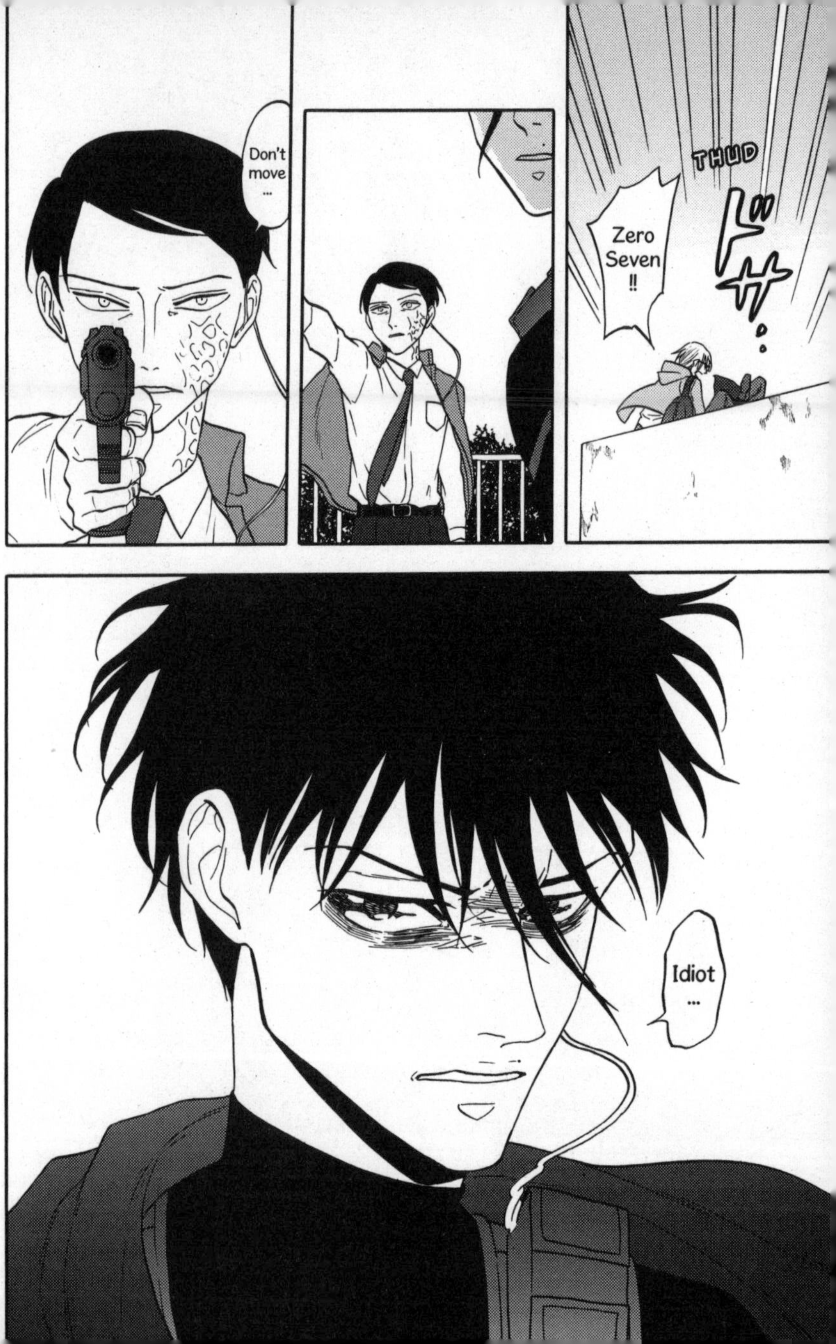
THUD
ドサ
Zero Seven!!
Don't move...
Idiot...

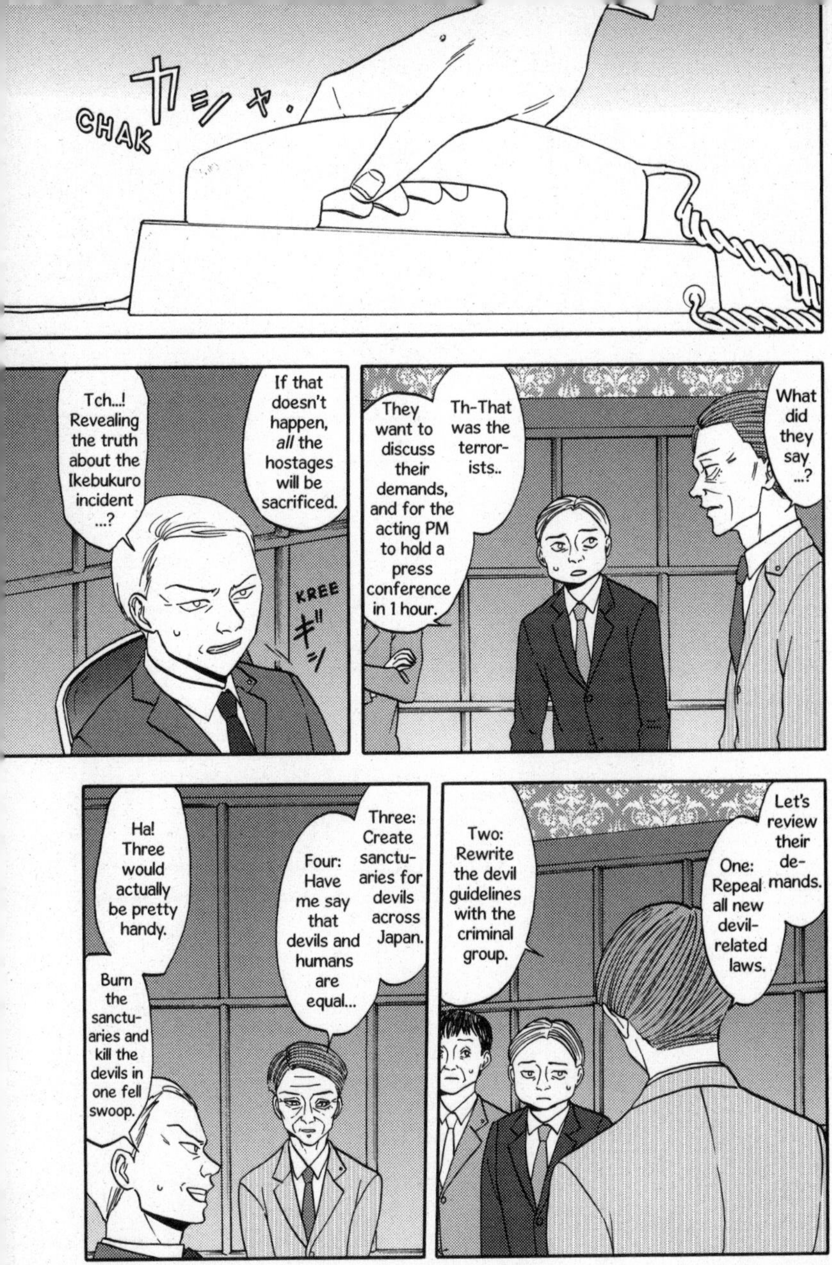

CHAK
カシャ.
What did they say ...?
Th-That was the terror-ists..
They want to discuss their demands, and for the acting PM to hold a press conference in 1 hour.
If that doesn't happen, *all* the hostages will be sacrificed.
Tch...! Revealing the truth about the Ikebukuro incident ...?
KREE
ギッ
Let's review their de-mands.
One: Repeal all new devil-related laws.
Two: Rewrite the devil guidelines with the criminal group.
Three: Create sanctu-aries for devils across Japan.
Four: Have me say that devils and humans are equal...
Ha! Three would actually be pretty handy.
Burn the sanctu-aries and kill the devils in one fell swoop.

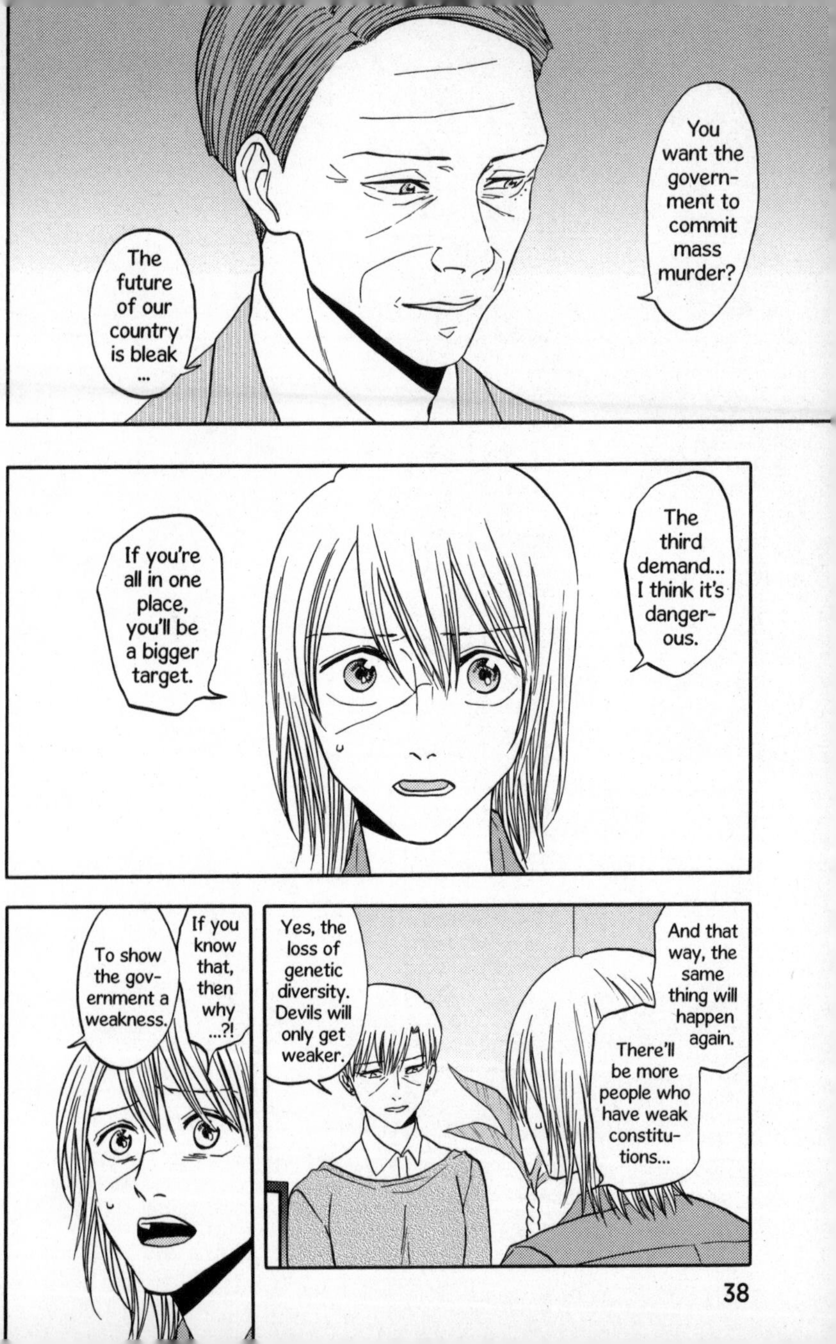
You want the government to commit mass murder?
The future of our country is bleak...
The third demand... I think it's dangerous.
If you're all in one place, you'll be a bigger target.
And that way, the same thing will happen again.
There'll be more people who have weak constitutions...
Yes, the loss of genetic diversity. Devils will only get weaker.
If you know that, then why...?!
To show the government a weakness.

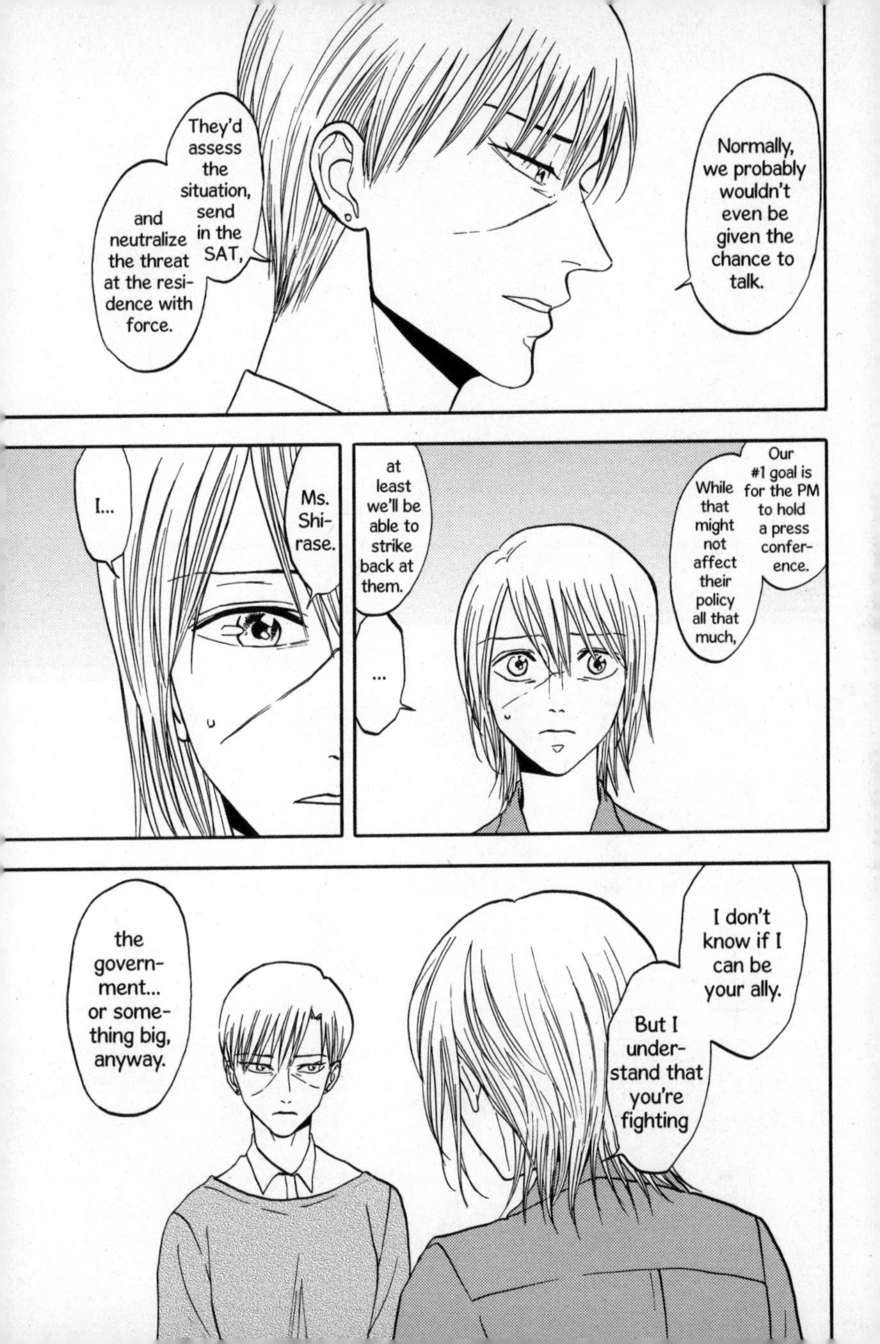
Normally, we probably wouldn't even be given the chance to talk.
They'd assess the situation, send in the SAT, and neutralize the threat at the residence with force.
Our #1 goal is for the PM to hold a press conference.
While that might not affect their policy all that much,
at least we'll be able to strike back at them.
...
Ms. Shirase.
I...
I don't know if I can be your ally.
But I understand that you're fighting
the government... or something big, anyway.

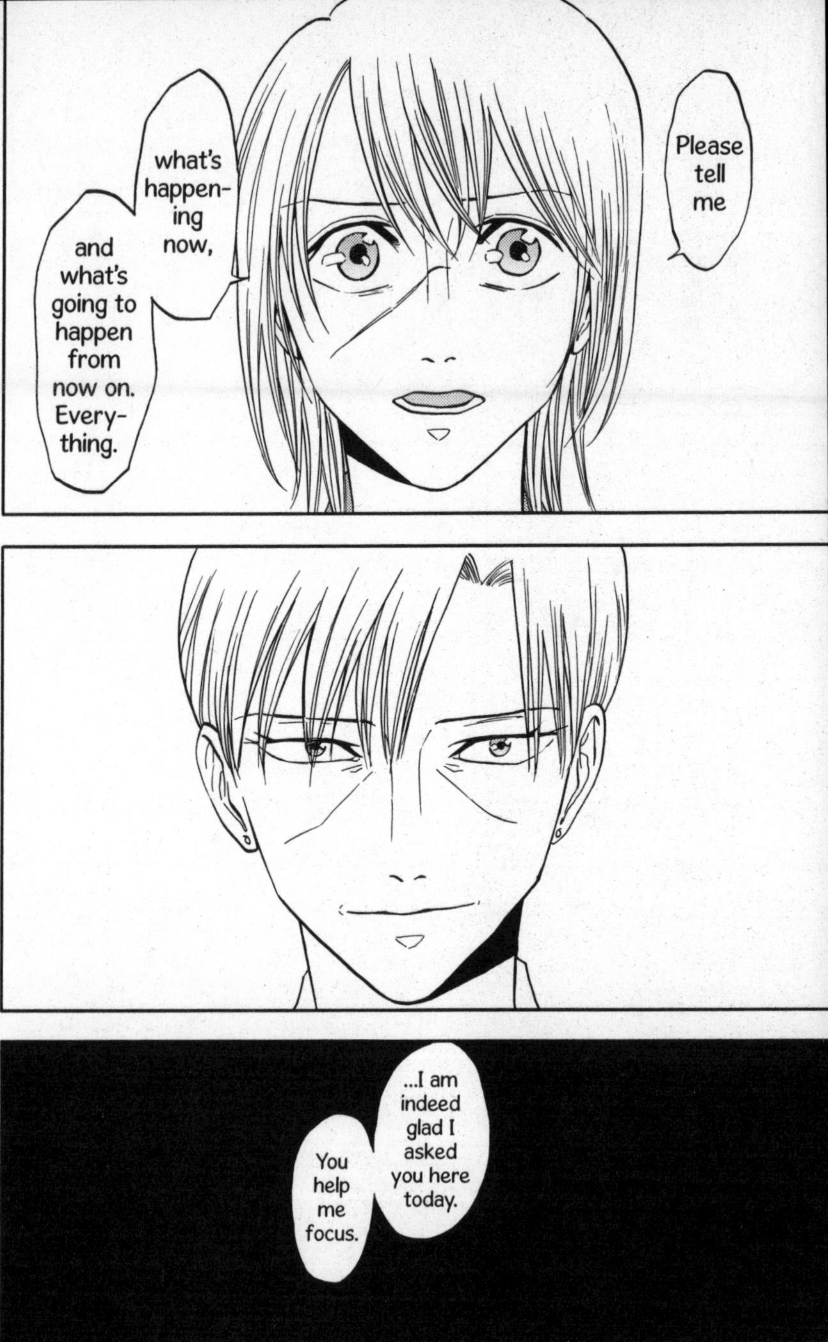
Please tell me
what's happening now,
and what's going to happen from now on. Everything.
...I am indeed glad I asked you here today.
You help me focus.

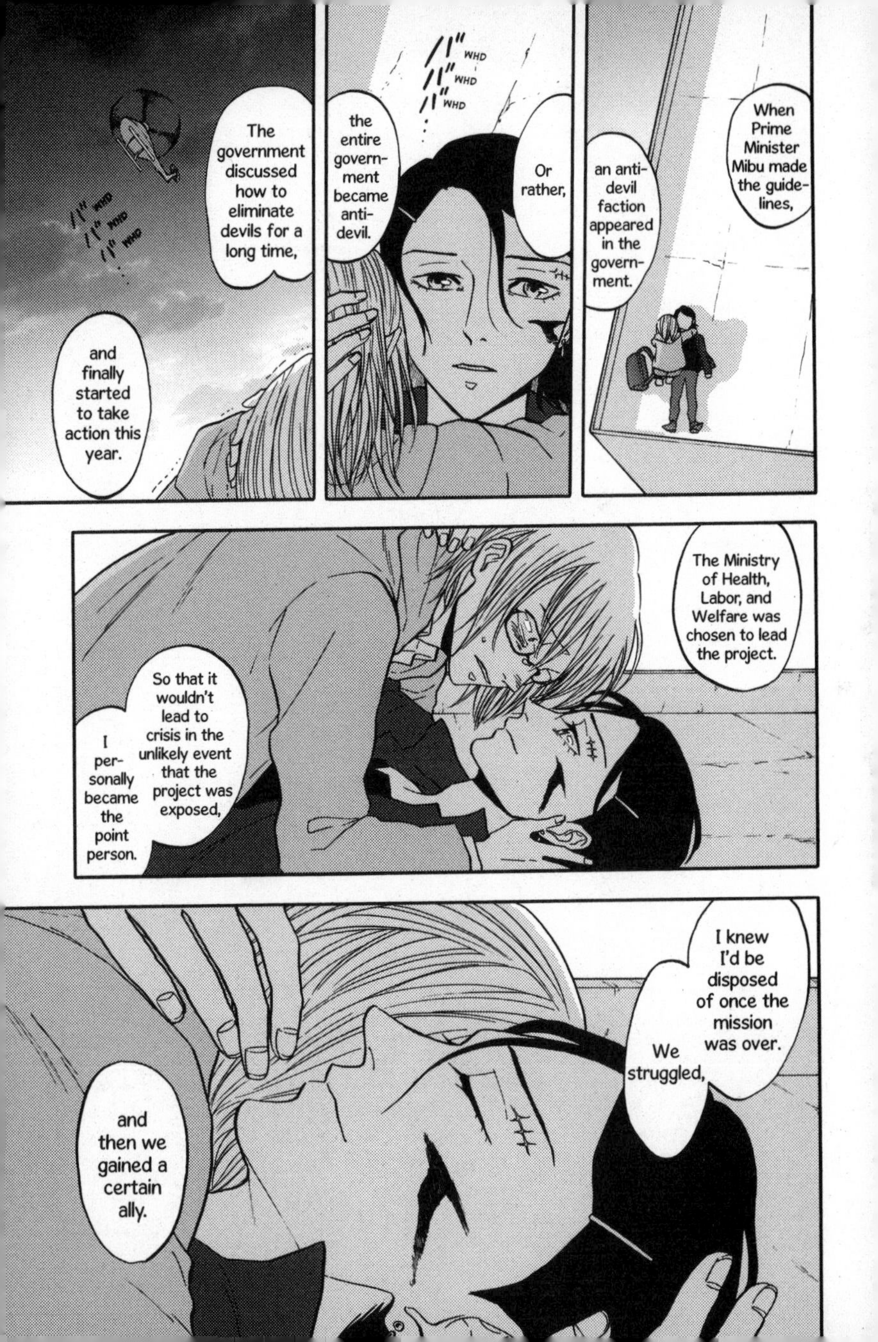
When Prime Minister Mibu made the guidelines,
an anti-devil faction appeared in the government.
WHD WHD WHD
Or rather,
the entire government became anti-devil.
WHD WHD WHD
The government discussed how to eliminate devils for a long time,
and finally started to take action this year.
The Ministry of Health, Labor, and Welfare was chosen to lead the project.
So that it wouldn't lead to crisis in the unlikely event that the project was exposed,
I personally became the point person.
I knew I'd be disposed of once the mission was over.
We struggled,
and then we gained a certain ally.

Minister of Labor Susumu Sofue.

He has a strong sense of justice and a secret understanding of devils.

He was also a candidate for interim prime minister.

We submit demands leaving an opening for the government.

With him as PM, he can create the opportunity for a press conference,

and then he can tell everything about what the government has done.

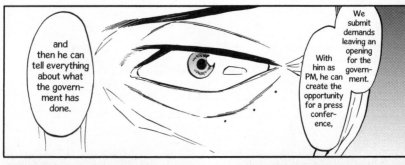

It won't be Queen who reveals the truth about the Ikebukuro incident.

It will be the current leader of our country.

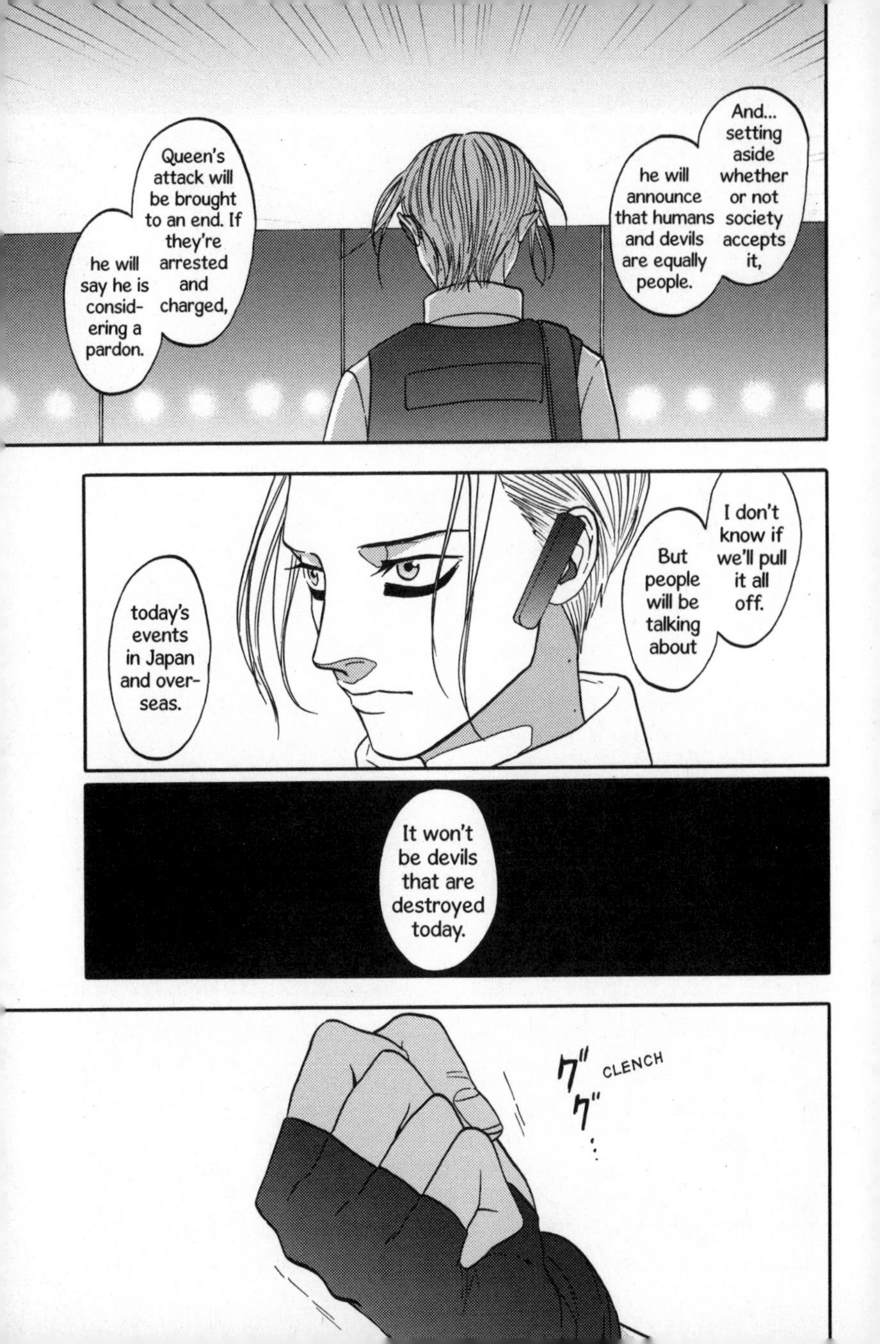

And... setting aside whether or not society accepts it,
he will announce that humans and devils are equally people.
Queen's attack will be brought to an end. If they're arrested and charged,
he will say he is consid-ering a pardon.
I don't know if we'll pull it all off.
But people will be talking about
today's events in Japan and over-seas.
It won't be devils that are destroyed today.
グッグッ
CLENCH

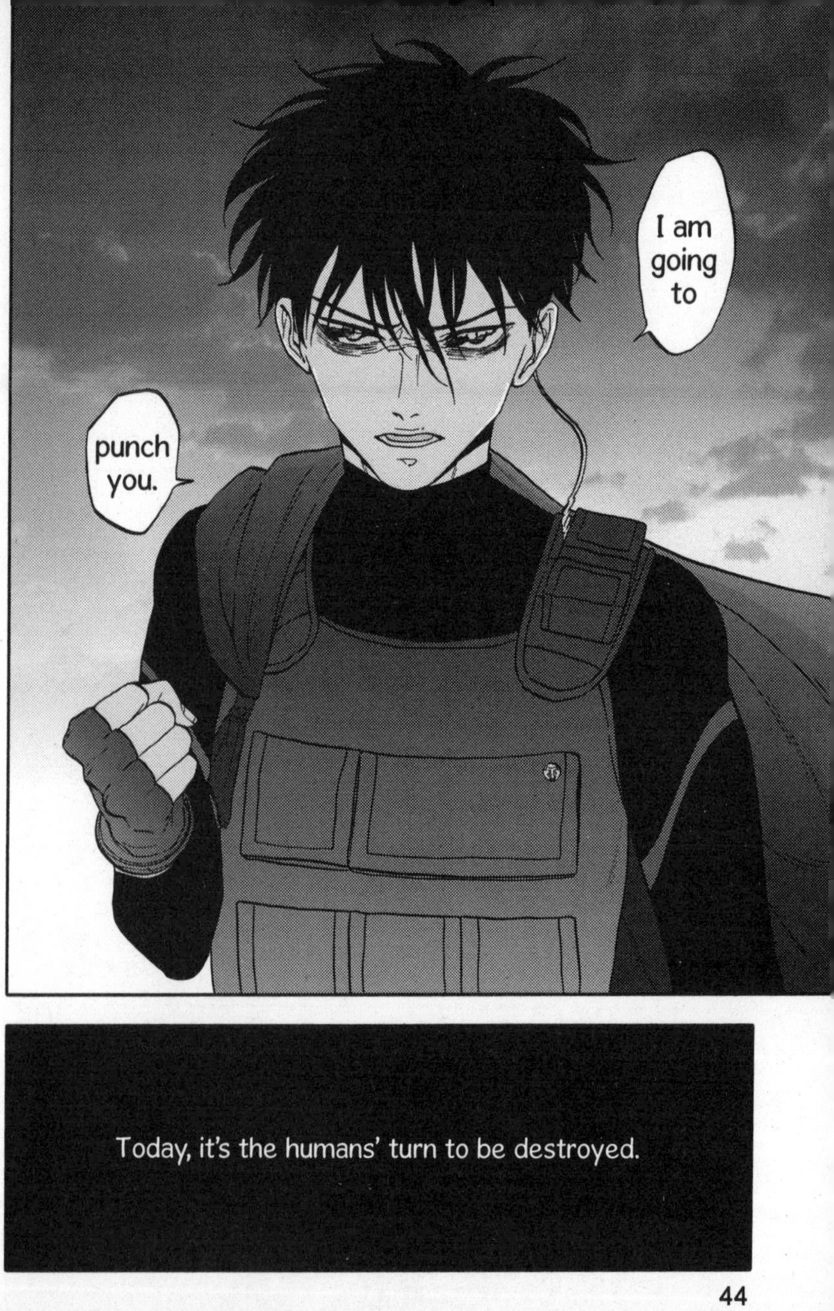
I am going to
punch you.

Today, it's the humans' turn to be destroyed.

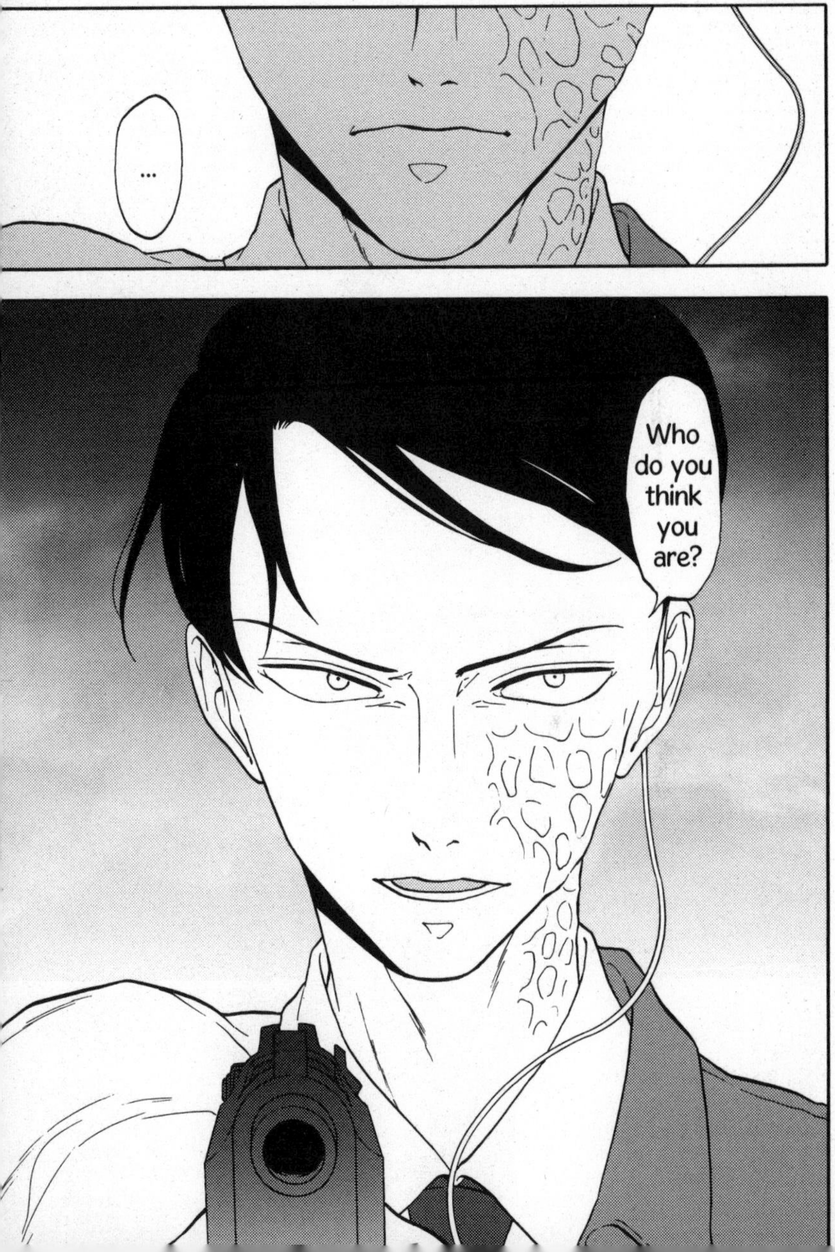
...
Who do you think you are?

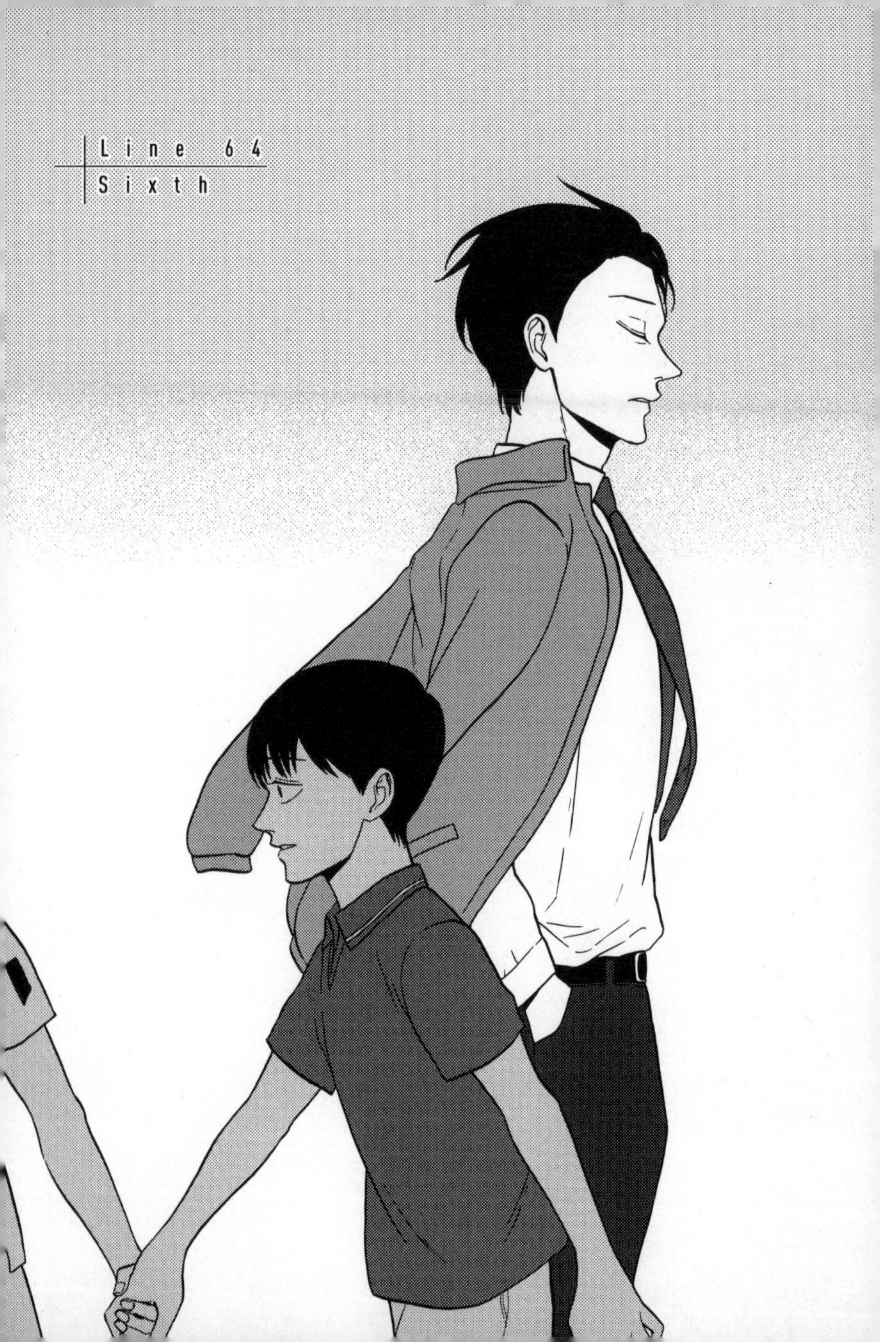
Line 64
Sixth

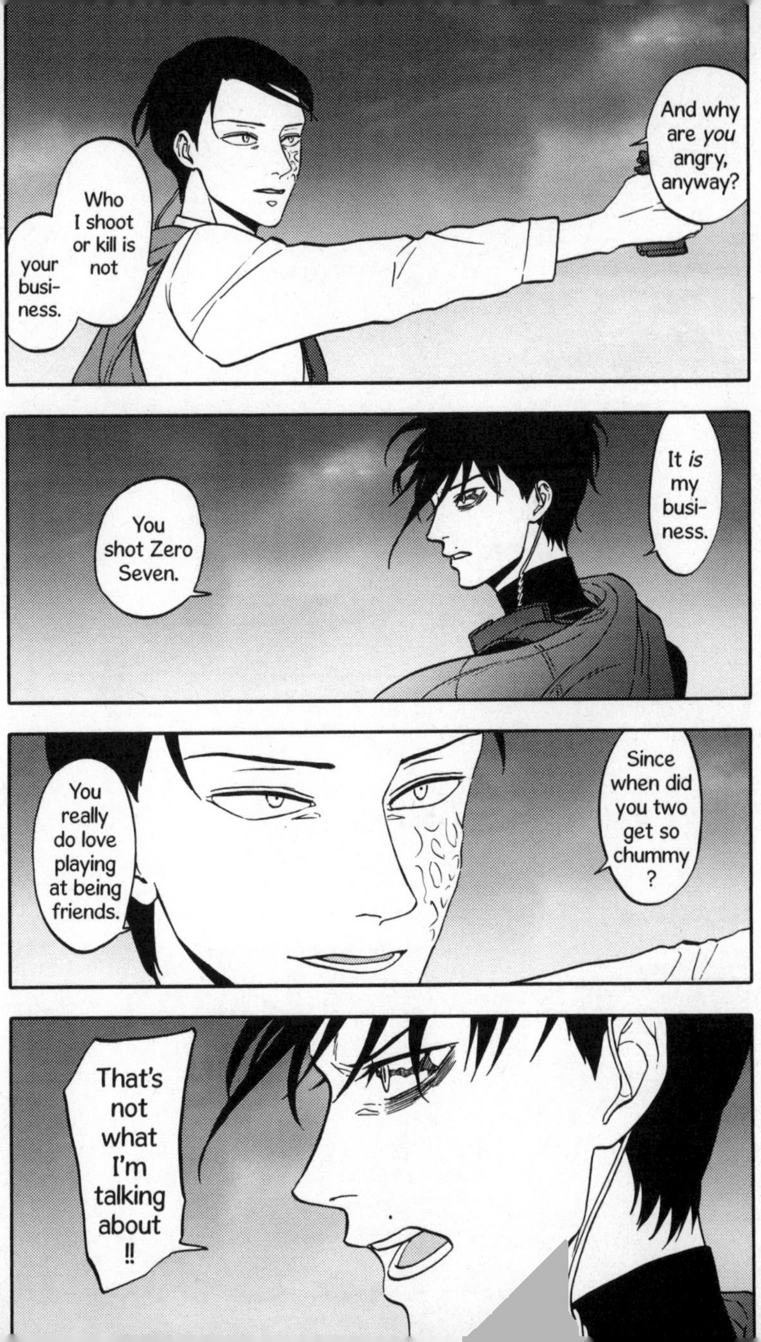
And why are *you* angry, anyway?
Who I shoot or kill is not your business.
It *is* my business.
You shot Zero Seven.
Since when did you two get so chummy?
You really do love playing at being friends.
That's not what I'm talking about!!

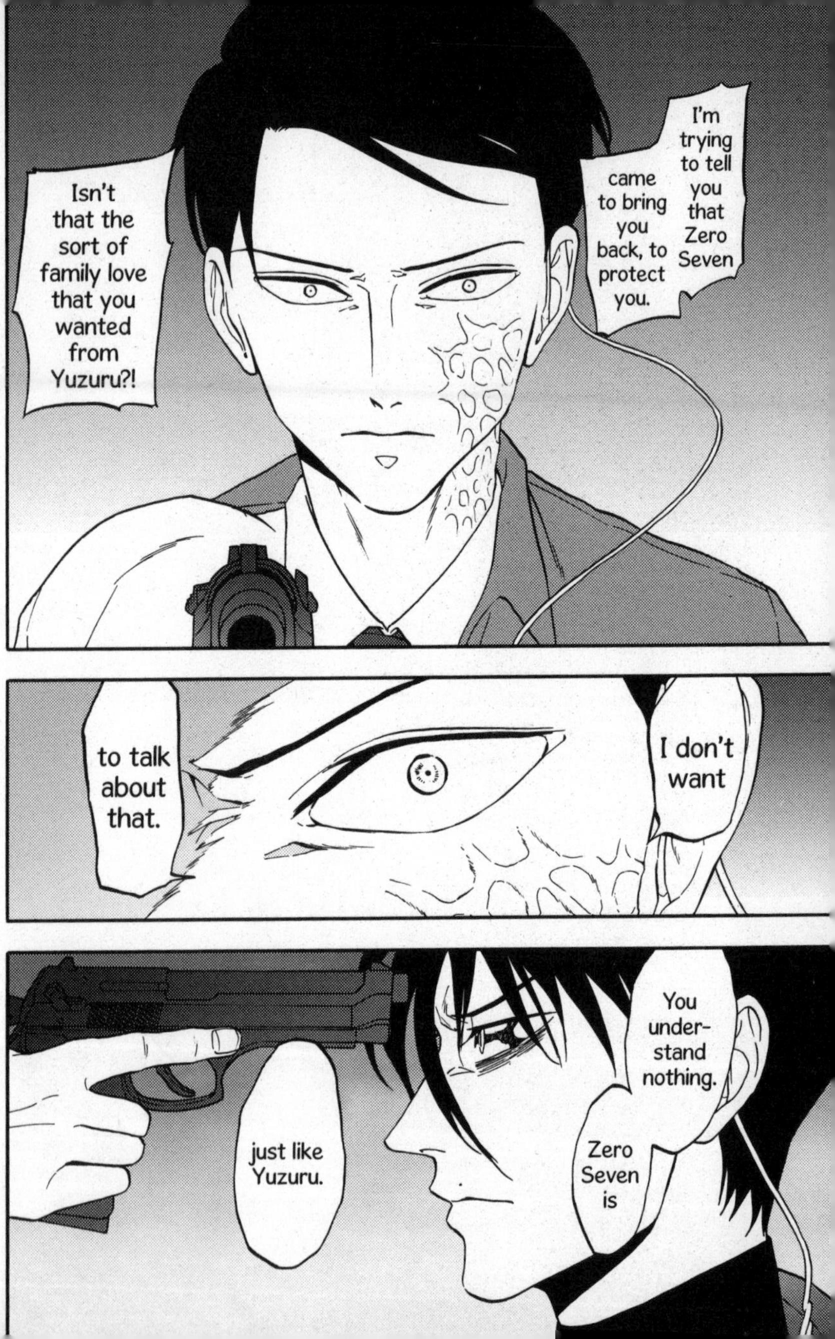
I'm trying to tell you that Zero Seven
came to bring you back, to protect you.
Isn't that the sort of family love that you wanted from Yuzuru?!
I don't want
to talk about that.
You under-stand nothing.
Zero Seven is
just like Yuzuru.

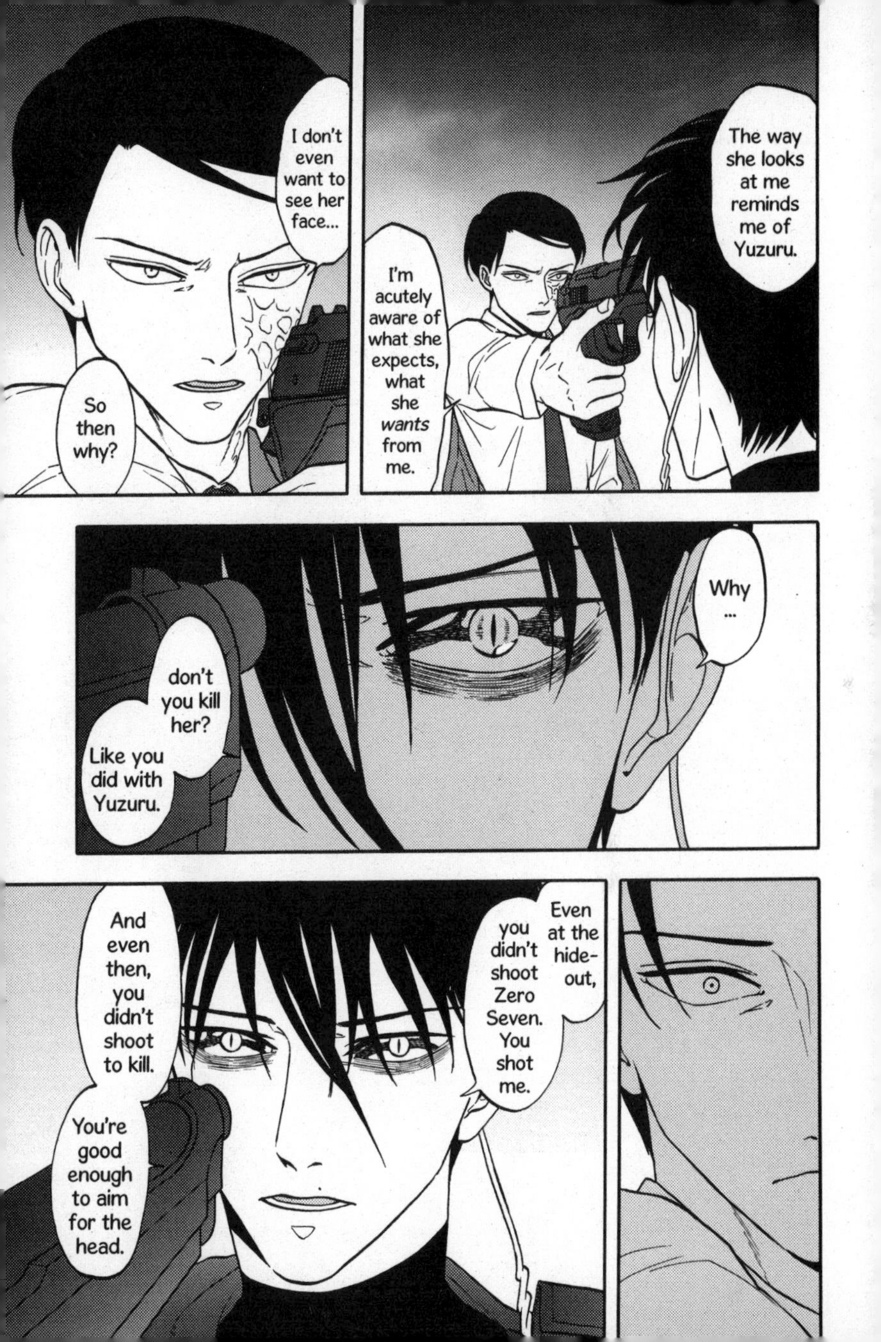
The way she looks at me reminds me of Yuzuru.
I'm acutely aware of what she expects, what she *wants* from me.
I don't even want to see her face...
So then why?
Why ...
don't you kill her?
Like you did with Yuzuru.
Even at the hide-out, you didn't shoot Zero Seven. You shot me.
And even then, you didn't shoot to kill.
You're good enough to aim for the head.

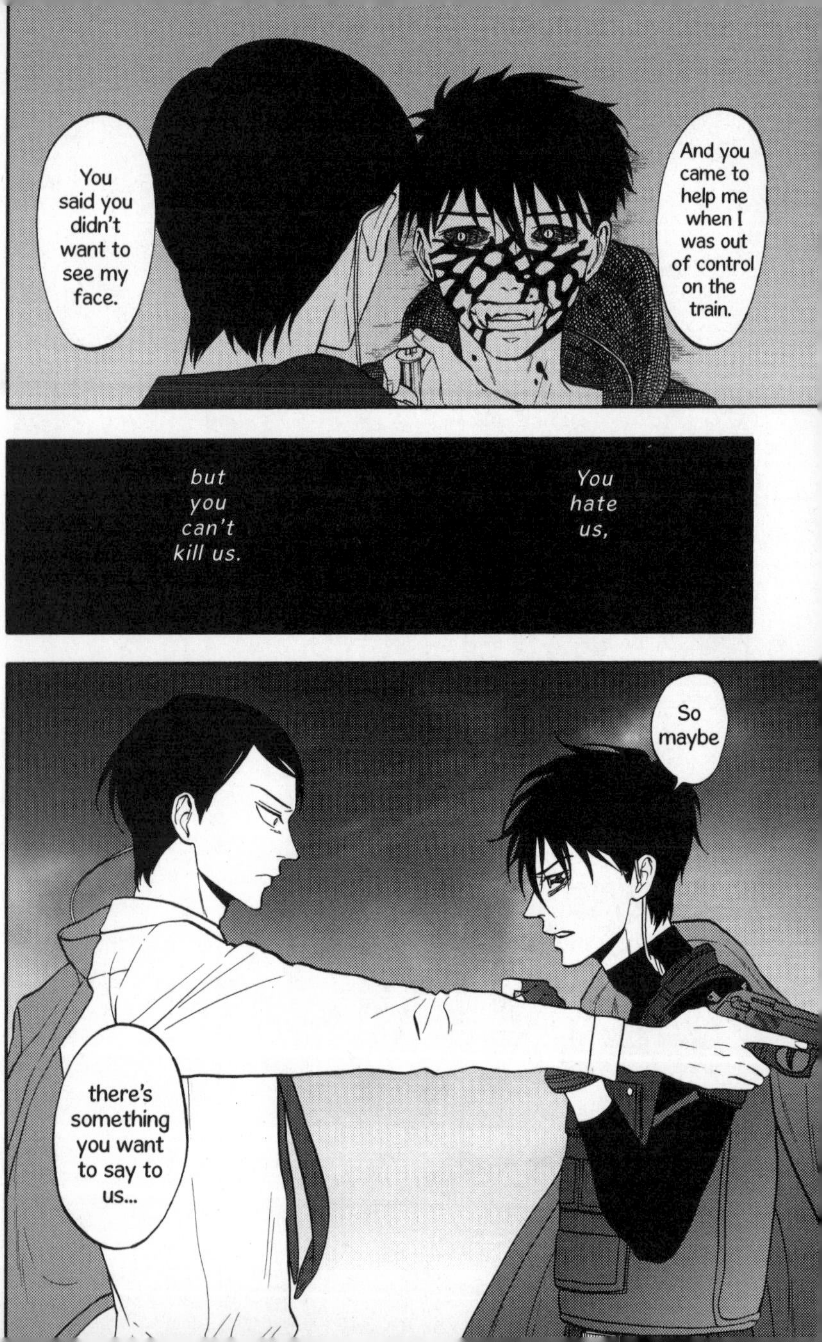
And you came to help me when I was out of control on the train.
You said you didn't want to see my face.
You hate us,
but you can't kill us.
So maybe
there's something you want to say to us...

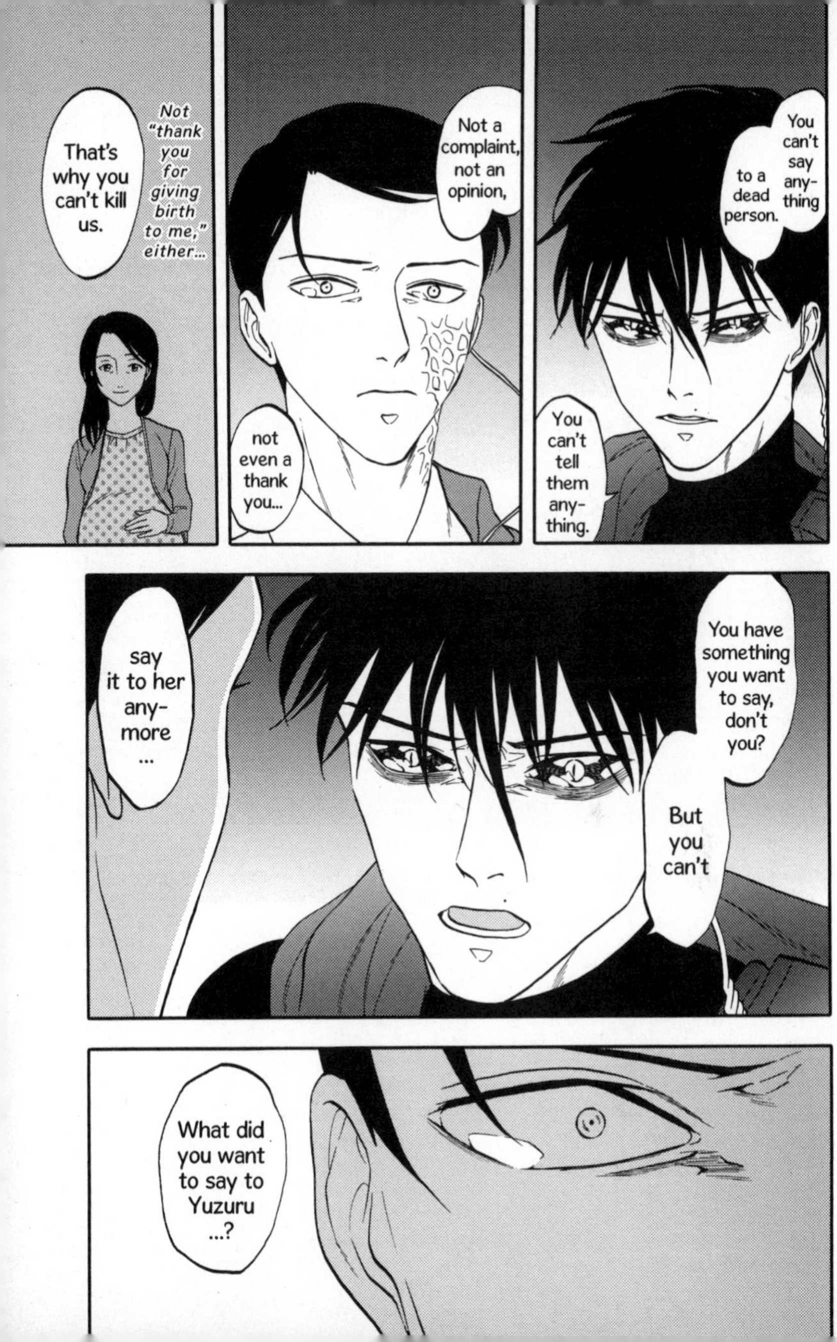
You can't say any-thing
to a dead person.
You can't tell them any-thing.
Not a complaint, not an opinion,
not even a thank you...
Not "thank you for giving birth to me," either...
That's why you can't kill us.
You have something you want to say, don't you?
But you can't
say it to her any-more ...
What did you want to say to Yuzuru ...?

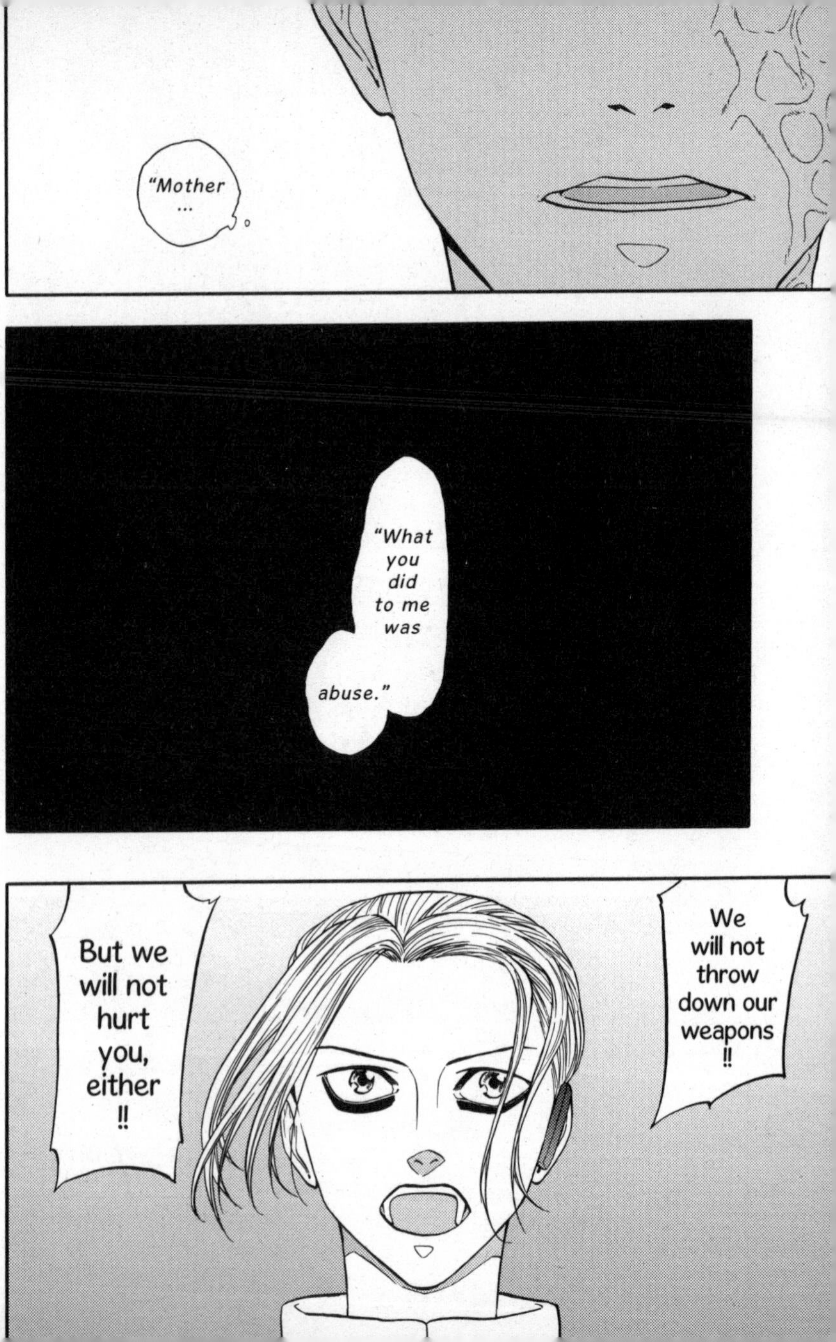
"Mother ...
"What you did to me was
abuse."
We will not throw down our weapons !!
But we will not hurt you, either !!

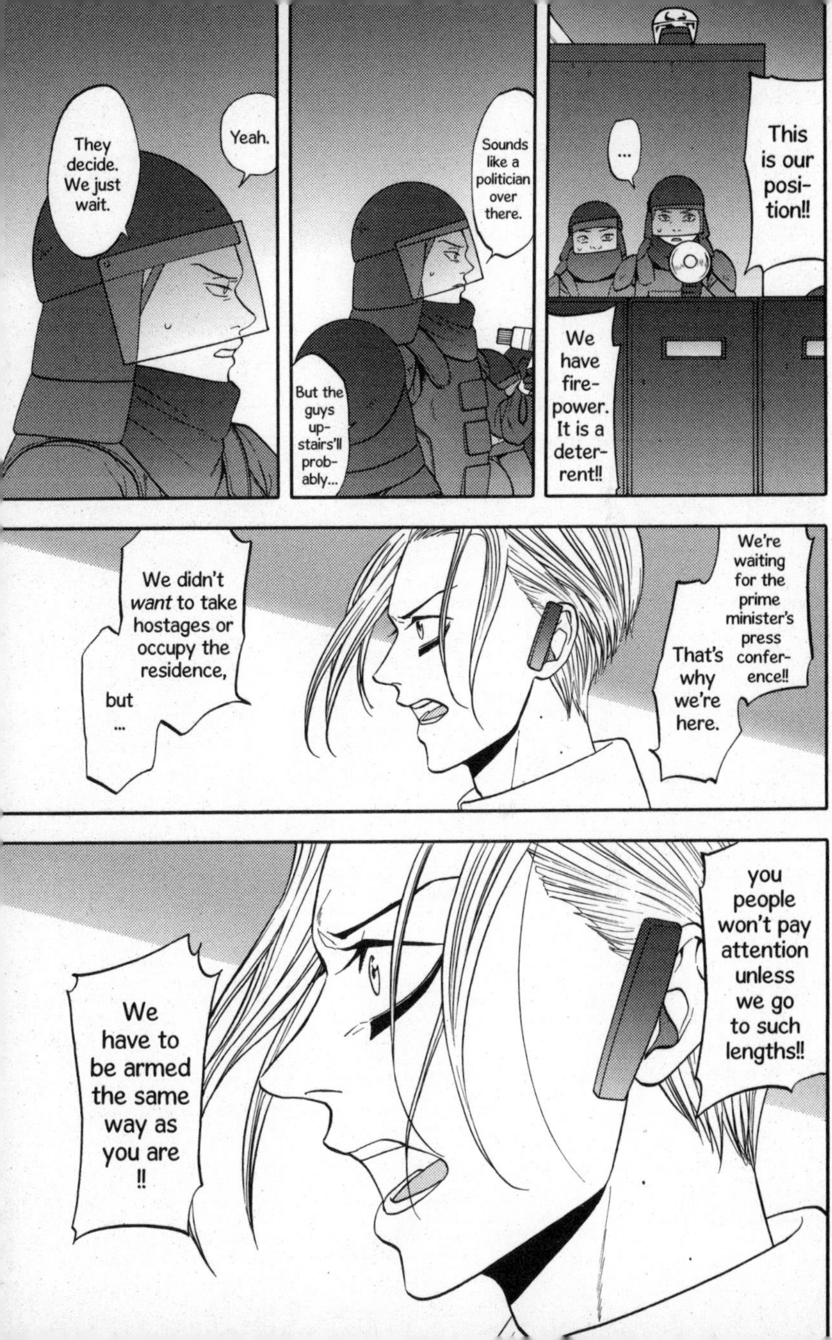
This is our position!!
...
We have firepower. It is a deterrent!!
Sounds like a politician over there.
But the guys upstairs'll probably...
Yeah.
They decide. We just wait.
We're waiting for the prime minister's press conference!!
That's why we're here.
We didn't *want* to take hostages or occupy the residence,
but...
you people won't pay attention unless we go to such lengths!!
We have to be armed the same way as you are!!

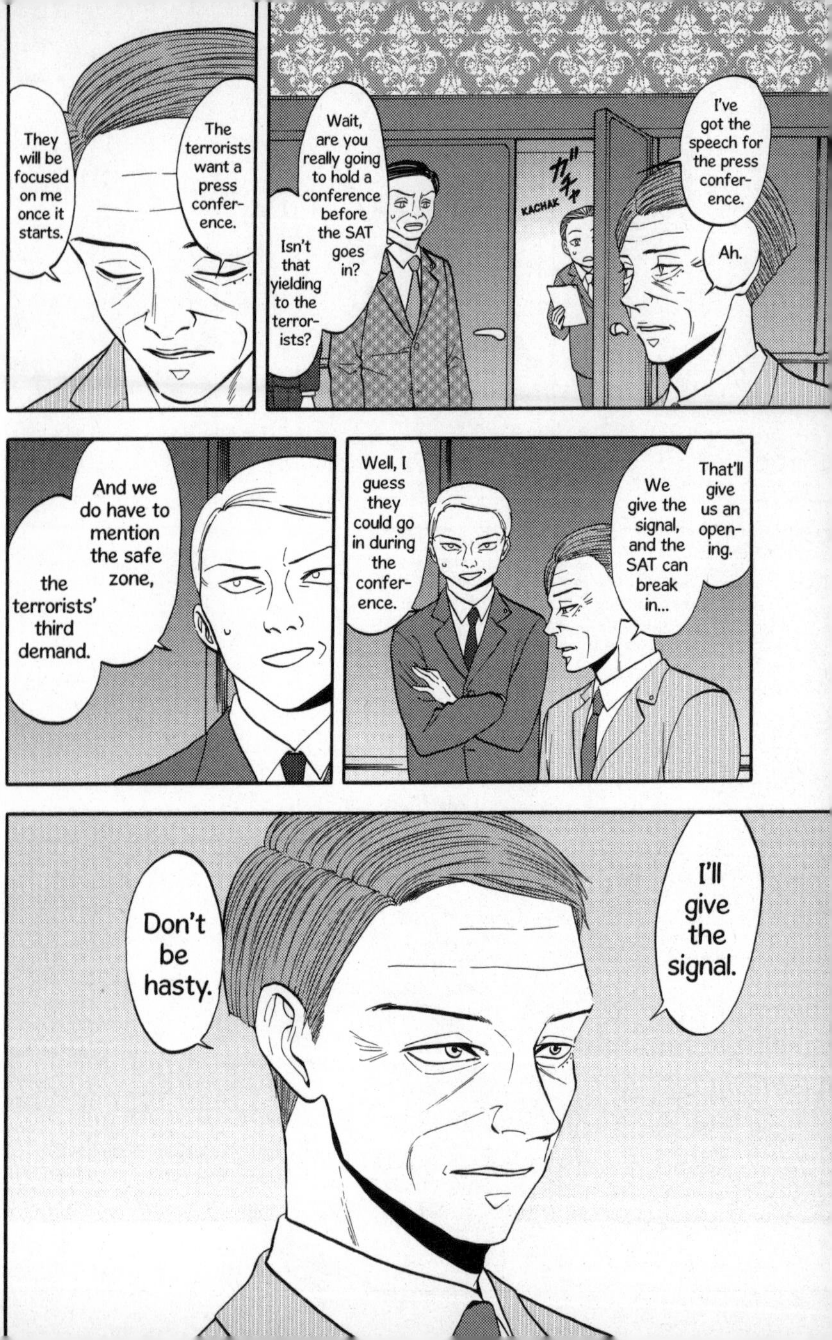
I've got the speech for the press conference.
Ah.
ガチャ
KACHAK
Wait, are you really going to hold a conference before the SAT goes in?
Isn't that yielding to the terrorists?
The terrorists want a press conference.
They will be focused on me once it starts.
That'll give us an opening.
We give the signal, and the SAT can break in...
Well, I guess they could go in during the conference.
And we do have to mention the safe zone,
the terrorists' third demand.
I'll give the signal.
Don't be hasty.

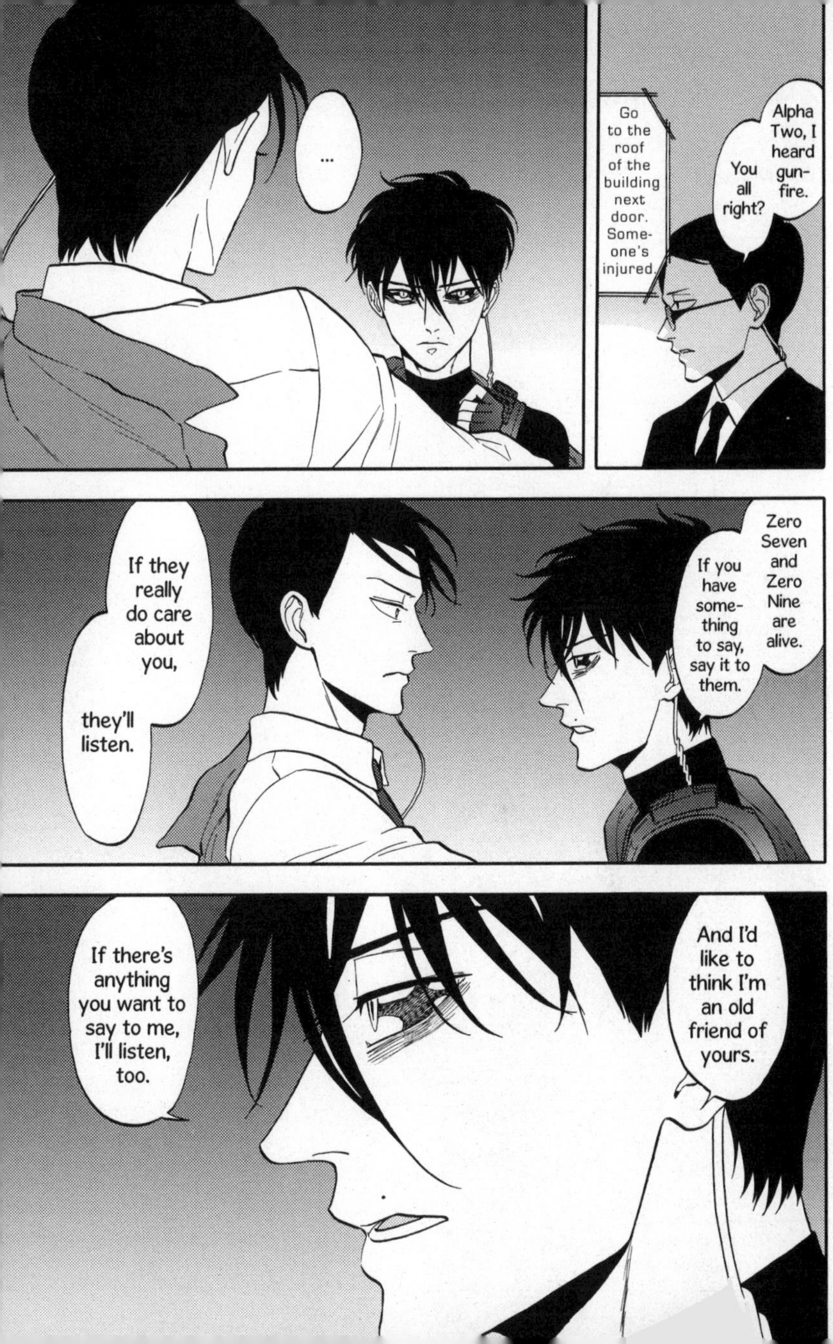

Alpha Two, I heard gunfire.
You all right?
Go to the roof of the building next door. Someone's injured.
...
Zero Seven and Zero Nine are alive.
If you have something to say, say it to them.
If they really do care about you,
they'll listen.
And I'd like to think I'm an old friend of yours.
If there's anything you want to say to me, I'll listen, too.

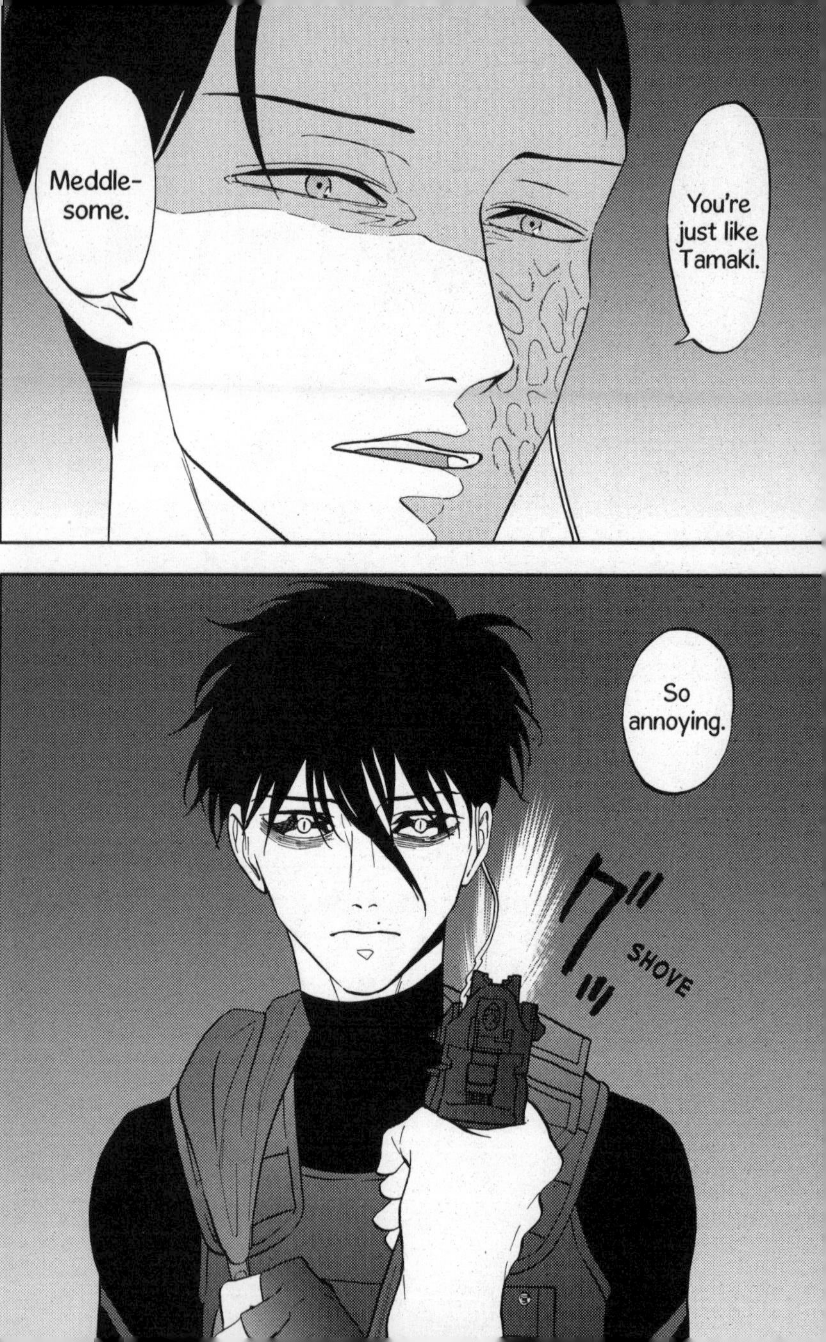
You're just like Tamaki.
Meddle-some.
So annoying.
SHOVE

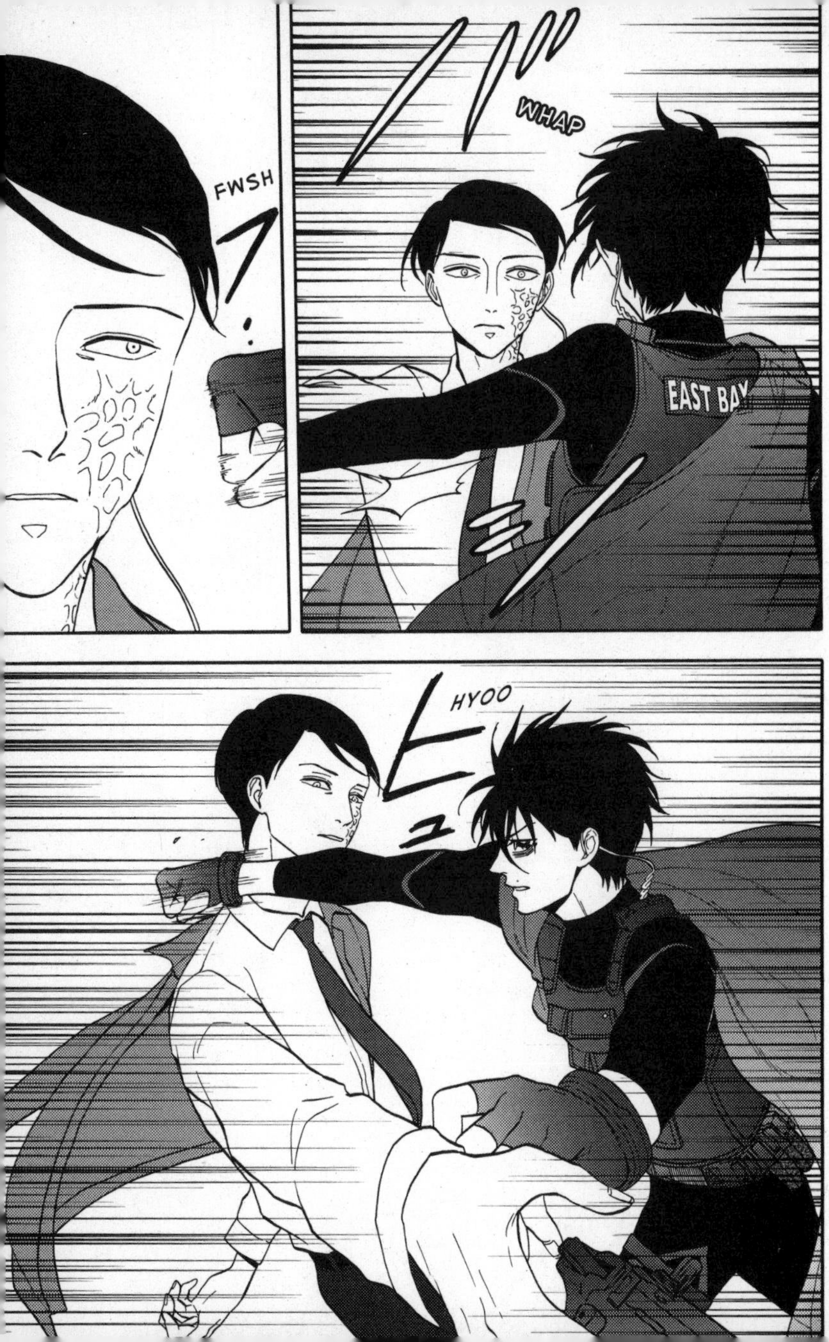
WHAP
EAST BAY
FWSH
HYOO

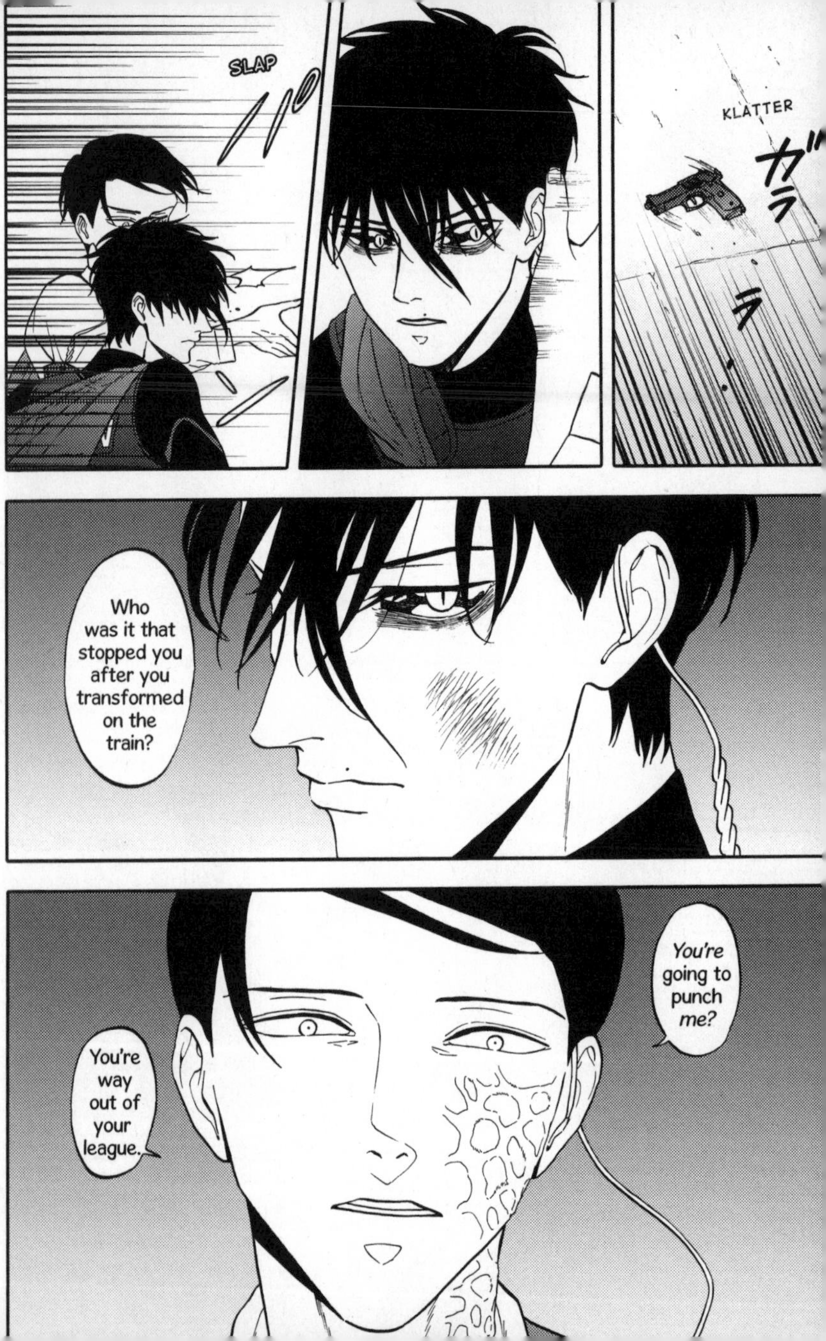
KLATTER
ガラ
ラ
SLAP
Who was it that stopped you after you transformed on the train?
You're going to punch *me?*
You're way out of your league.

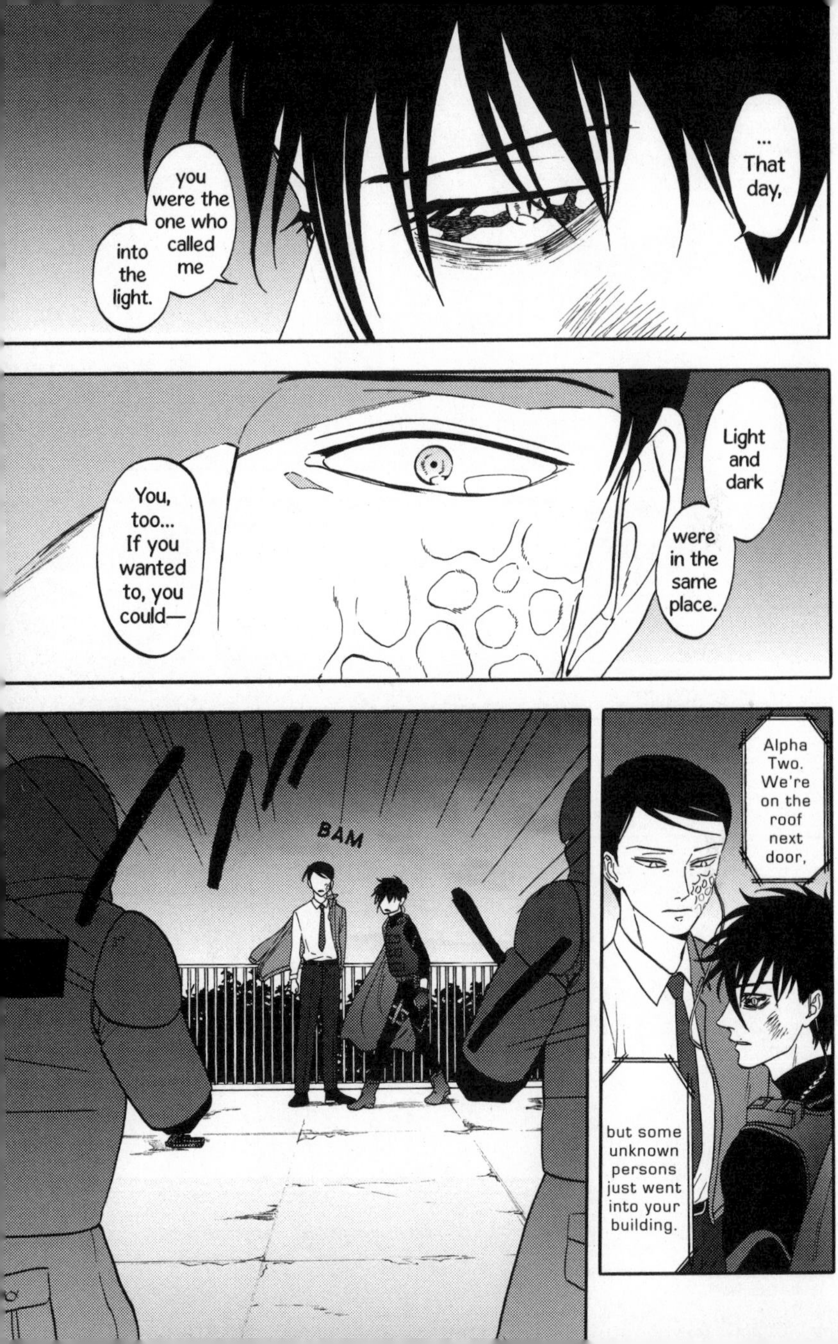
... That day,
you were the one who called me into the light.
Light and dark were in the same place.
You, too... If you wanted to, you could—
Alpha Two. We're on the roof next door,
but some unknown persons just went into your building.
BAM

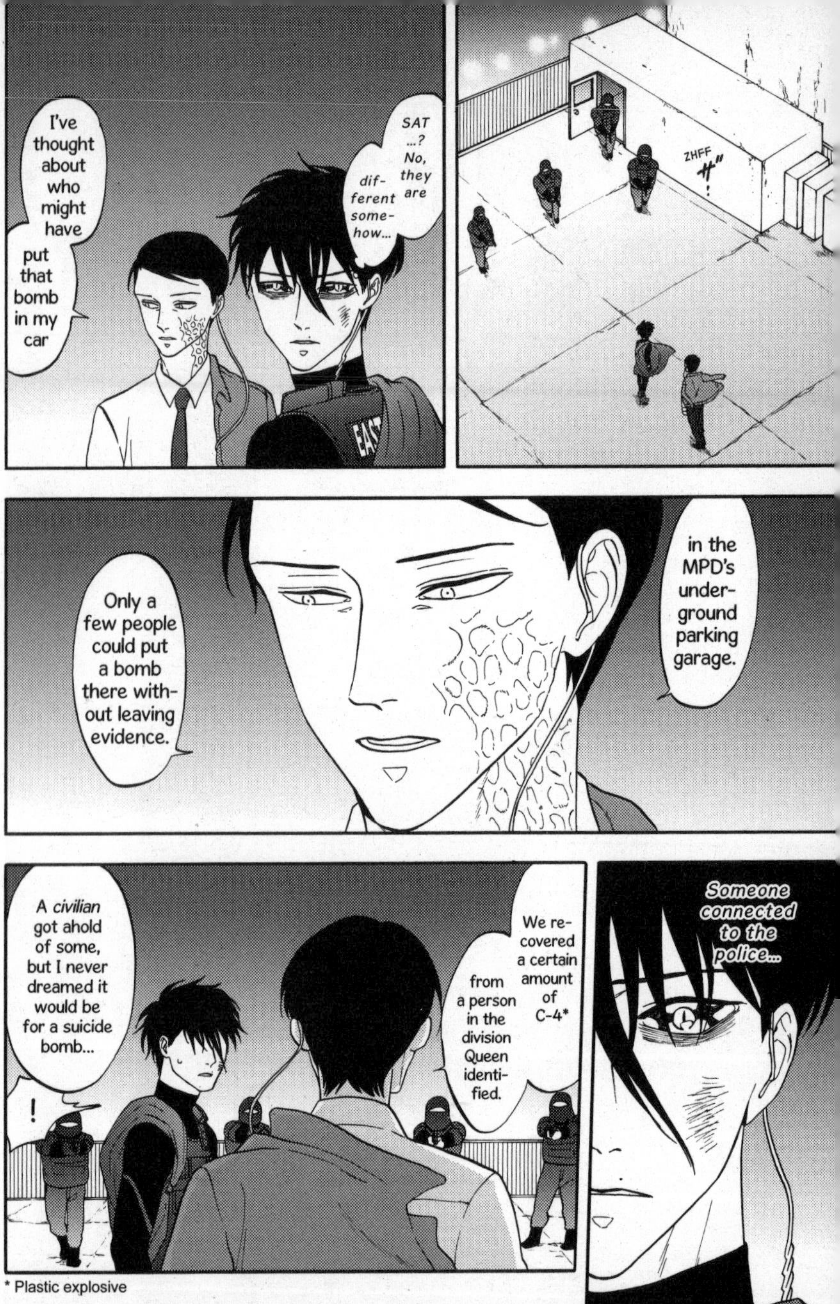
ZHFF
SAT ...? No, they are different somehow...
I've thought about who might have put that bomb in my car
in the MPD's underground parking garage.
Only a few people could put a bomb there without leaving evidence.
Someone connected to the police...
We recovered a certain amount of C-4*
from a person in the division Queen identified.
A civilian got ahold of some, but I never dreamed it would be for a suicide bomb...
!

* Plastic explosive

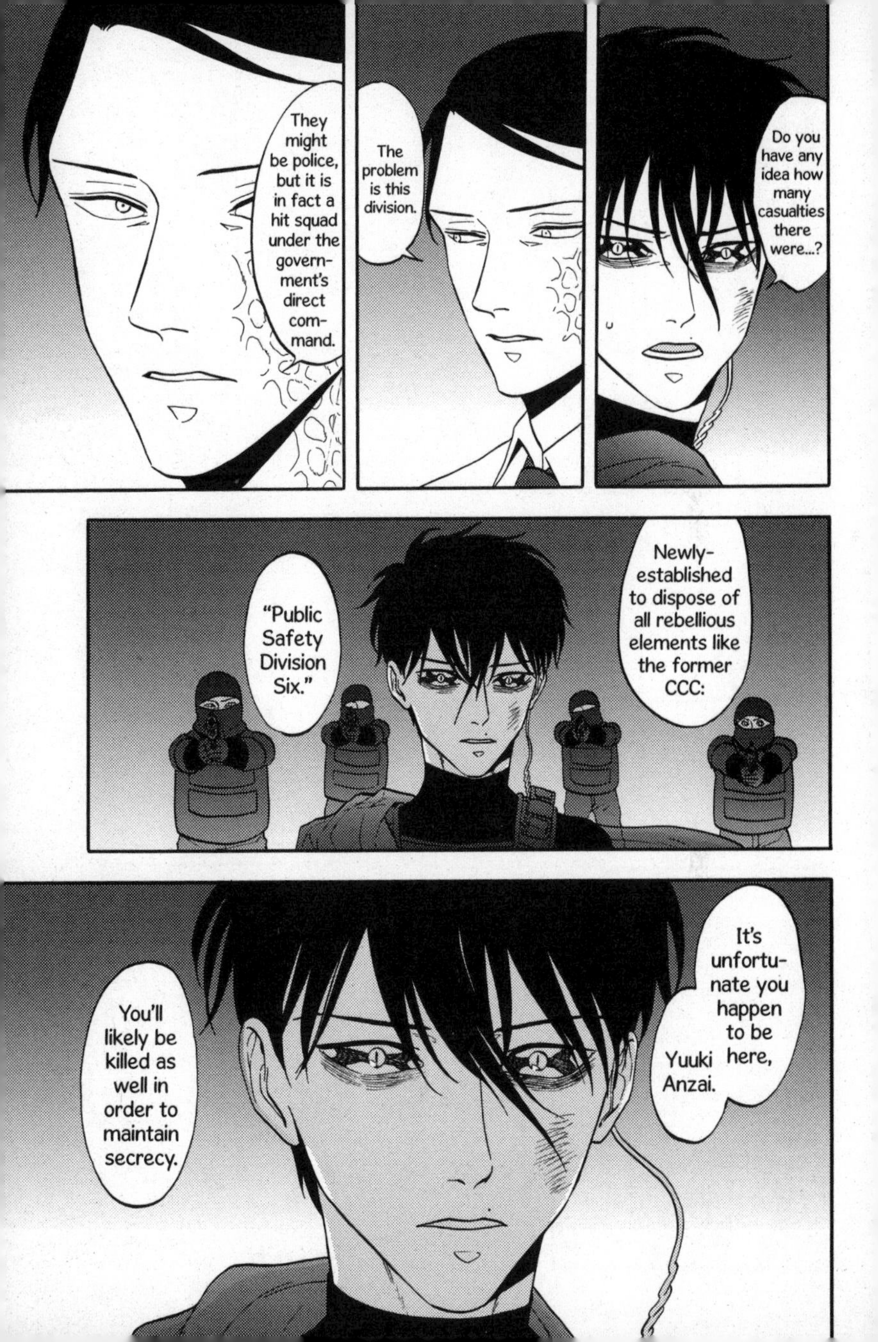
Do you have any idea how many casualties there were...?
The problem is this division.
They might be police, but it is in fact a hit squad under the government's direct command.
Newly-established to dispose of all rebellious elements like the former CCC:
"Public Safety Division Six."
It's unfortunate you happen to be here,
Yuuki Anzai.
You'll likely be killed as well in order to maintain secrecy.

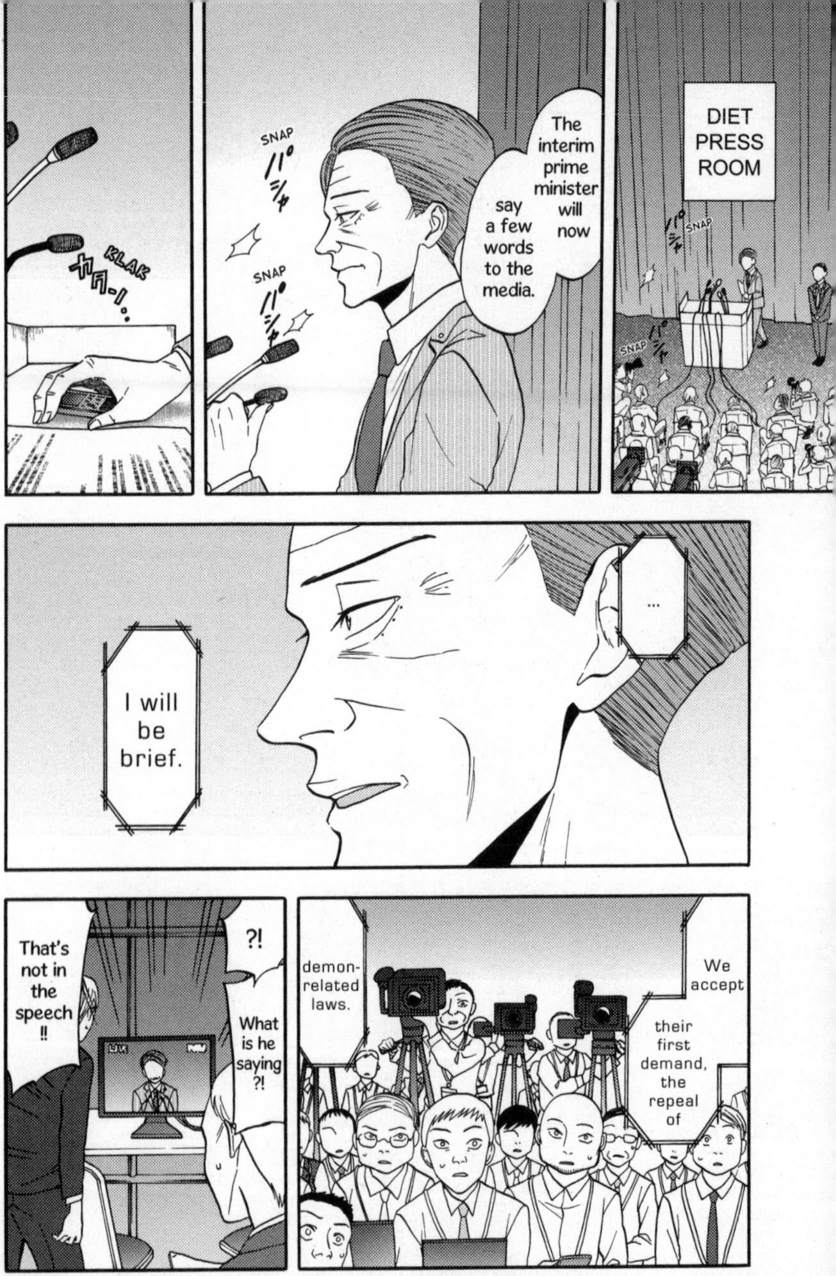
DIET PRESS ROOM
SNAP
SNAP
The interim prime minister will now say a few words to the media.
SNAP
SNAP
KLAK
...
I will be brief.
We accept their first demand, the repeal of demon-related laws.
?!
What is he saying ?!
That's not in the speech !!

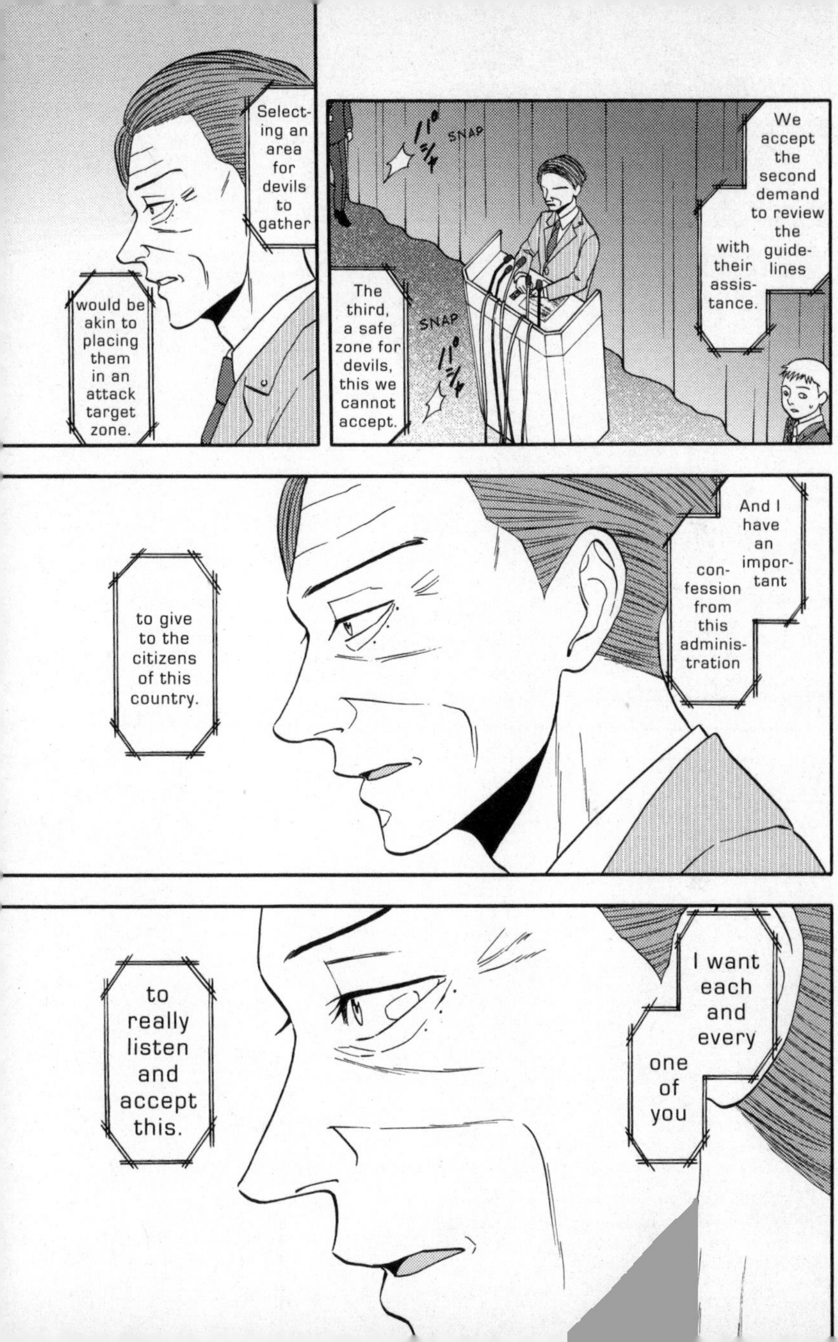
We accept the second demand to review the guidelines with their assistance.
SNAP
SNAP
The third, a safe zone for devils, this we cannot accept.
Selecting an area for devils to gather
would be akin to placing them in an attack target zone.
And I have an important confession from this administration
to give to the citizens of this country.
I want each and every one of you
to really listen and accept this.

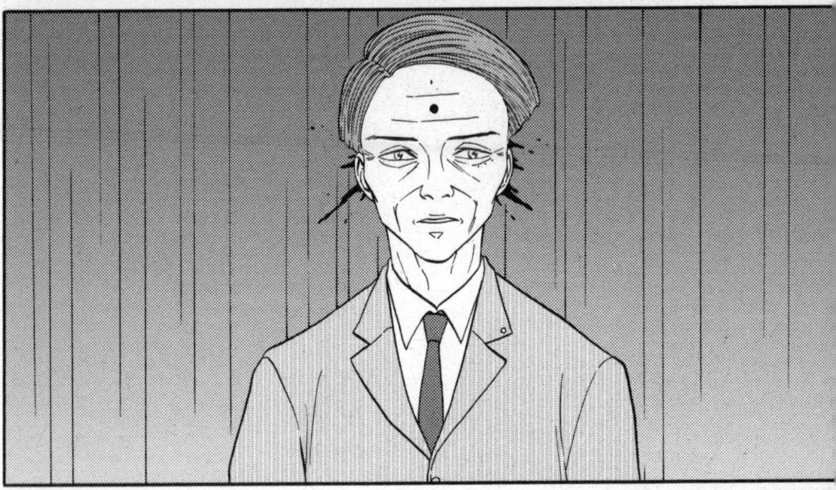
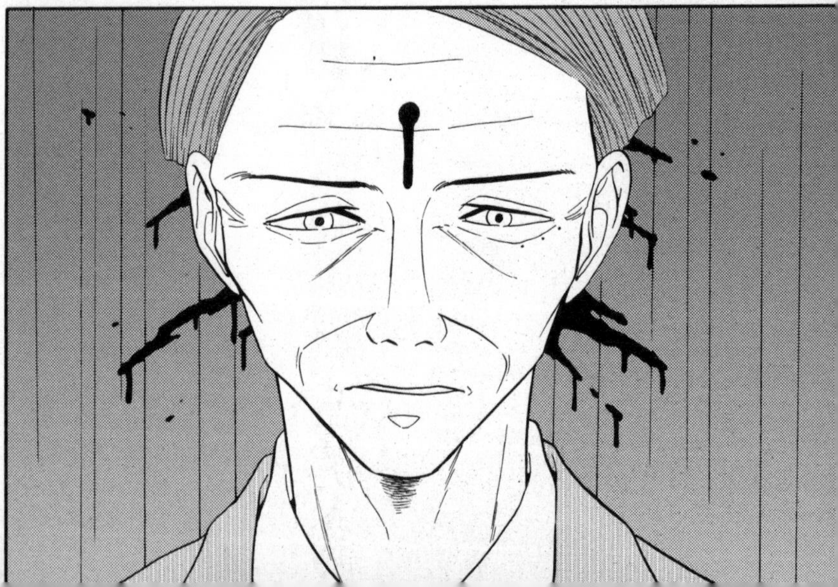

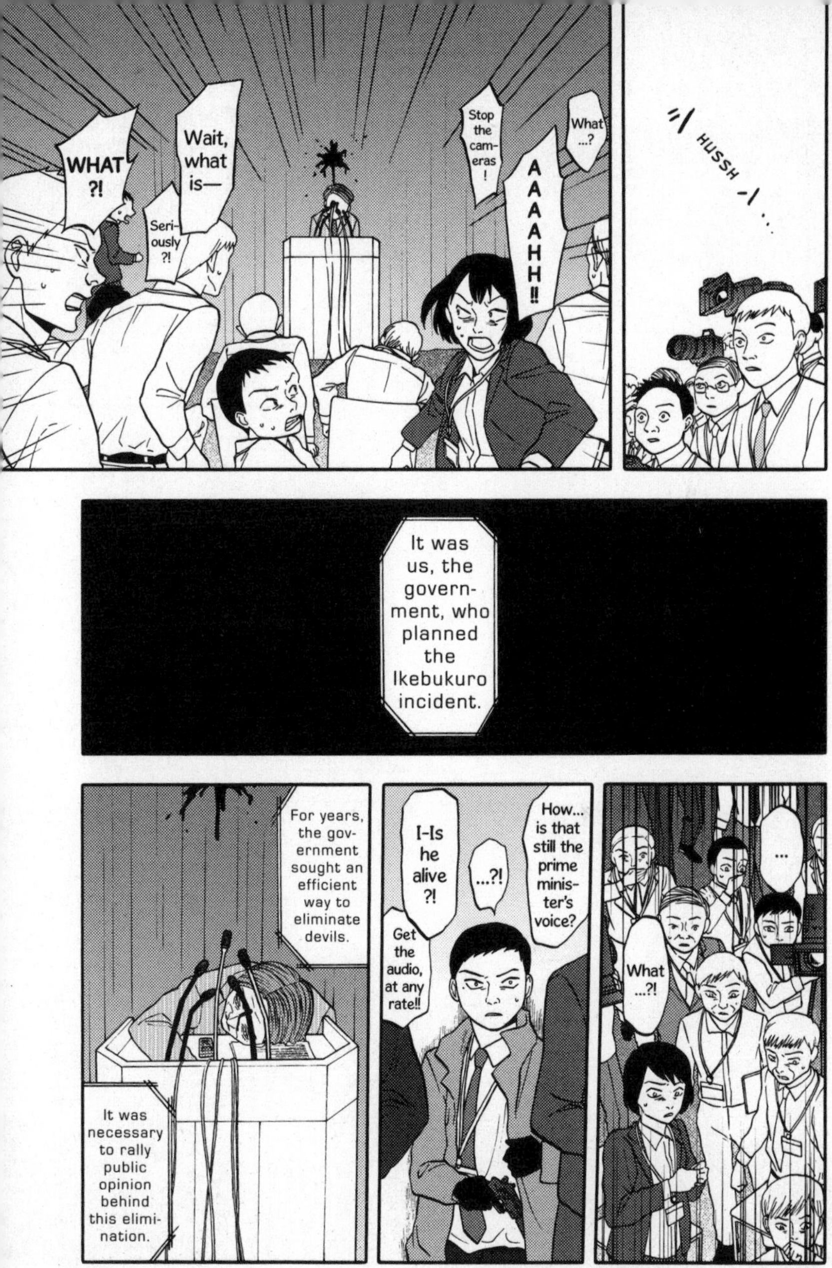
HUSSH...
What ...?
Stop the cameras!
AAAAHH!!
Wait, what is—
Seriously?!
WHAT?!
It was us, the government, who planned the Ikebukuro incident.
...
What ...?!
How... is that still the prime minister's voice?
...?!
I-Is he alive?!
Get the audio, at any rate!!
For years, the government sought an efficient way to eliminate devils.
It was necessary to rally public opinion behind this elimination.

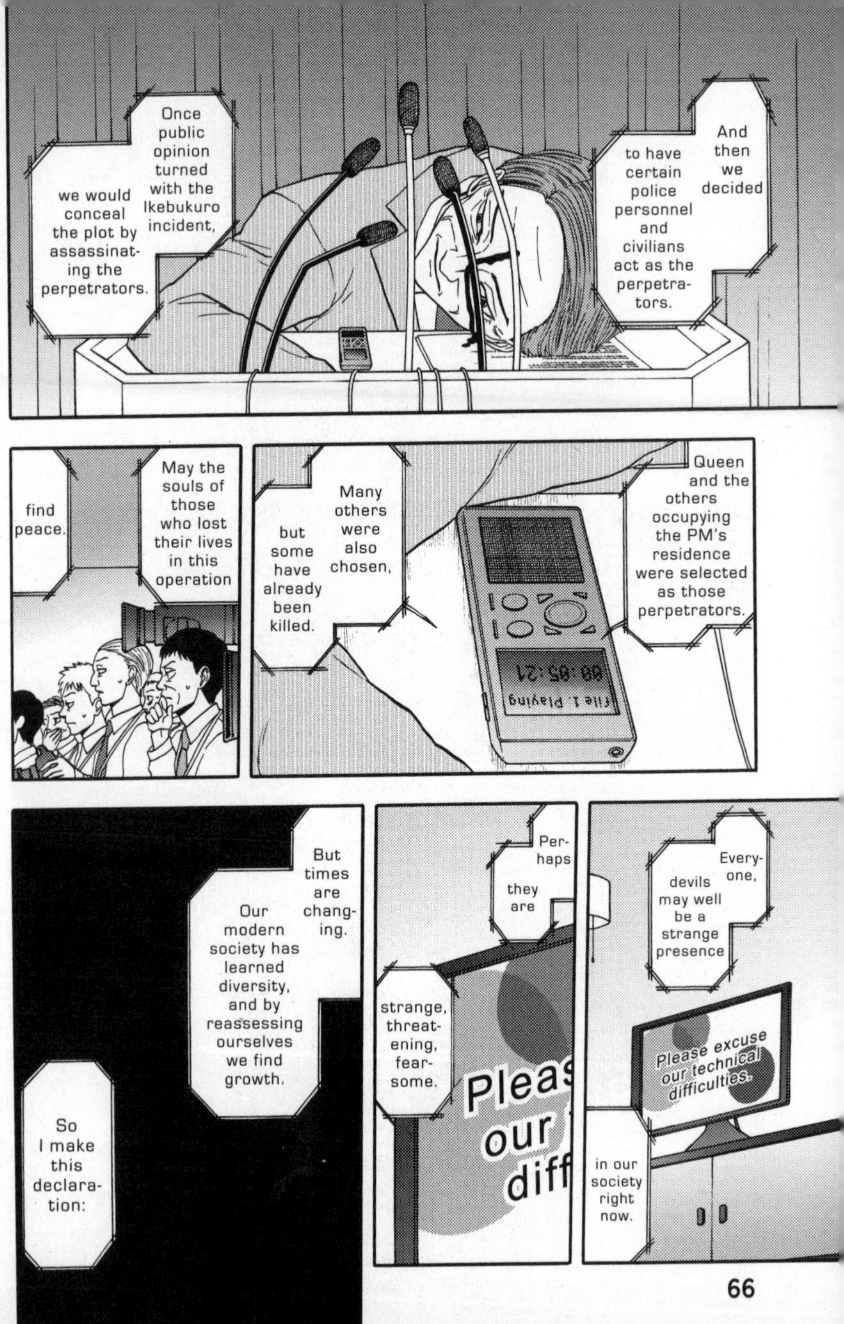
And then we decided to have certain police personnel and civilians act as the perpetra-tors.
Once public opinion turned with the Ikebukuro incident, we would conceal the plot by assassinat-ing the perpetrators.
Queen and the others occupying the PM's residence were selected as those perpetrators.
Many others were also chosen, but some have already been killed.
May the souls of those who lost their lives in this operation find peace.
Every-one, devils may well be a strange presence in our society right now.
Please excuse our technical difficulties.
Per-haps they are strange, threat-ening, fear-some.
But times are chang-ing. Our modern society has learned diversity, and by reassessing ourselves we find growth.
So I make this declara-tion:

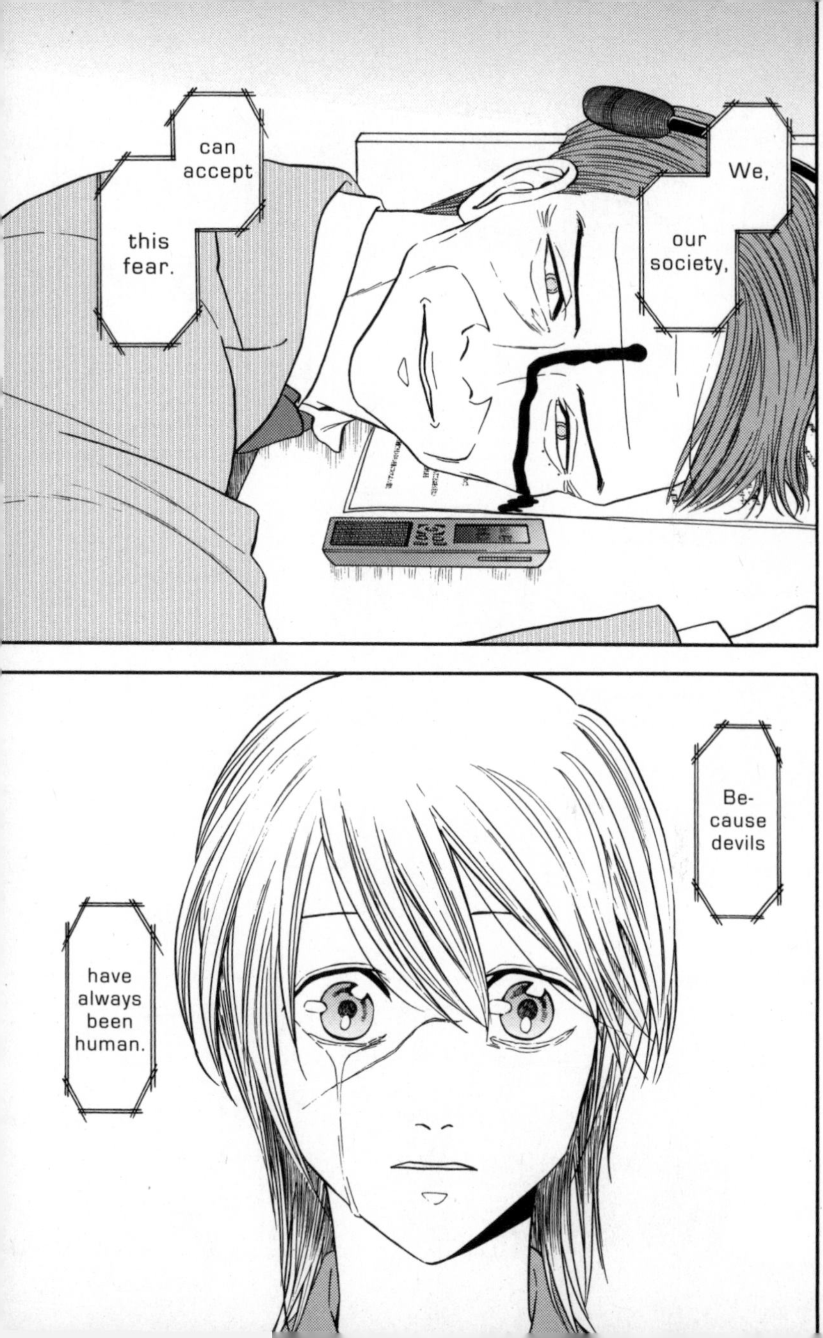
We, our society,
can accept this fear.
Be-cause devils
have always been human.

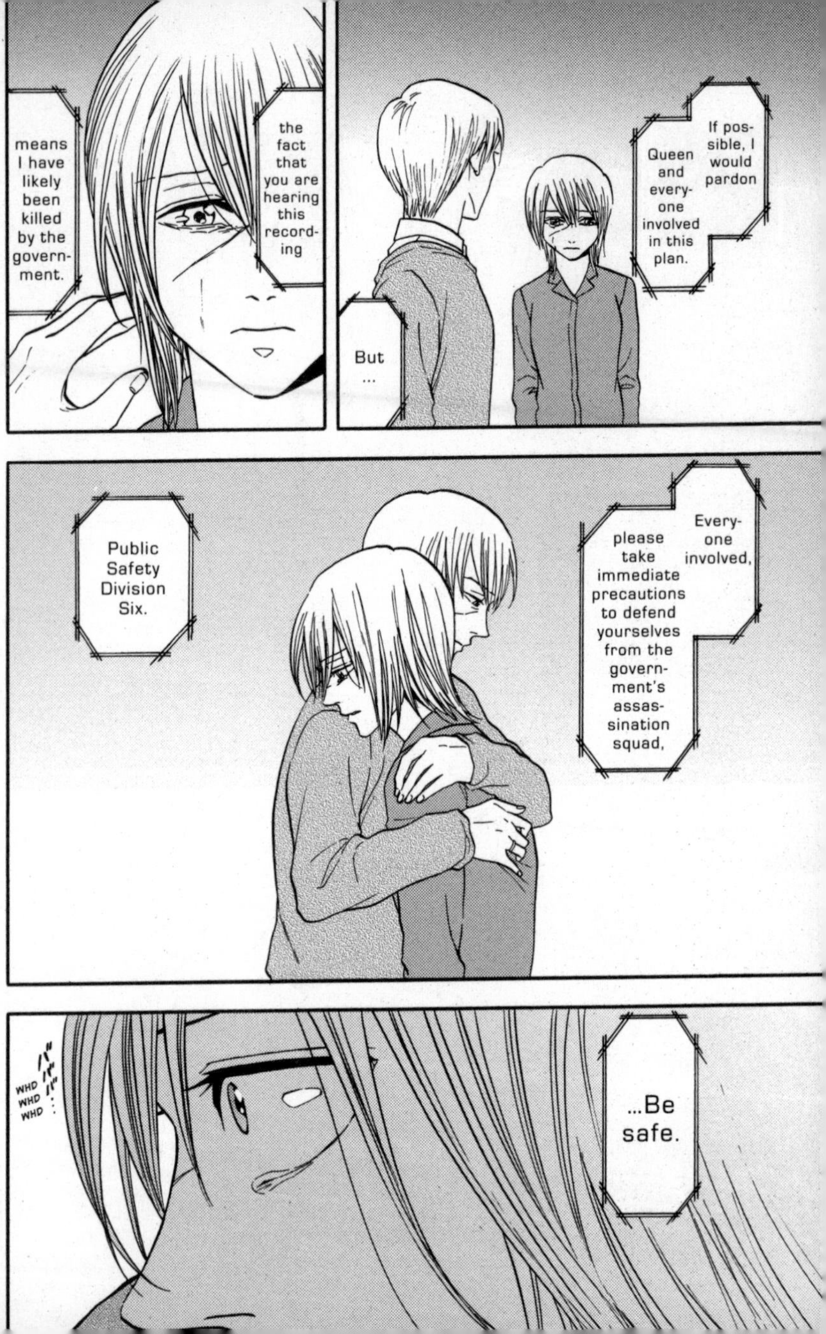

If possible, I would pardon Queen and everyone involved in this plan.
But ...
the fact that you are hearing this recording
means I have likely been killed by the government.
Everyone involved, please take immediate precautions to defend yourselves from the government's assassination squad,
Public Safety Division Six.
...Be safe.
バ バ バ…
WHD WHD WHD

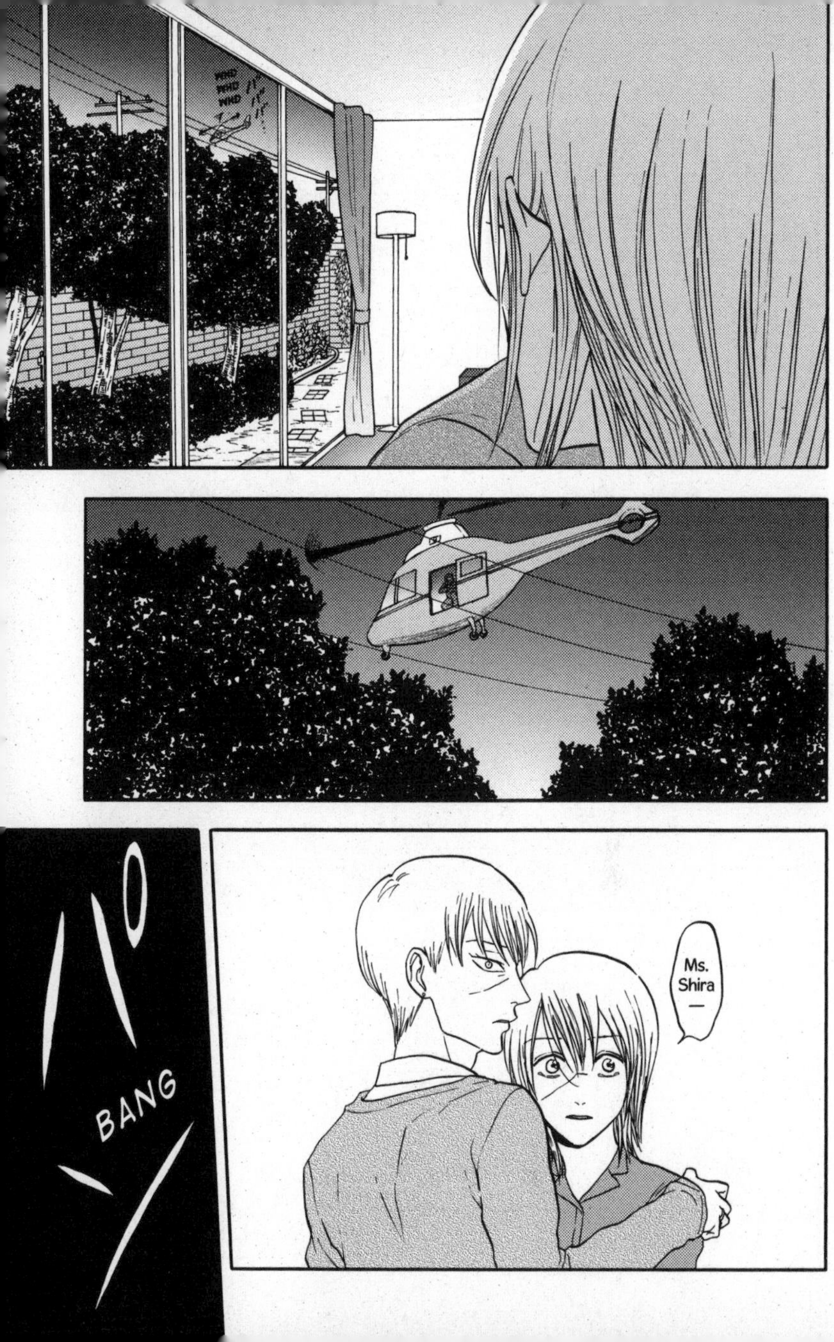
WHD
WHD
WHD
Ms. Shira —
BANG

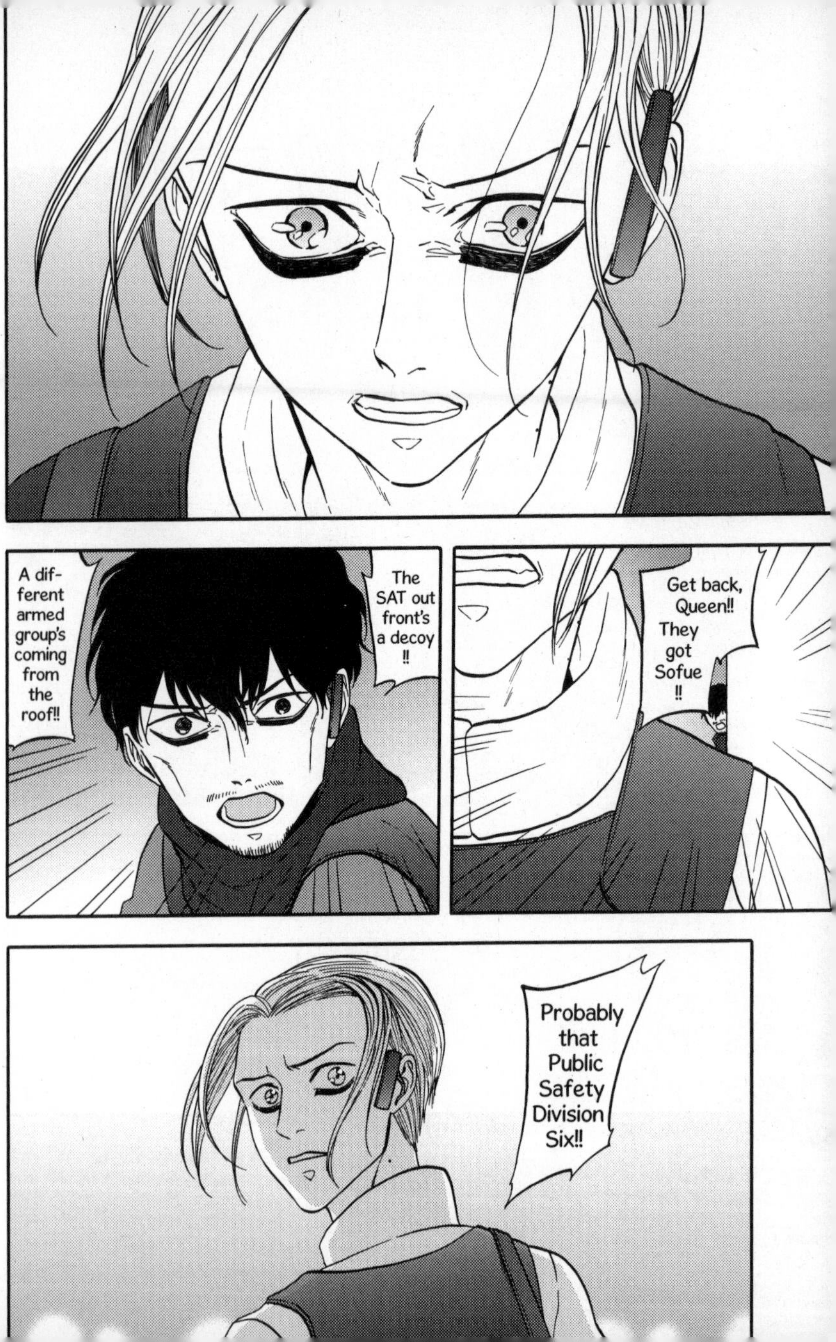
Get back, Queen!! They got Sofue!!
The SAT out front's a decoy!!
A different armed group's coming from the roof!!
Probably that Public Safety Division Six!!

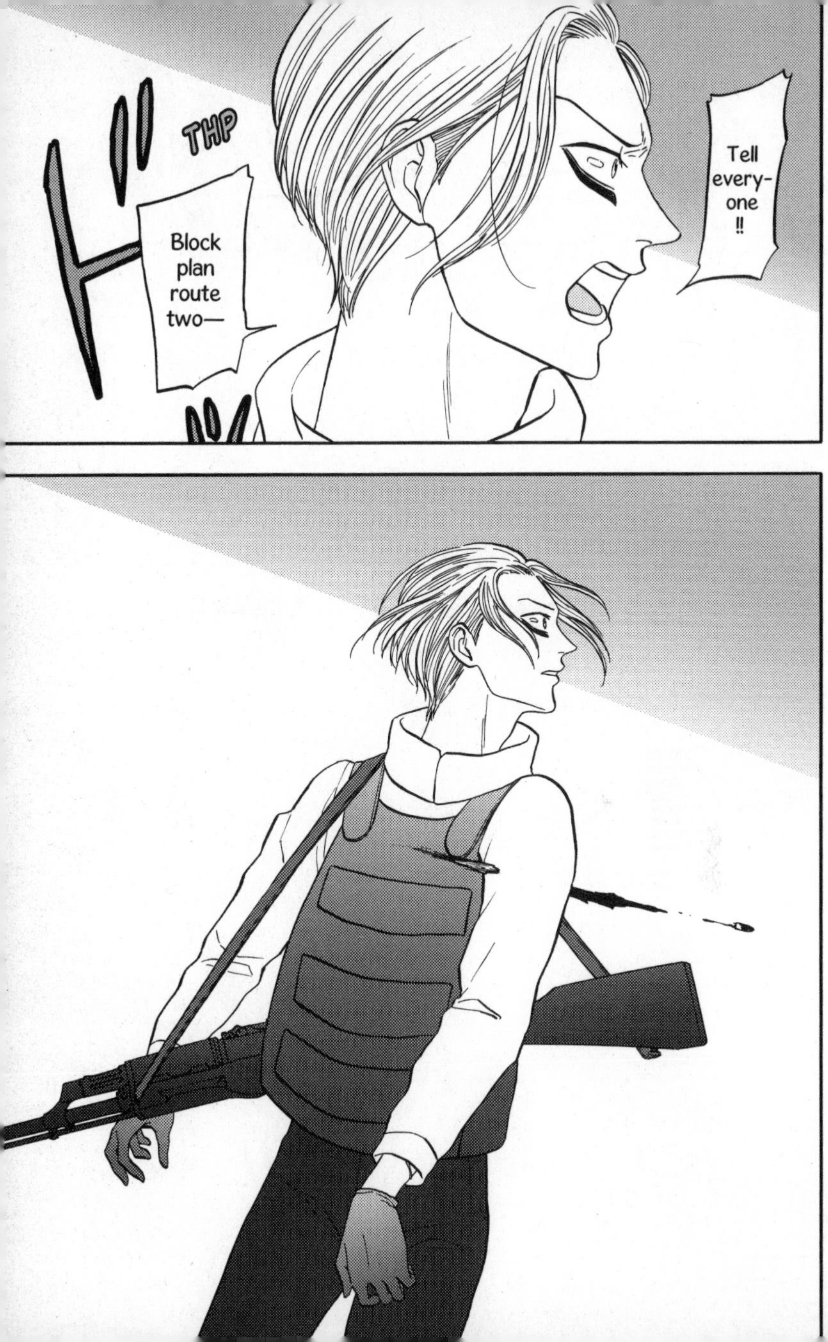
Tell every-one ‼
Block plan route two—
THP

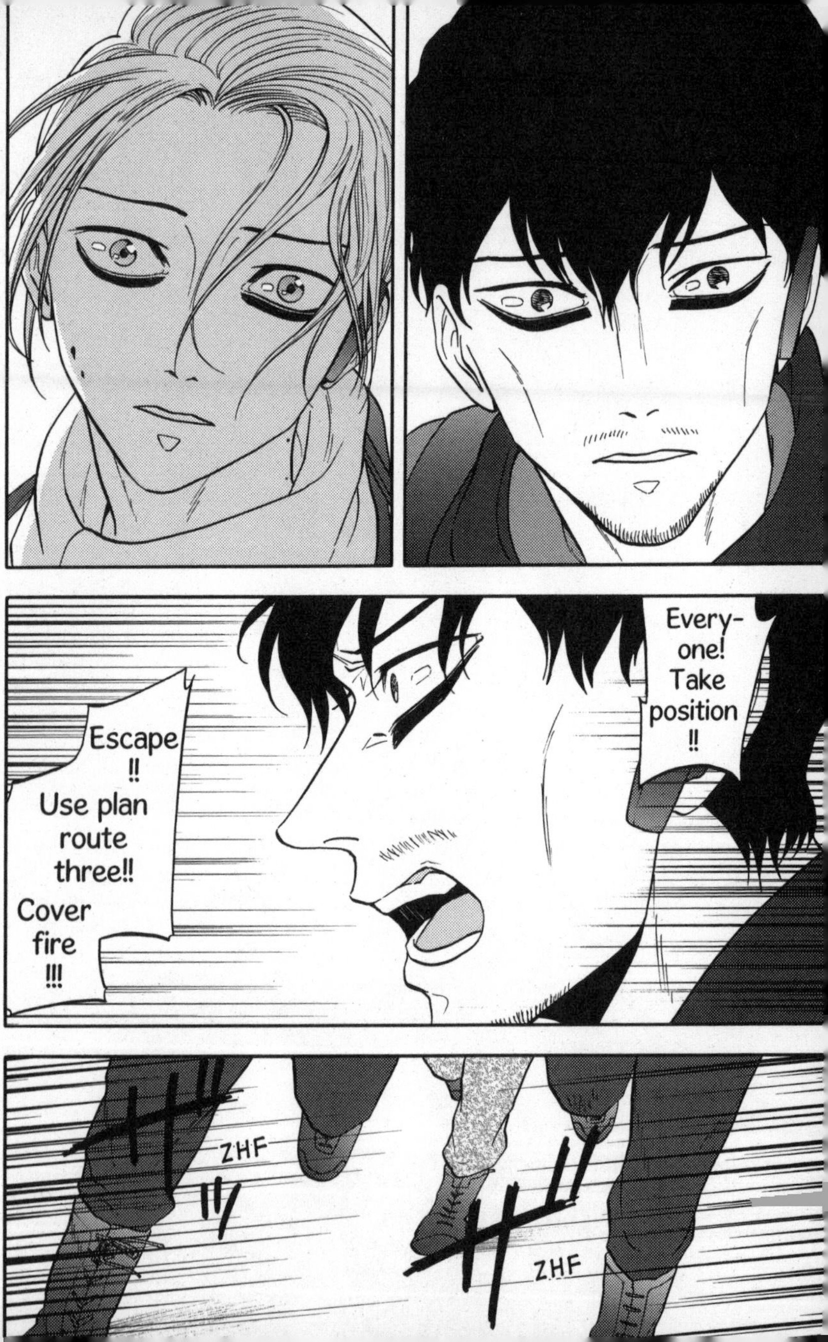
Every-one! Take position!!
Escape!! Use plan route three!! Cover fire!!!
ZHF
ZHF

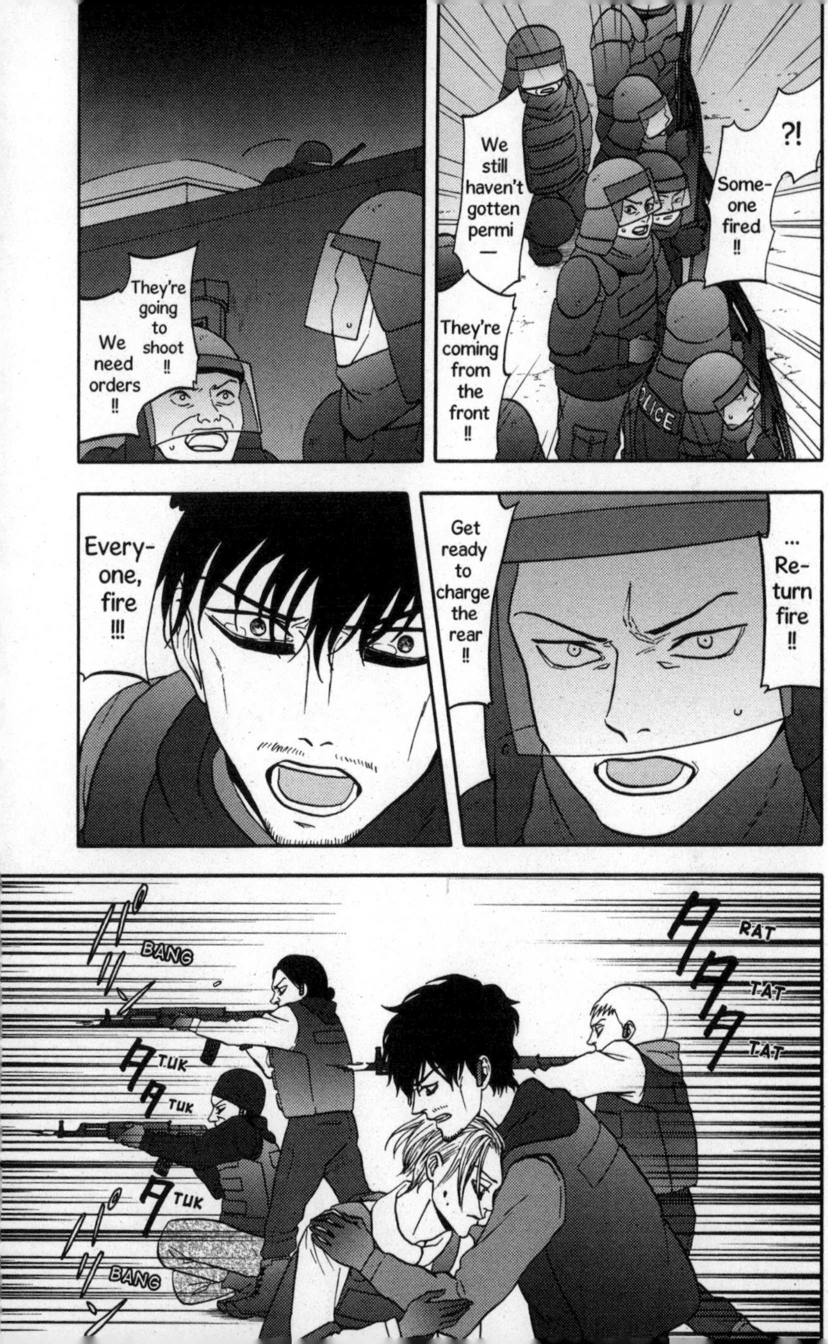
?!
Some-one fired!!
We still haven't gotten permi—
They're coming from the front!!
They're going to shoot!!
We need orders!!
...Re-turn fire!!
Get ready to charge the rear!!
Every-one, fire!!!
RAT
TAT
TAT
BANG
TUK
TUK
TUK
BANG

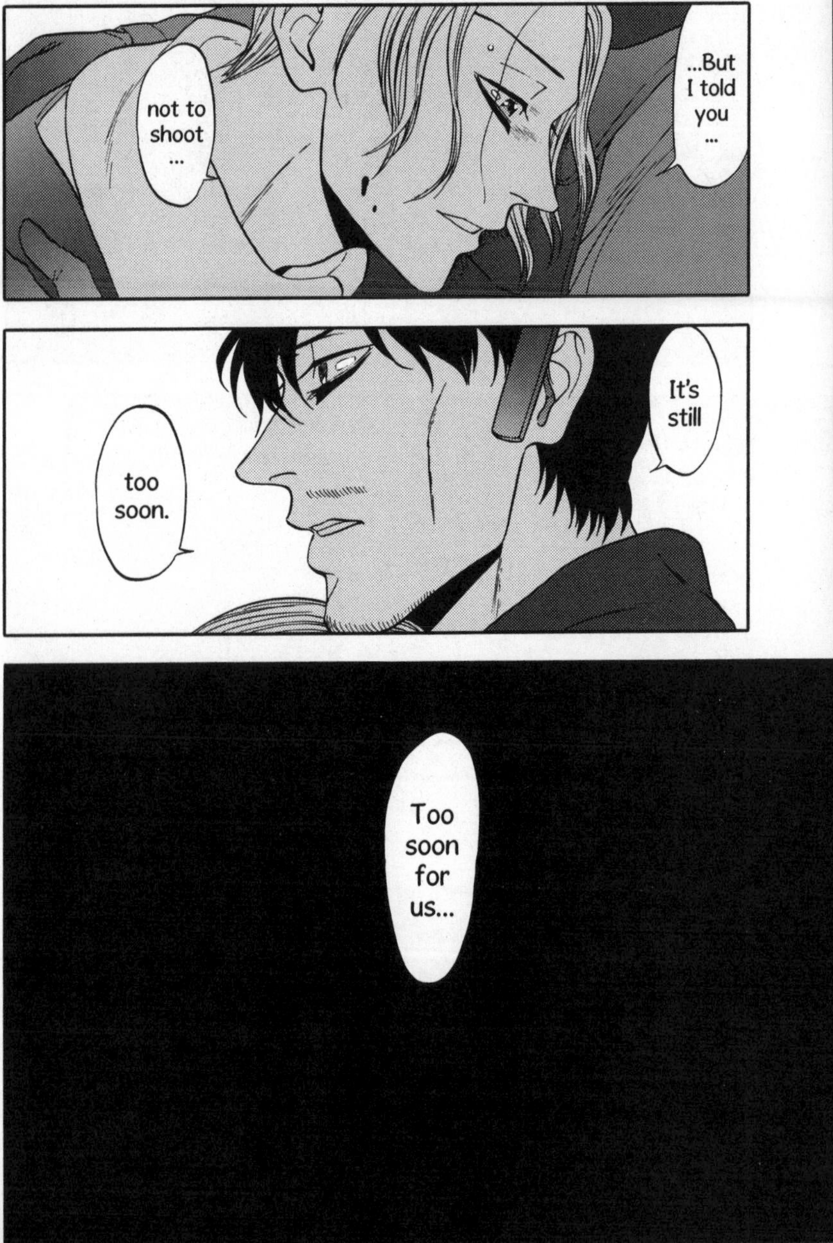
...But I told you ...
not to shoot ...
It's still
too soon.
Too soon for us...

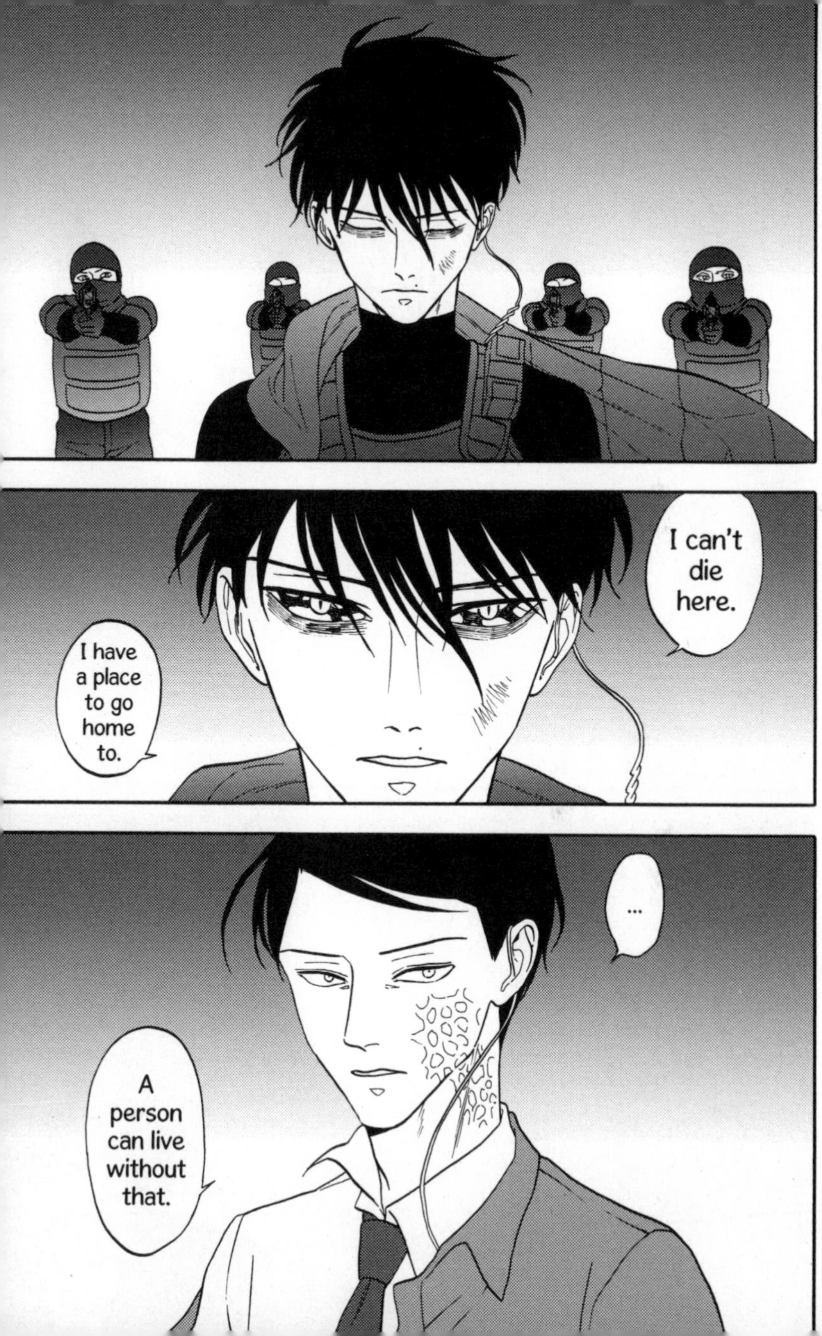
I can't die here.
I have a place to go home to.
...
A person can live without that.

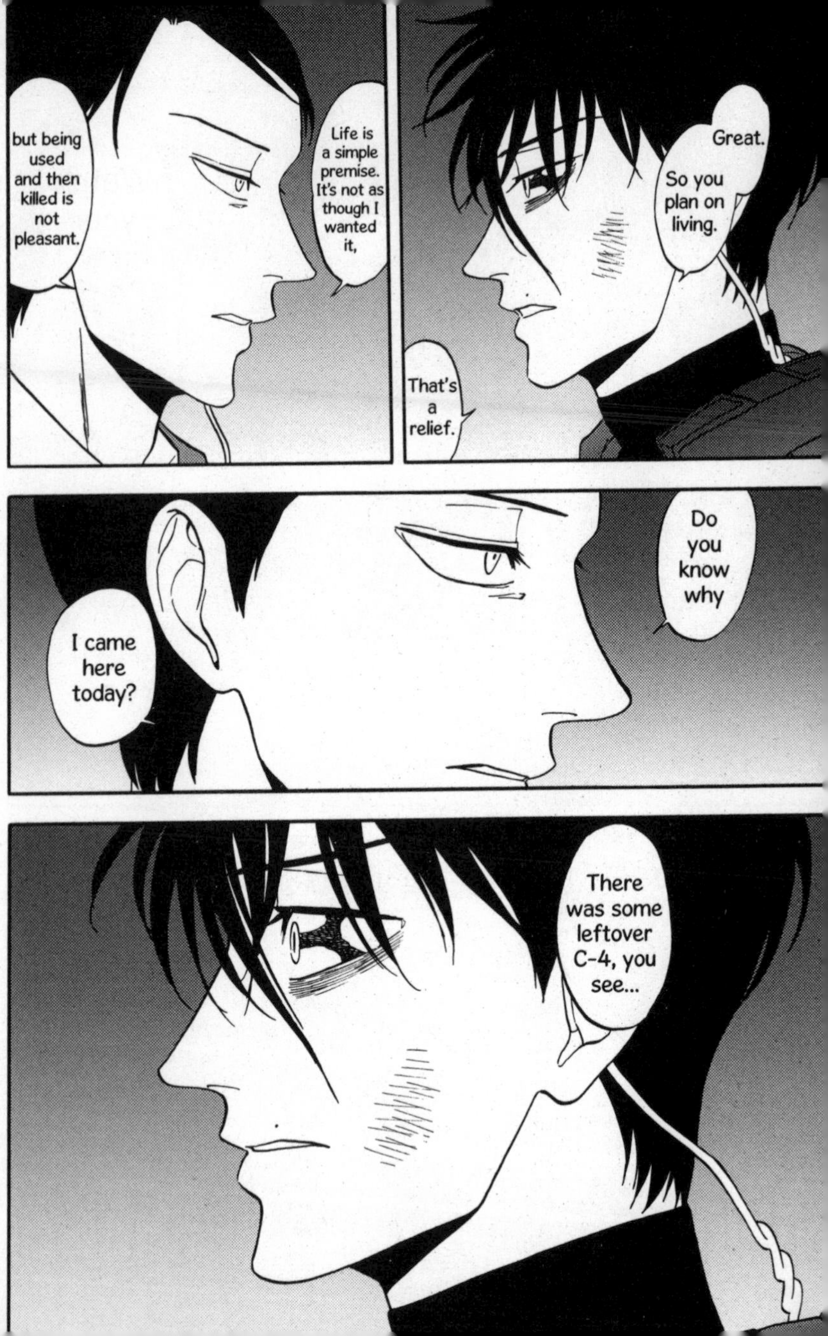
Great.
So you plan on living.
That's a relief.
Life is a simple premise. It's not as though I wanted it,
but being used and then killed is not pleasant.
Do you know why
I came here today?
There was some leftover C-4, you see...

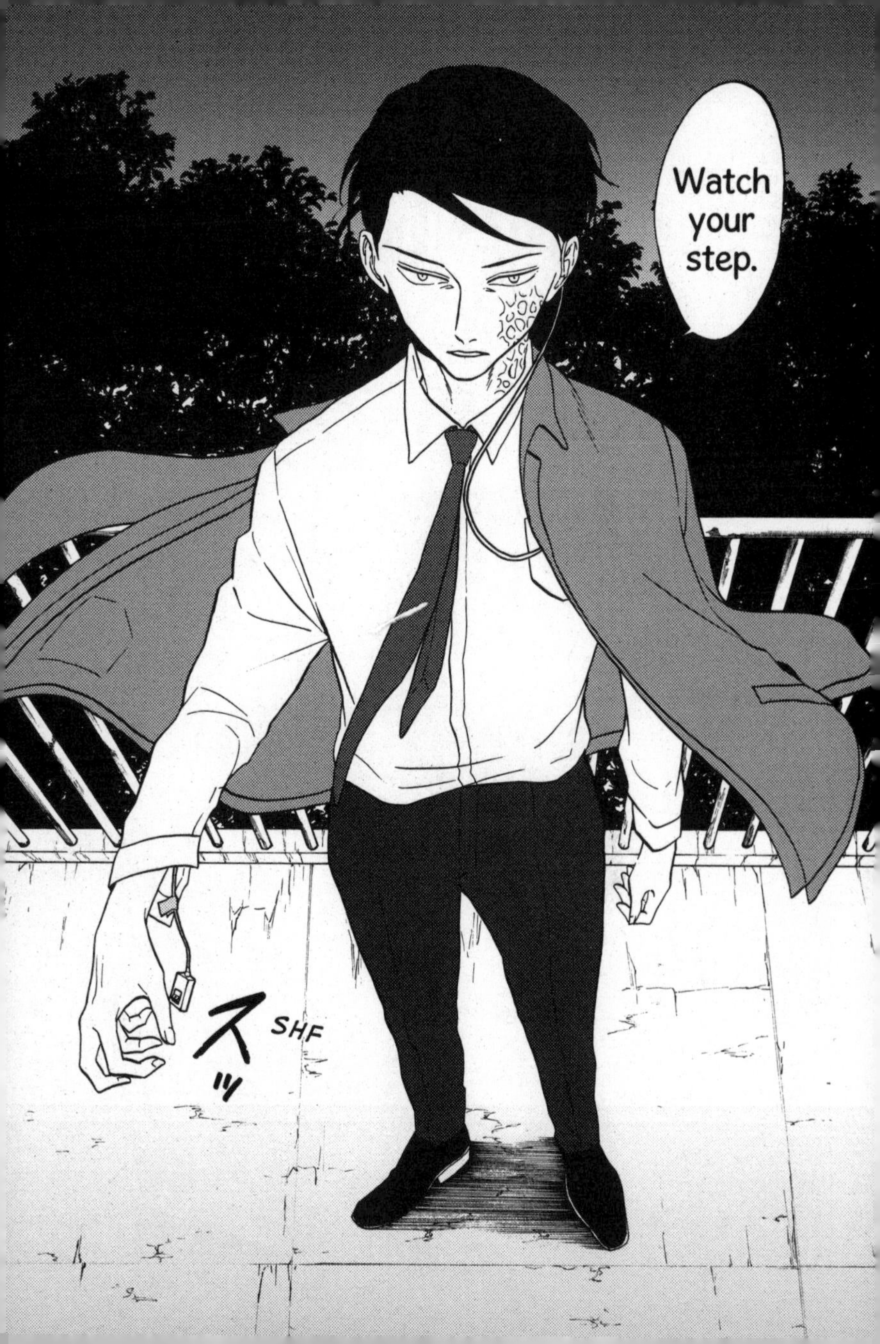
Watch your step.
スッ
SHF

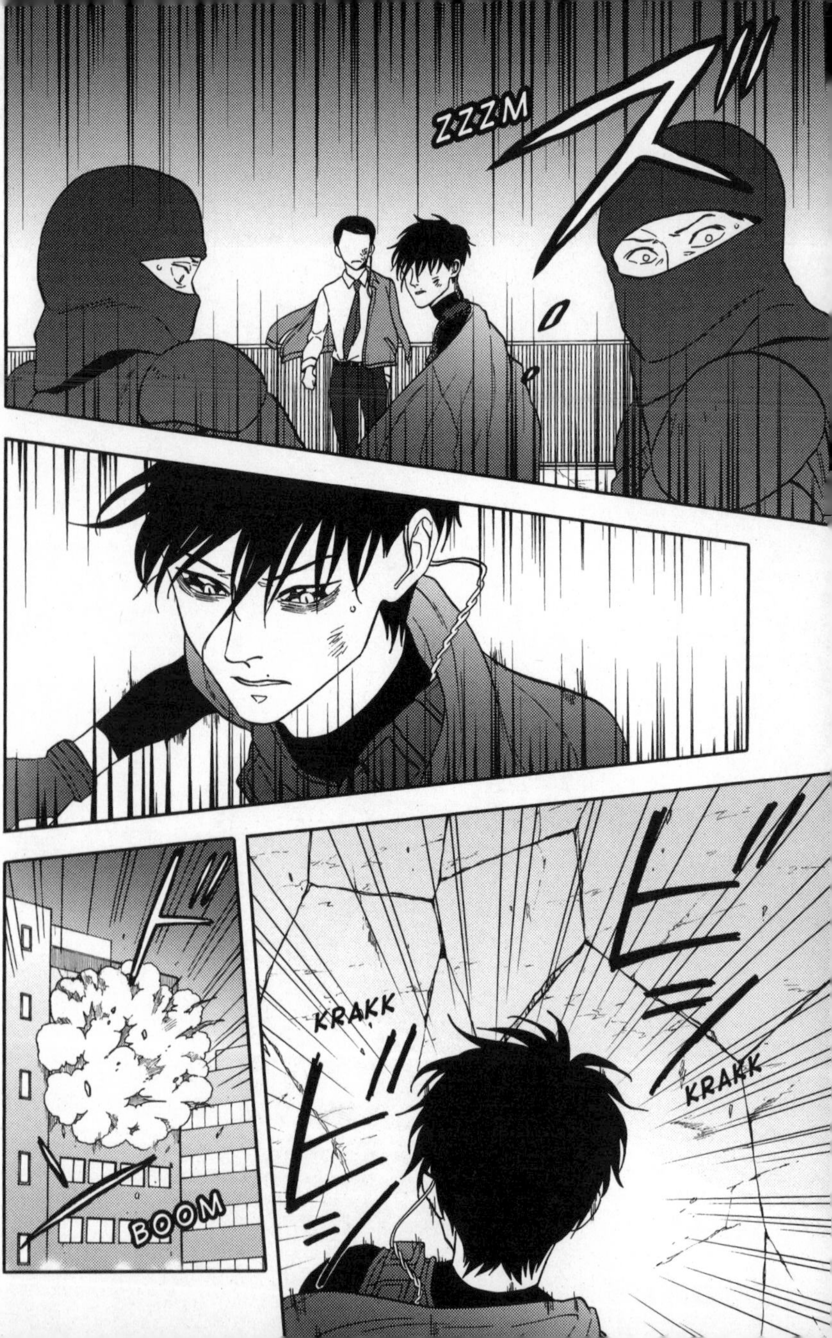
ZZZM
KRAKK
KRAKK
BOOM

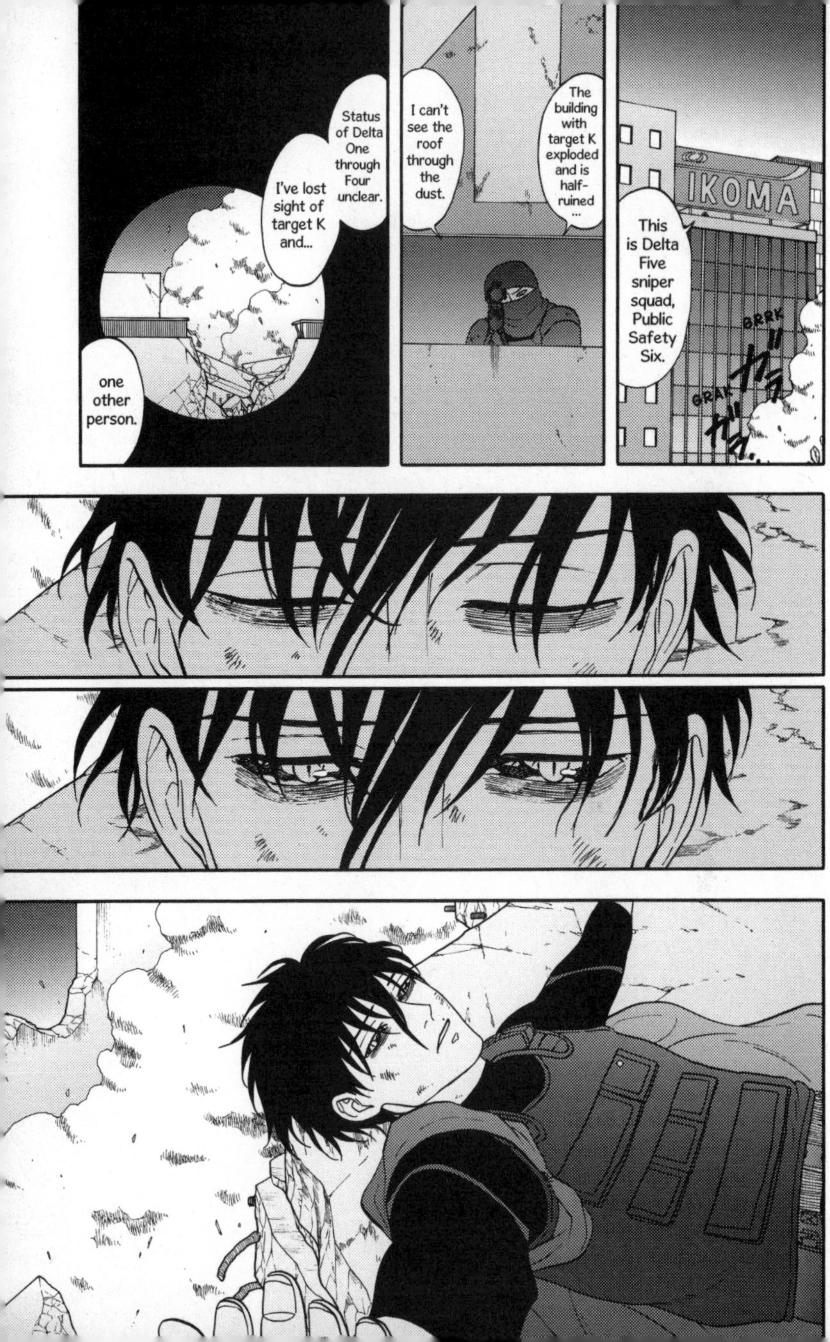
This is Delta Five sniper squad, Public Safety Six.
GRRK
GRAK
The building with target K exploded and is half-ruined ...
I can't see the roof through the dust.
Status of Delta One through Four unclear.
I've lost sight of target K and...
one other person.

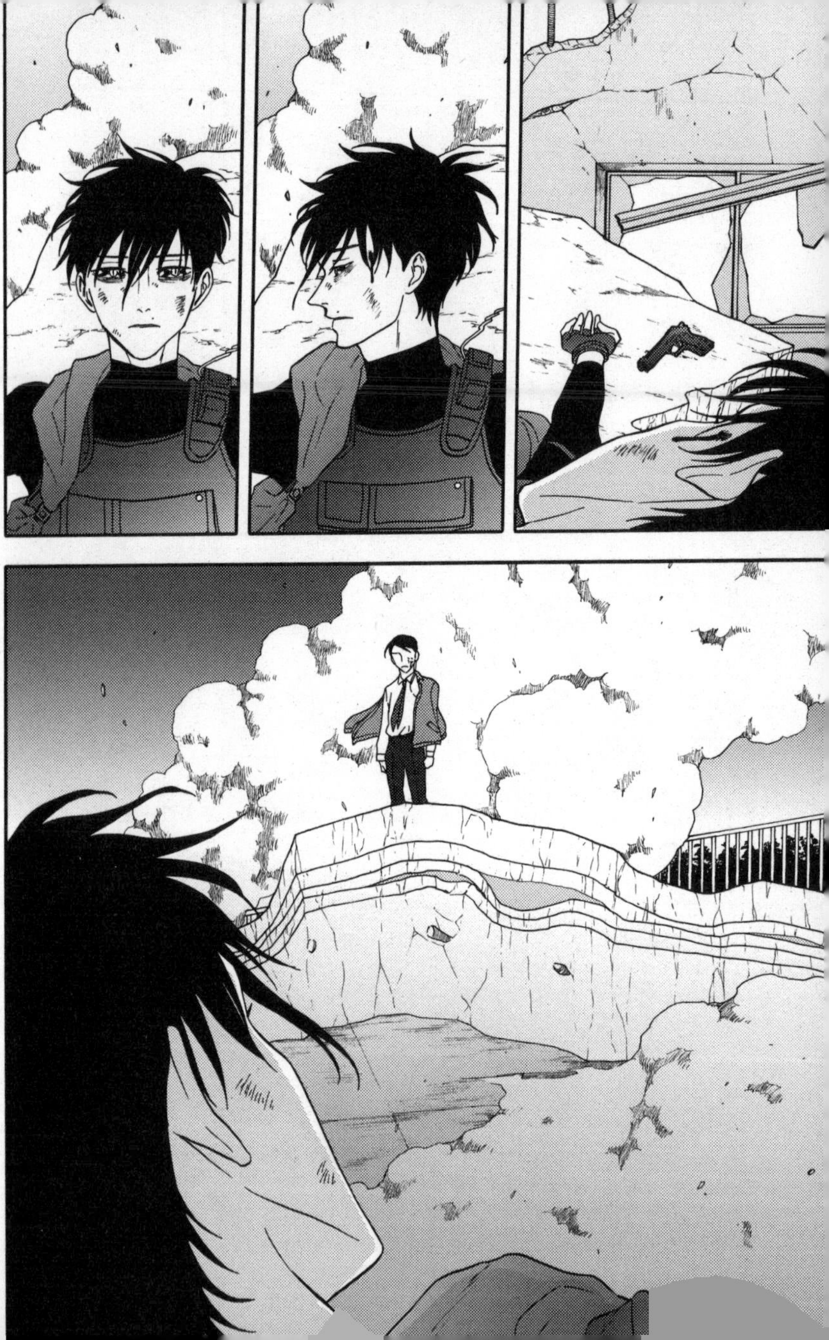

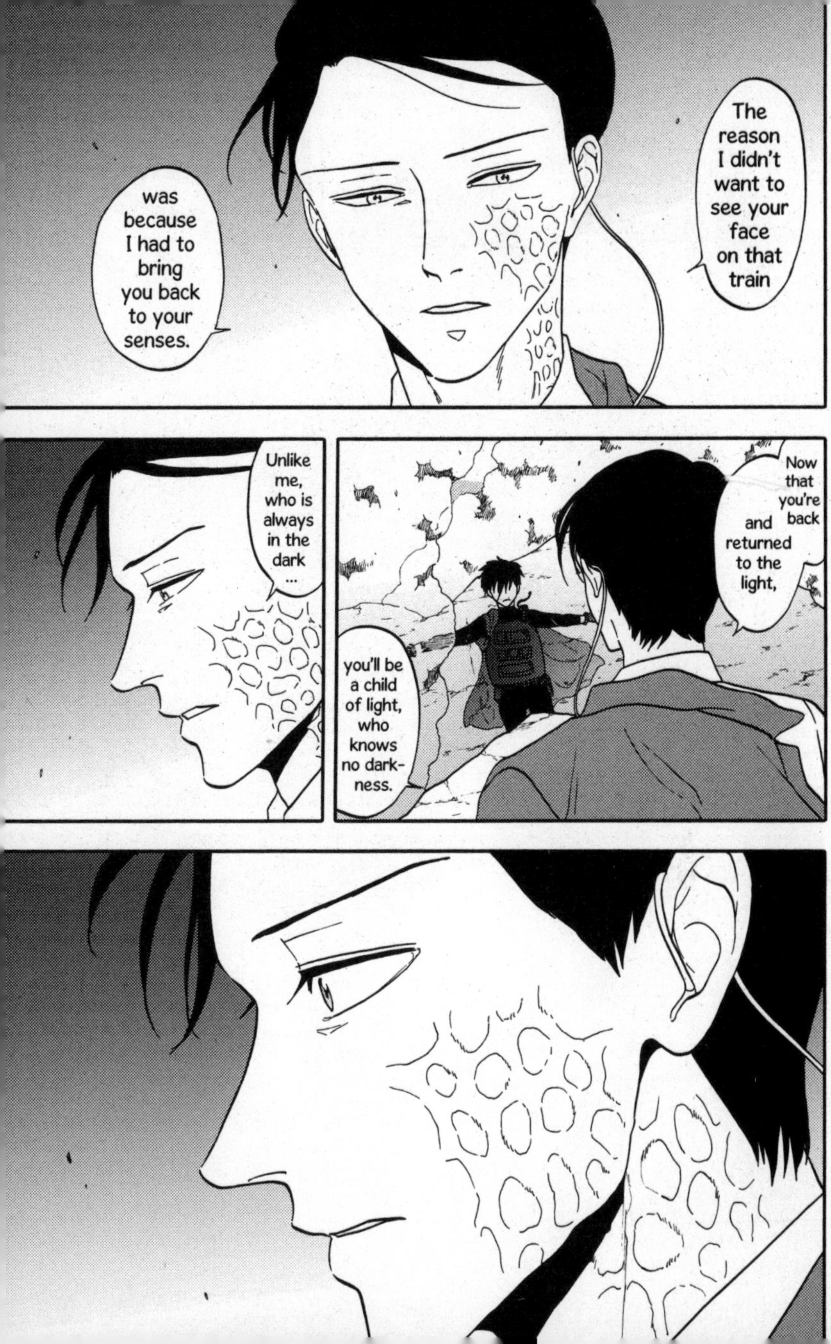
The reason I didn't want to see your face on that train
was because I had to bring you back to your senses.
Now that you're back and returned to the light,
you'll be a child of light, who knows no dark-ness.
Unlike me, who is always in the dark ...

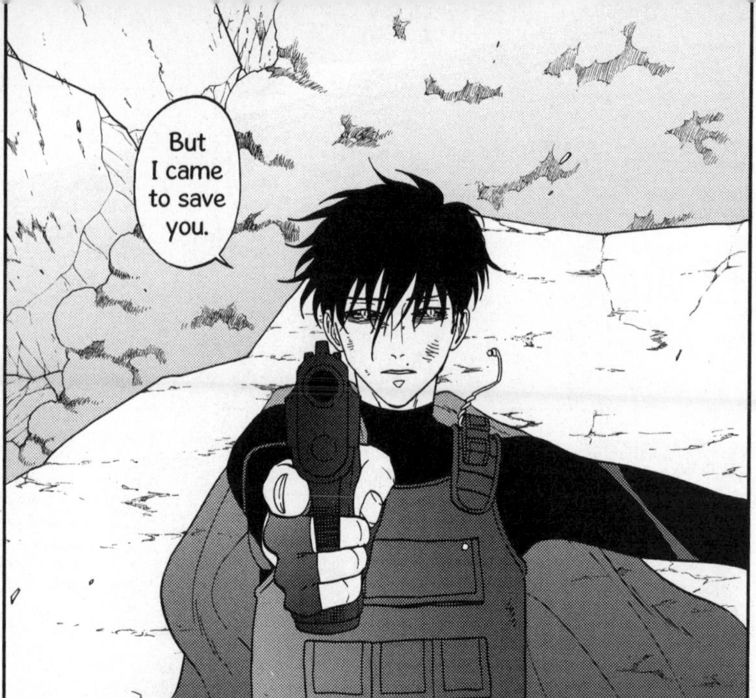
But I came to save you.
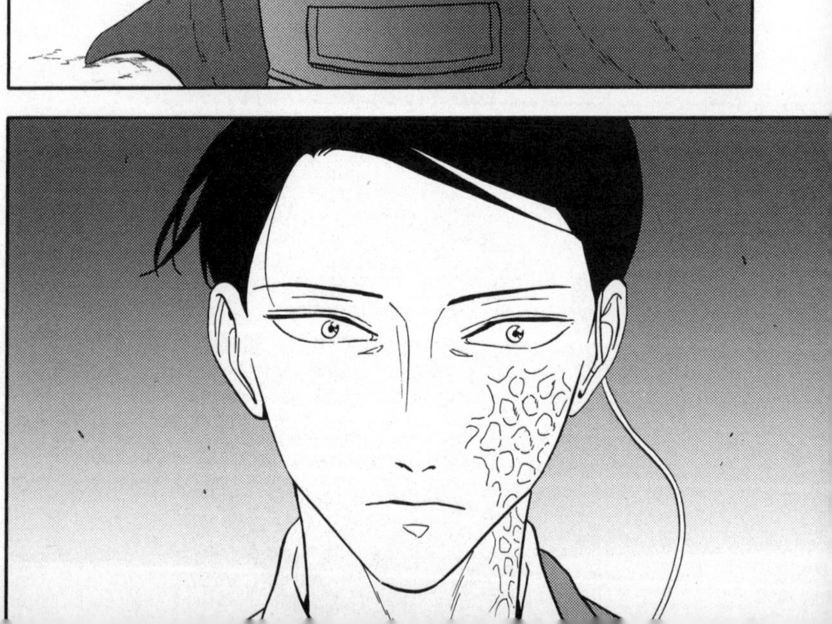

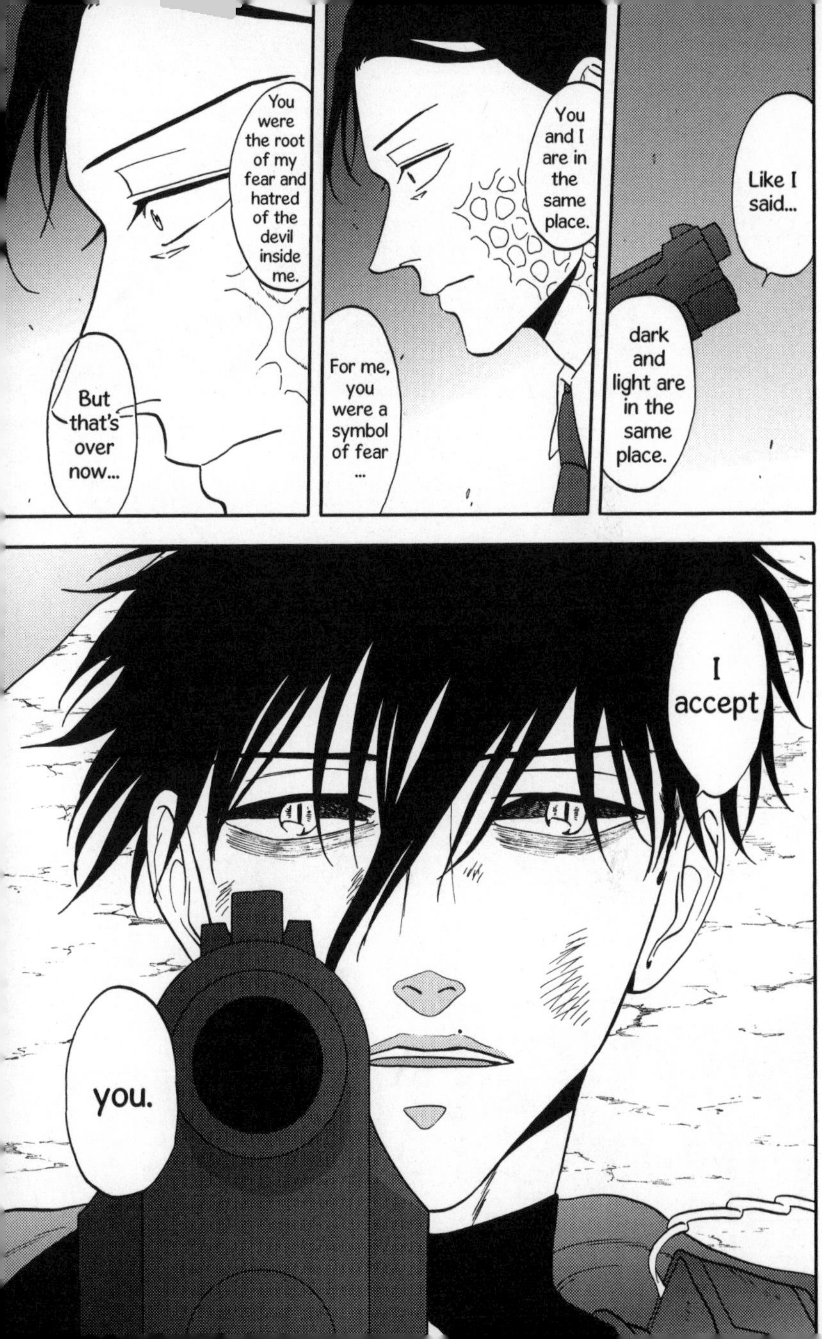
Like I said...
dark and light are in the same place.
You and I are in the same place.
For me, you were a symbol of fear ...
You were the root of my fear and hatred of the devil inside me.
But that's over now...
I accept
you.

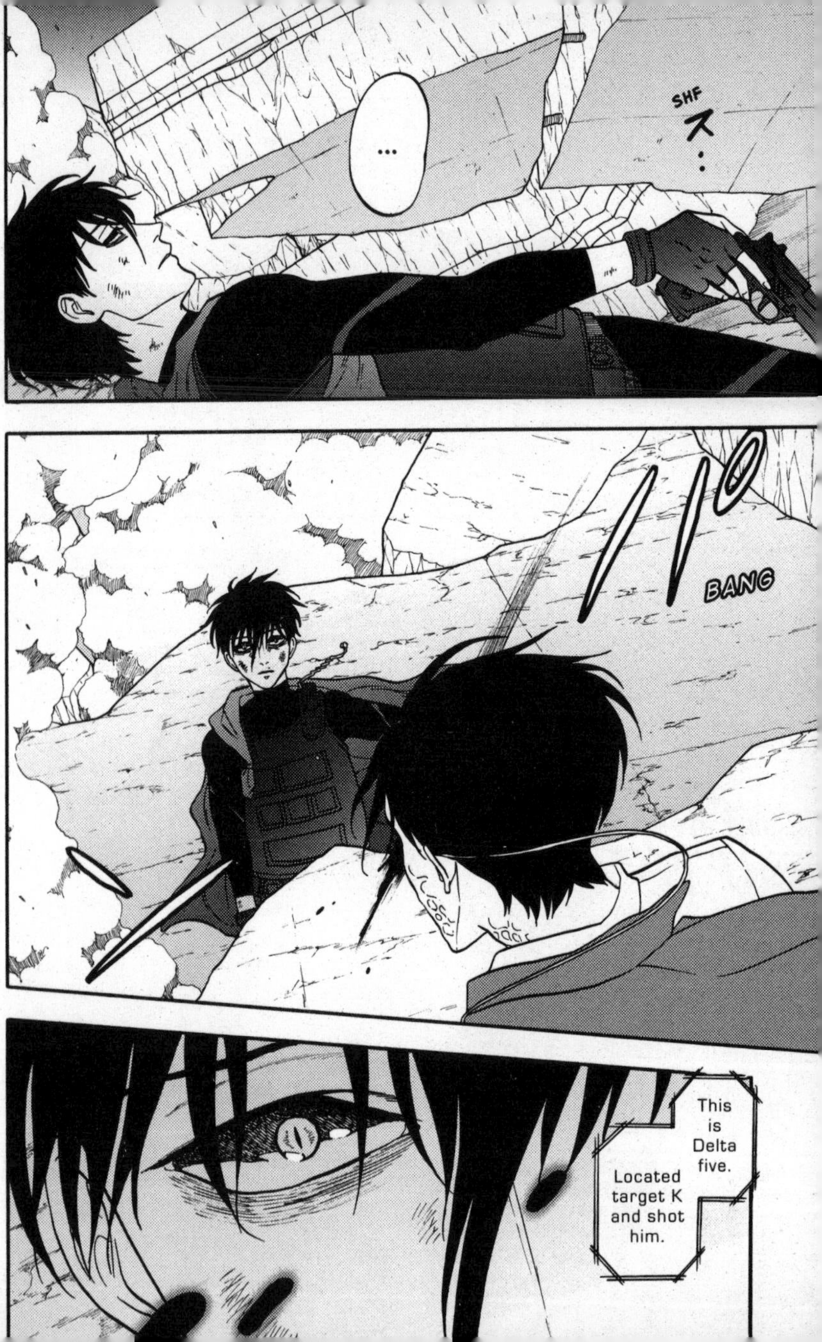
...
SHF
ス・・
BANG
This is Delta five.
Located target K and shot him.

Line 65
Who Are We

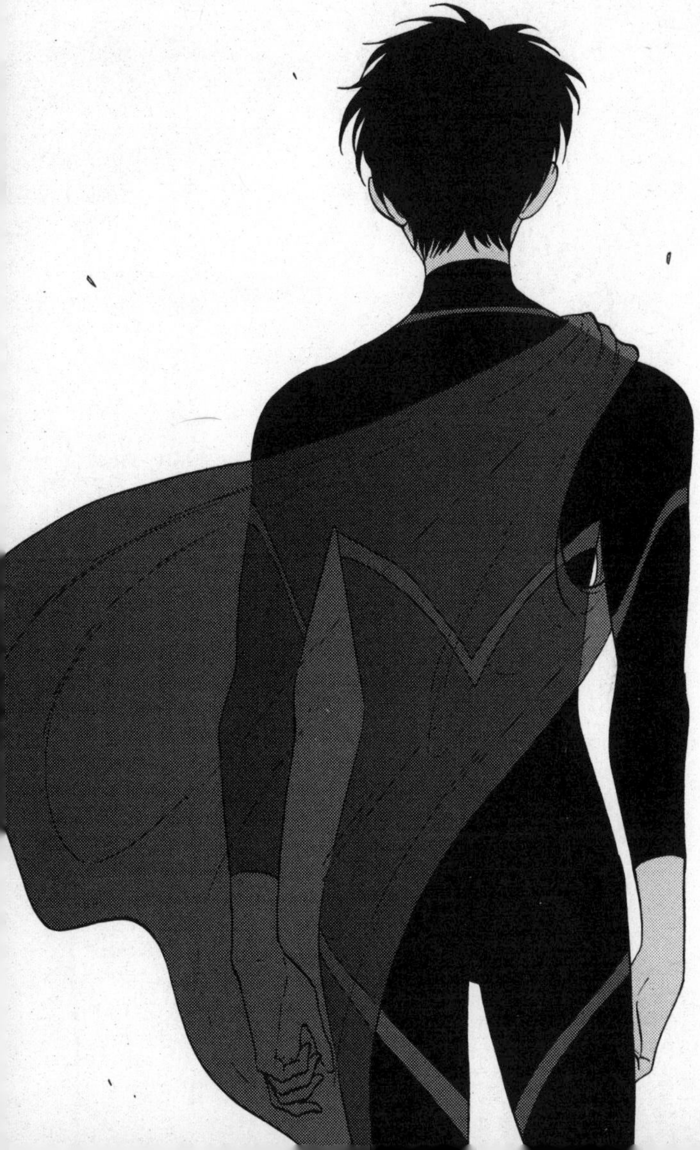

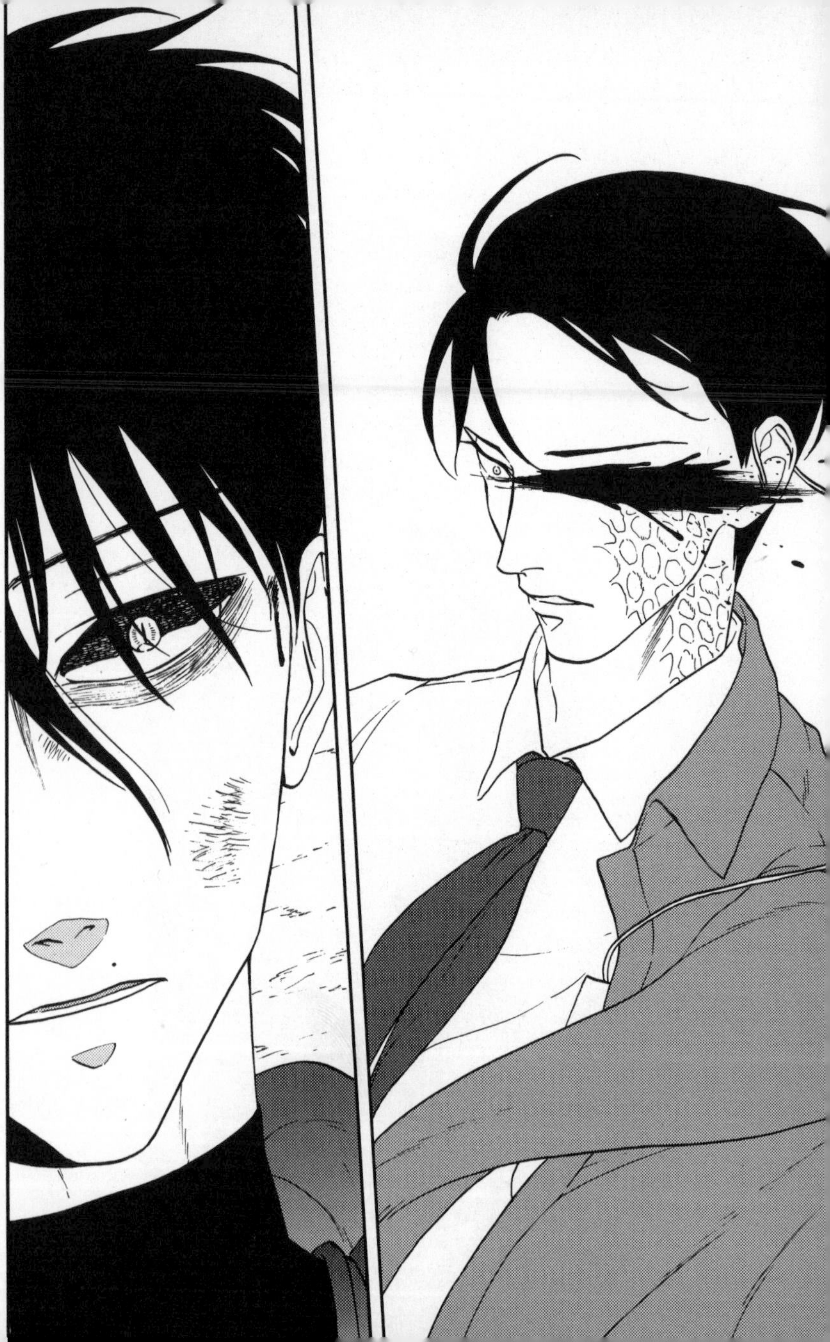

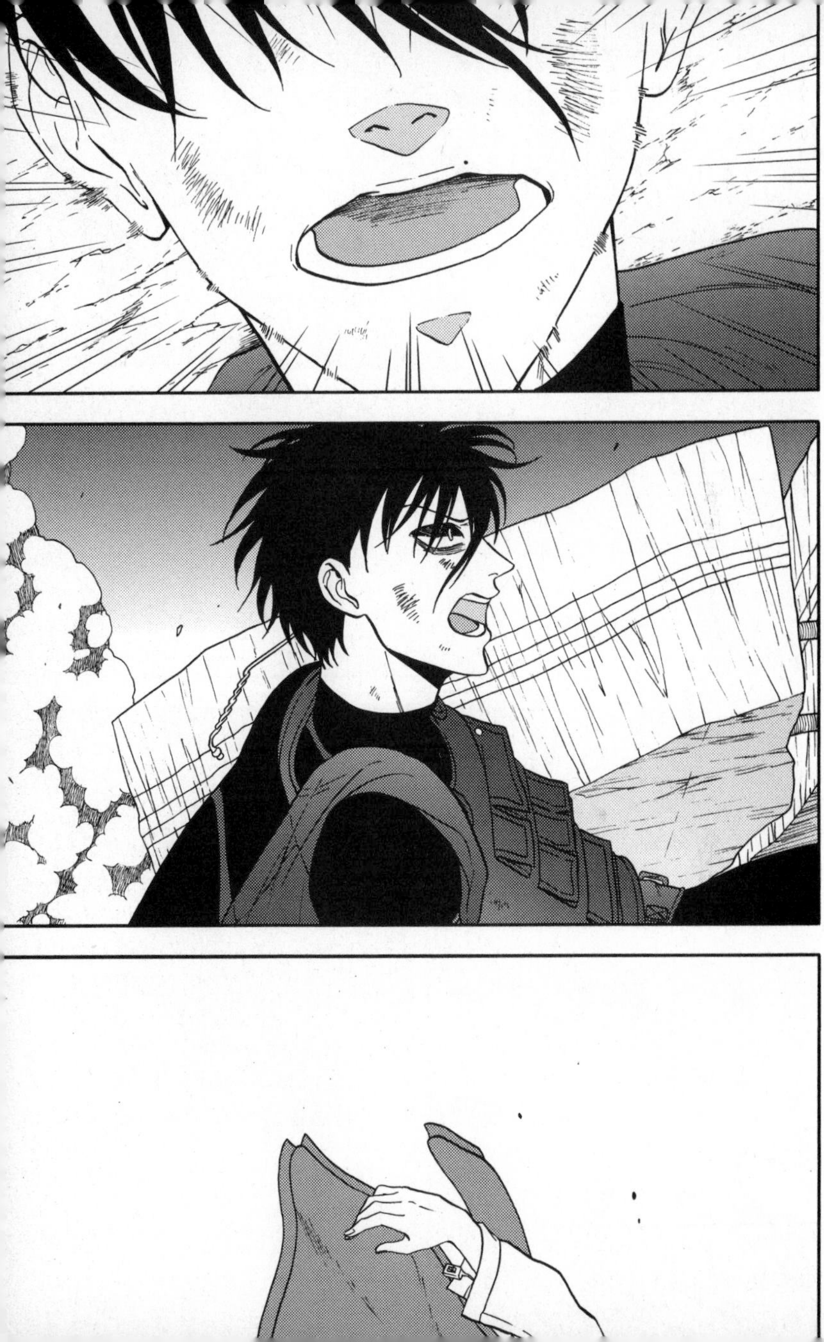

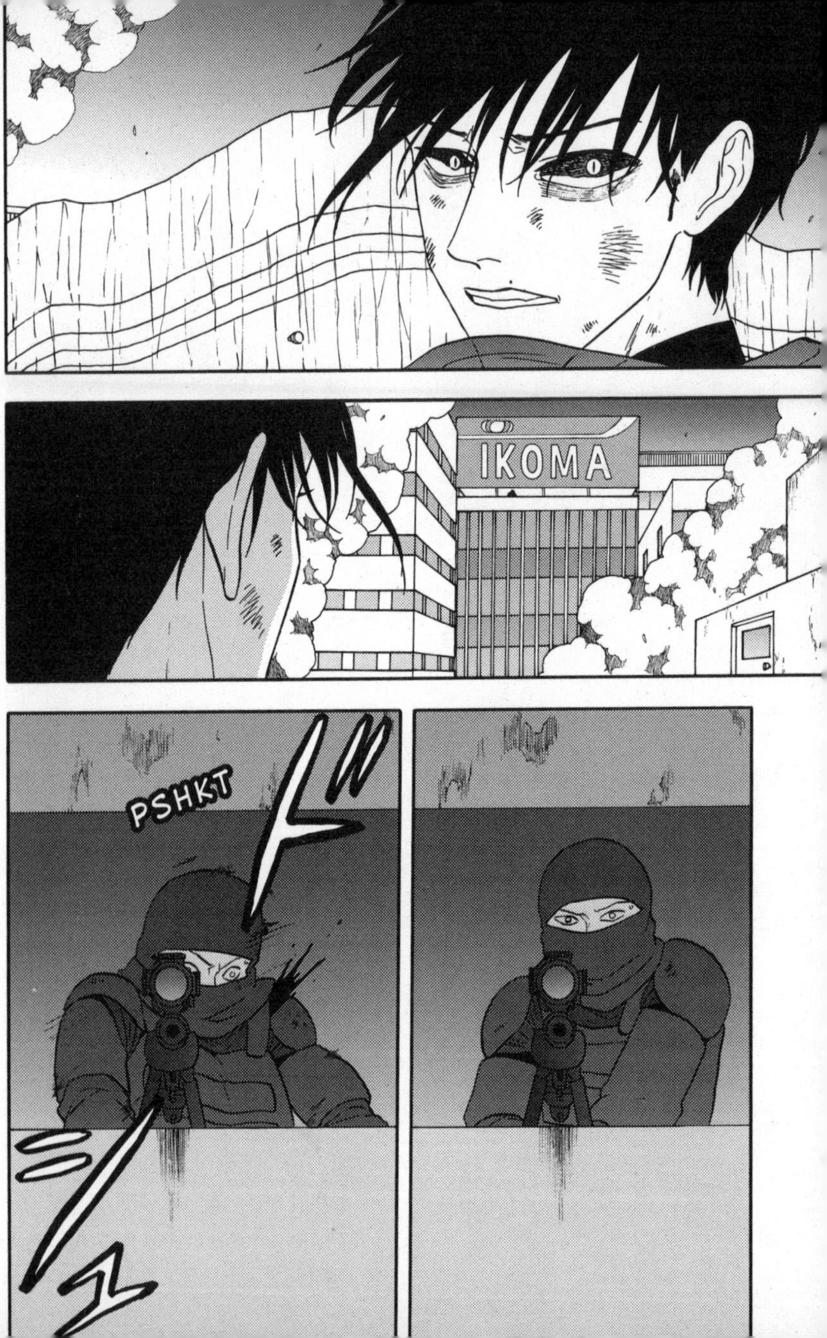
IKOMA
PSHKT

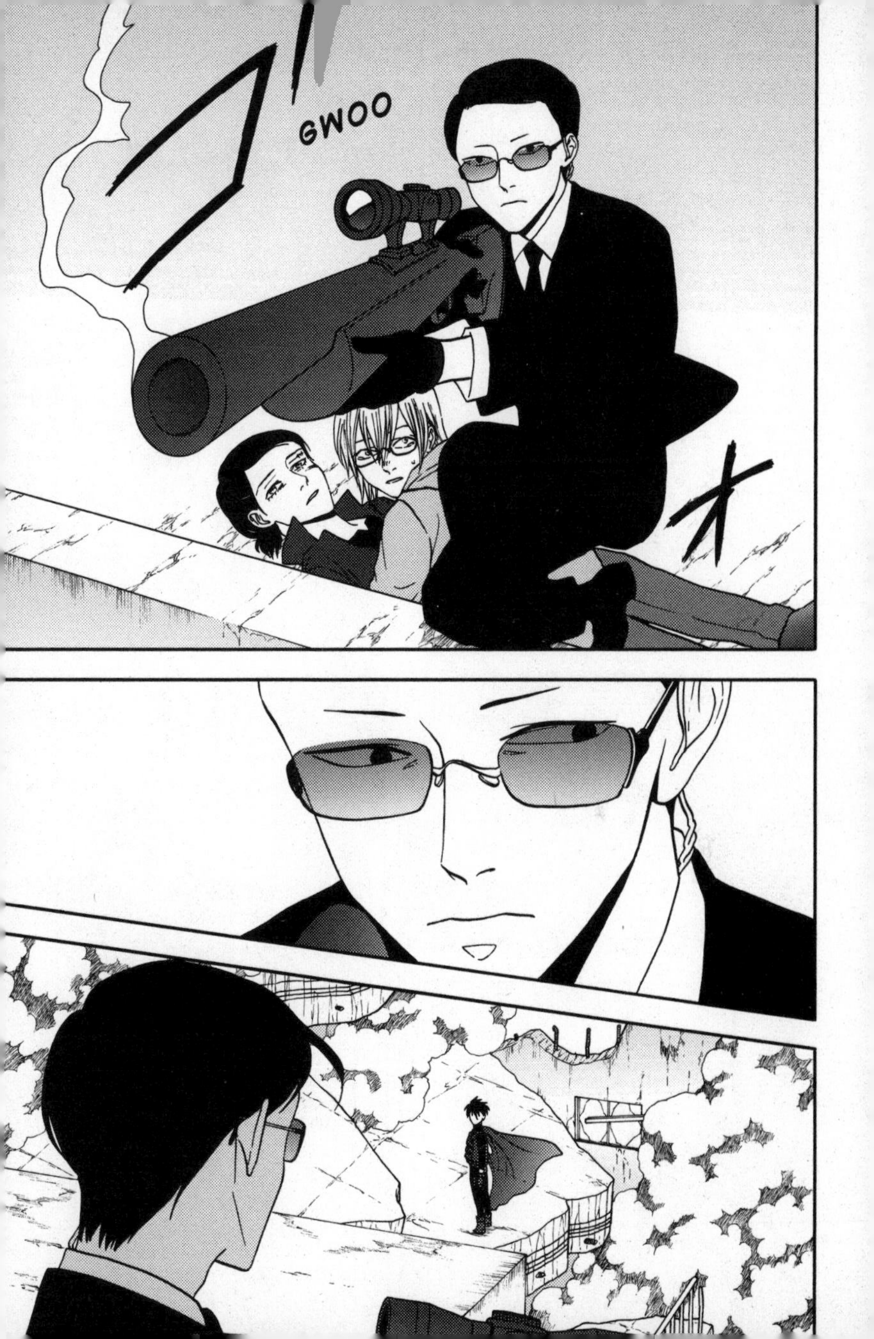
GWOO

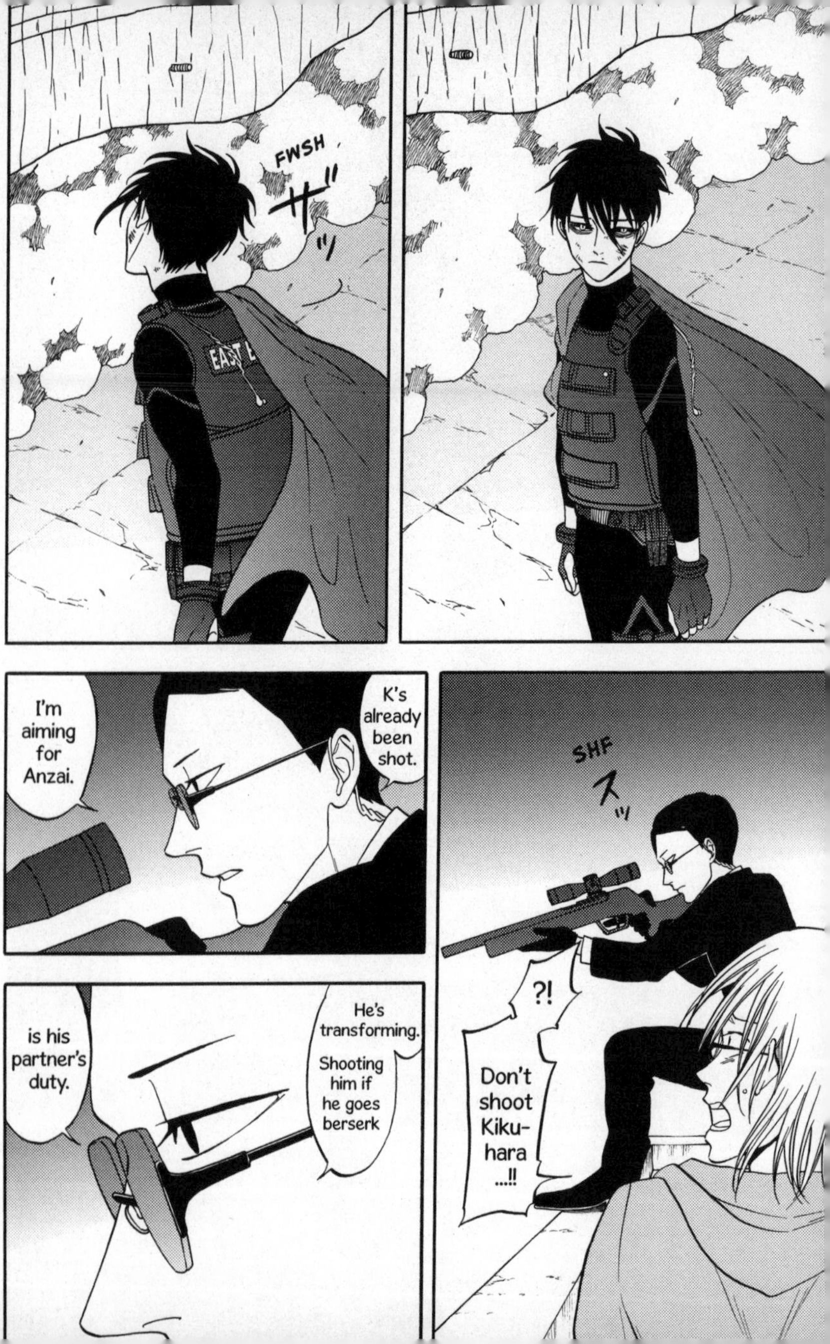
FWSH
ザッ
SHF
スッ
?!
Don't shoot Kiku-hara ...!!
K's already been shot.
I'm aiming for Anzai.
He's transforming.
Shooting him if he goes berserk
is his partner's duty.

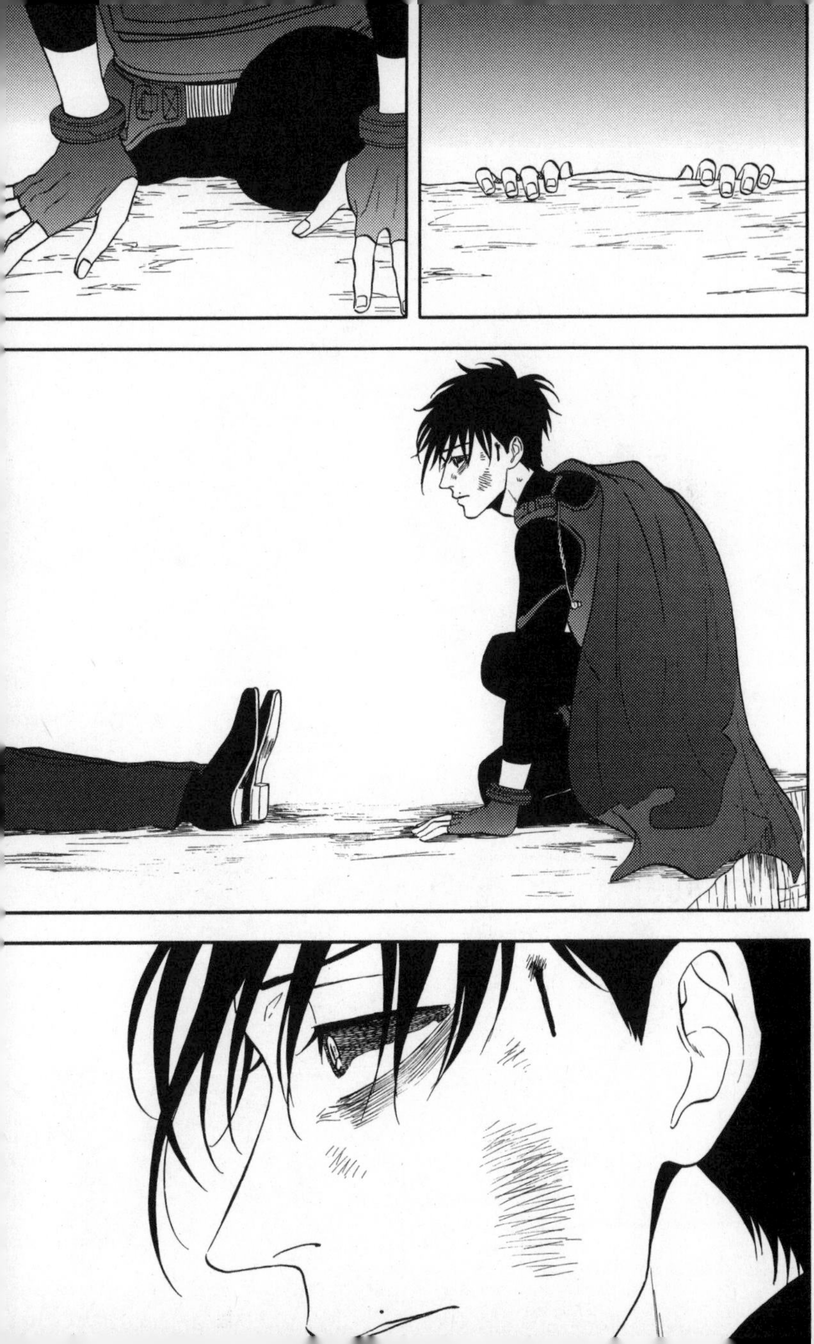

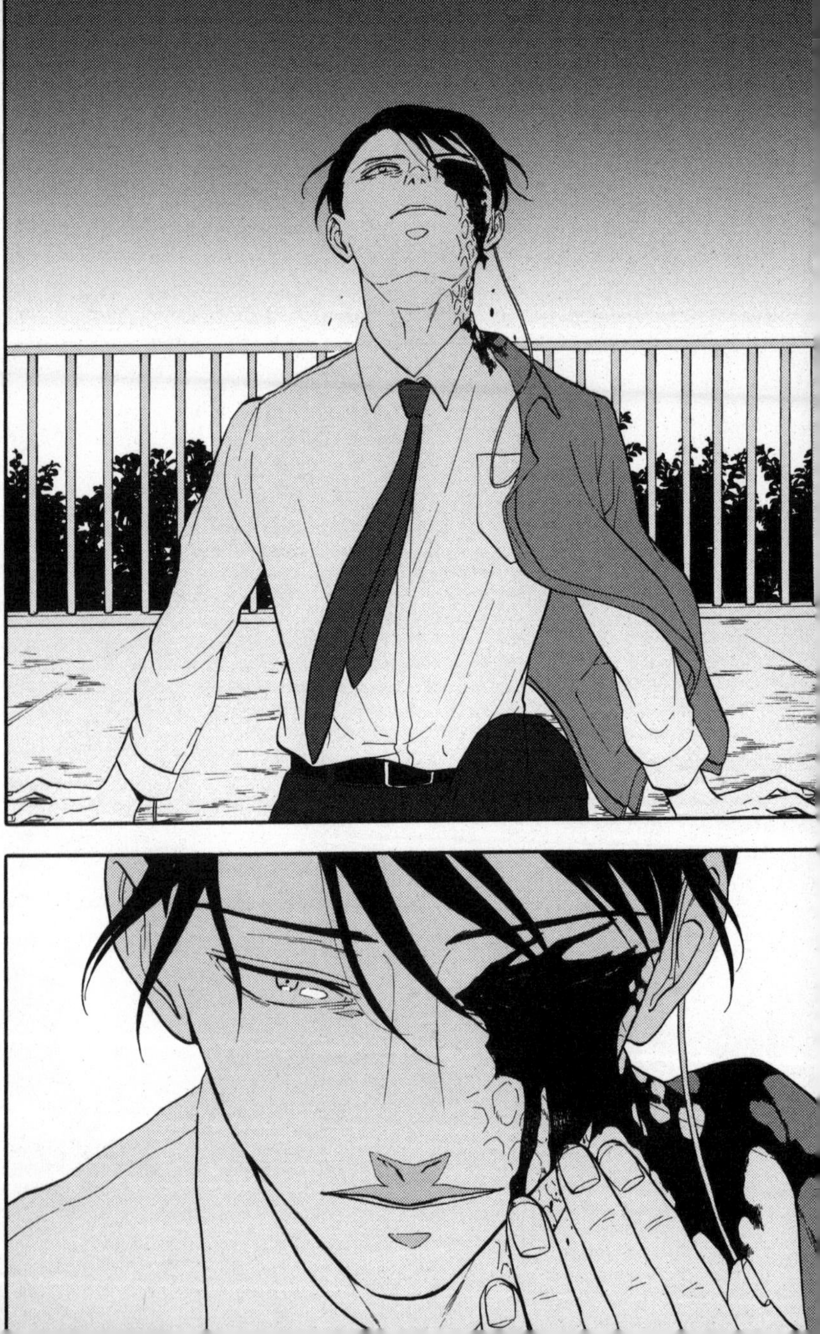

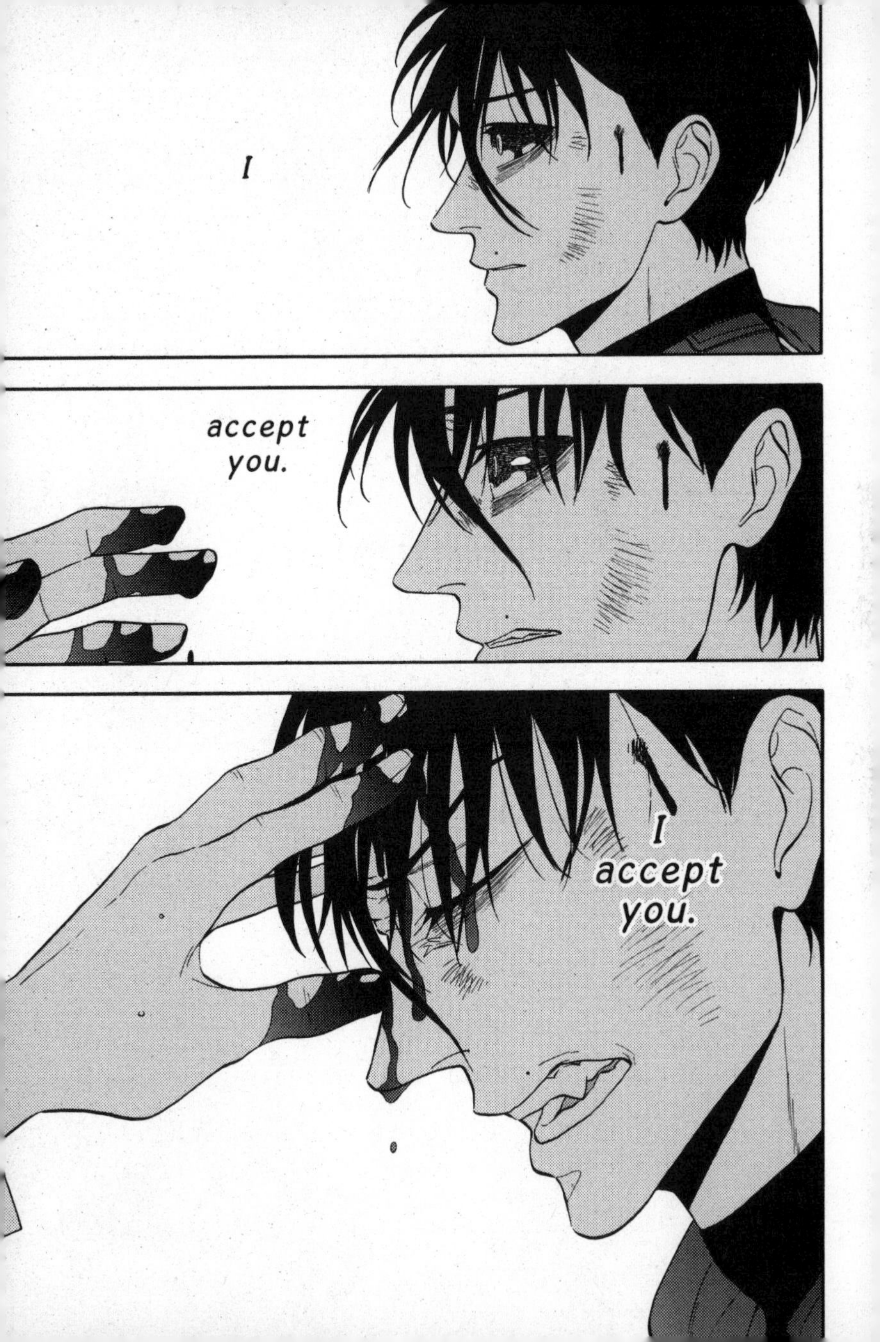
I
accept you.
I accept you.

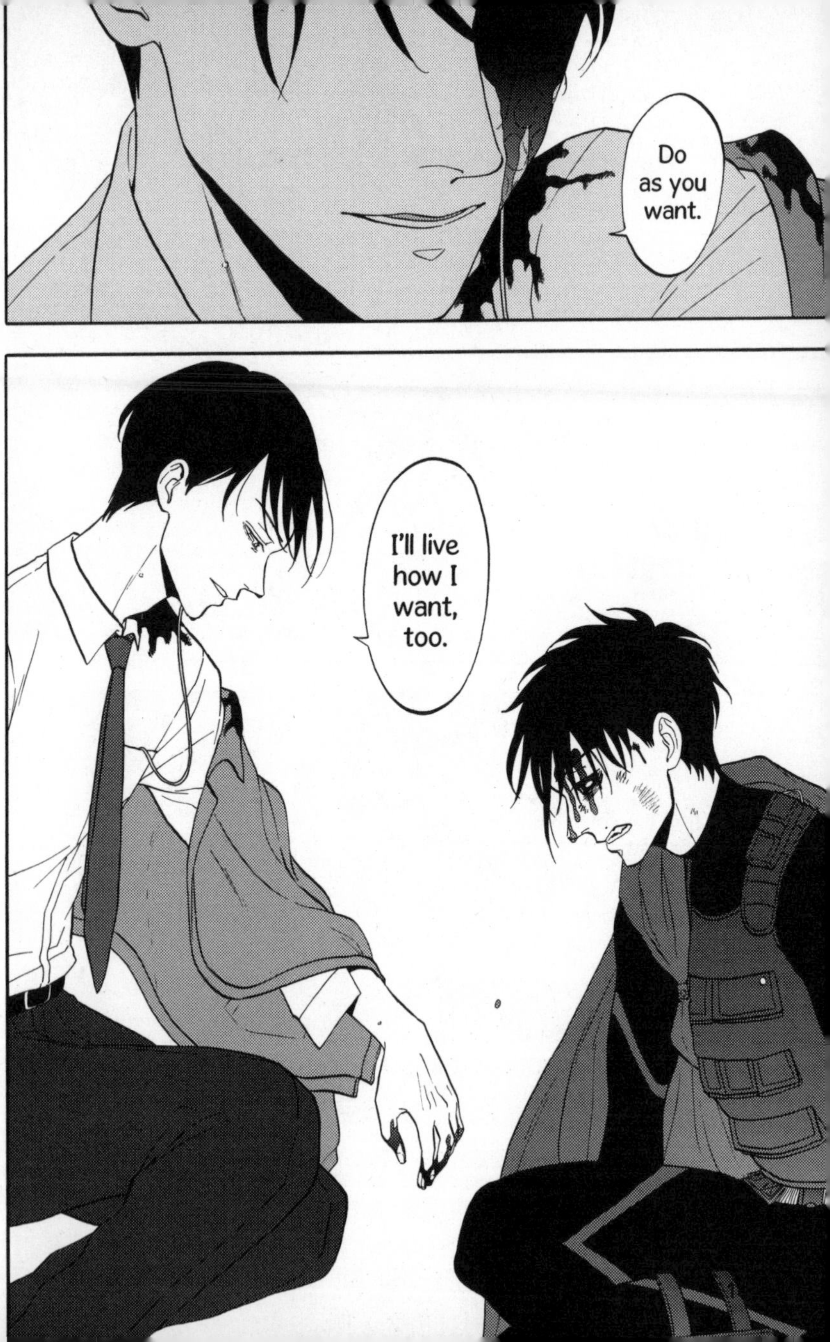
Do as you want.
I'll live how I want, too.

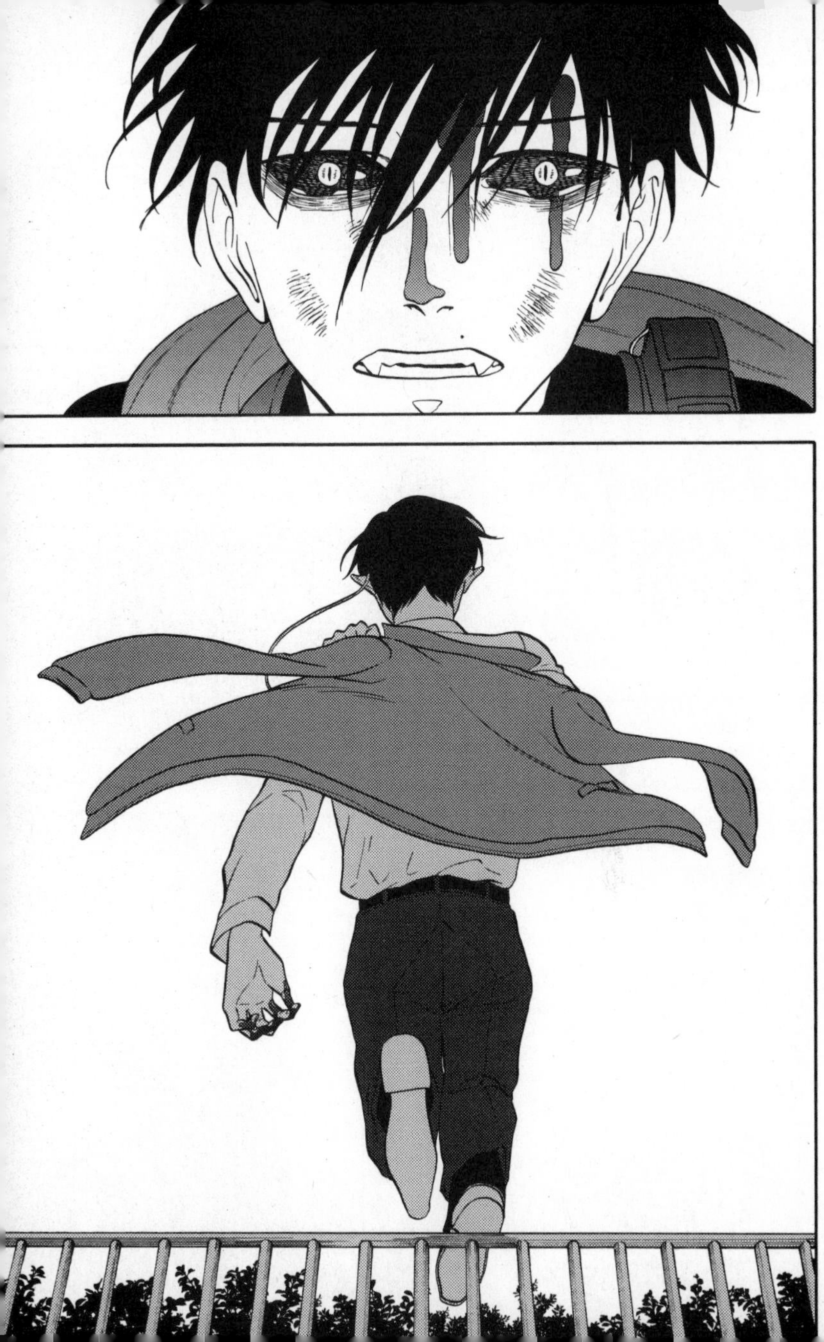

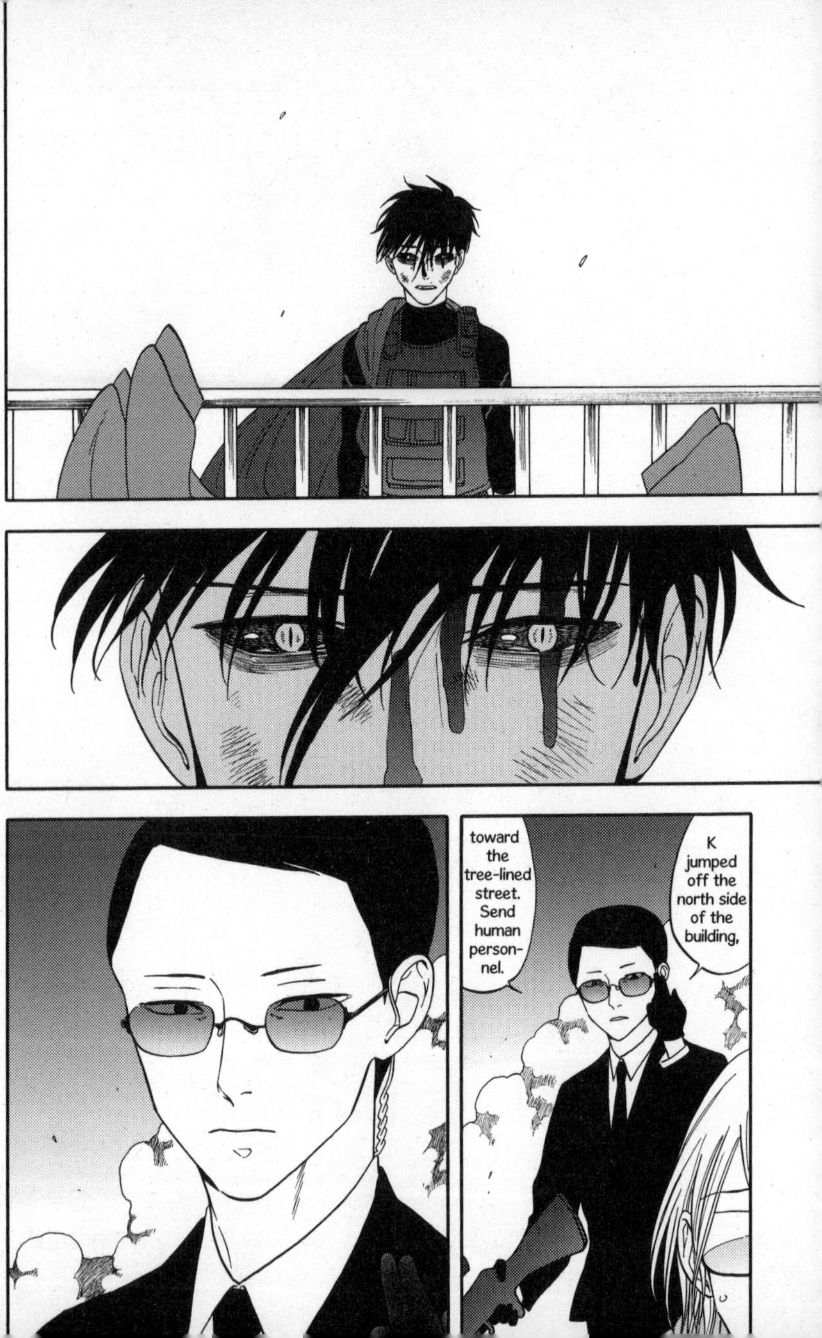
K jumped off the north side of the building,
toward the tree-lined street. Send human person-nel.

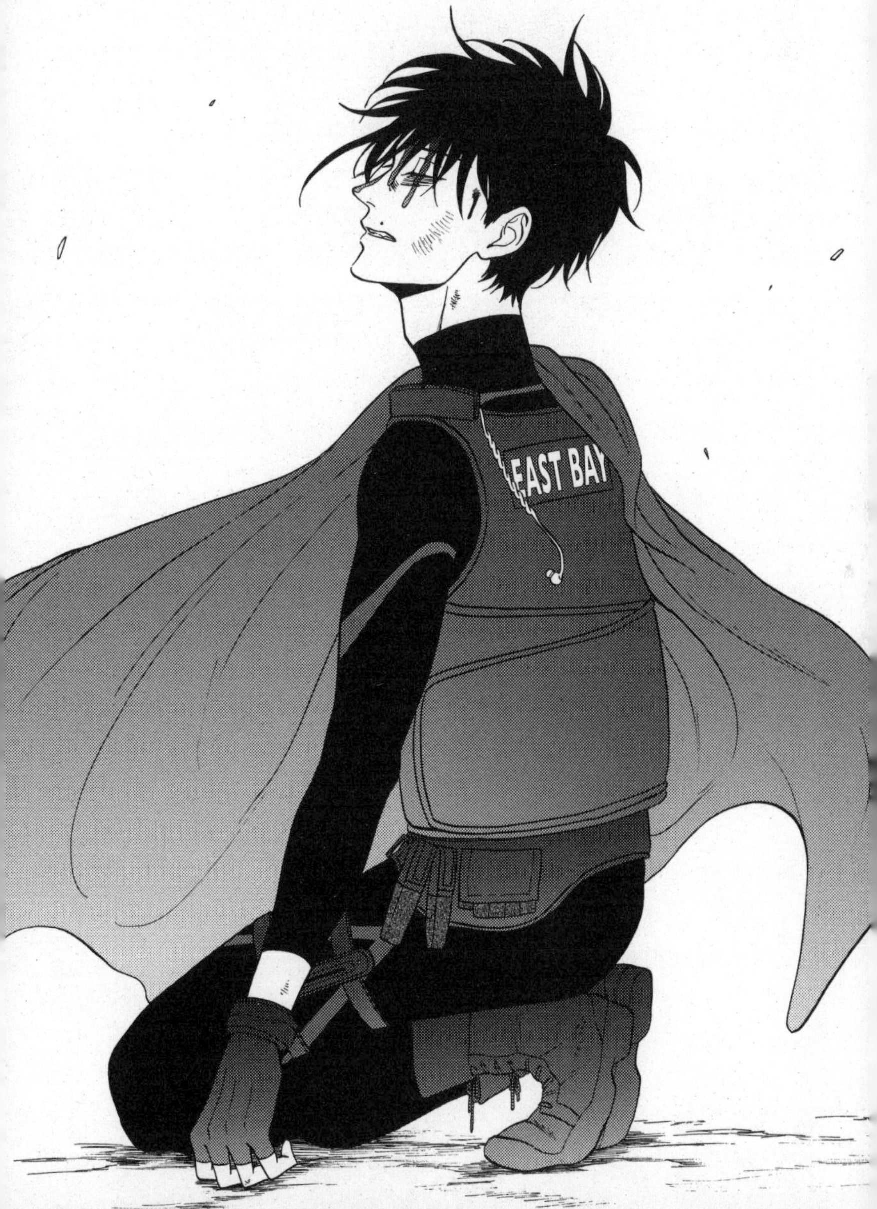
EAST BAY

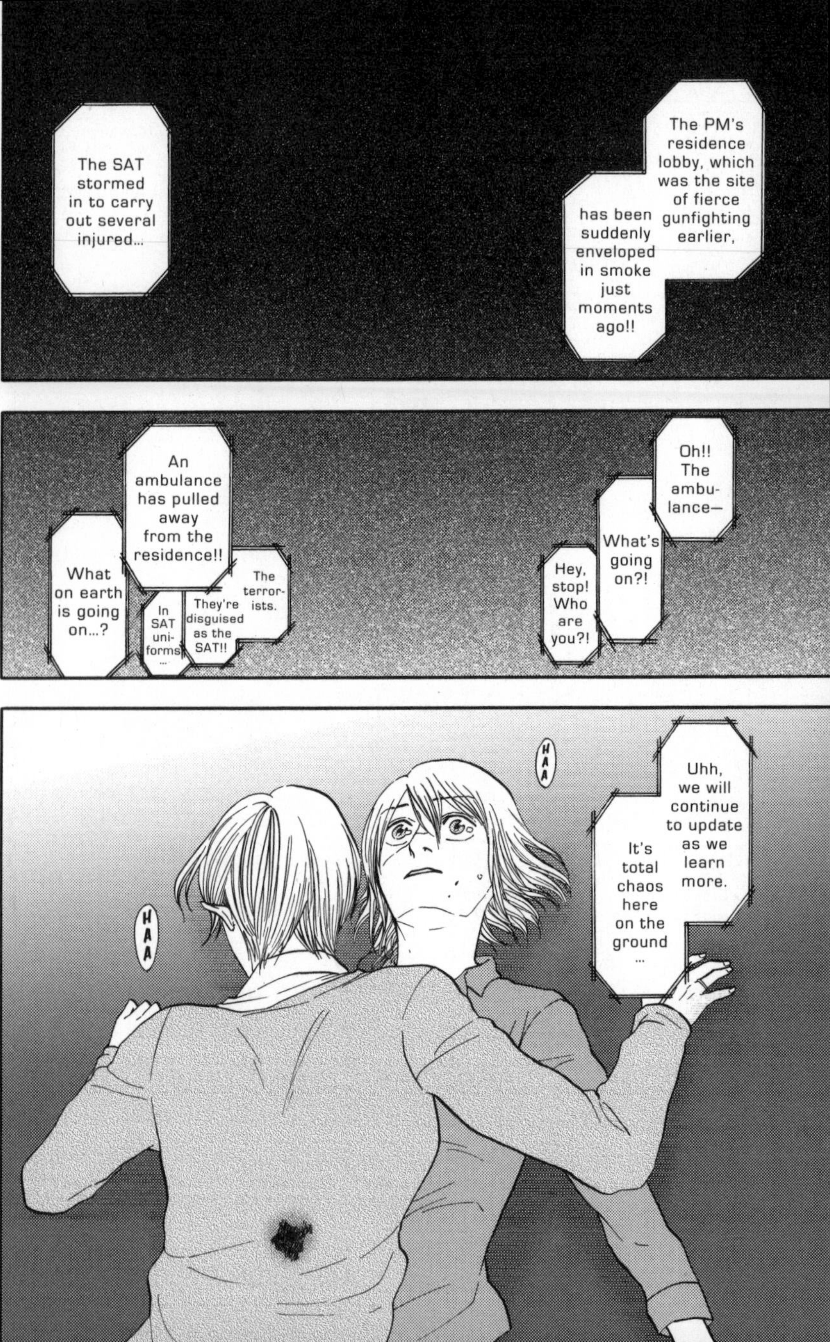
The PM's residence lobby, which was the site of fierce gunfighting earlier,
has been suddenly enveloped in smoke just moments ago!!
The SAT stormed in to carry out several injured...
Oh!! The ambulance—
What's going on?!
Hey, stop! Who are you?!
The terrorists.
They're disguised as the SAT!!
An ambulance has pulled away from the residence!!
In SAT uniforms...
What on earth is going on...?
HAA
Uhh, we will continue to update as we learn more.
It's total chaos here on the ground...
HAA

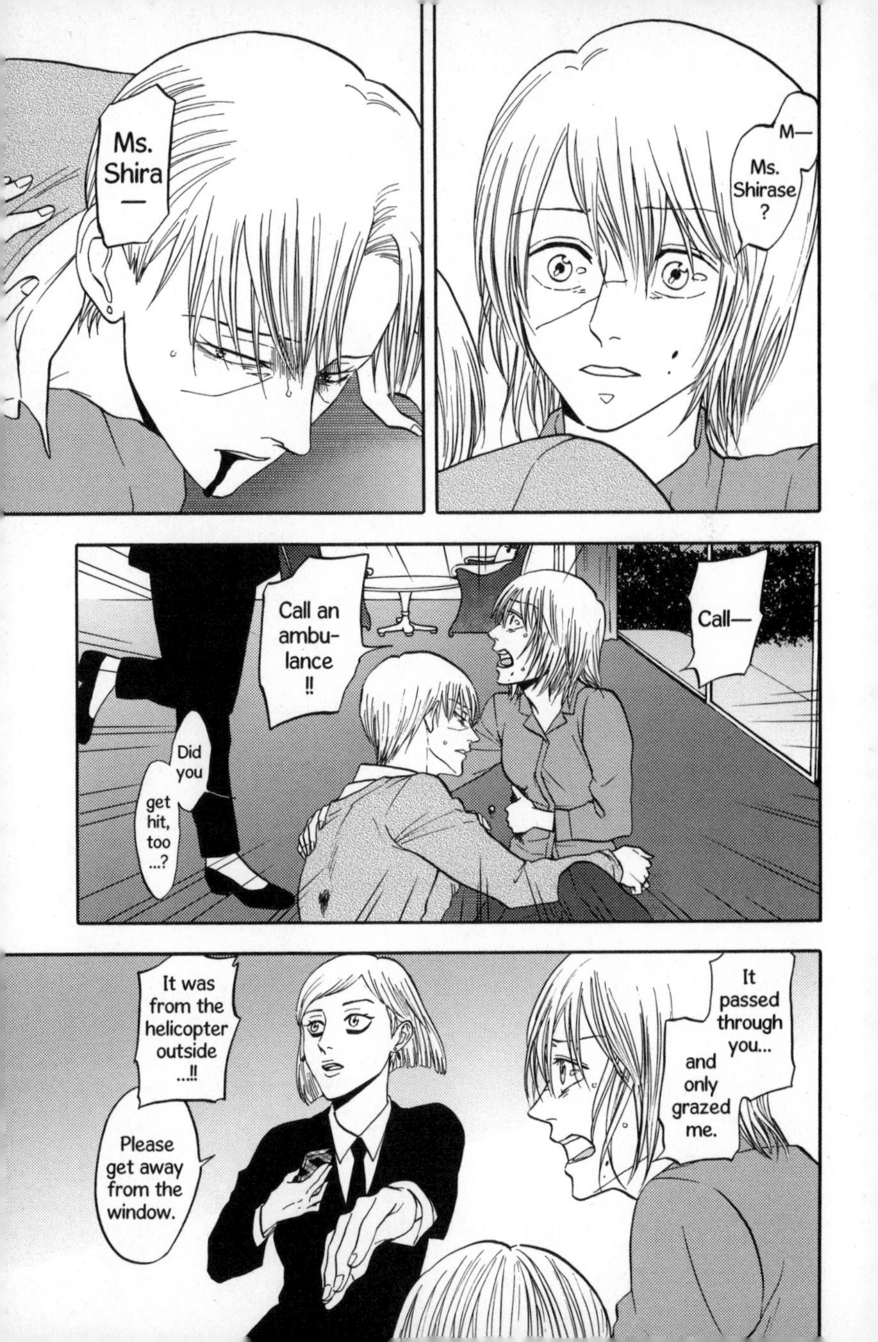
M— Ms. Shirase?
Ms. Shira—
Call—
Call an ambulance!!
Did you get hit, too...?
It passed through you... and only grazed me.
It was from the helicopter outside...!!
Please get away from the window.

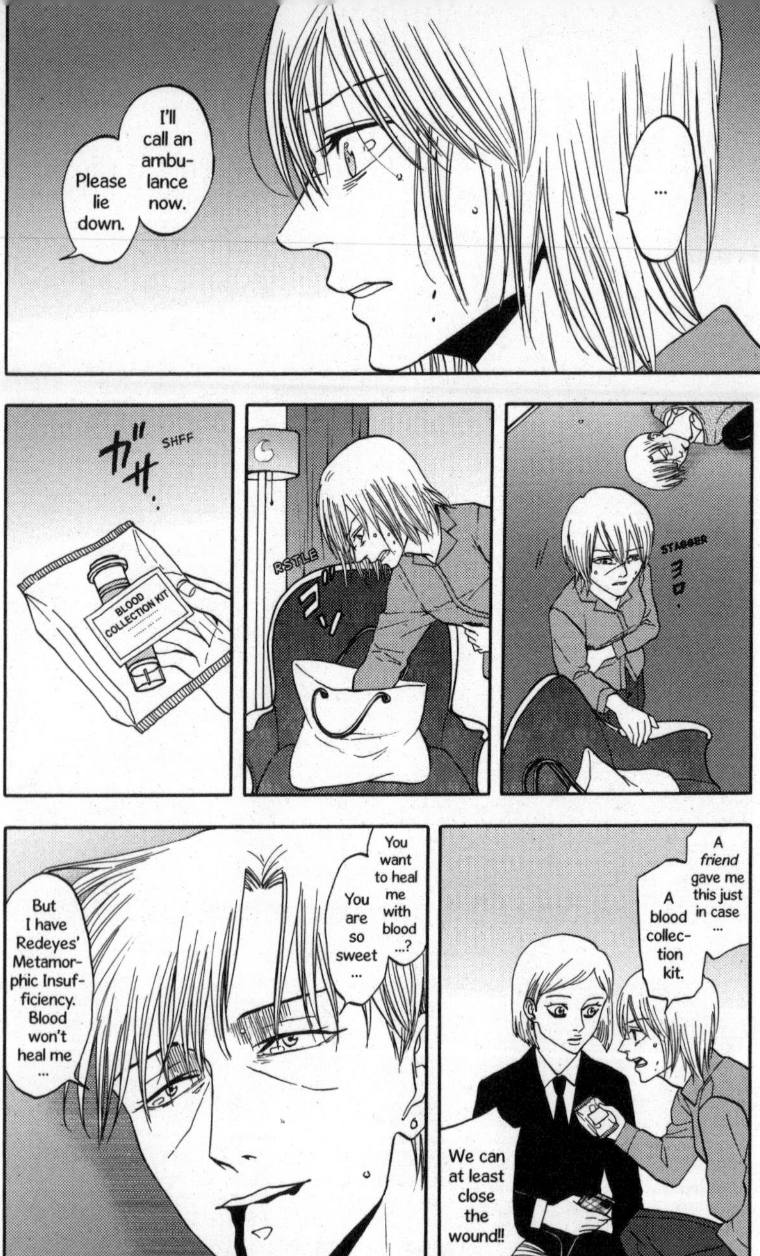

...
I'll call an ambulance now.
Please lie down.
STAGGER
ヨロ.
RSTLE
ゴソ
ガサ..
SHFF
BLOOD COLLECTION KIT
A *friend* gave me this just in case ...
A blood collection kit.
We can at least close the wound!!
You want to heal me with blood ...?
You are so sweet ...
But I have Redeyes' Metamorphic Insufficiency. Blood won't heal me ...

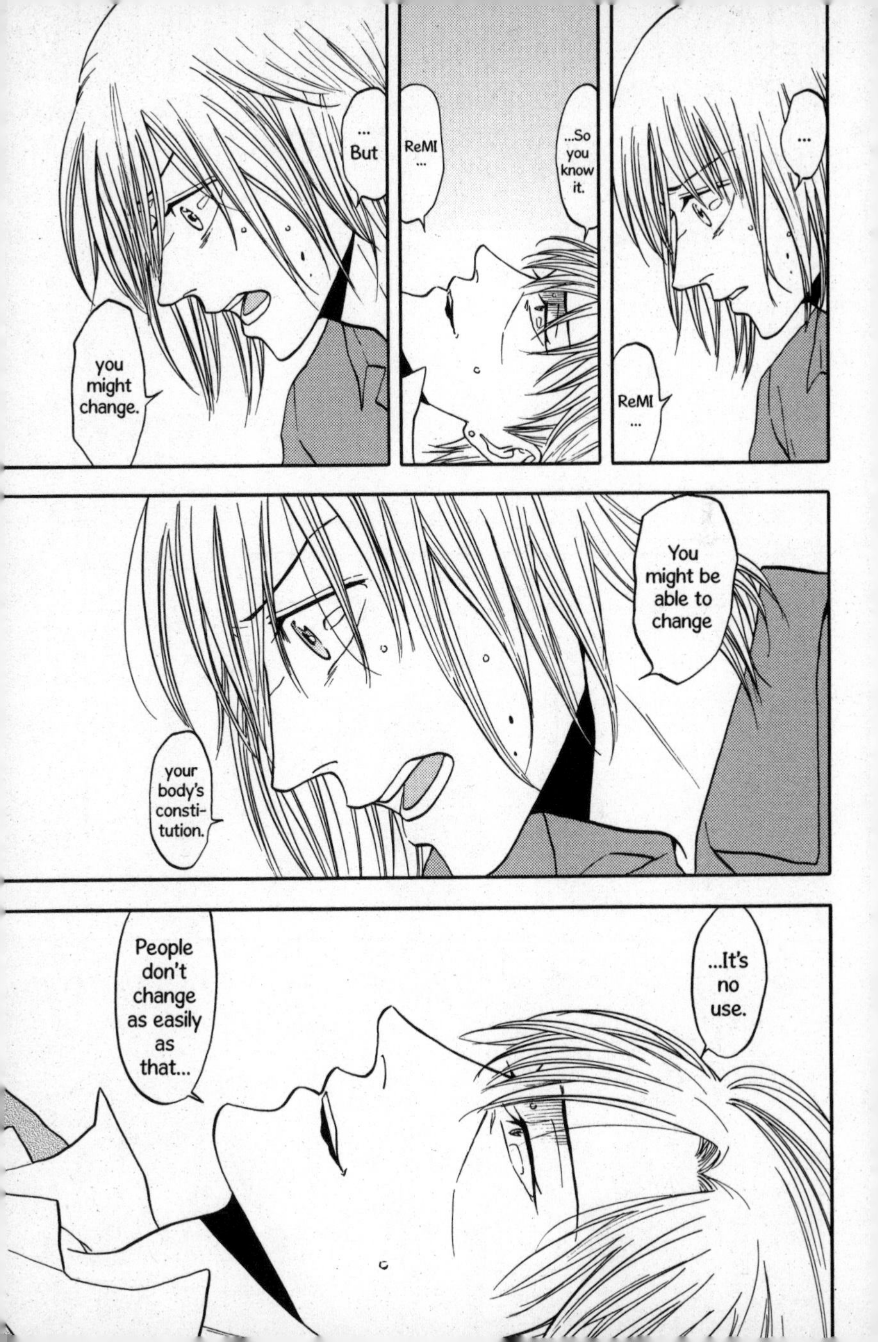
...
ReMI ...
...So you know it.
ReMI ...
... But
you might change.
You might be able to change
your body's constitution.
...It's no use.
People don't change as easily as that...

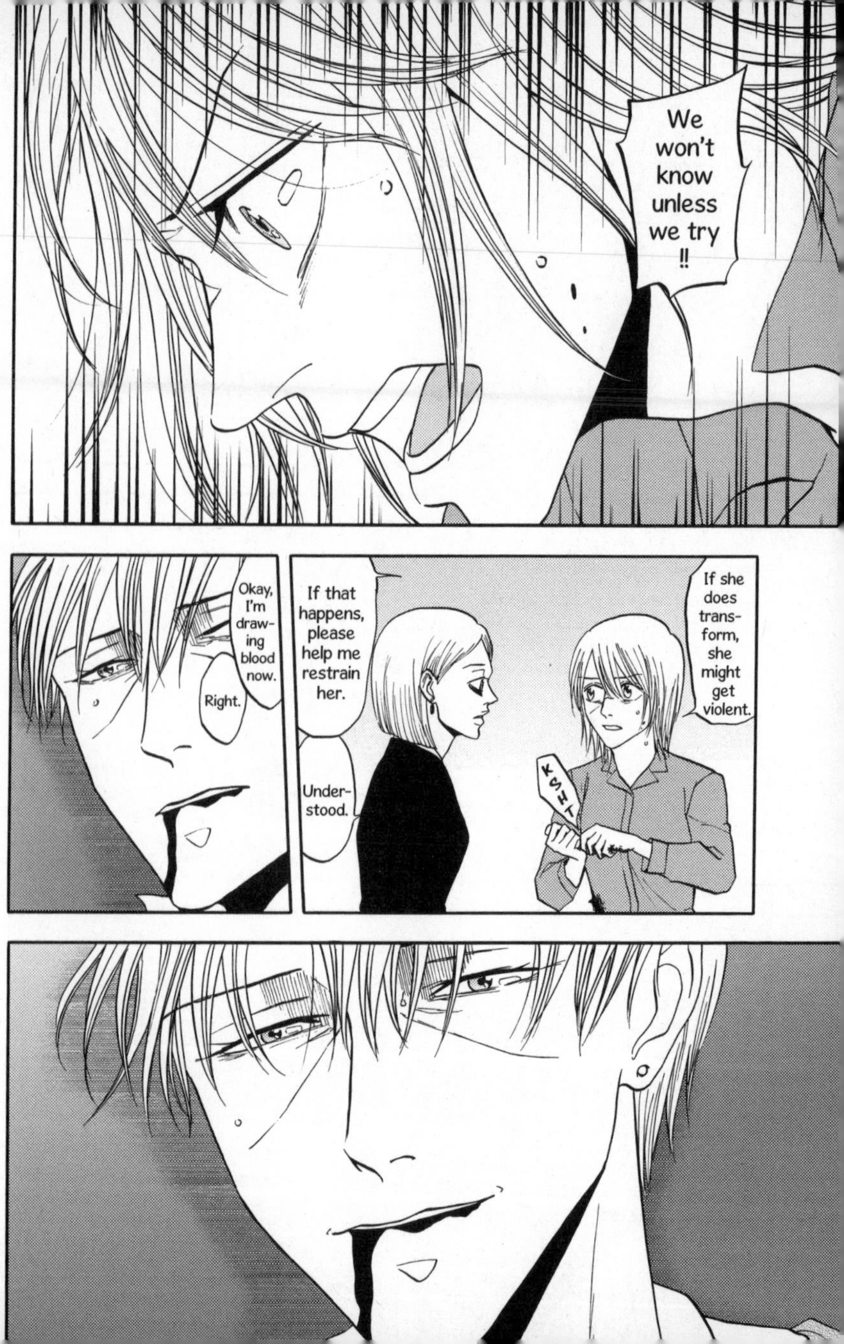
We won't know unless we try !!
If she does trans-form, she might get violent.
KSHT
If that happens, please help me restrain her.
Understood.
Okay, I'm draw-ing blood now.
Right.

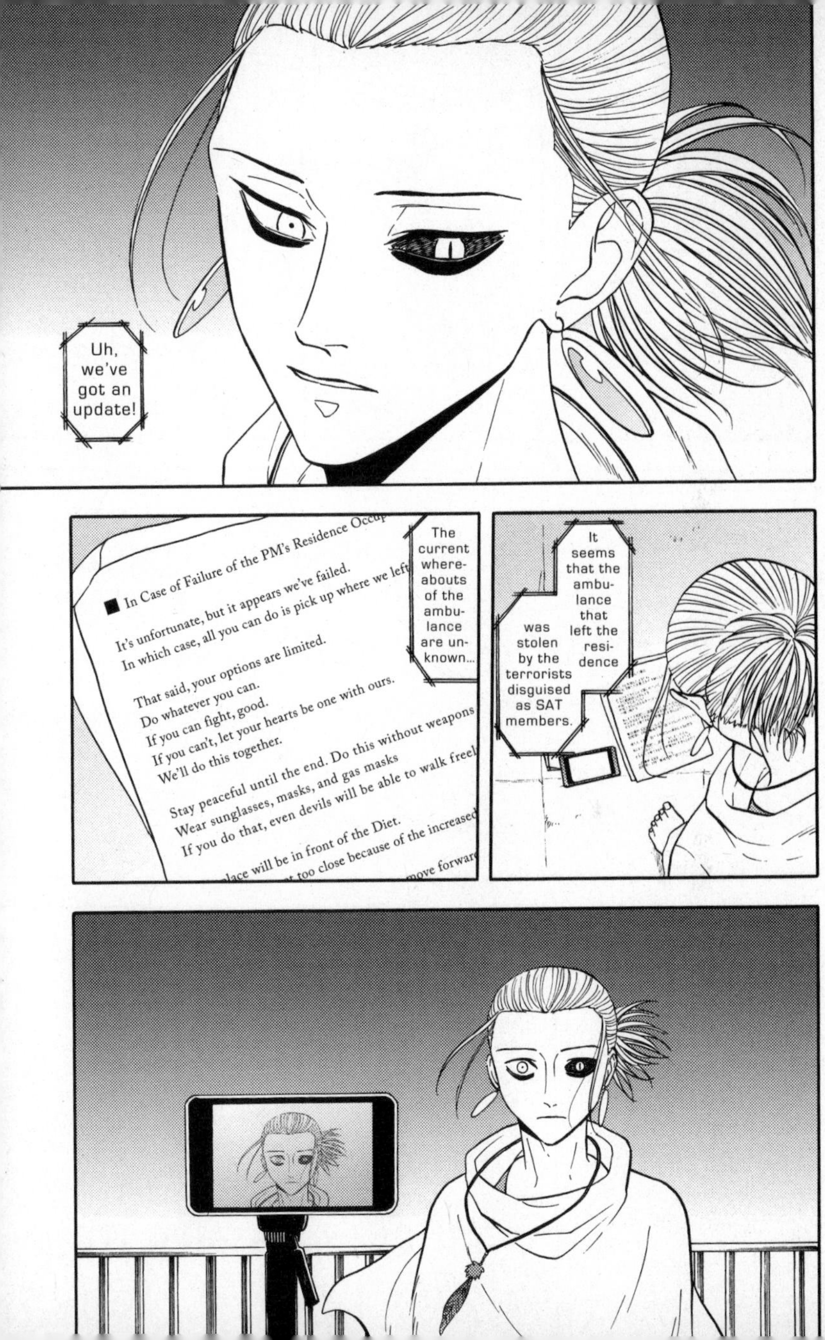
Uh, we've got an update!
It seems that the ambulance that left the residence was stolen by the terrorists disguised as SAT members.
The current whereabouts of the ambulance are unknown...
In Case of Failure of the PM's Residence Occup
It's unfortunate, but it appears we've failed.
In which case, all you can do is pick up where we left
That said, your options are limited.
Do whatever you can.
If you can fight, good.
If you can't, let your hearts be one with ours.
We'll do this together.
Stay peaceful until the end. Do this without weapons
Wear sunglasses, masks, and gas masks
If you do that, even devils will be able to walk freel
If you do that, even devils will be able to walk freel
If you do that, even devils will be able to walk freel

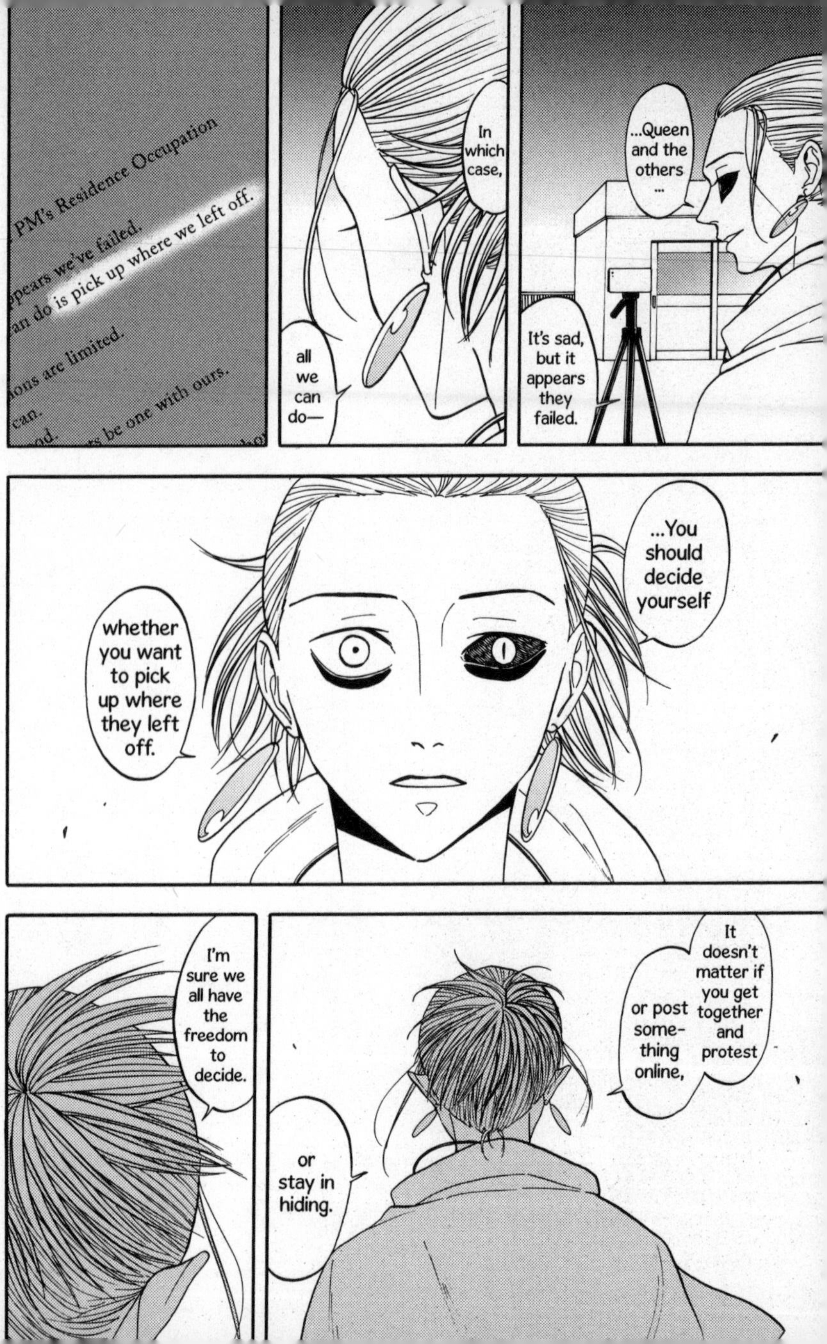
...Queen and the others ...
It's sad, but it appears they failed.
In which case,
all we can do—
PM's Residence Occupation
we've failed.
is pick up where we left off.
are limited.
can.
be one with ours.
...You should decide yourself
whether you want to pick up where they left off.
It doesn't matter if you get together and protest
or post some-thing online,
or stay in hiding.
I'm sure we all have the freedom to decide.

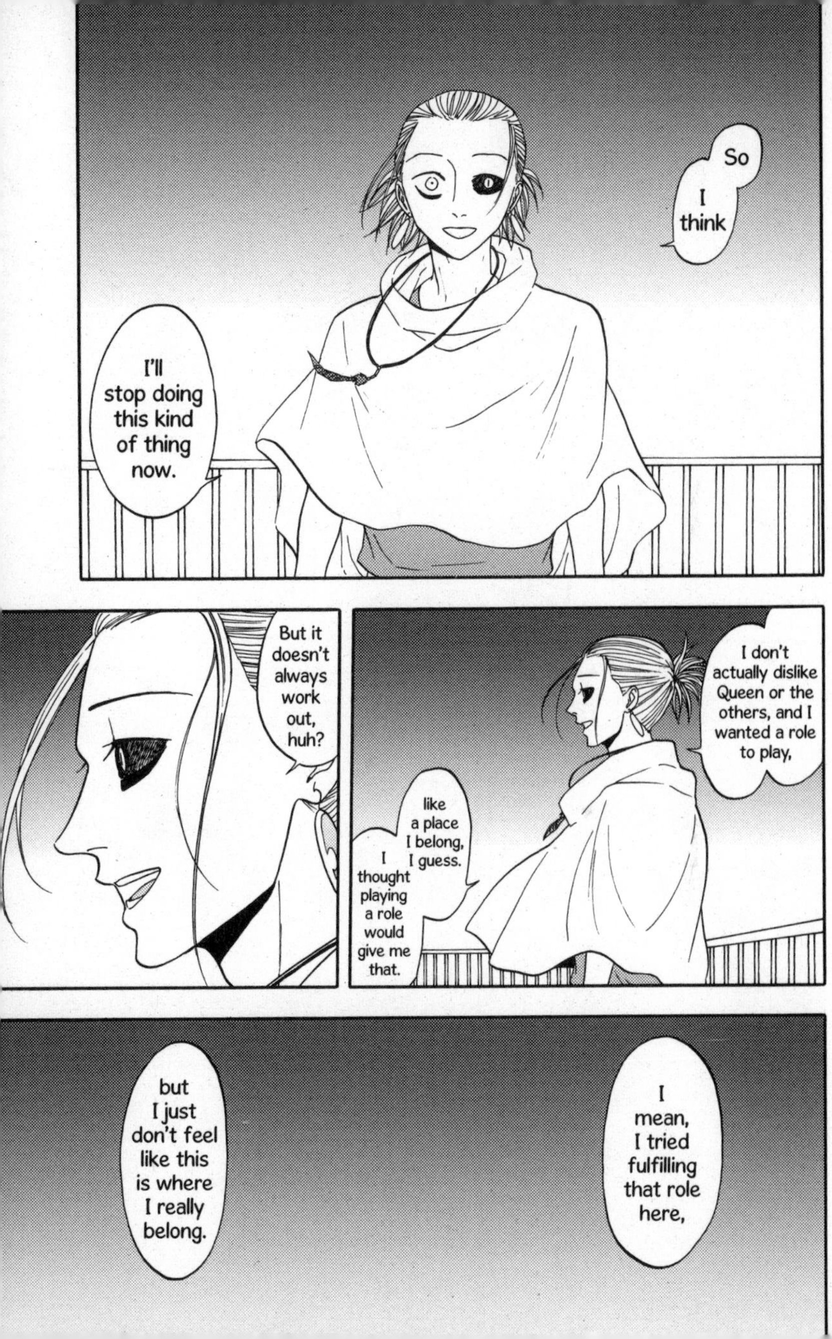
So I think
I'll stop doing this kind of thing now.
I don't actually dislike Queen or the others, and I wanted a role to play,
like a place I belong, I guess.
I thought playing a role would give me that.
But it doesn't always work out, huh?
I mean, I tried fulfilling that role here,
but I just don't feel like this is where I really belong.

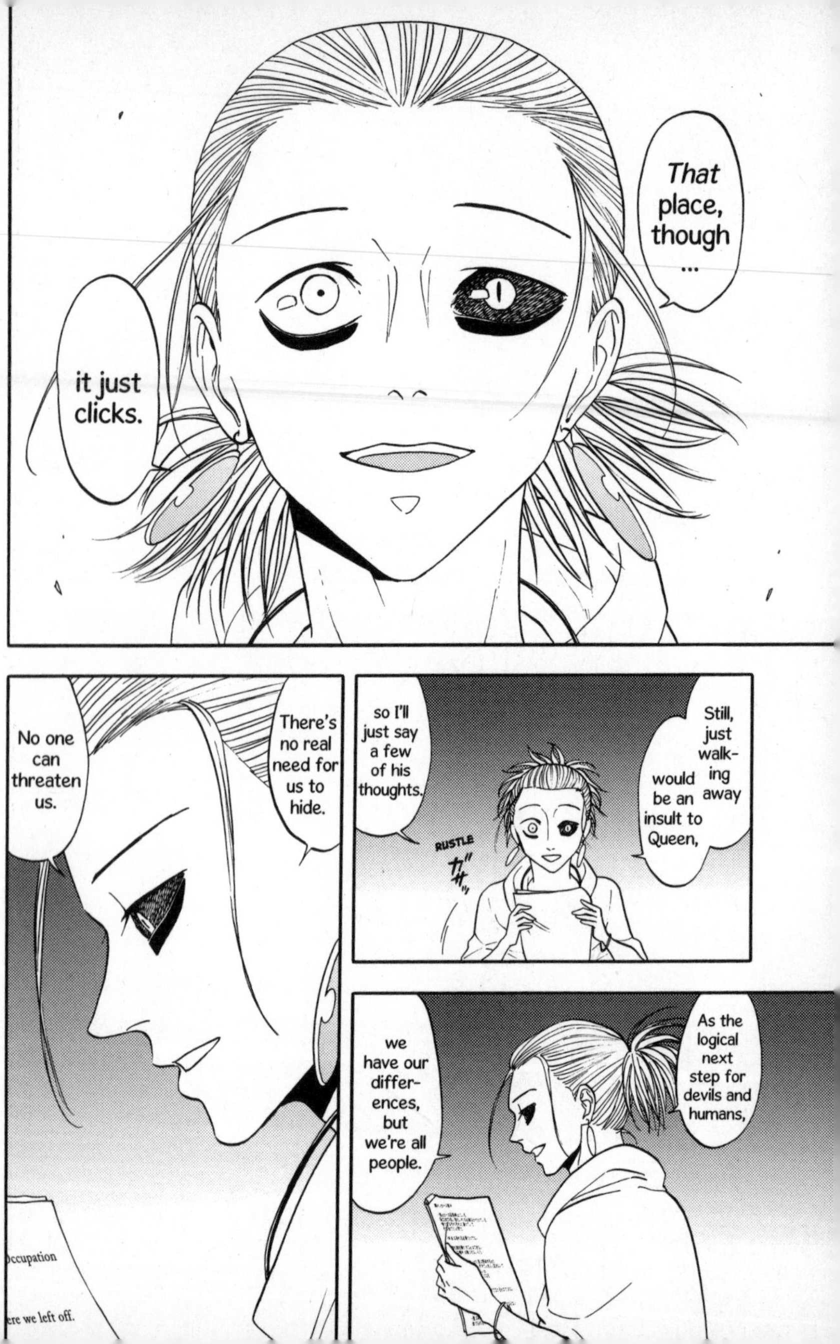
That place, though ...
it just clicks.
Still, just walking away would be an insult to Queen,
so I'll just say a few of his thoughts.
RUSTLE
As the logical next step for devils and humans,
we have our differences, but we're all people.
There's no real need for us to hide.
No one can threaten us.

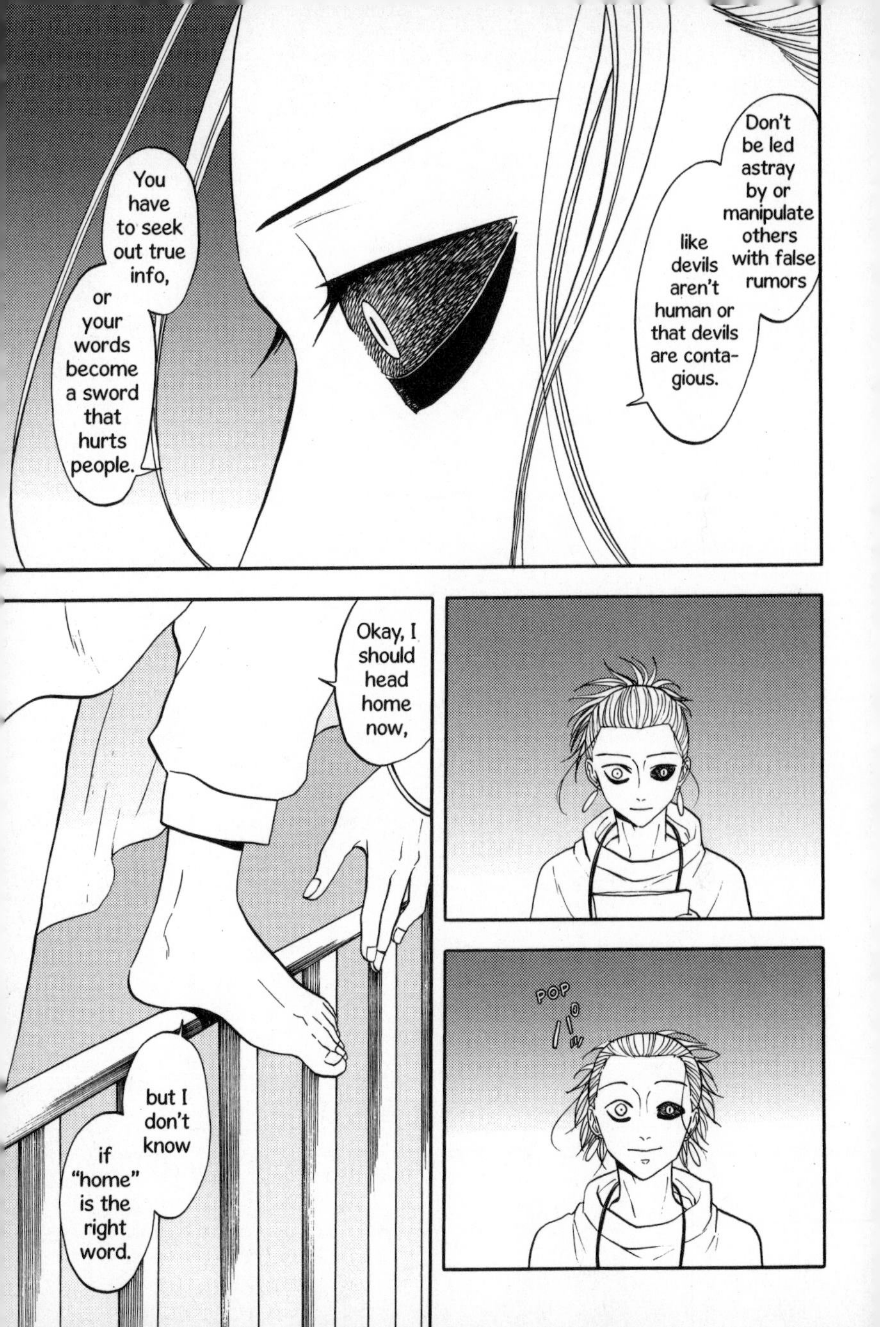
Don't be led astray by or manipulate others with false rumors
like devils aren't human or that devils are contagious.
You have to seek out true info,
or your words become a sword that hurts people.
POP
Okay, I should head home now,
but I don't know
if "home" is the right word.

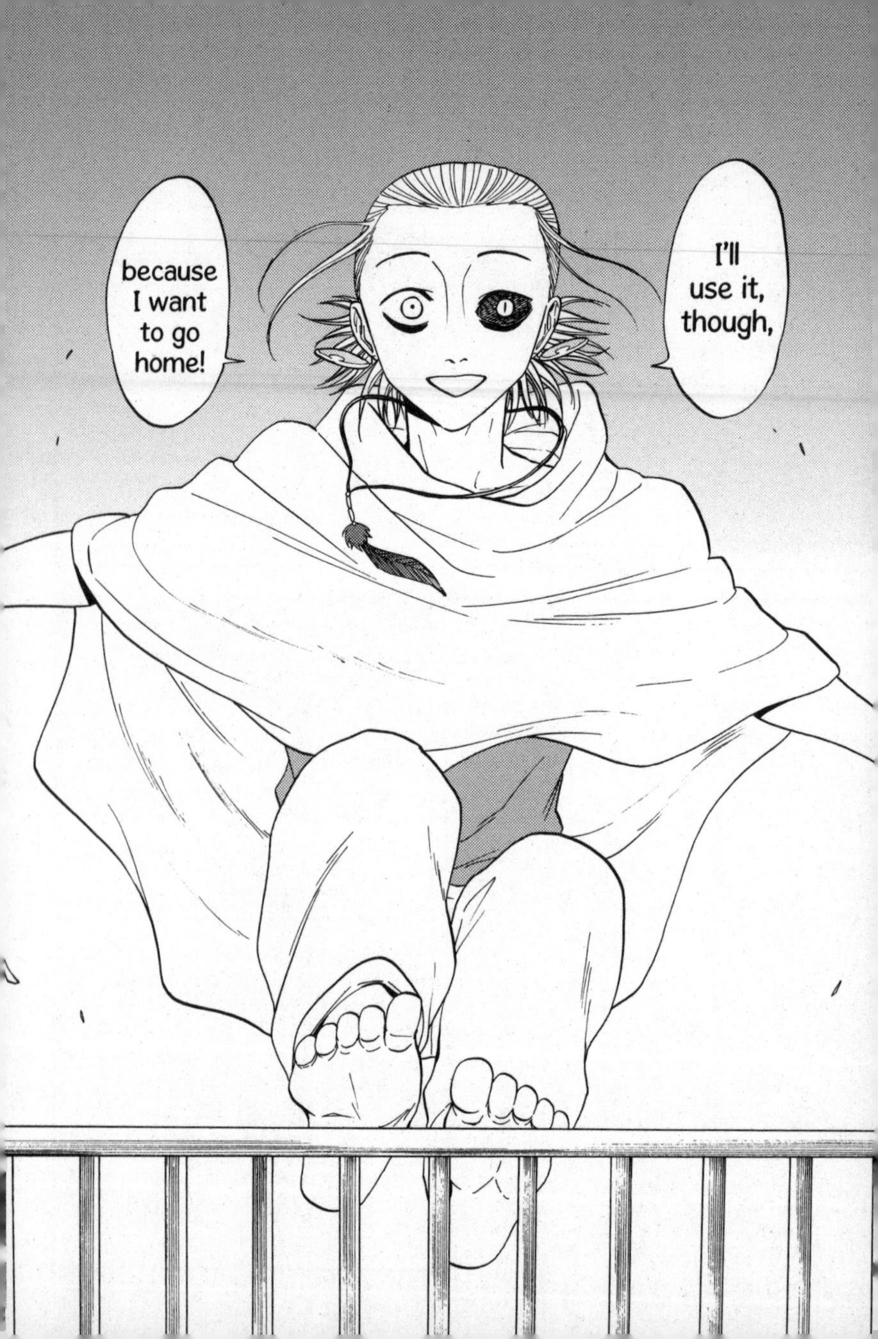
I'll use it, though,
because I want to go home!

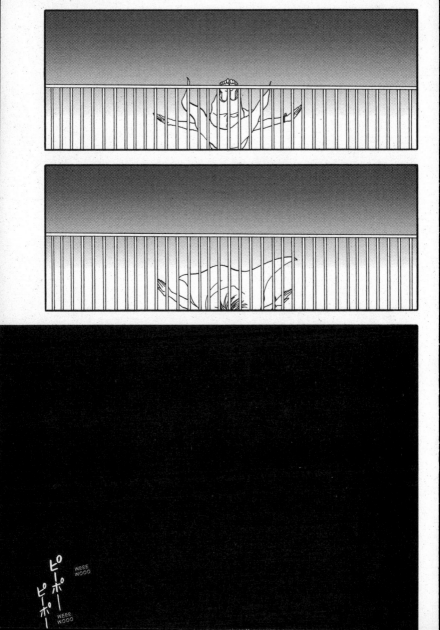

ピ
ー
ポ
ー
WEEE
WOOO

ピ
ー
ポ
ー
WEEE
WOOO

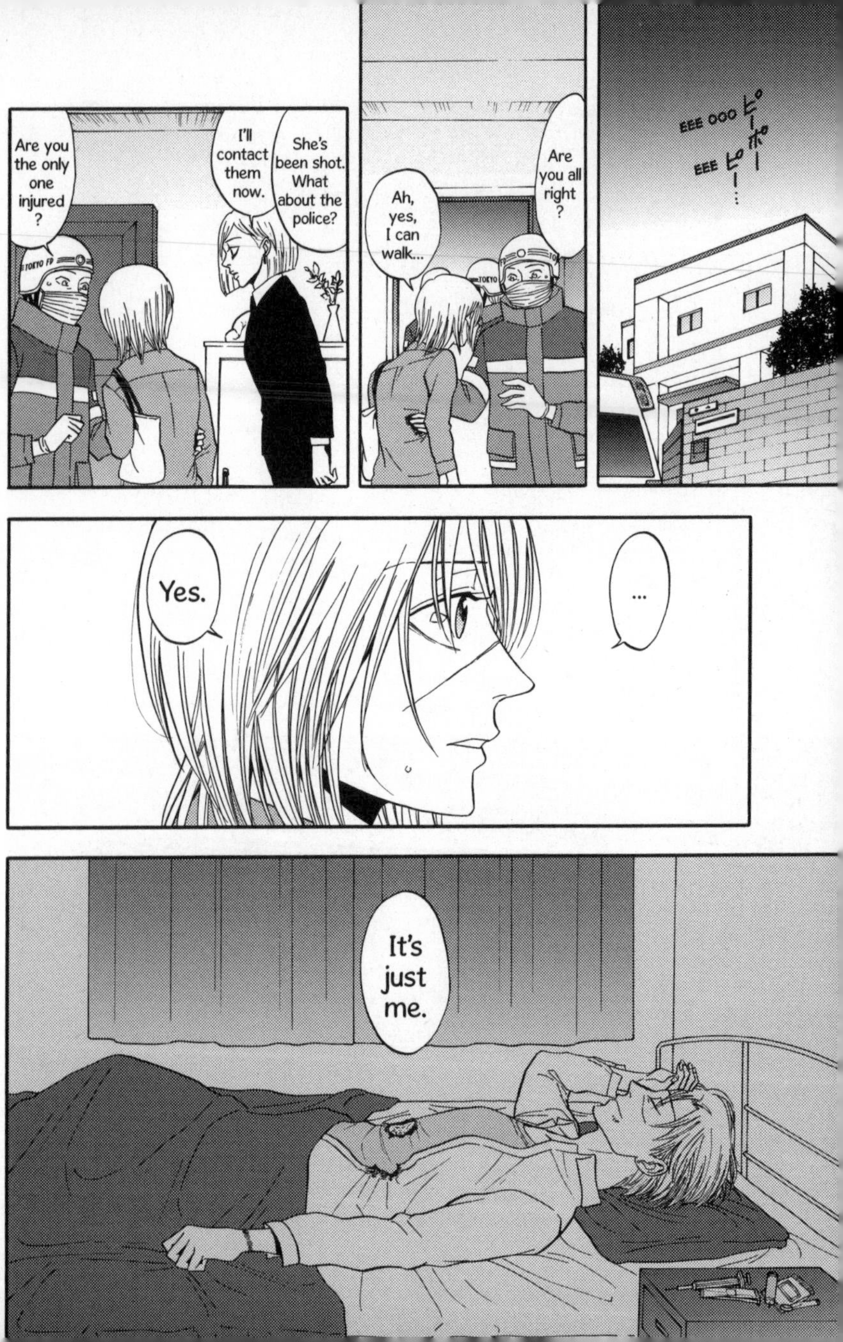
EEE OOO ピーポー
EEE ピー…
Are you all right?
Ah, yes, I can walk...
She's been shot. What about the police?
I'll contact them now.
Are you the only one injured?
...
Yes.
It's just me.

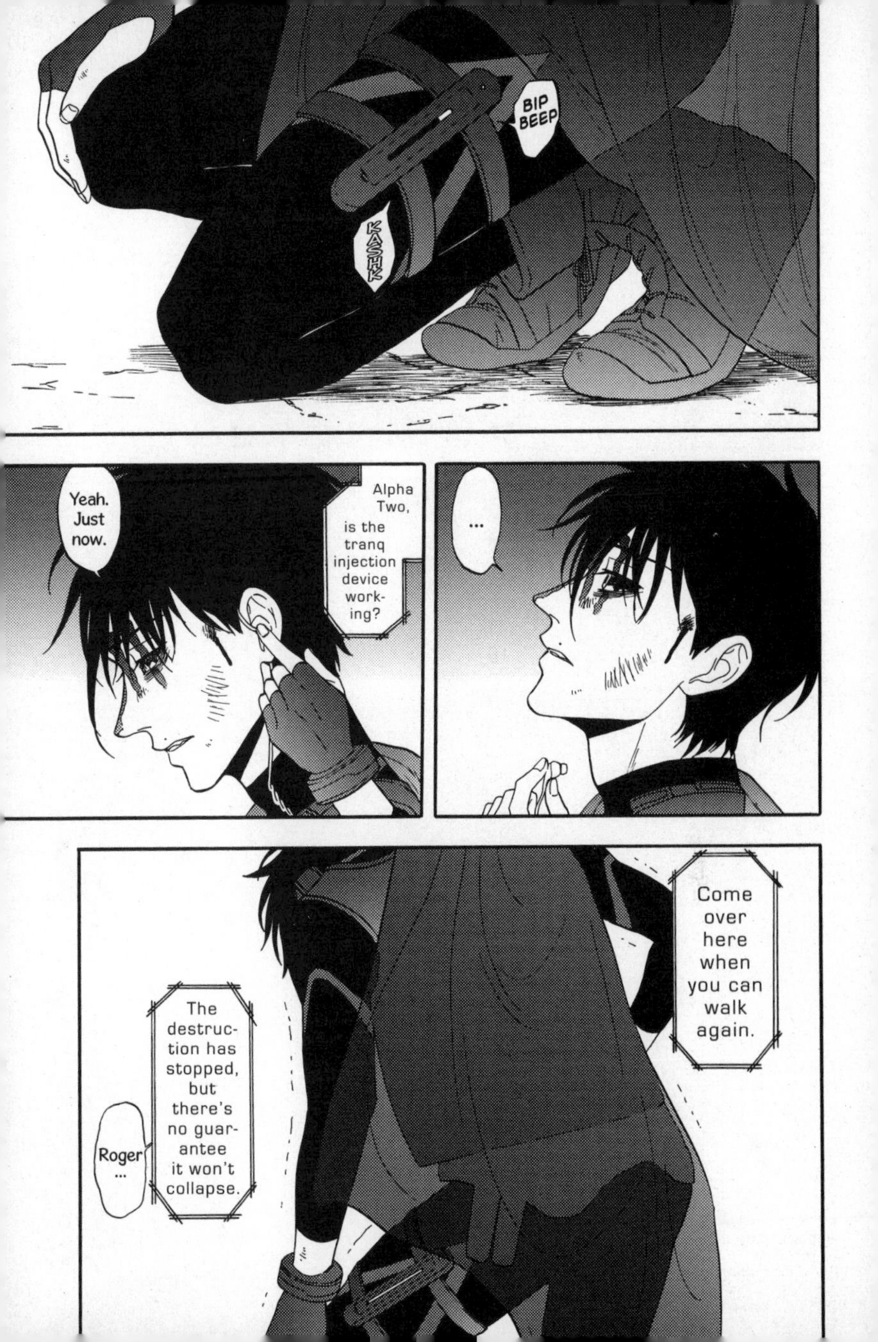
BIP BEEP
KASHK
...
Alpha Two, is the tranq injection device working?
Yeah. Just now.
Come over here when you can walk again.
The destruction has stopped, but there's no guarantee it won't collapse.
Roger...

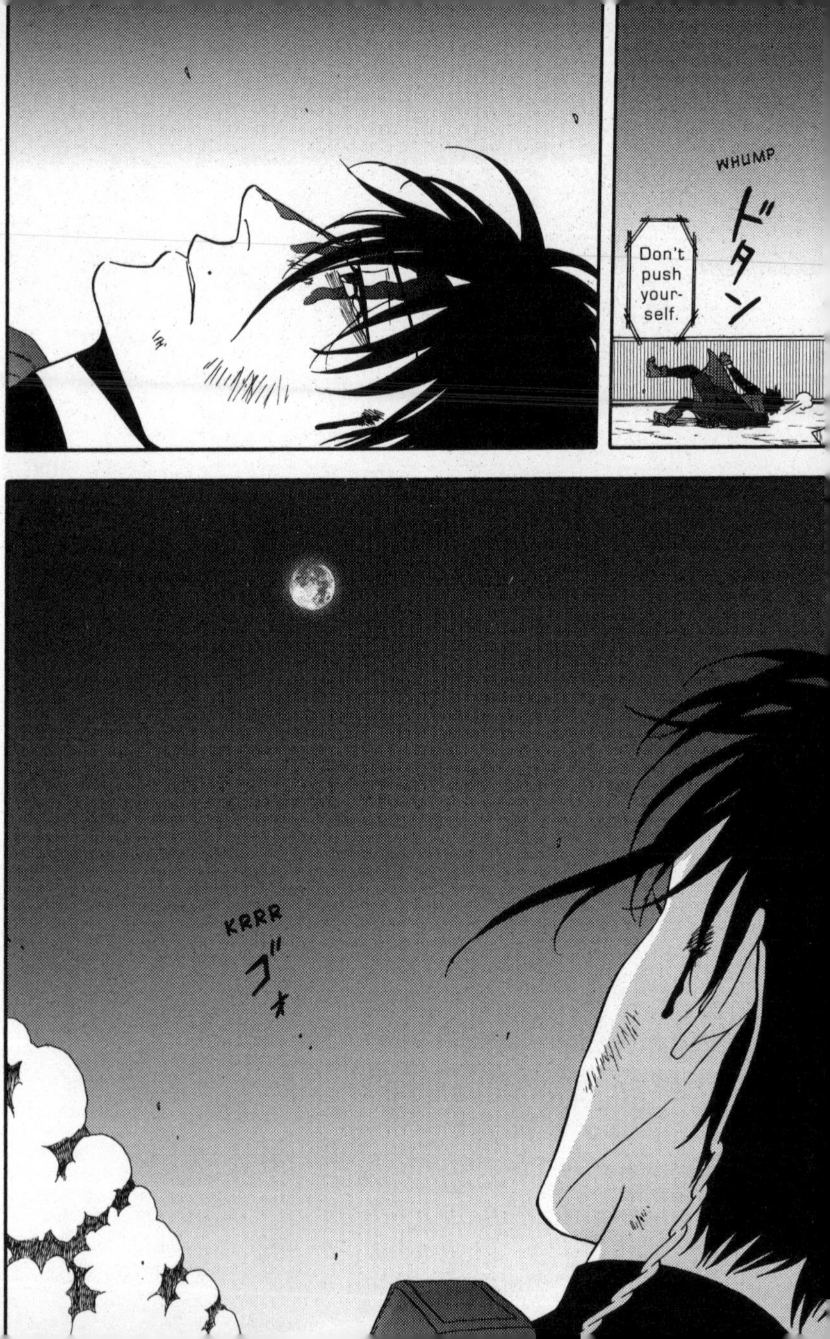
WHUMP
ドタン
Don't push your-self.
KRRR
ゴォ…

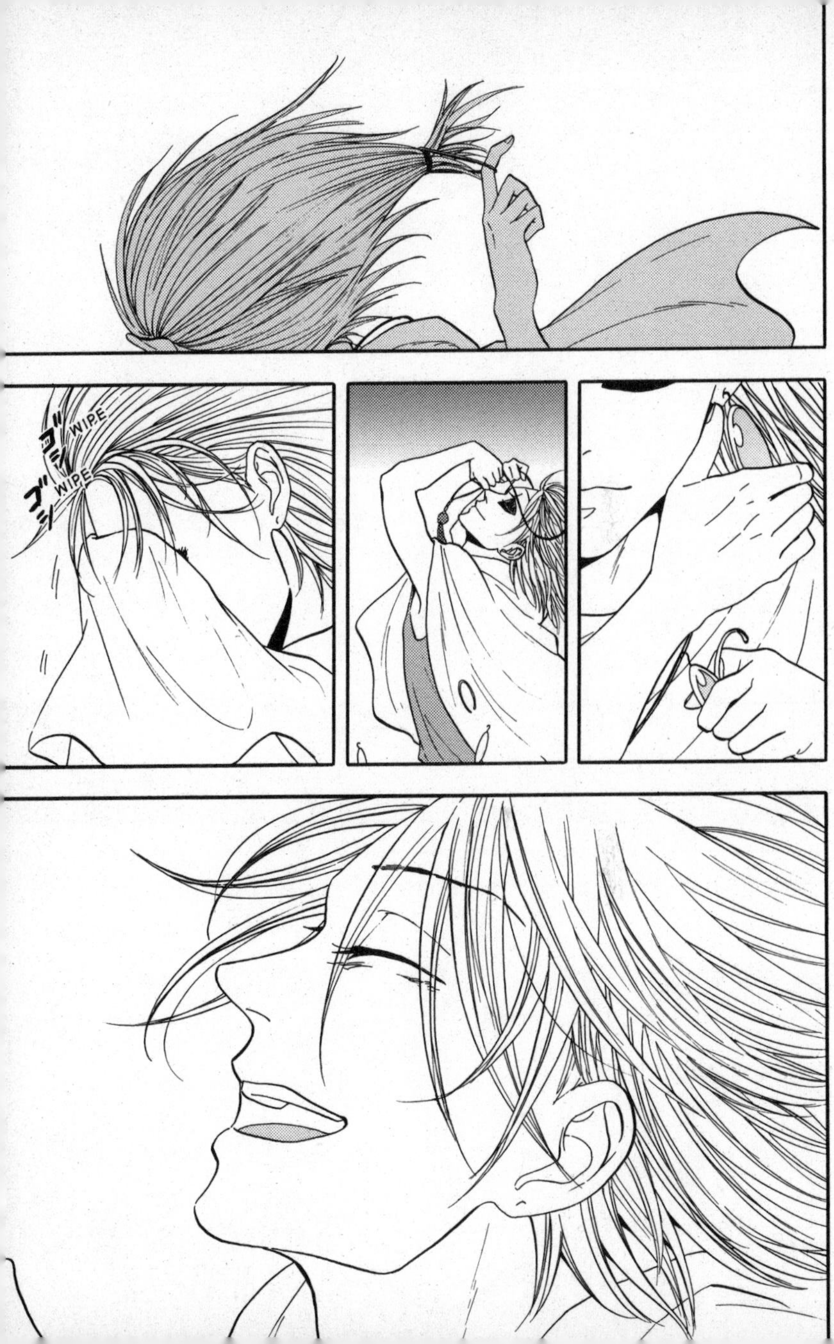
ゴシ WIPE
ゴシ WIPE

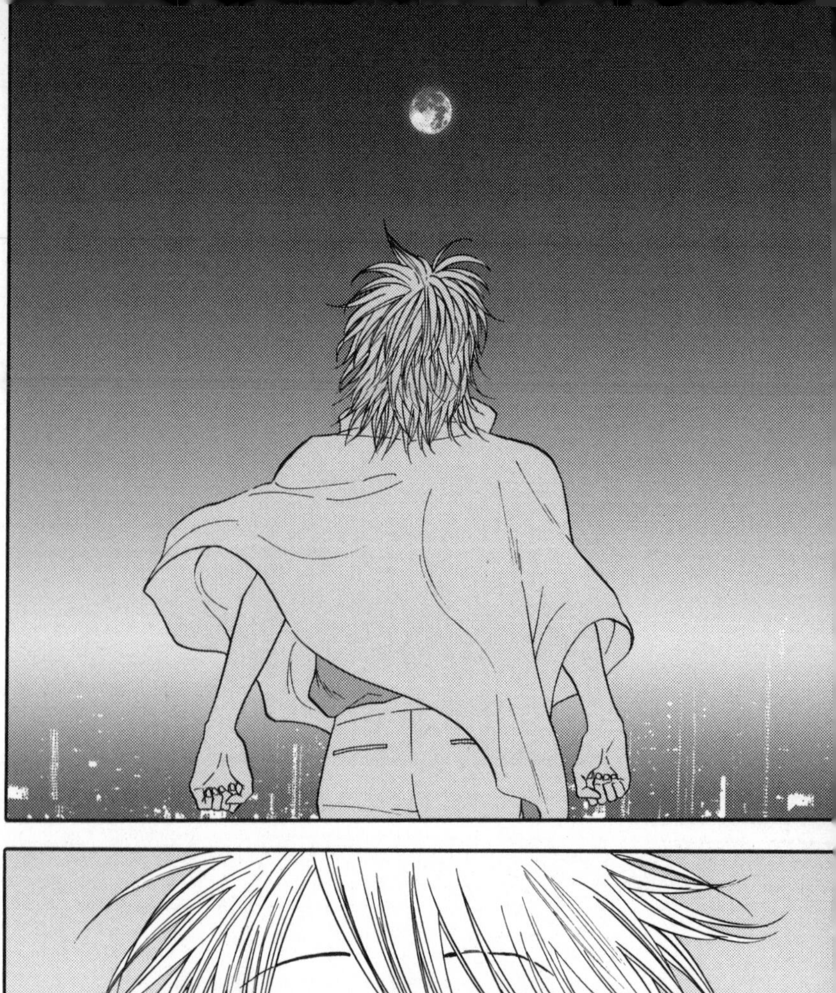
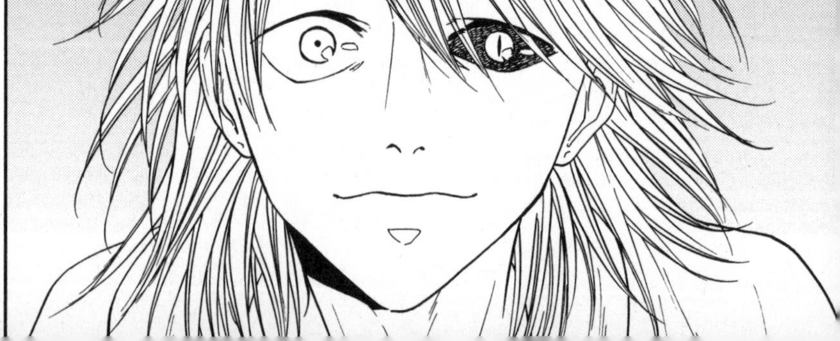

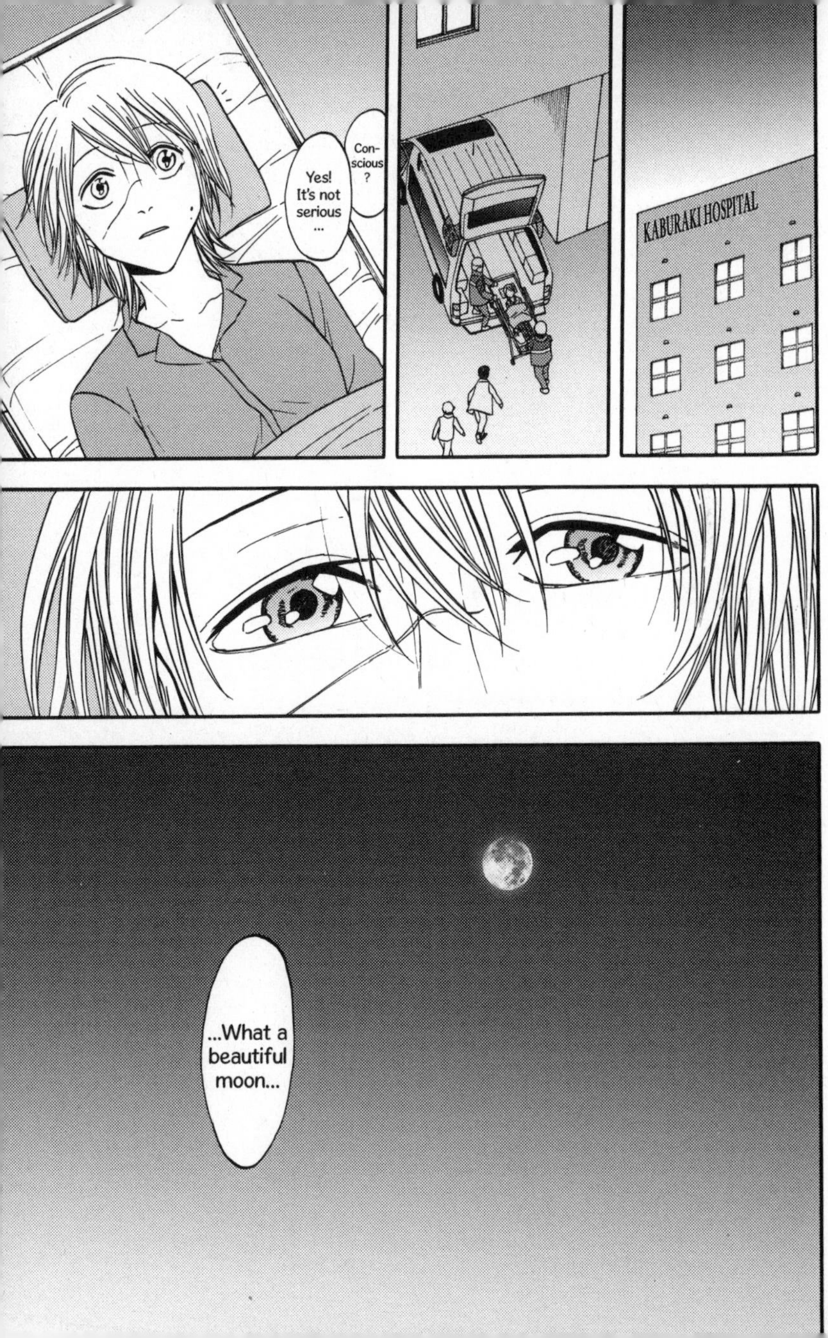
KABURAKI HOSPITAL
Con-scious?
Yes! It's not serious ...
...What a beautiful moon...

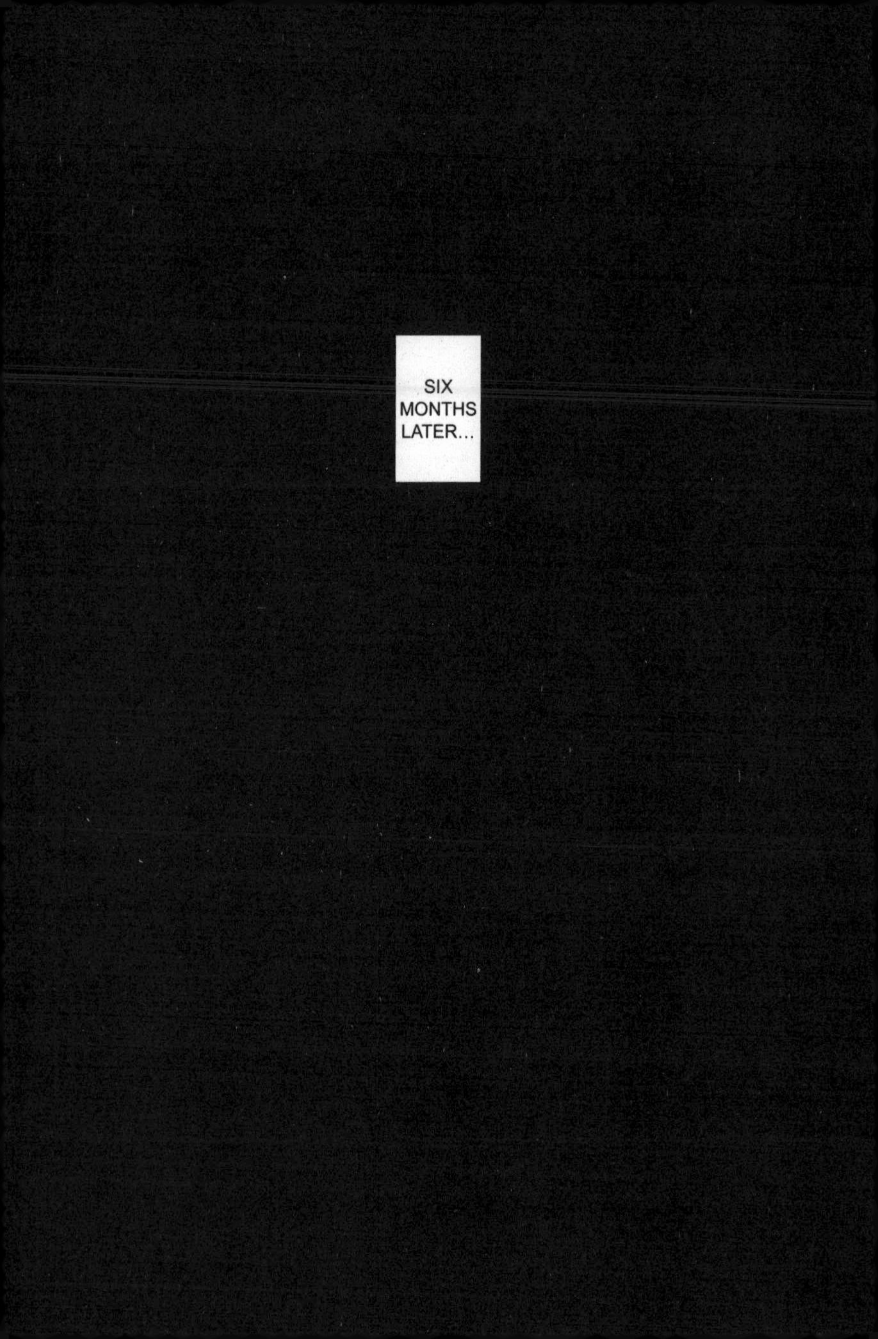
SIX MONTHS LATER...

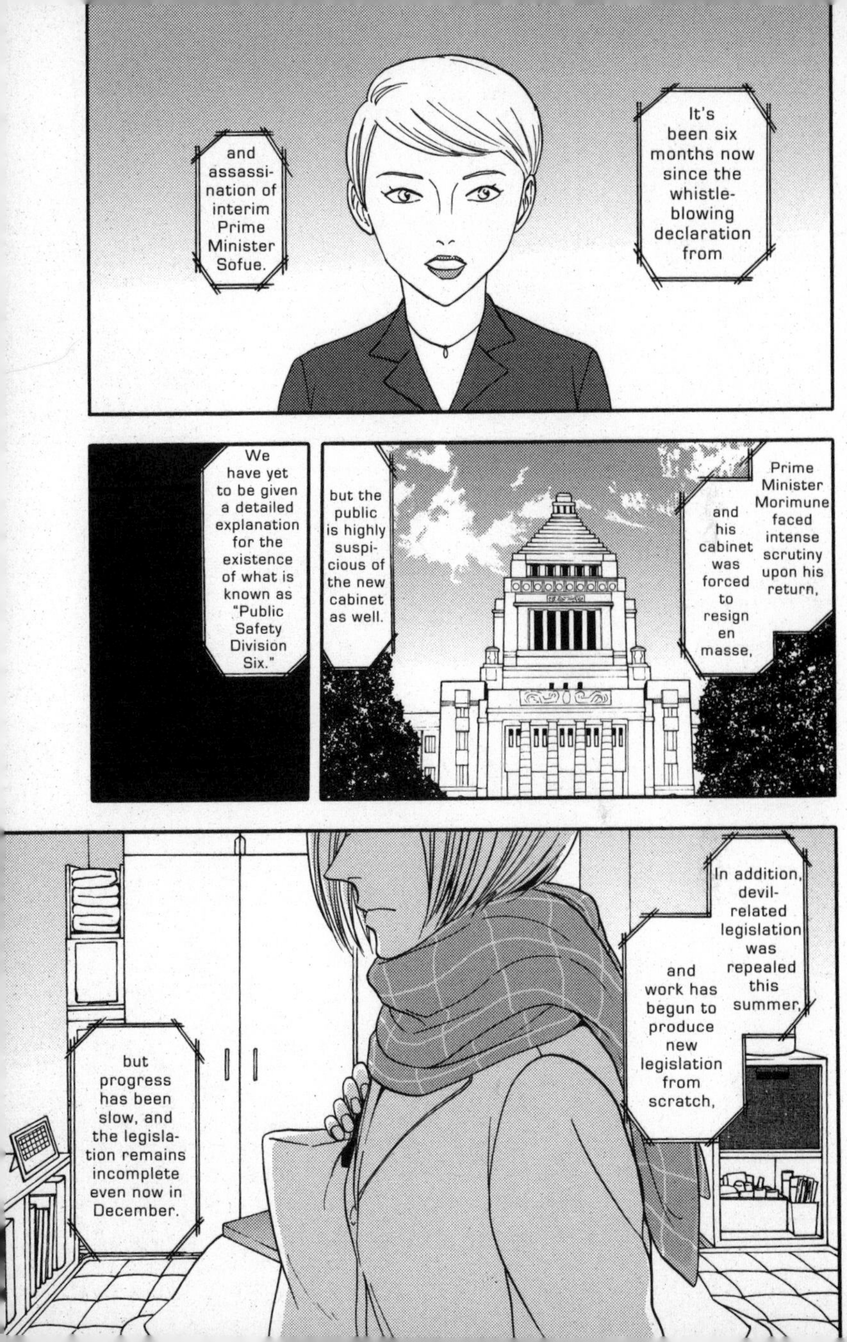
It's been six months now since the whistle-blowing declaration from
and assassination of interim Prime Minister Sofue.
Prime Minister Morimune faced intense scrutiny upon his return,
and his cabinet was forced to resign en masse,
but the public is highly suspicious of the new cabinet as well.
We have yet to be given a detailed explanation for the existence of what is known as "Public Safety Division Six."
In addition, devil-related legislation was repealed this summer,
and work has begun to produce new legislation from scratch,
but progress has been slow, and the legislation remains incomplete even now in December.

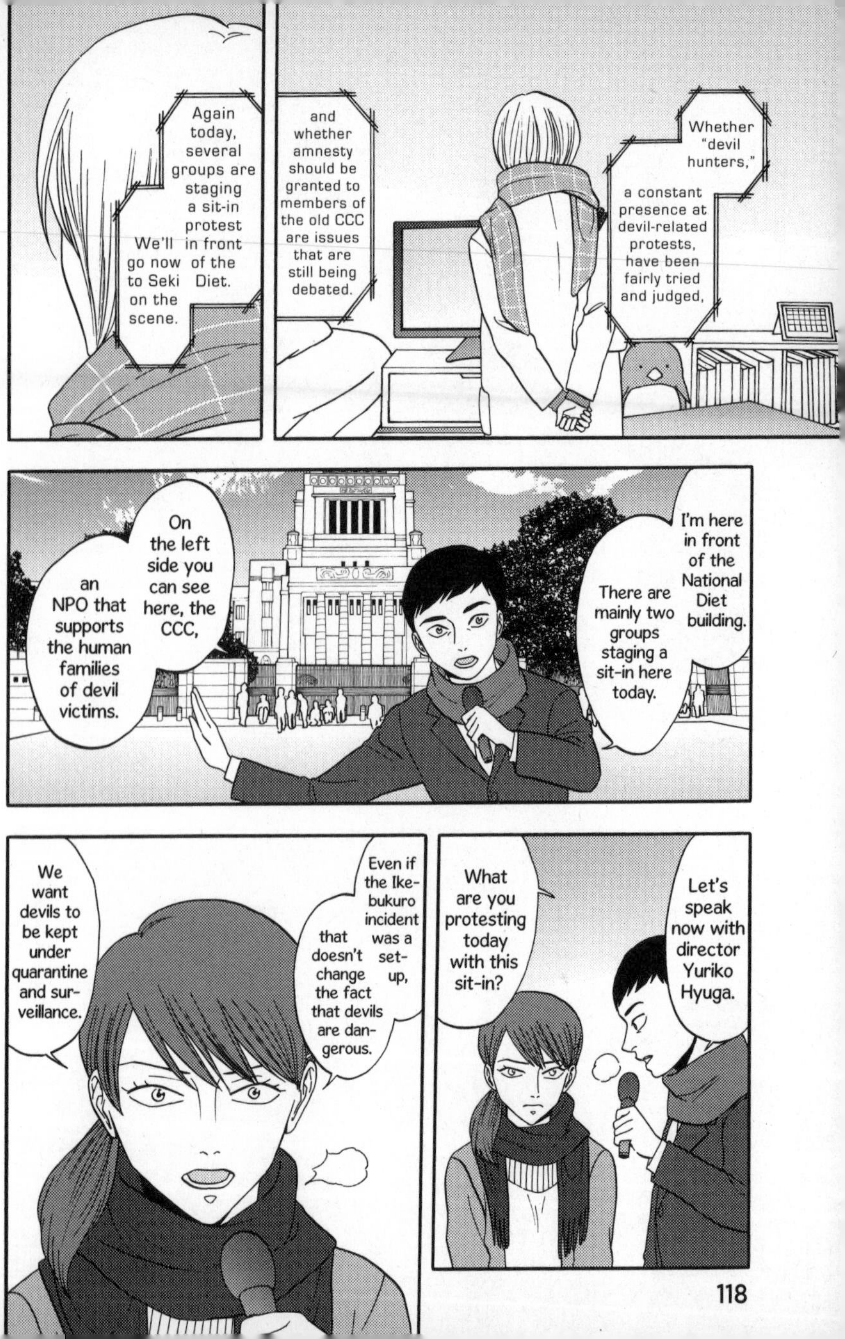
Whether "devil hunters," a constant presence at devil-related protests, have been fairly tried and judged,
and whether amnesty should be granted to members of the old CCC are issues that are still being debated.
Again today, several groups are staging a sit-in protest in front of the Diet.
We'll go now to Seki on the scene.
I'm here in front of the National Diet building.
There are mainly two groups staging a sit-in here today.
On the left side you can see here, the CCC,
an NPO that supports the human families of devil victims.
Let's speak now with director Yuriko Hyuga.
What are you protesting today with this sit-in?
Even if the Ike-bukuro incident was a set-up, that doesn't change the fact that devils are dan-gerous.
We want devils to be kept under quarantine and sur-veillance.

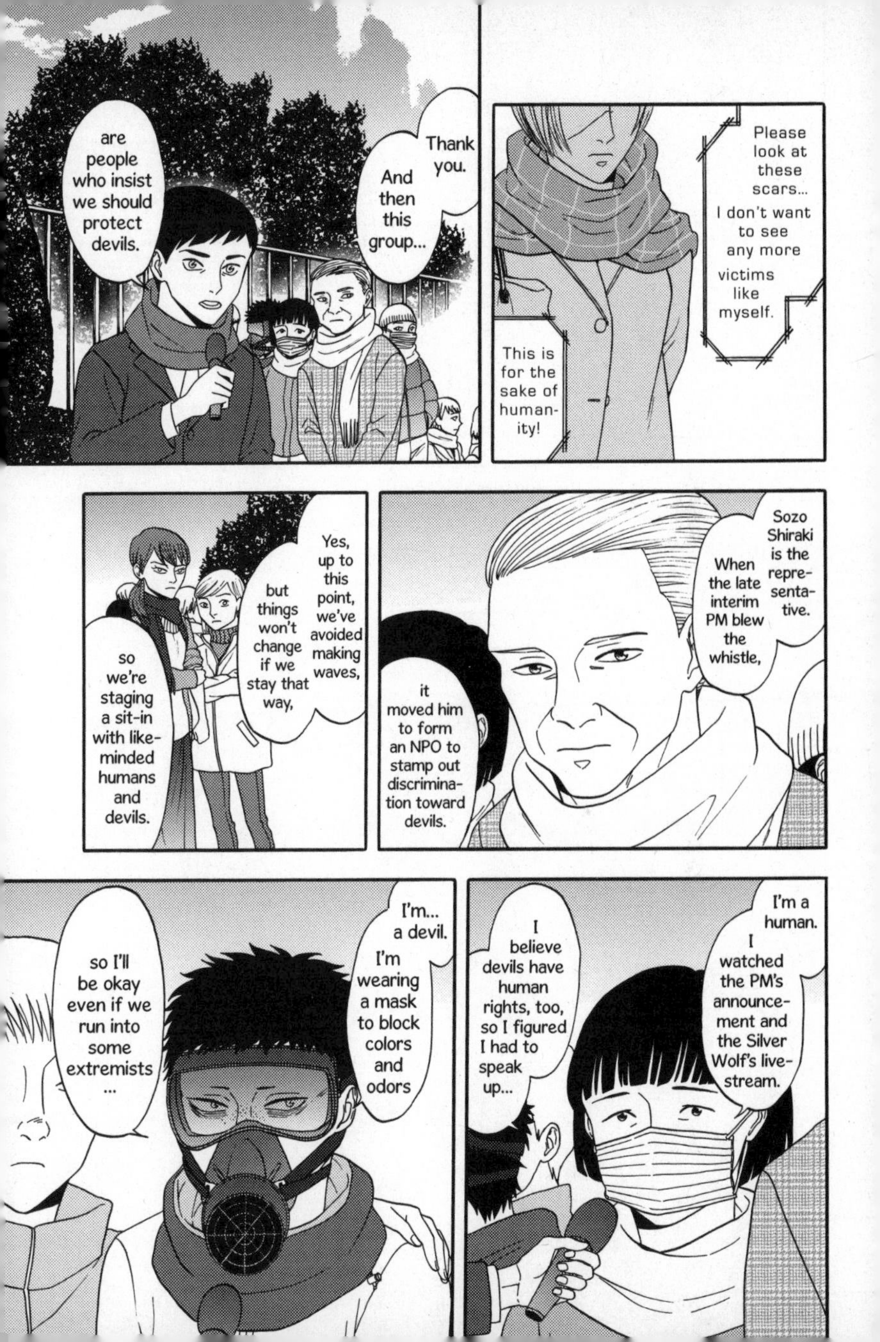
Please look at these scars... I don't want to see any more victims like myself.
This is for the sake of humanity!
Thank you.
And then this group...
are people who insist we should protect devils.
Sozo Shiraki is the representative.
When the late interim PM blew the whistle,
it moved him to form an NPO to stamp out discrimination toward devils.
Yes, up to this point, we've avoided making waves,
but things won't change if we stay that way,
so we're staging a sit-in with like-minded humans and devils.
I'm a human.
I watched the PM's announcement and the Silver Wolf's livestream.
I believe devils have human rights, too, so I figured I had to speak up...
I'm... a devil.
I'm wearing a mask to block colors and odors
so I'll be okay even if we run into some extremists...

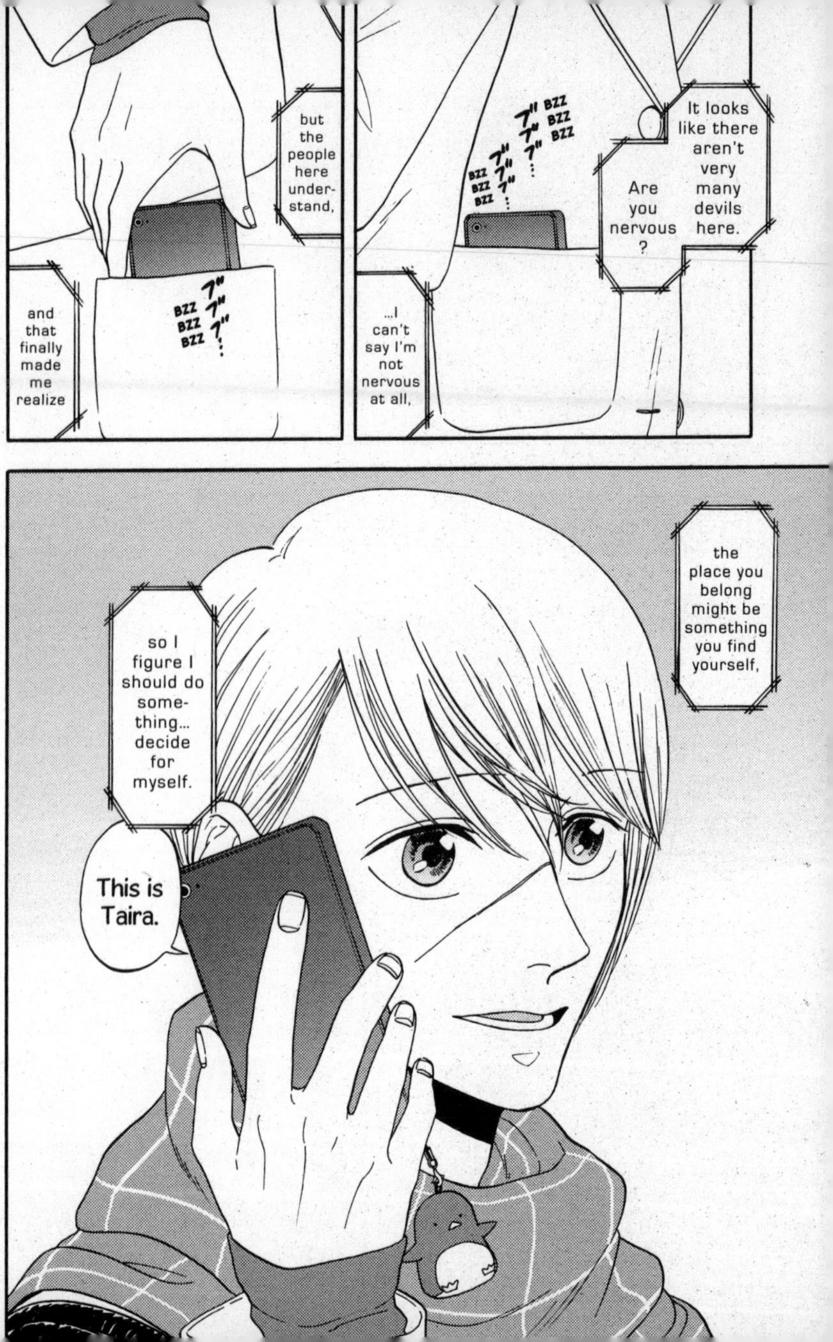
It looks like there aren't very many devils here.
Are you nervous?
BZZ BZZ BZZ...
BZZ BZZ BZZ...
...I can't say I'm not nervous at all,
but the people here understand,
BZZ BZZ BZZ...
and that finally made me realize
the place you belong might be something you find yourself,
so I figure I should do something... decide for myself.
This is Taira.

Line 66
Devils' Line

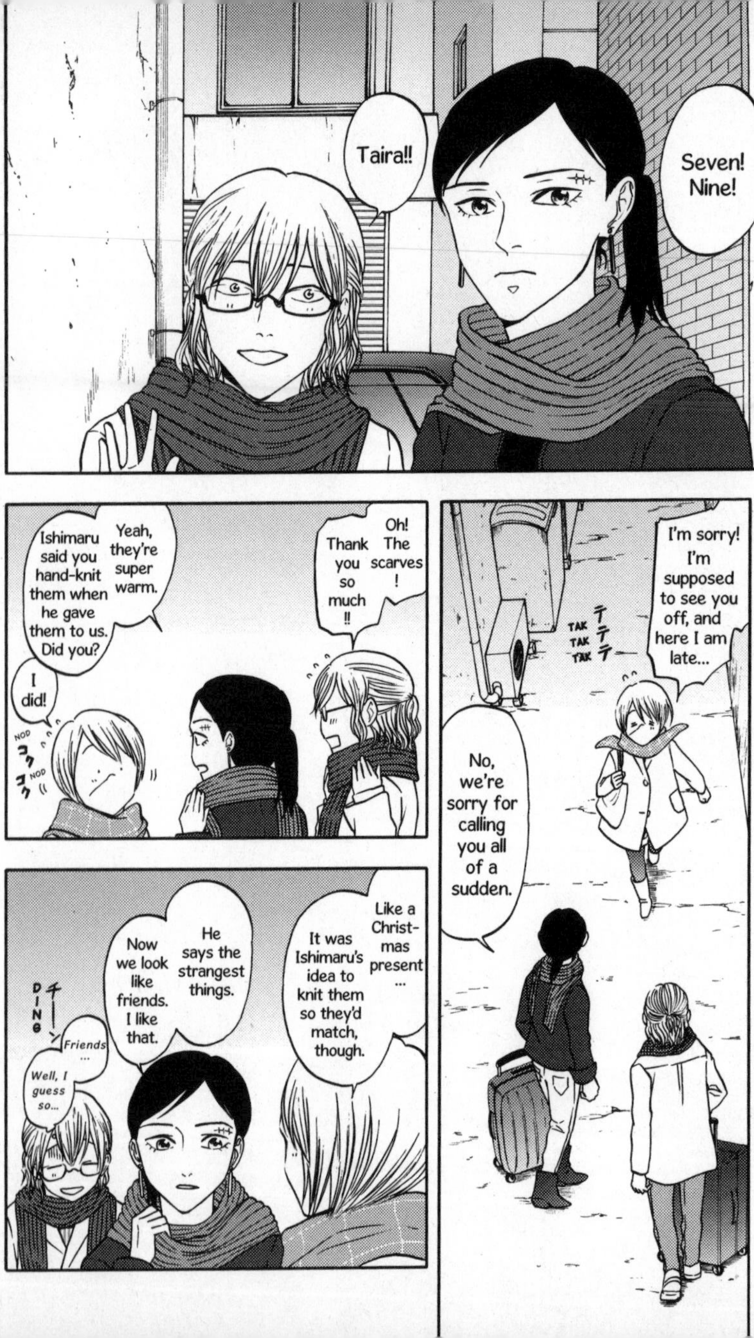
Seven! Nine!
Taira!!
I'm sorry! I'm supposed to see you off, and here I am late...
TAK TAK TAK
No, we're sorry for calling you all of a sudden.
Oh! The scarves!
Thank you so much!!
Yeah, they're super warm.
Ishimaru said you hand-knit them when he gave them to us. Did you?
I did!
NOD NOD
Like a Christmas present...
It was Ishimaru's idea to knit them so they'd match, though.
He says the strangest things.
Now we look like friends. I like that.
DING
Friends...
Well, I guess so...

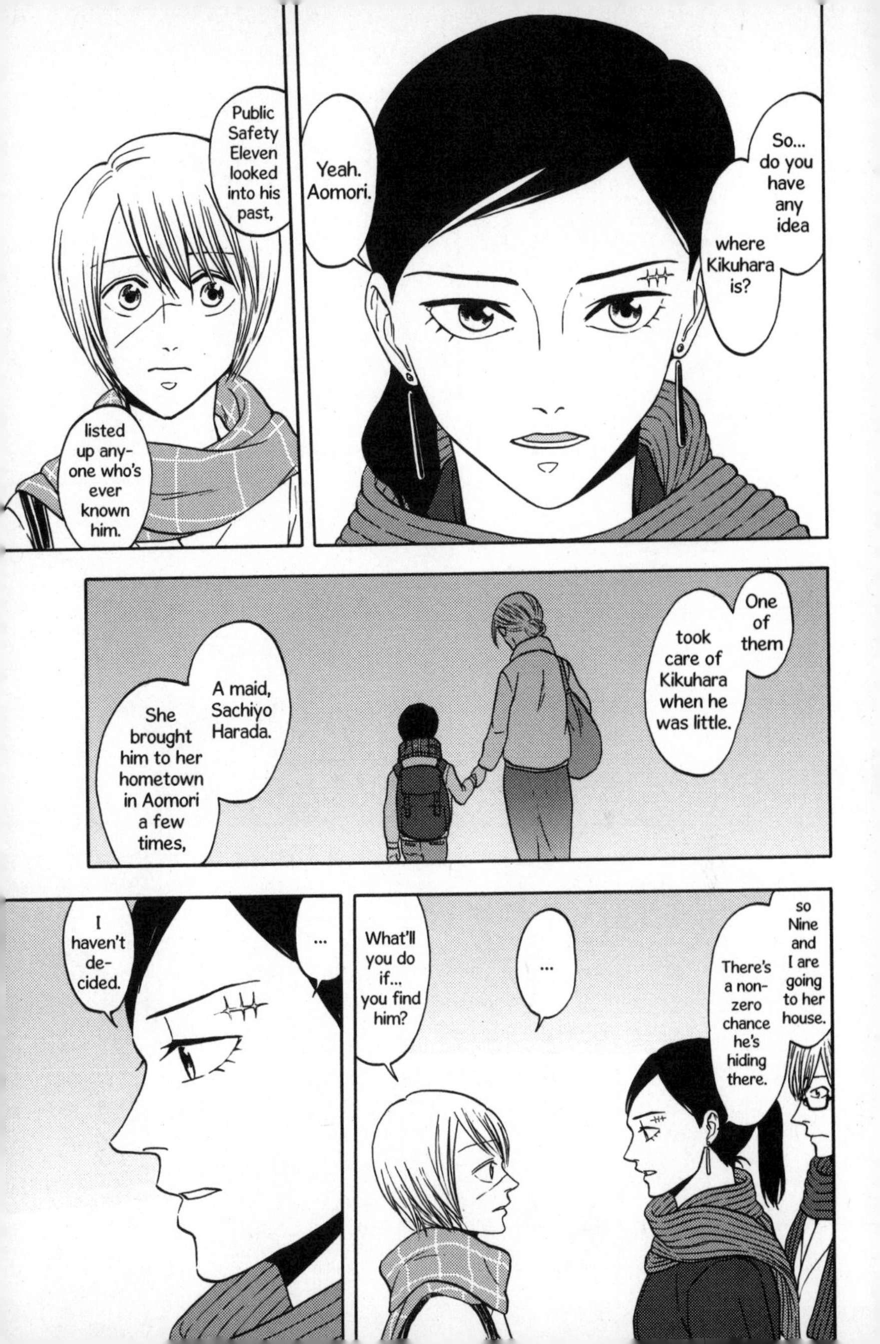
So... do you have any idea where Kikuhara is?
Yeah. Aomori.
Public Safety Eleven looked into his past,
listed up any-one who's ever known him.
One of them took care of Kikuhara when he was little.
A maid, Sachiyo Harada.
She brought him to her hometown in Aomori a few times,
so Nine and I are going to her house.
There's a non-zero chance he's hiding there.
...
What'll you do if... you find him?
...
I haven't de-cided.

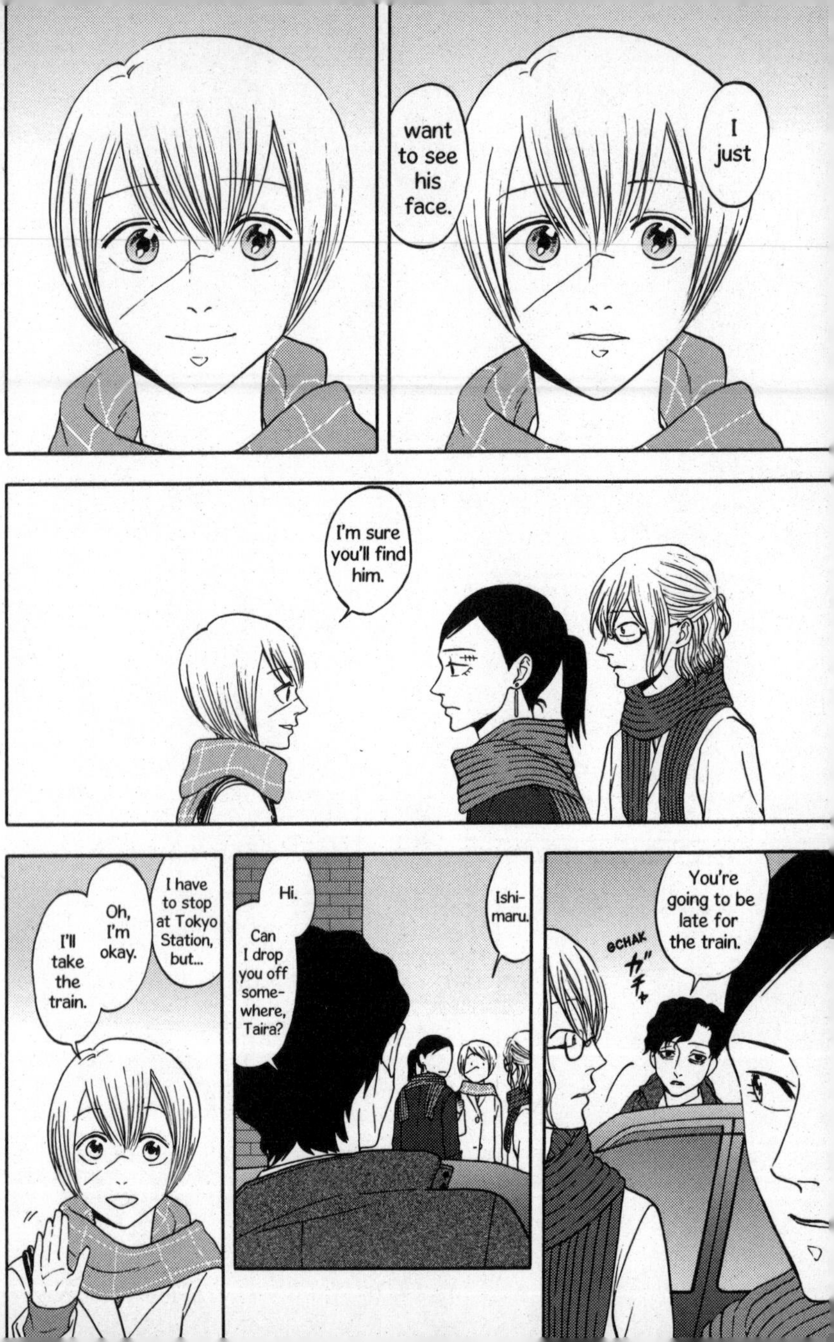
I just
want to see his face.
I'm sure you'll find him.
You're going to be late for the train.
GCHAK
ガチャ
Ishi-maru.
Hi.
Can I drop you off some-where, Taira?
I have to stop at Tokyo Station, but...
Oh, I'm okay.
I'll take the train.

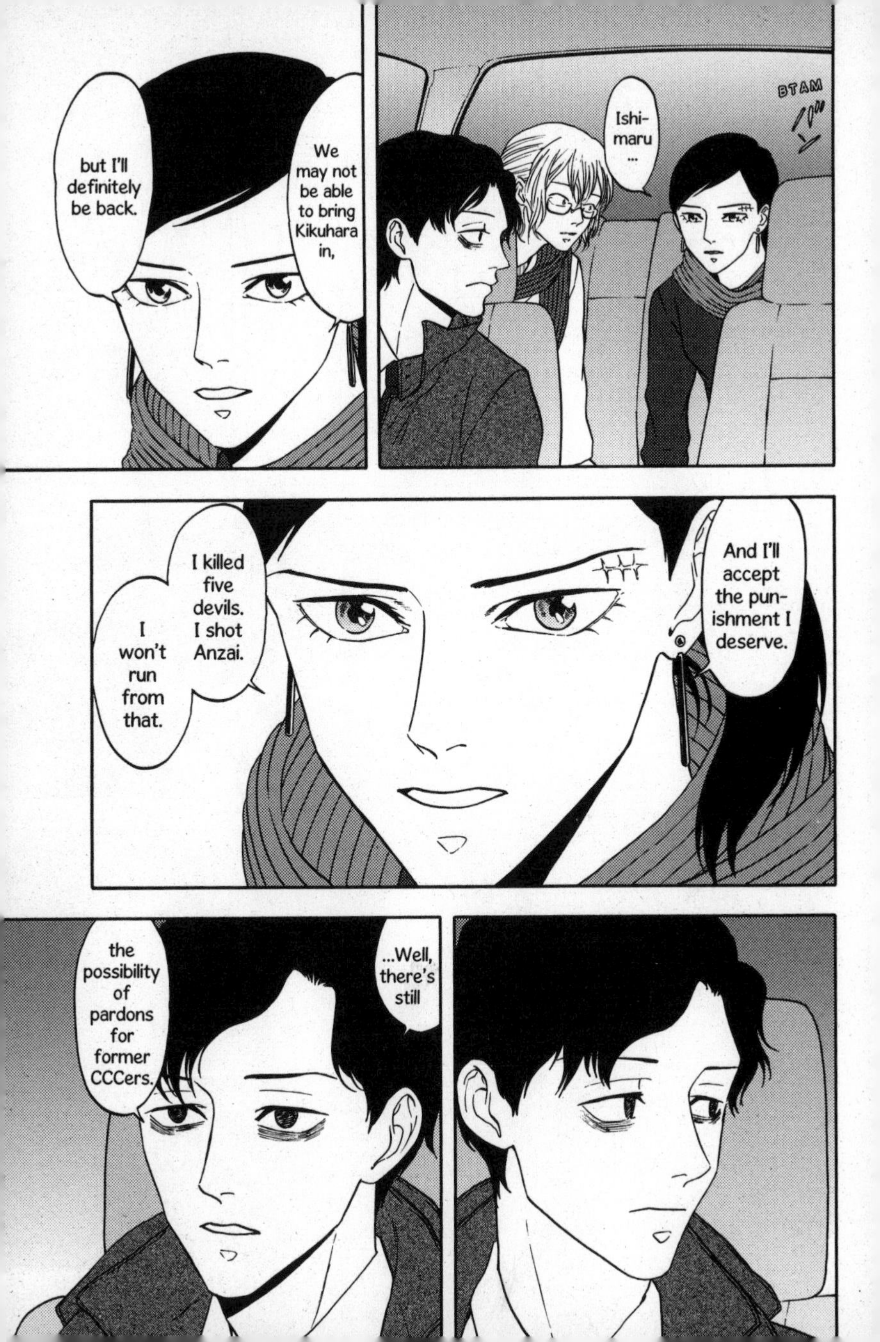
BTAM
Ishi-maru...
We may not be able to bring Kikuhara in,
but I'll definitely be back.
And I'll accept the punishment I deserve.
I killed five devils. I shot Anzai.
I won't run from that.
...Well, there's still
the possibility of pardons for former CCCers.

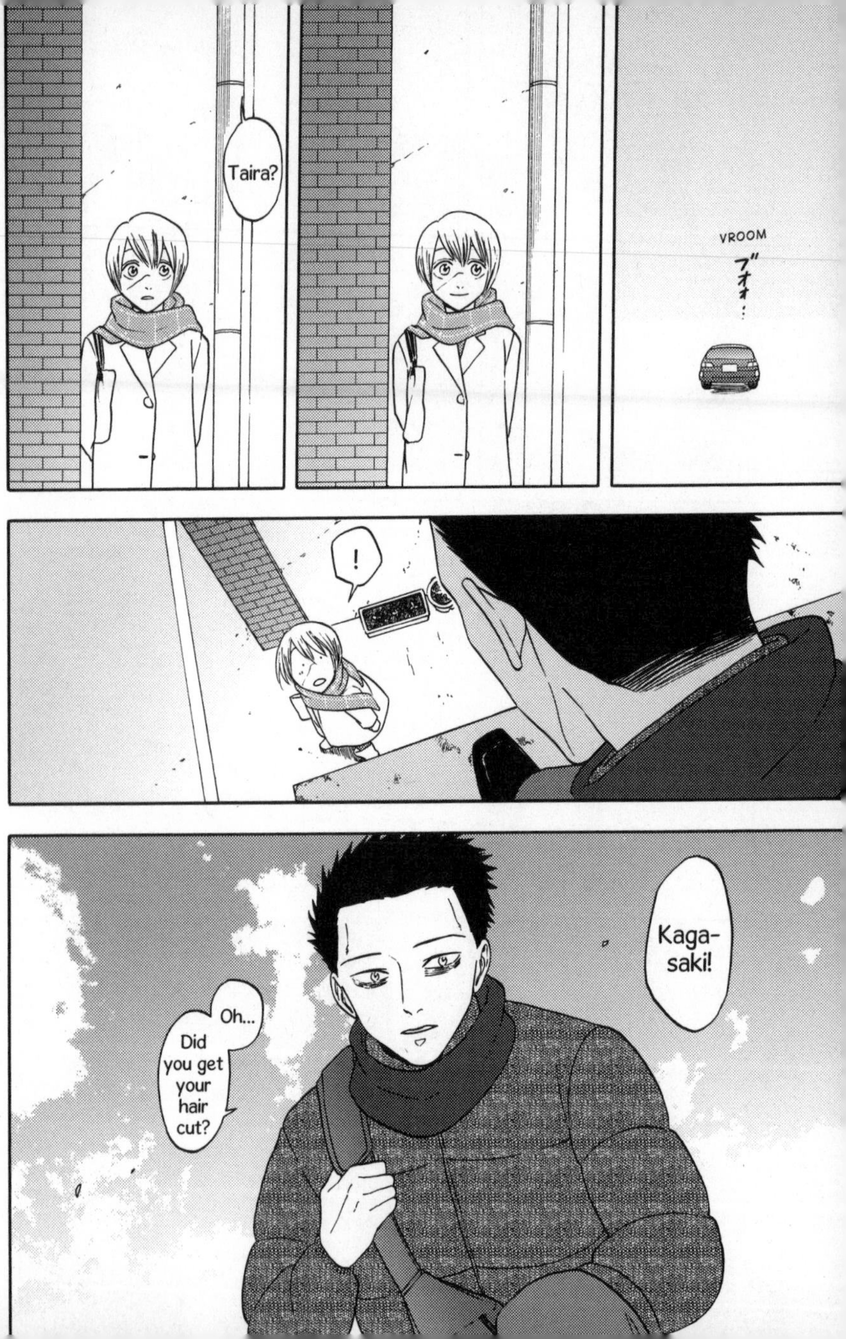
VROOM
ブォォ!
Taira?
!
Kaga-saki!
Oh... Did you get your hair cut?

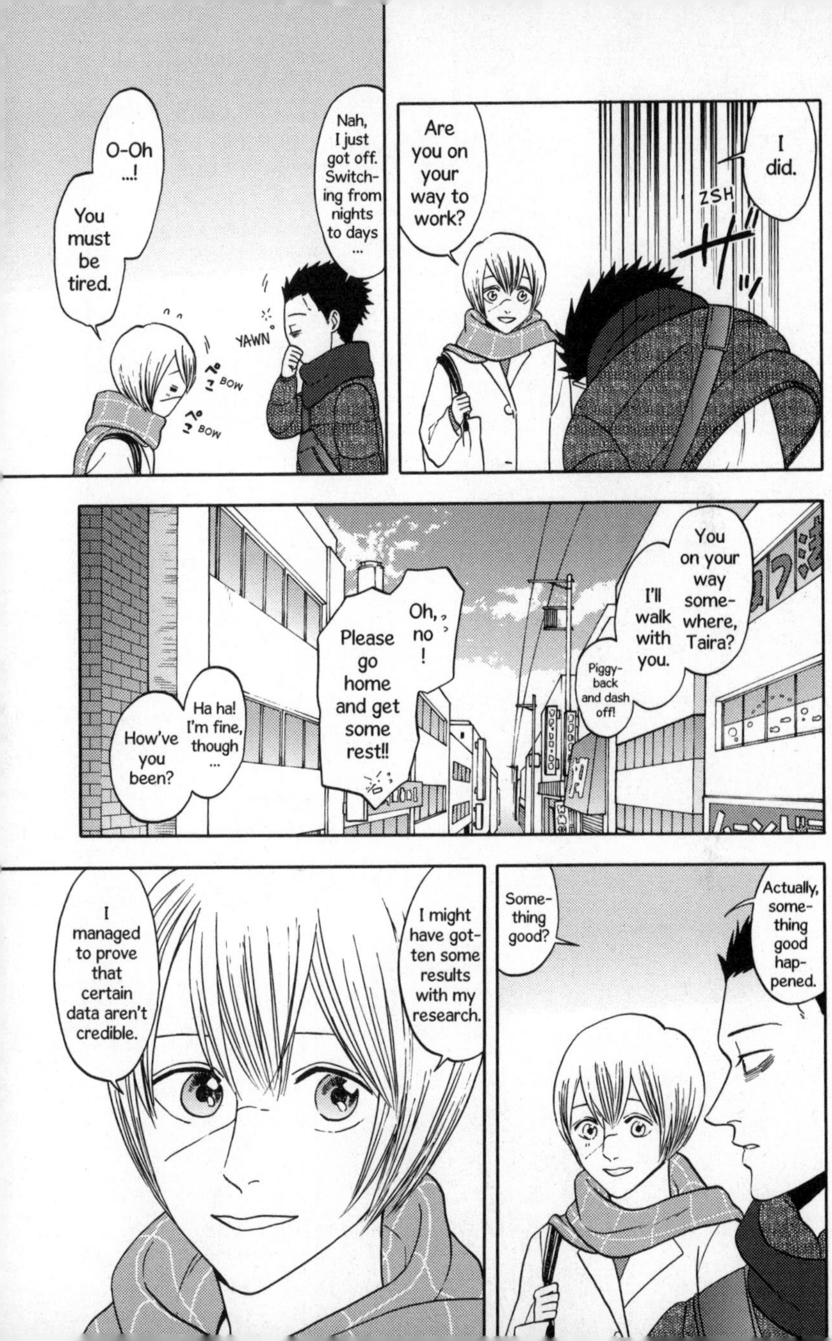
I did.
ZSH
Are you on your way to work?
Nah, I just got off. Switching from nights to days ...
O-Oh ...!
You must be tired.
YAWN
BOW
BOW
You on your way somewhere, Taira?
I'll walk with you.
Piggy-back and dash off!
Oh, no!
Please go home and get some rest!!
Ha ha! I'm fine, though ...
How've you been?
Actually, something good happened.
Something good?
I might have gotten some results with my research.
I managed to prove that certain data aren't credible.

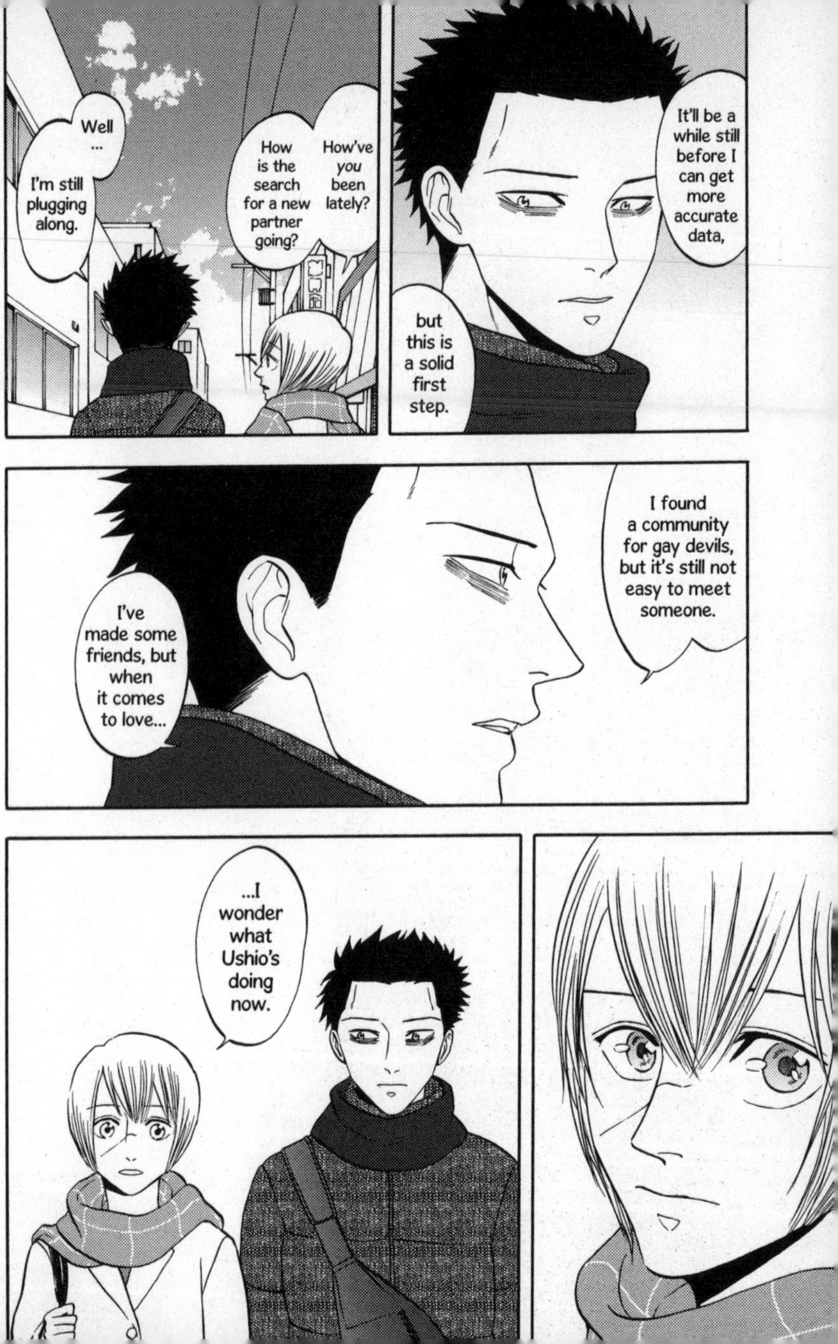
It'll be a while still before I can get more accurate data,
but this is a solid first step.
How've *you* been lately?
How is the search for a new partner going?
Well ...
I'm still plugging along.
I found a community for gay devils, but it's still not easy to meet someone.
I've made some friends, but when it comes to love...
...I wonder what Ushio's doing now.

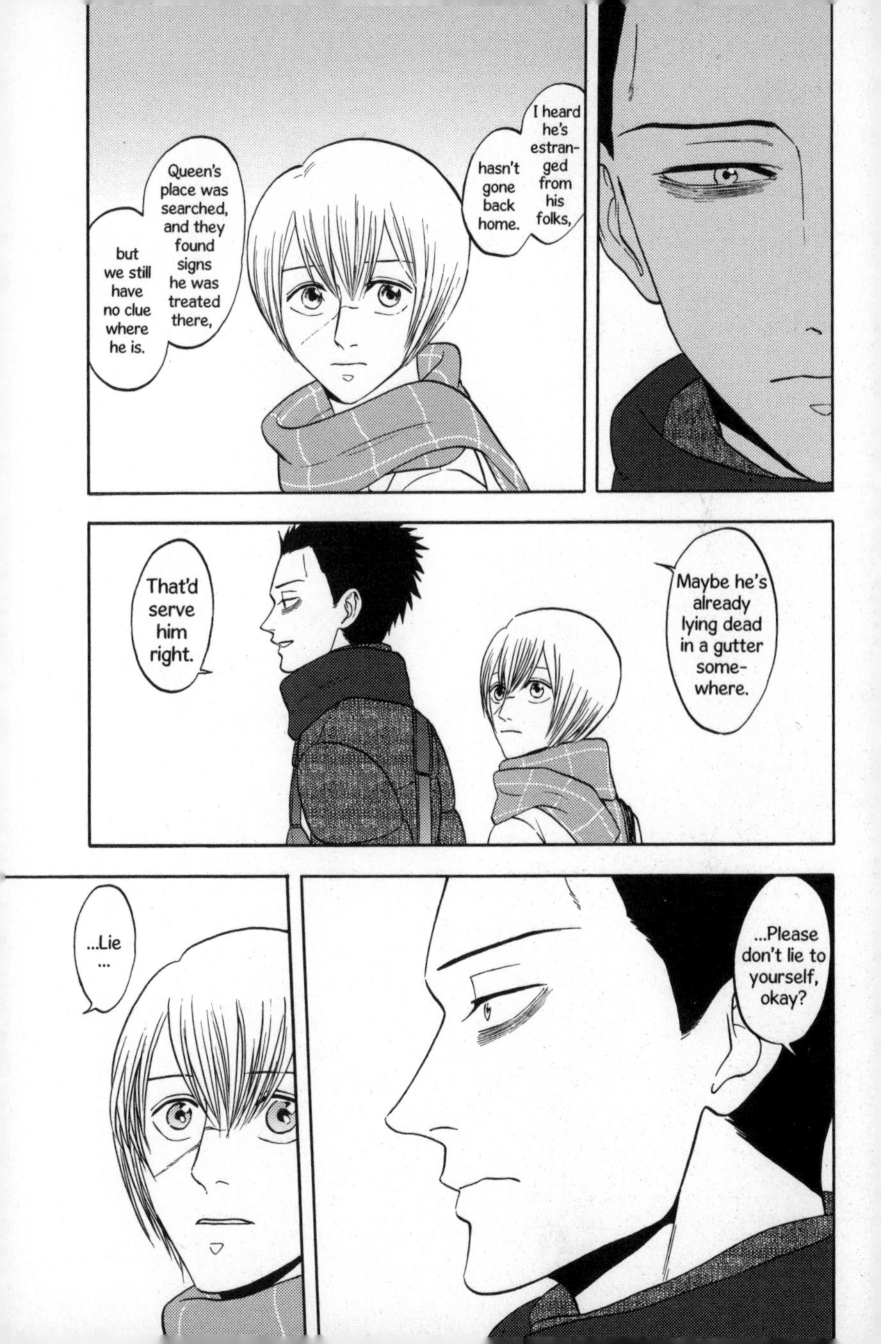
I heard he's estranged from his folks,
hasn't gone back home.
Queen's place was searched, and they found signs he was treated there,
but we still have no clue where he is.
Maybe he's already lying dead in a gutter somewhere.
That'd serve him right.
...Please don't lie to yourself, okay?
...Lie ...

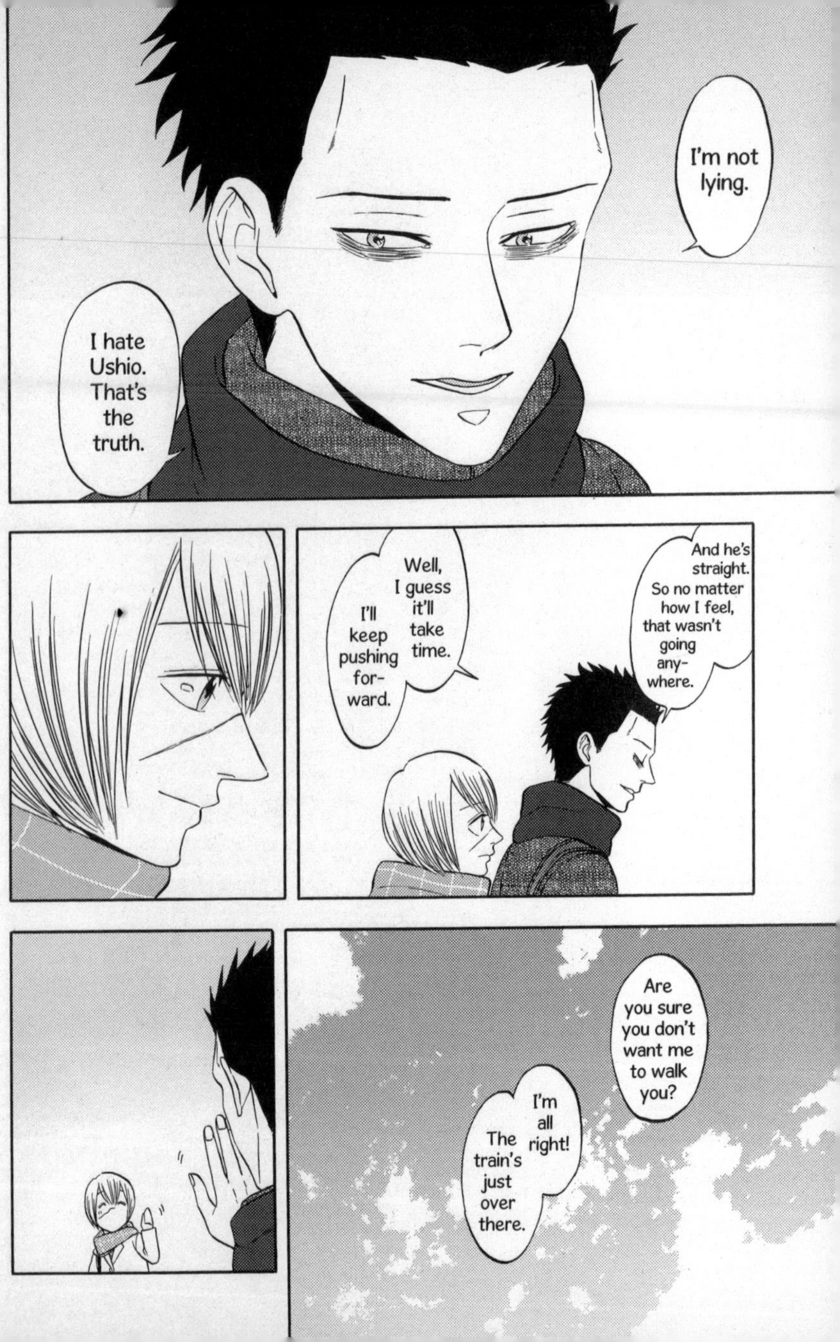
I'm not lying.
I hate Ushio. That's the truth.
And he's straight. So no matter how I feel, that wasn't going anywhere.
Well, I guess it'll take time.
I'll keep pushing for-ward.
Are you sure you don't want me to walk you?
I'm all right!
The train's just over there.

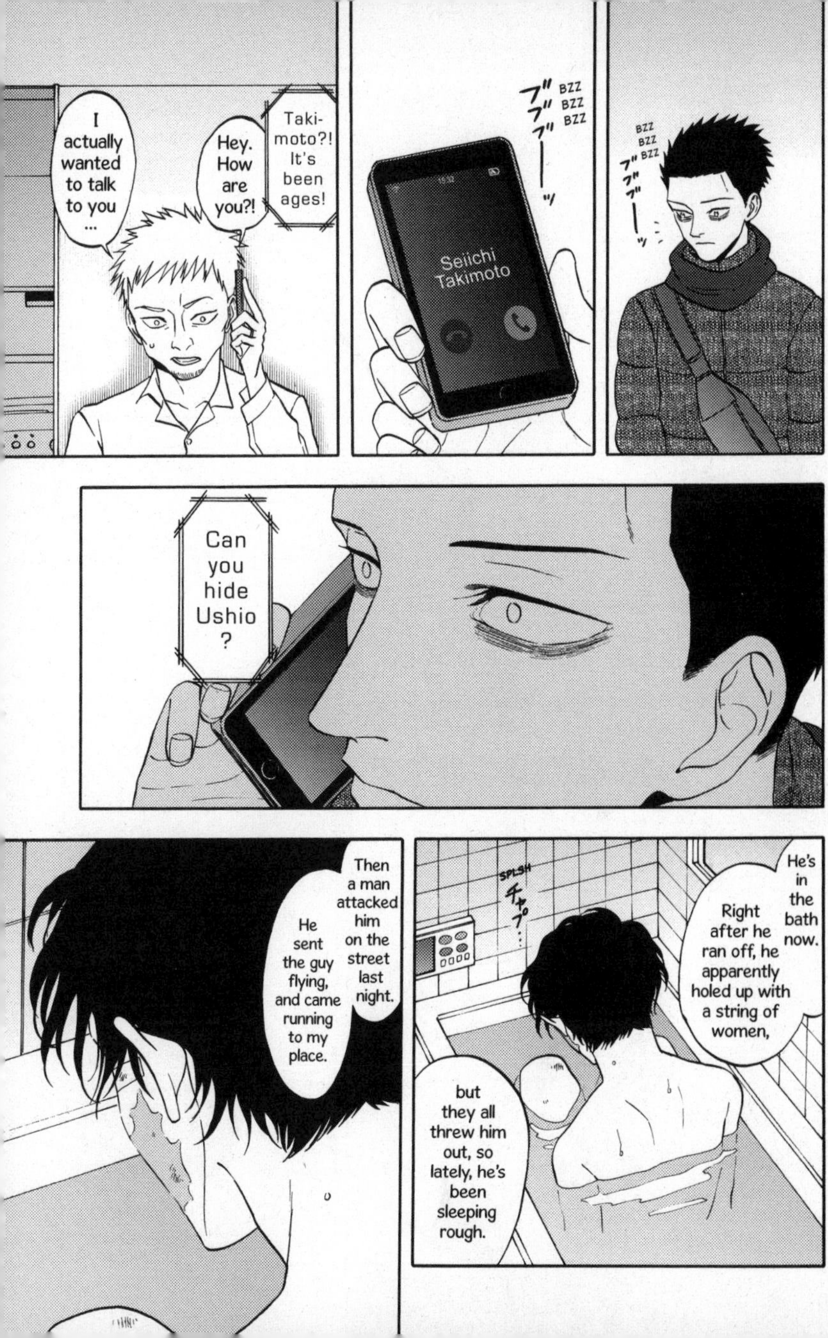
BZZ BZZ BZZ
ブブブーッ
BZZ BZZ BZZ
ブブブーッ
Seiichi Takimoto
Taki-moto?! It's been ages!
Hey. How are you?!
I actually wanted to talk to you ...
Can you hide Ushio?
He's in the bath now.
Right after he ran off, he apparently holed up with a string of women,
SPLSH
チャプ…
but they all threw him out, so lately, he's been sleeping rough.
Then a man attacked him on the street last night.
He sent the guy flying, and came running to my place.

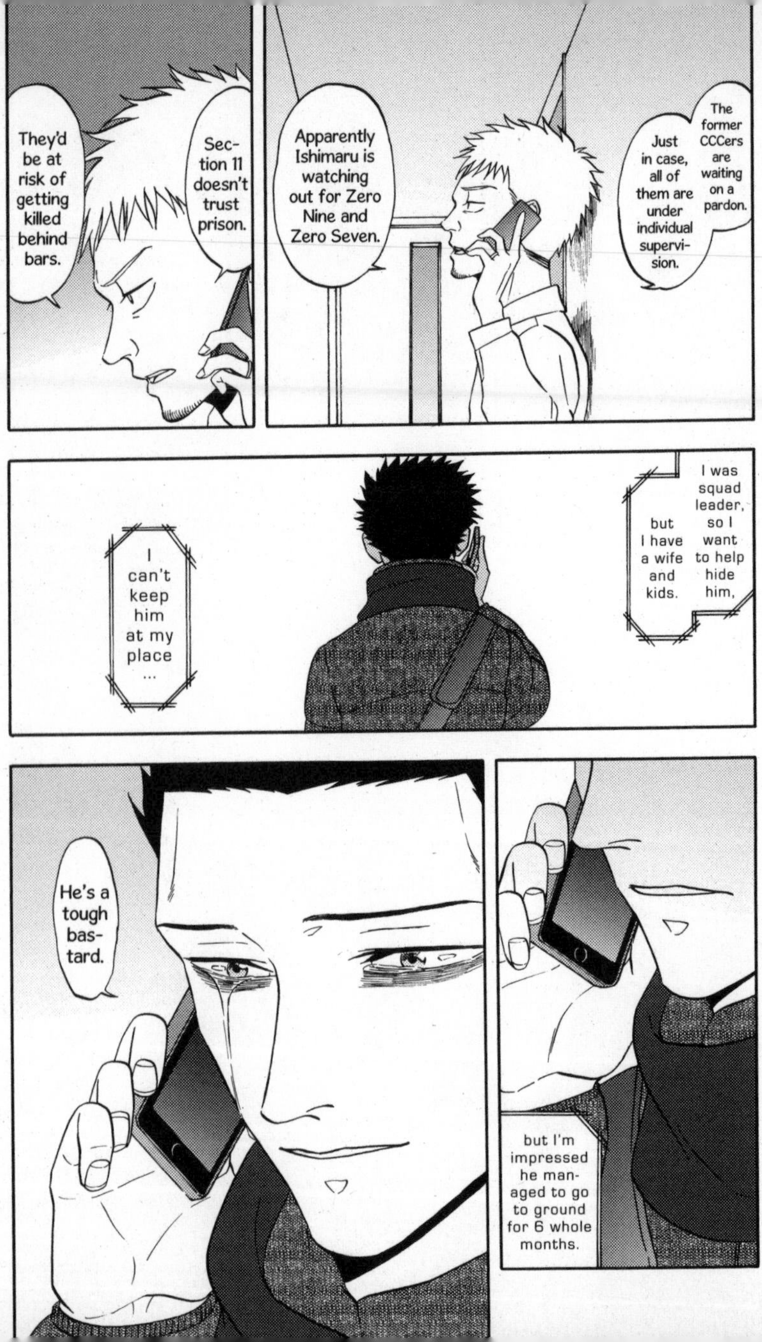
The former CCCers are waiting on a pardon.
Just in case, all of them are under individual supervision.
Apparently Ishimaru is watching out for Zero Nine and Zero Seven.
Section 11 doesn't trust prison.
They'd be at risk of getting killed behind bars.
I was squad leader, so I want to help hide him,
but I have a wife and kids.
I can't keep him at my place...
but I'm impressed he managed to go to ground for 6 whole months.
He's a tough bastard.

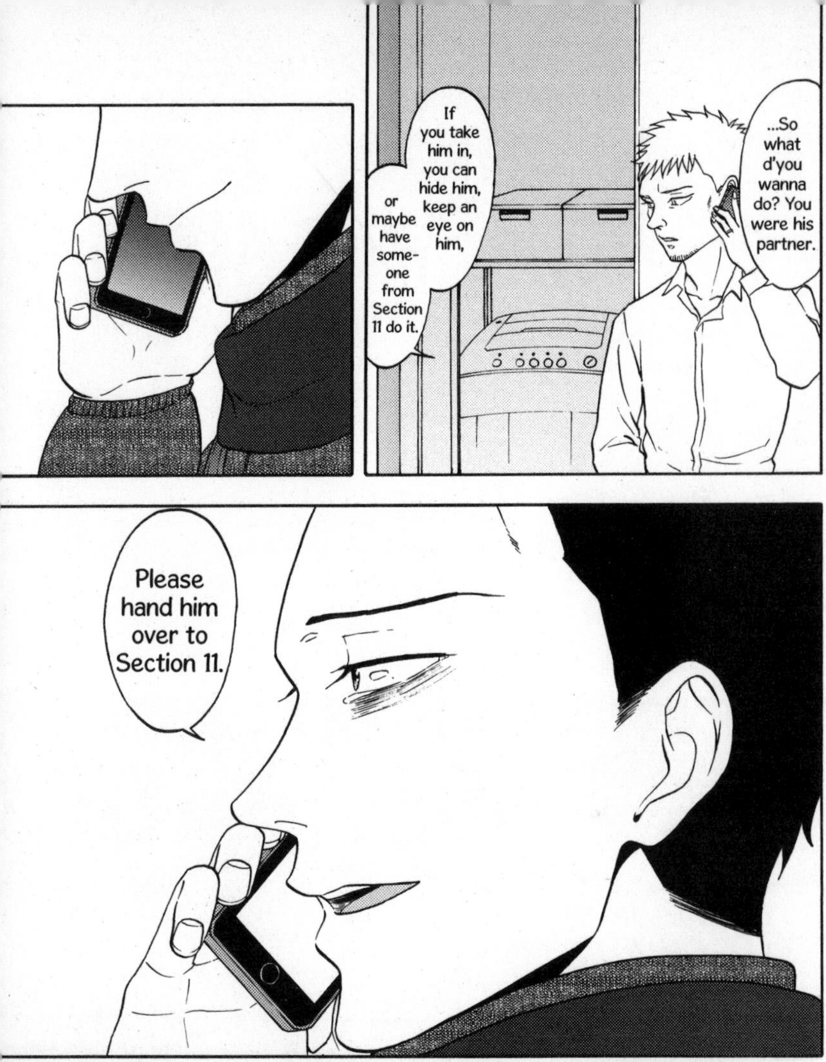
...So what d'you wanna do? You were his partner.
If you take him in, you can hide him, keep an eye on him,
or maybe have some-one from Section 11 do it.
Please hand him over to Section 11.

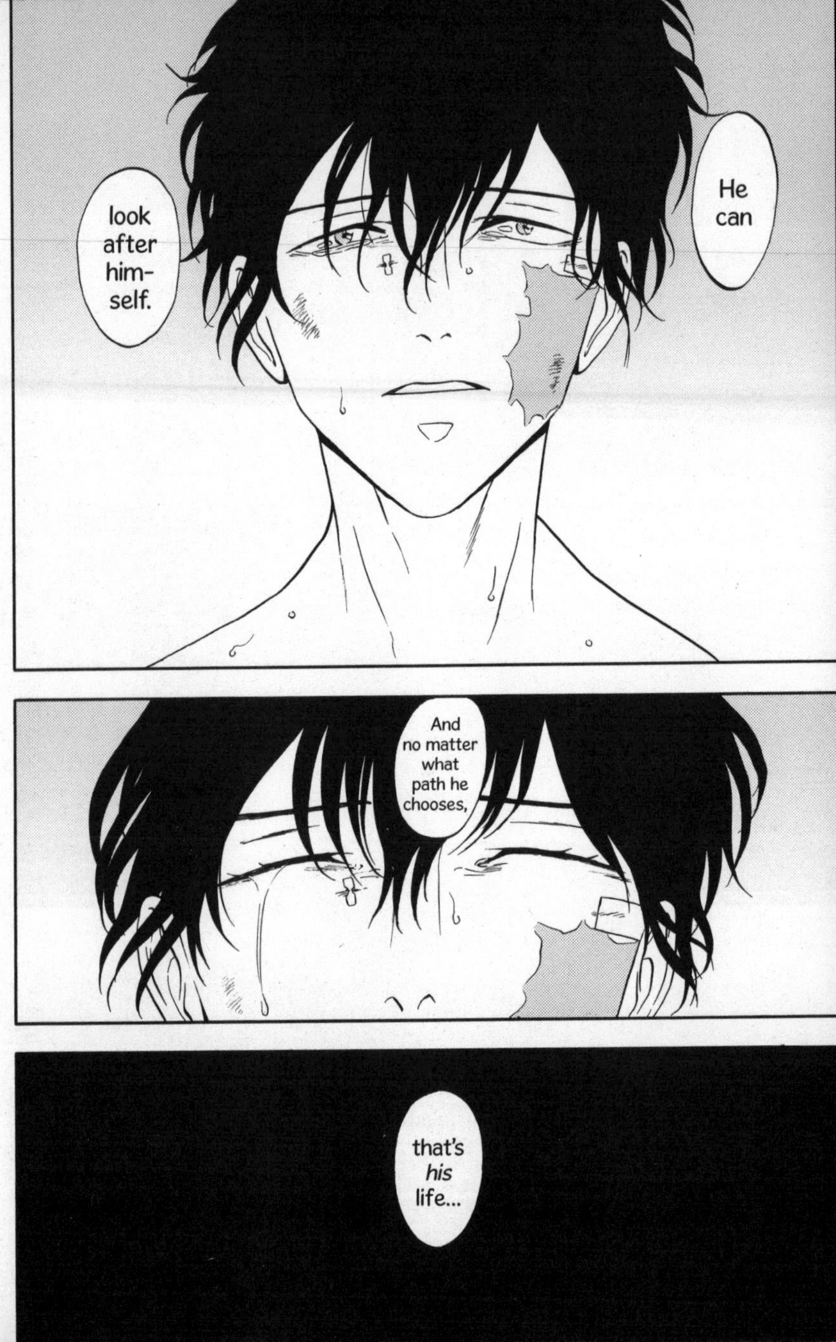
He can
look after him-self.
And no matter what path he chooses,
that's *his* life...

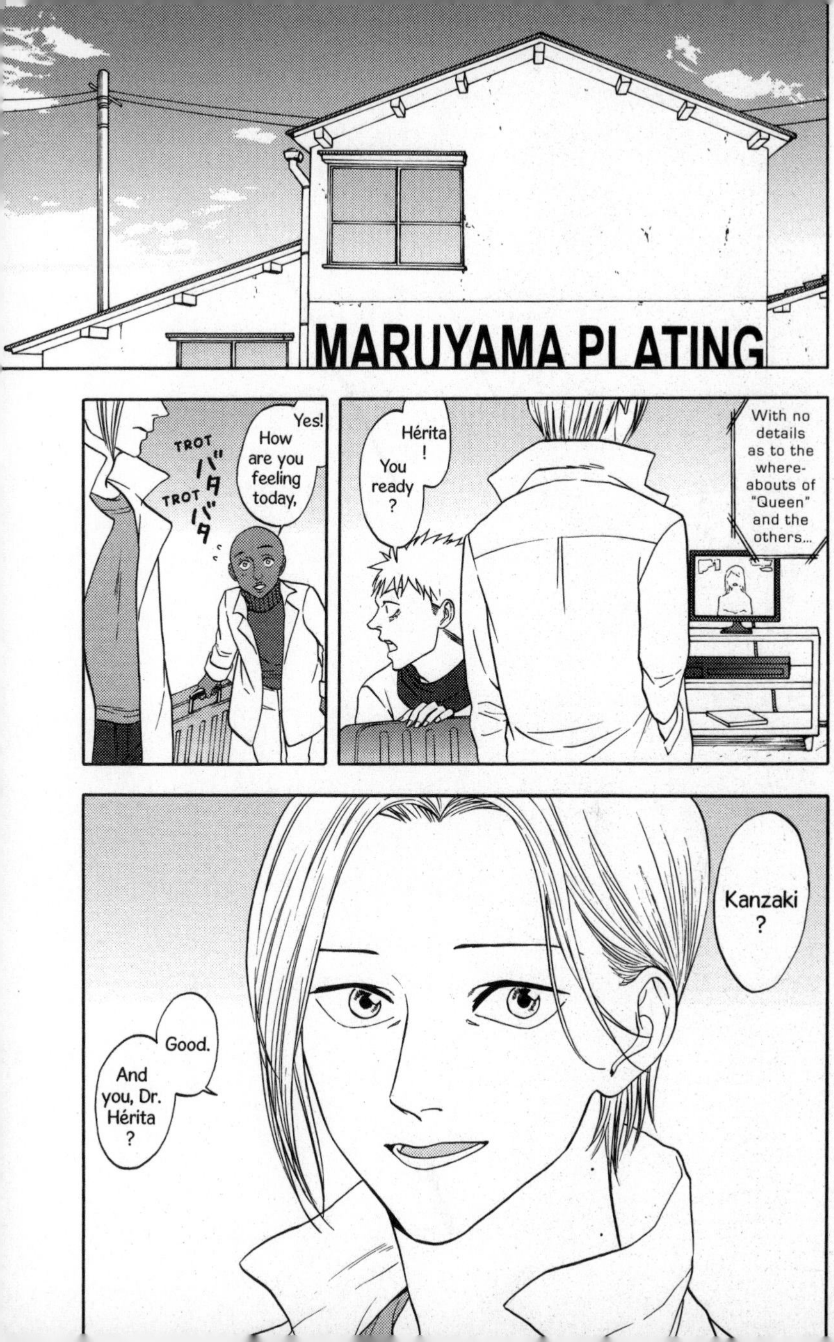
MARUYAMA PLATING
With no details as to the whereabouts of "Queen" and the others...
Hérita! You ready?
Yes! How are you feeling today,
TROT バタ TROT バタ
Kanzaki?
Good. And you, Dr. Hérita?

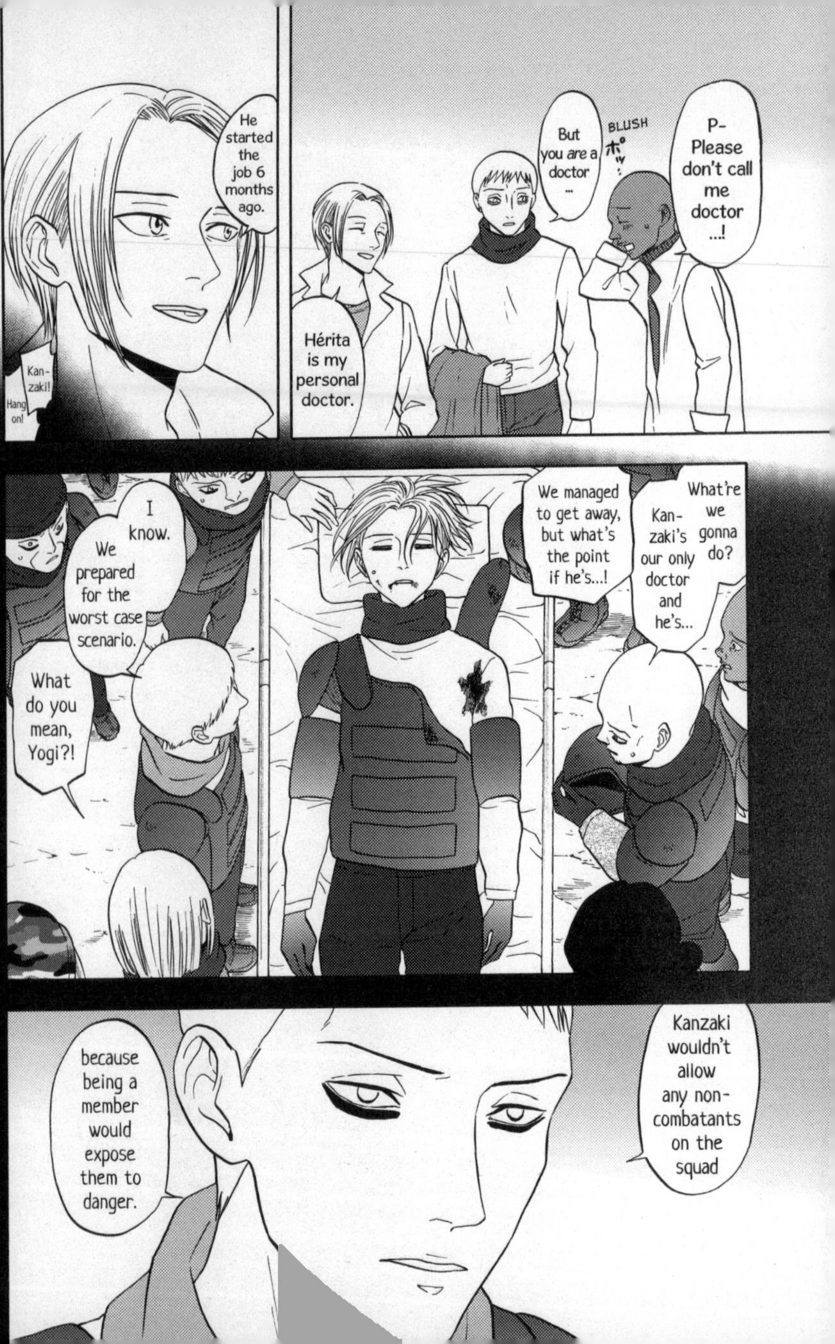
P- Please don't call me doctor ...!
BLUSH
ポッ
But you *are* a doctor ...
Hérita is my personal doctor.
He started the job 6 months ago.
Kan-zaki!
Hang on!
What're we gonna do?
Kan-zaki's our only doctor and he's...
We managed to get away, but what's the point if he's...!
I know.
We prepared for the worst case scenario.
What do you mean, Yogi?!
Kanzaki wouldn't allow any non-combatants on the squad
because being a member would expose them to danger.

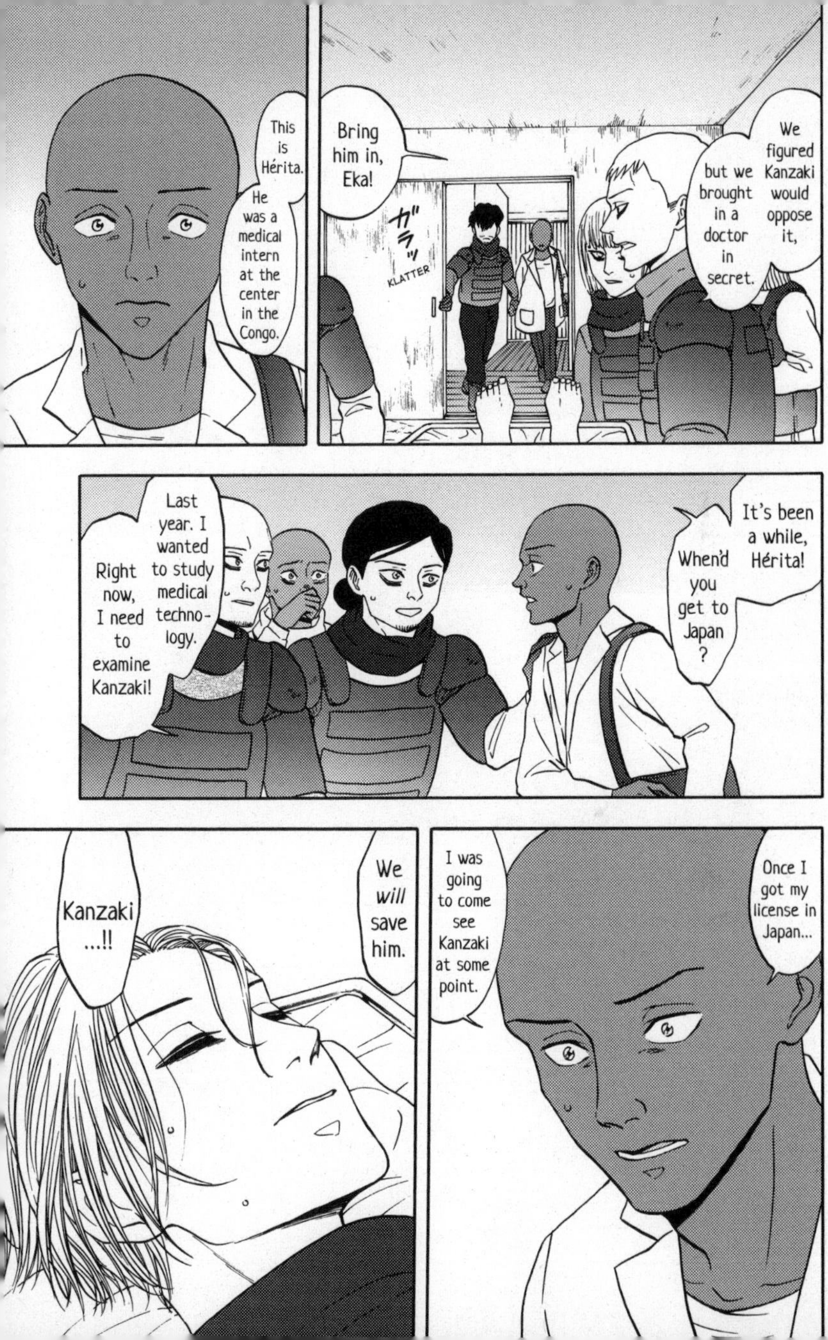

We figured Kanzaki would oppose it,
but we brought in a doctor in secret.
Bring him in, Eka!
ガラッ
KLATTER
This is Hérita.
He was a medical intern at the center in the Congo.
It's been a while, Hérita!
When'd you get to Japan?
Last year. I wanted to study medical techno-logy.
Right now, I need to examine Kanzaki!
Once I got my license in Japan...
I was going to come see Kanzaki at some point.
We *will* save him.
Kanzaki ...!!

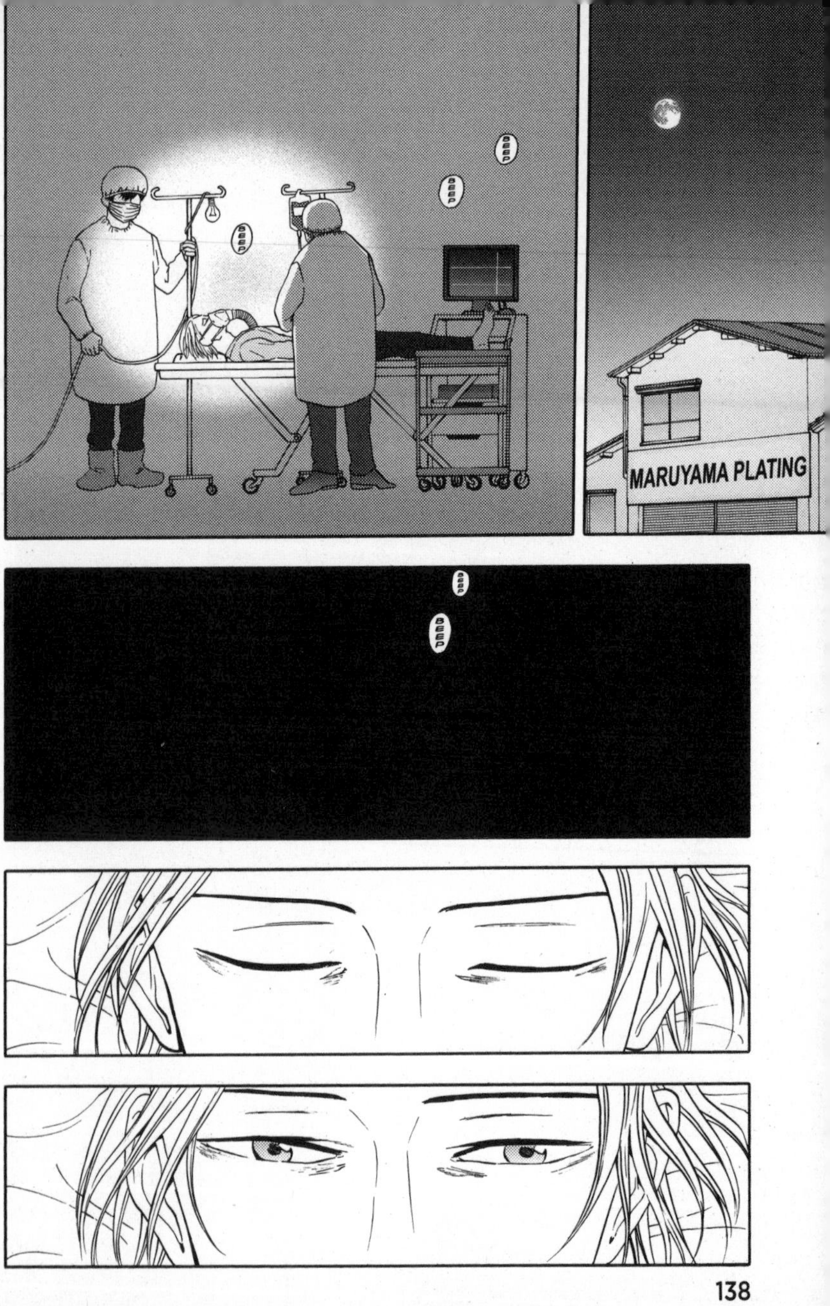
MARUYAMA PLATING
BEEP
BEEP
BEEP
BEEP
BEEP

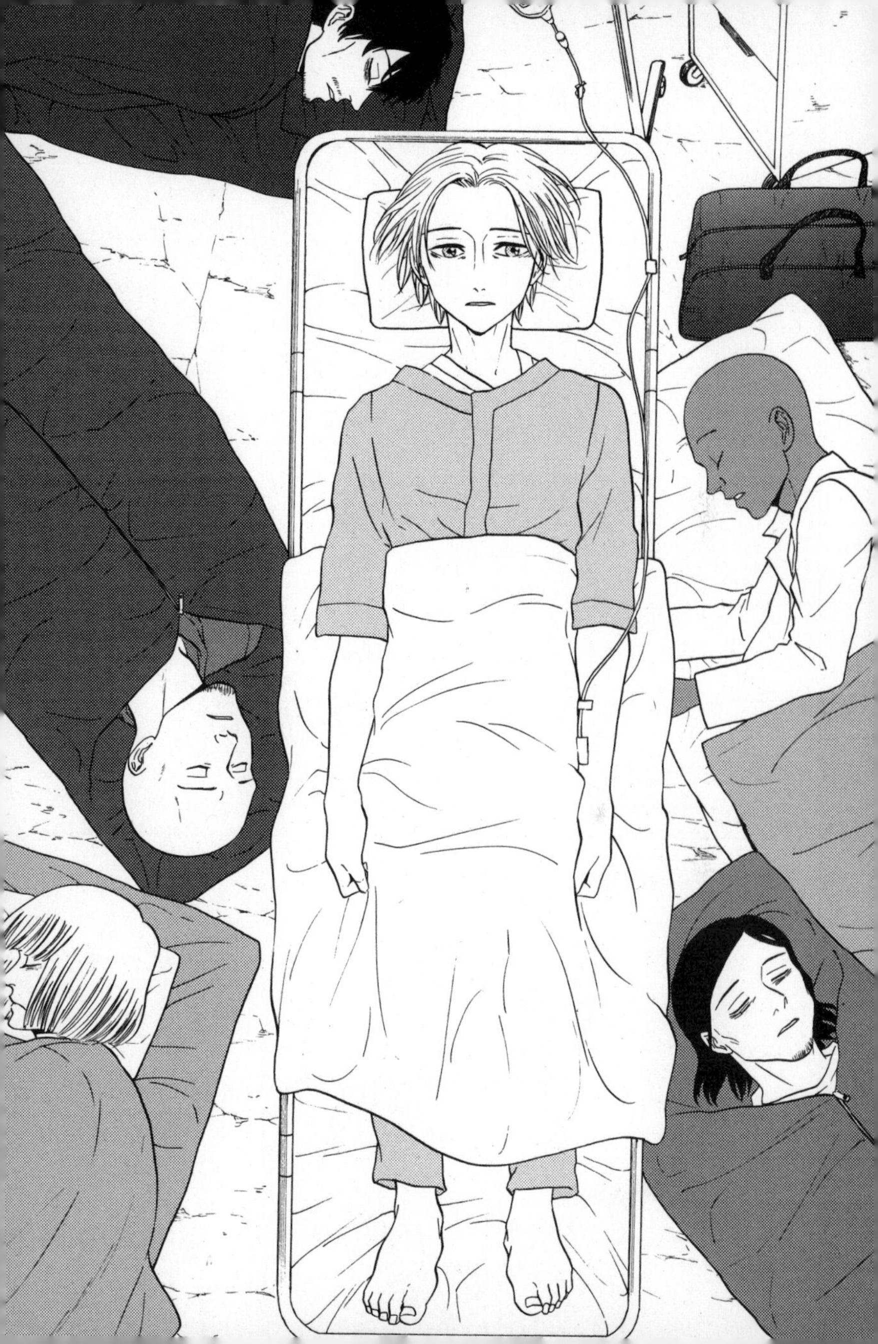

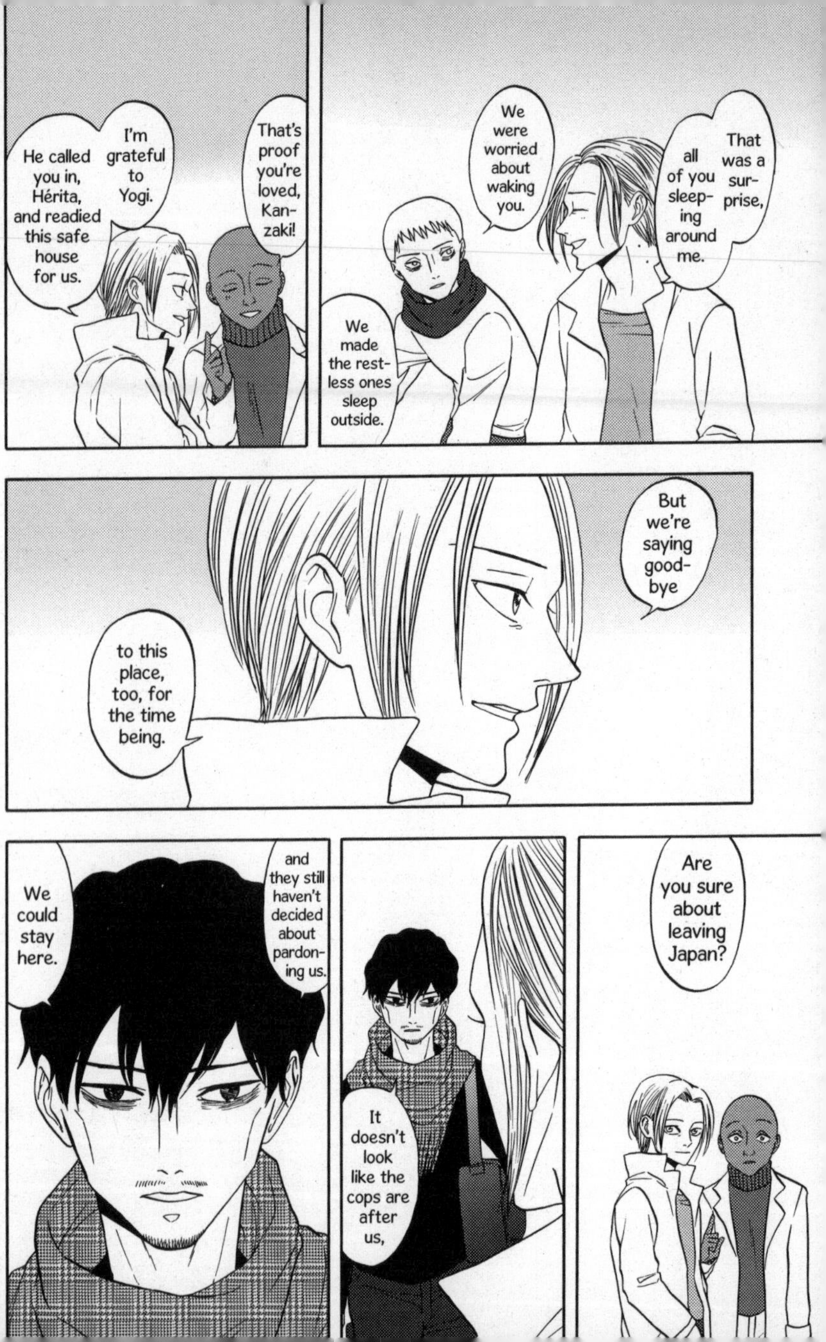
That was a surprise,
all of you sleeping around me.
We were worried about waking you.
We made the restless ones sleep outside.
That's proof you're loved, Kanzaki!
I'm grateful to Yogi.
He called you in, Hérita, and readied this safe house for us.
But we're saying goodbye
to this place, too, for the time being.
Are you sure about leaving Japan?
It doesn't look like the cops are after us,
and they still haven't decided about pardoning us.
We could stay here.

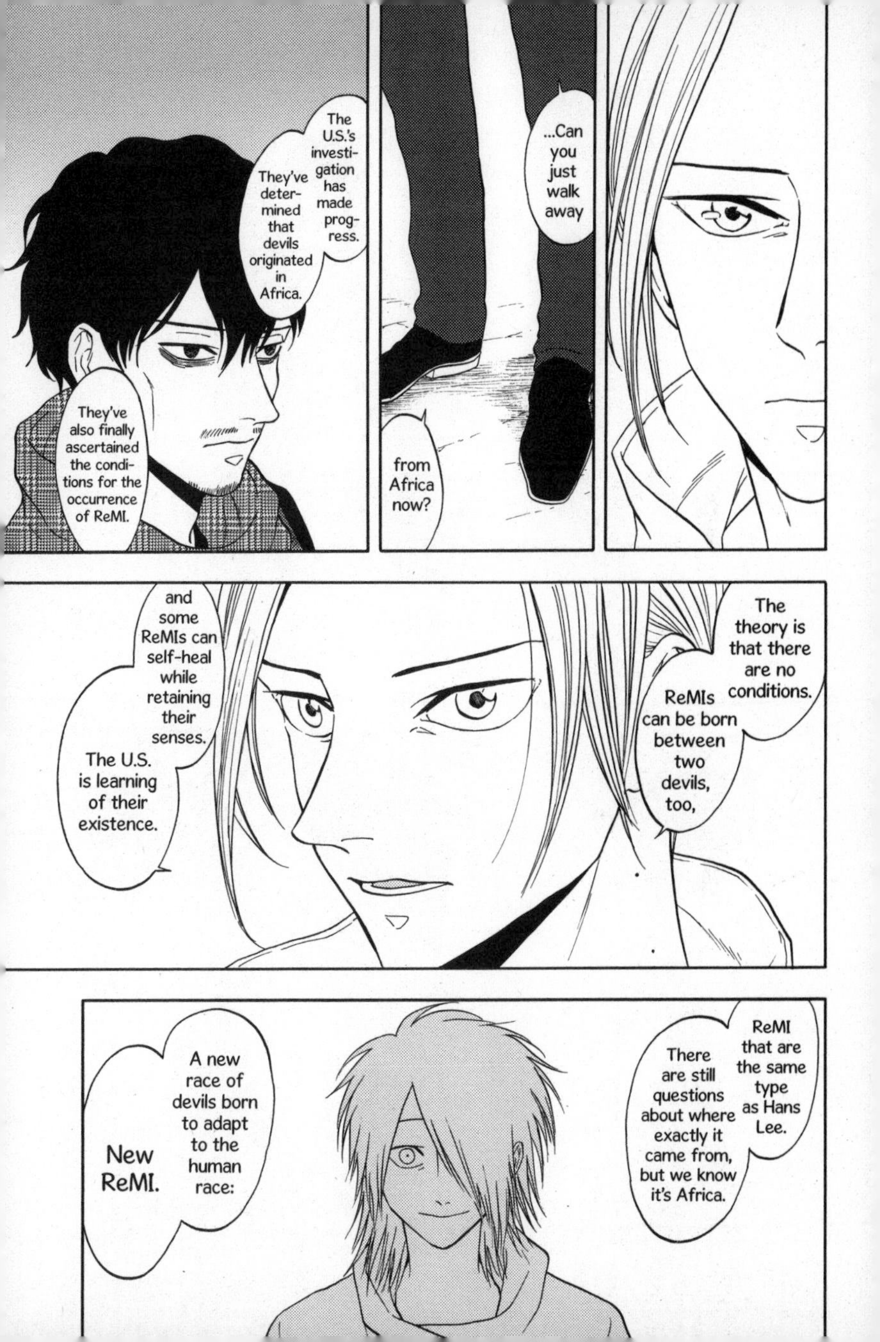
...Can you just walk away
from Africa now?
The U.S.'s investigation has made progress.
They've determined that devils originated in Africa.
They've also finally ascertained the conditions for the occurrence of ReMI.
The theory is that there are no conditions.
ReMIs can be born between two devils, too,
and some ReMIs can self-heal while retaining their senses.
The U.S. is learning of their existence.
ReMI that are the same type as Hans Lee.
There are still questions about where exactly it came from, but we know it's Africa.
A new race of devils born to adapt to the human race:
New ReMI.

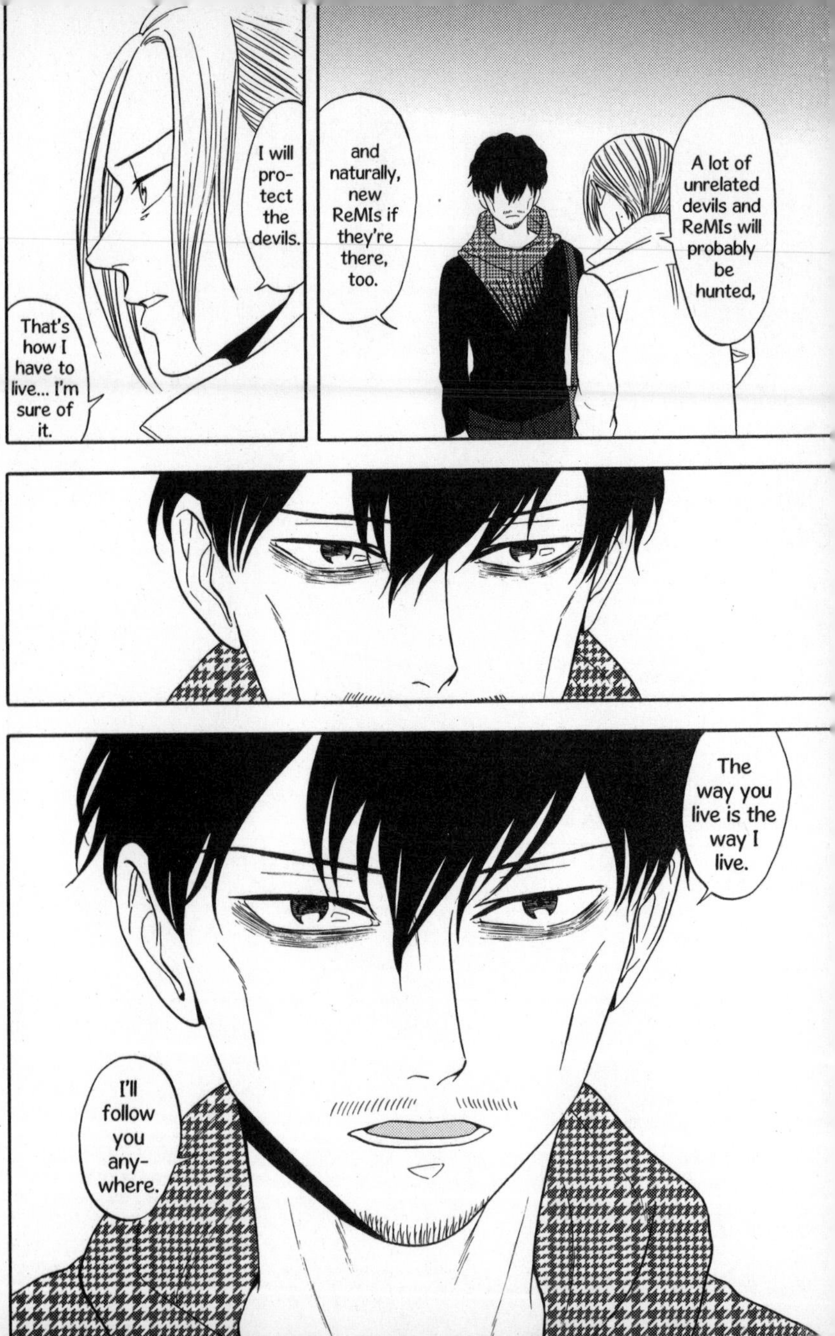
A lot of unrelated devils and ReMIs will probably be hunted,
and naturally, new ReMIs if they're there, too.
I will protect the devils.
That's how I have to live... I'm sure of it.
The way you live is the way I live.
I'll follow you anywhere.

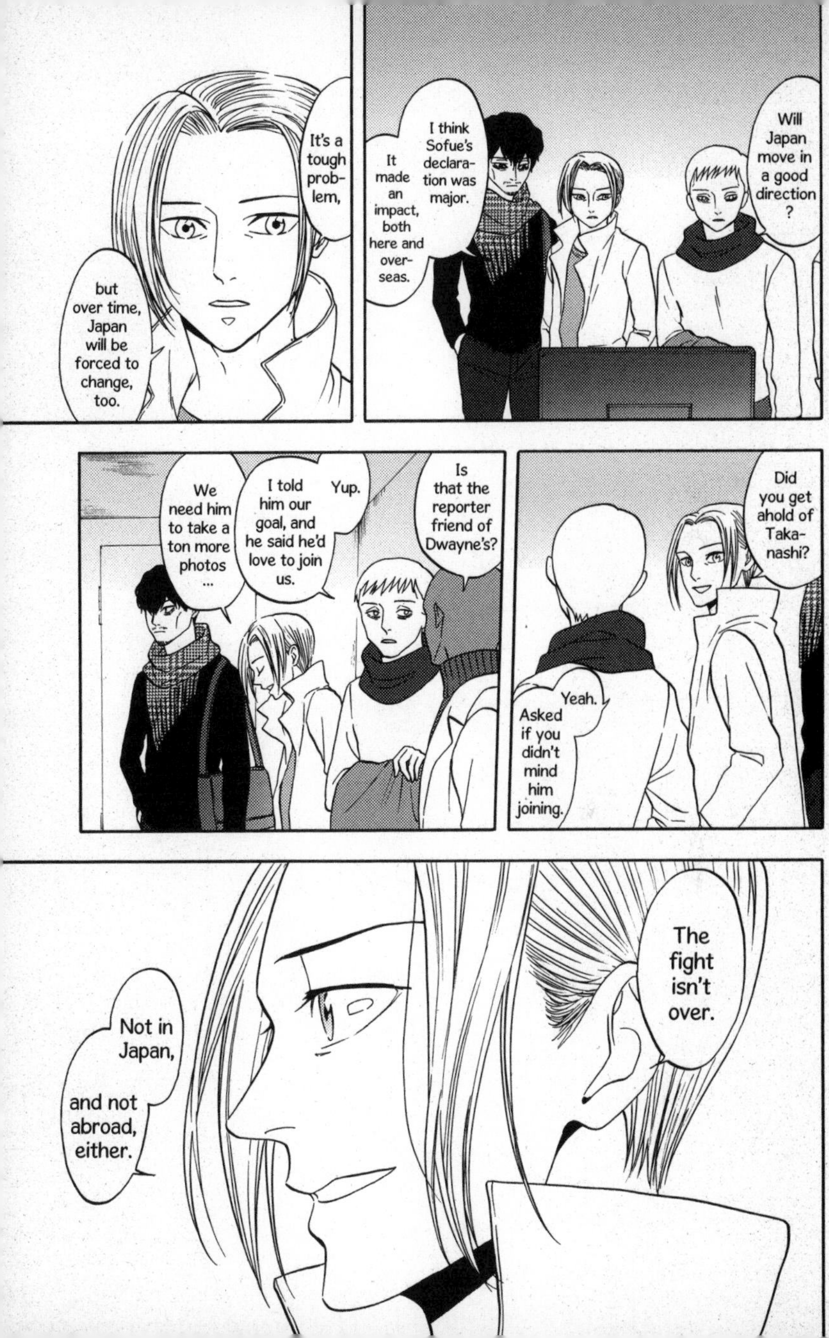
Will Japan move in a good direction?
I think Sofue's declaration was major.
It made an impact, both here and overseas.
It's a tough problem,
but over time, Japan will be forced to change, too.
Did you get ahold of Takanashi?
Yeah. Asked if you didn't mind him joining.
Is that the reporter friend of Dwayne's?
Yup.
I told him our goal, and he said he'd love to join us.
We need him to take a ton more photos ...
The fight isn't over.
Not in Japan,
and not abroad, either.

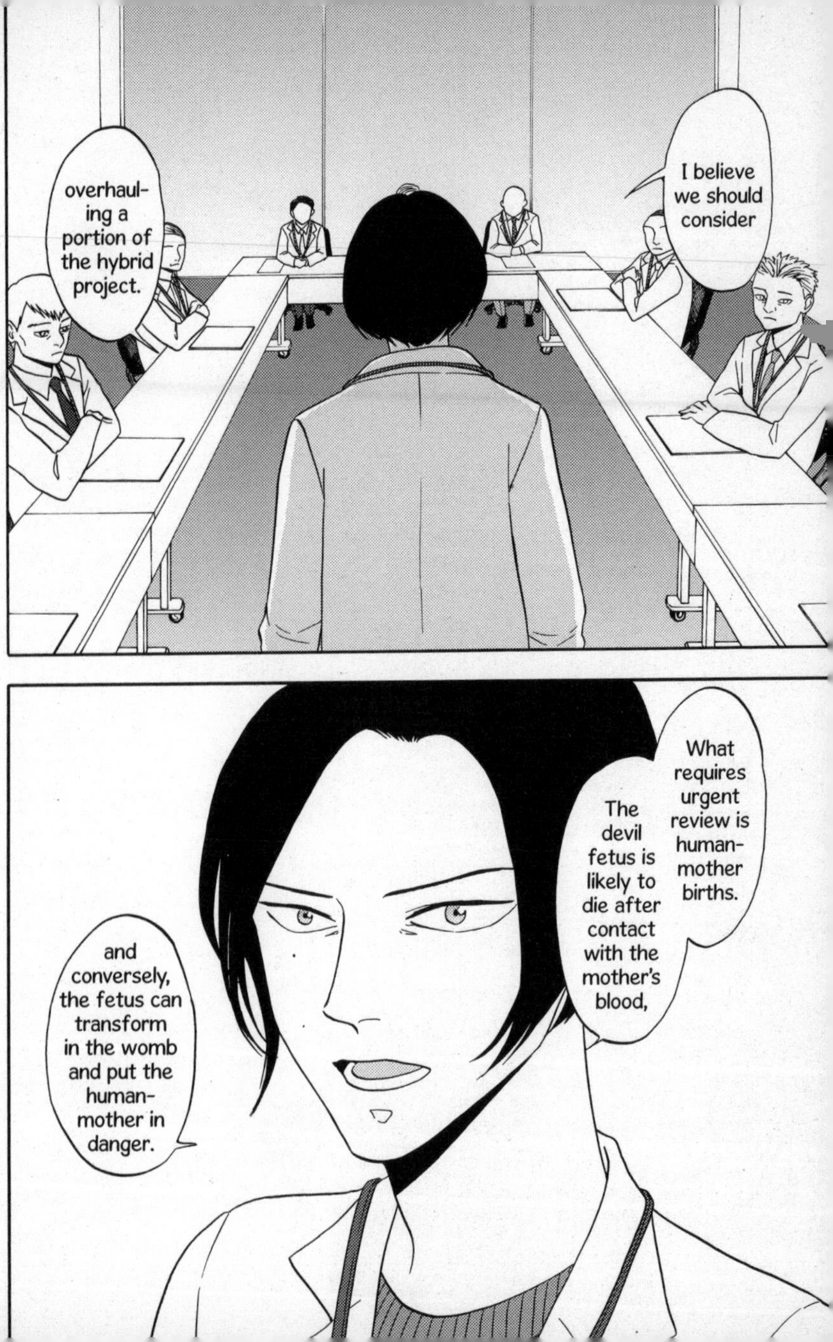
I believe we should consider
overhaul-ing a portion of the hybrid project.
What requires urgent review is human-mother births.
The devil fetus is likely to die after contact with the mother's blood,
and conversely, the fetus can transform in the womb and put the human-mother in danger.

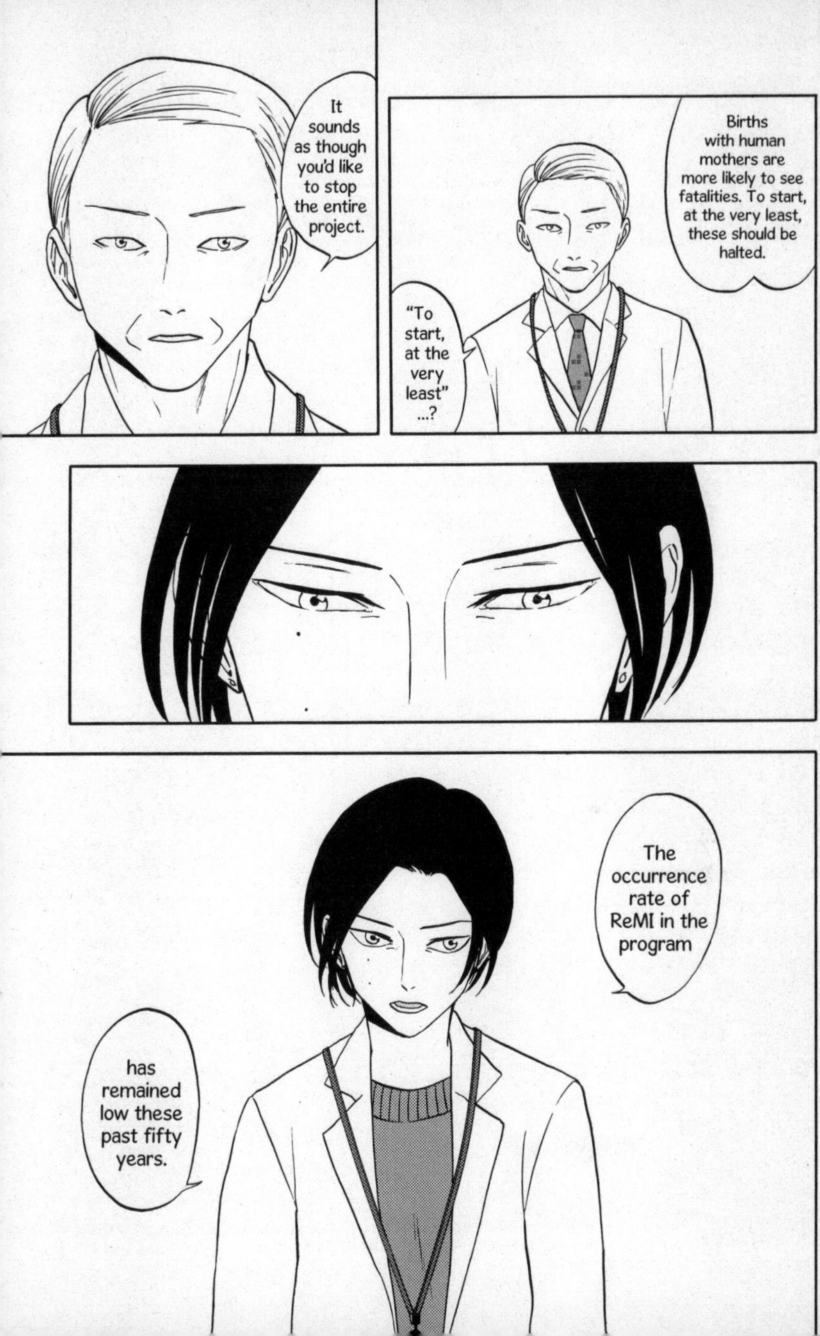
Births with human mothers are more likely to see fatalities. To start, at the very least, these should be halted.
"To start, at the very least" ...?
It sounds as though you'd like to stop the entire project.
The occurrence rate of ReMI in the program
has remained low these past fifty years.

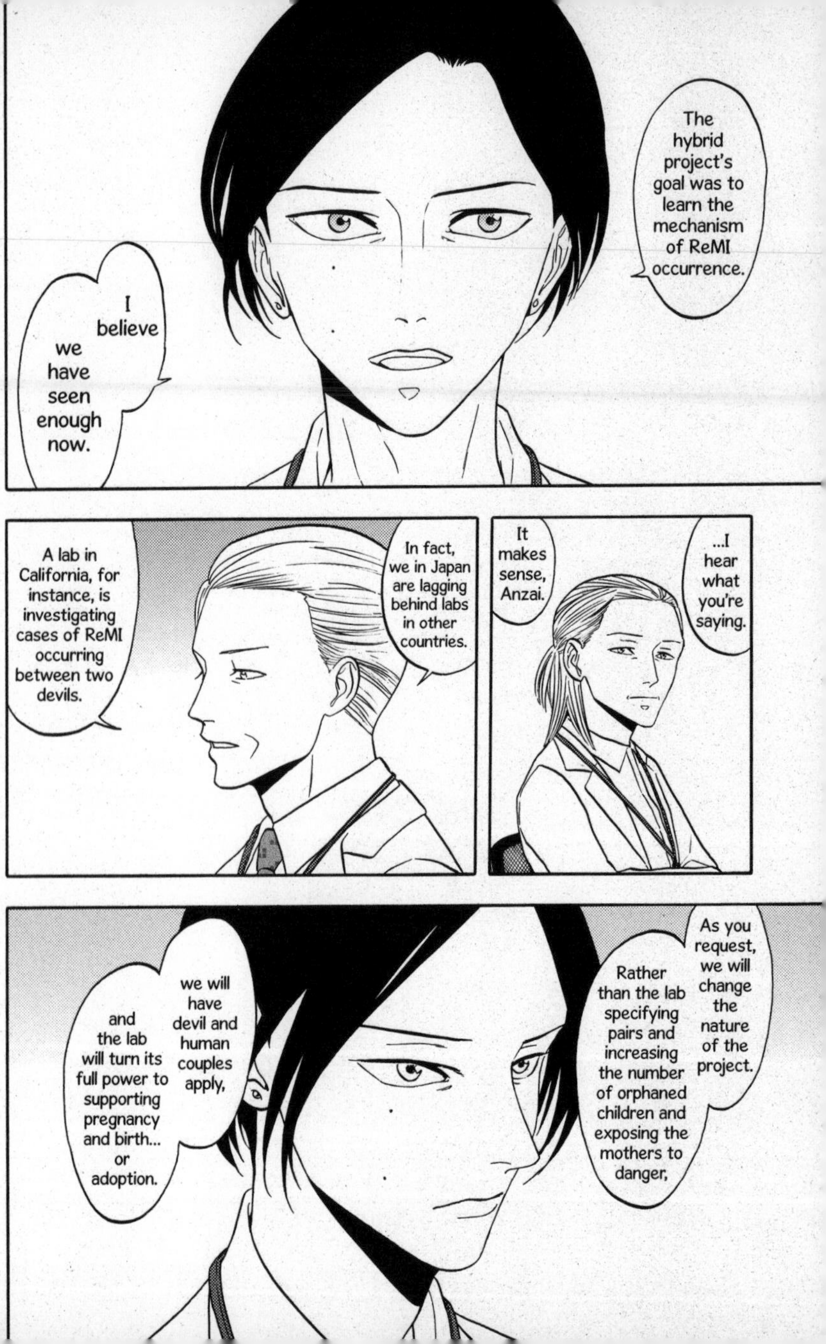
The hybrid project's goal was to learn the mechanism of ReMI occurrence.
I believe we have seen enough now.
...I hear what you're saying.
It makes sense, Anzai.
In fact, we in Japan are lagging behind labs in other countries.
A lab in California, for instance, is investigating cases of ReMI occurring between two devils.
As you request, we will change the nature of the project.
Rather than the lab specifying pairs and increasing the number of orphaned children and exposing the mothers to danger,
we will have devil and human couples apply,
and the lab will turn its full power to supporting pregnancy and birth... or adoption.

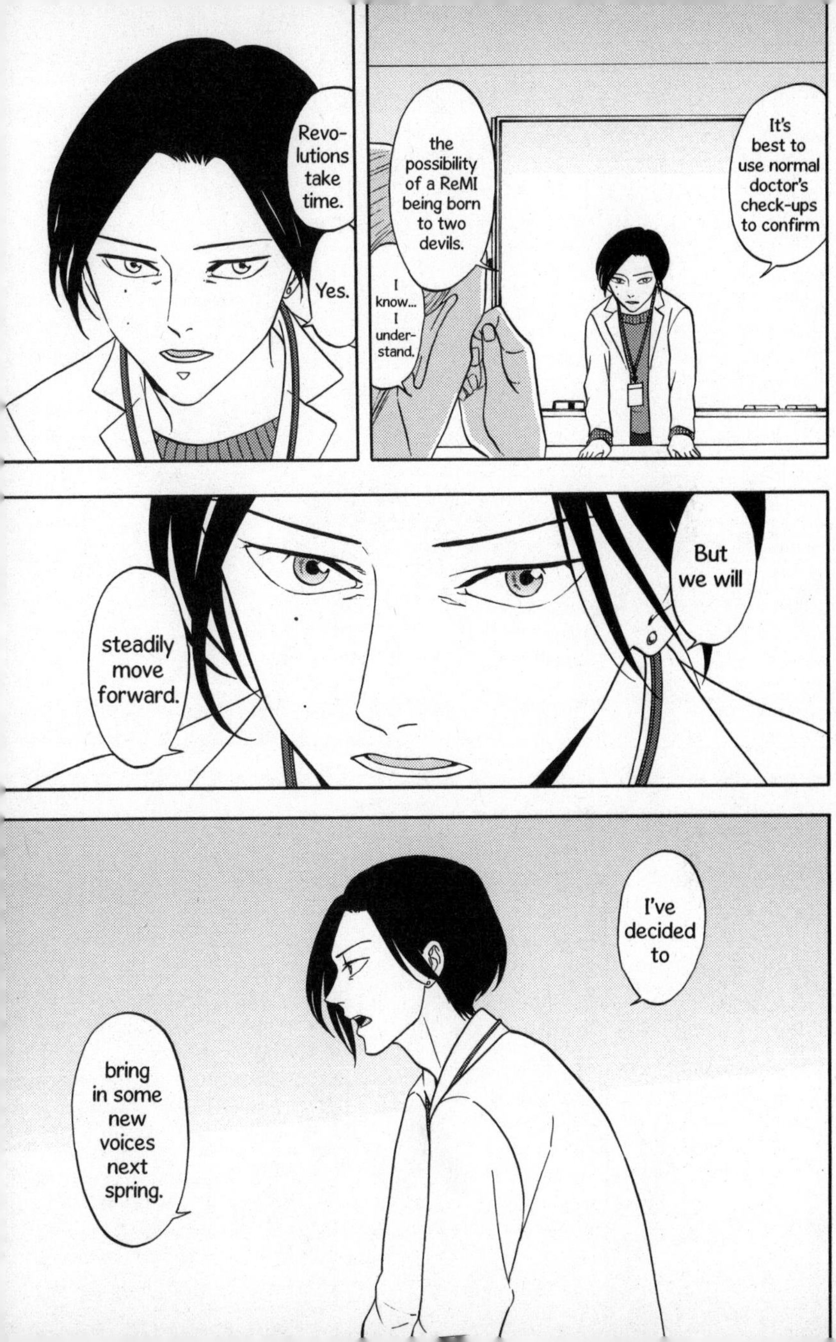
It's best to use normal doctor's check-ups to confirm
the possibility of a ReMI being born to two devils.
I know... I understand.
Revo-lutions take time.
Yes.
But we will
steadily move forward.
I've decided to
bring in some new voices next spring.

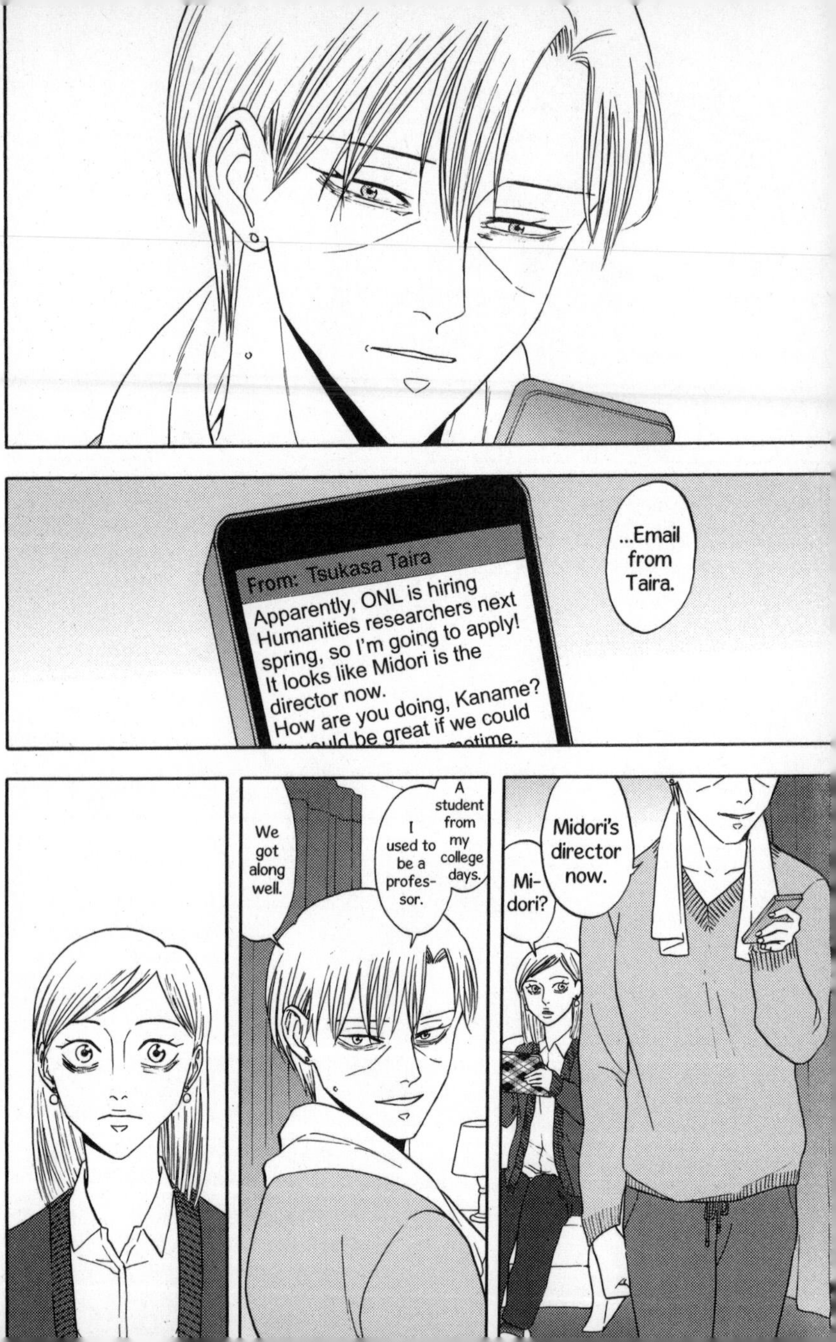
...Email from Taira.
From: Tsukasa Taira
Apparently, ONL is hiring
Humanities researchers next
spring, so I'm going to apply!
It looks like Midori is the
director now.
How are you doing, Kaname?
Midori's director now.
Mi-dori?
A student from my college days.
I used to be a profes-sor.
We got along well.

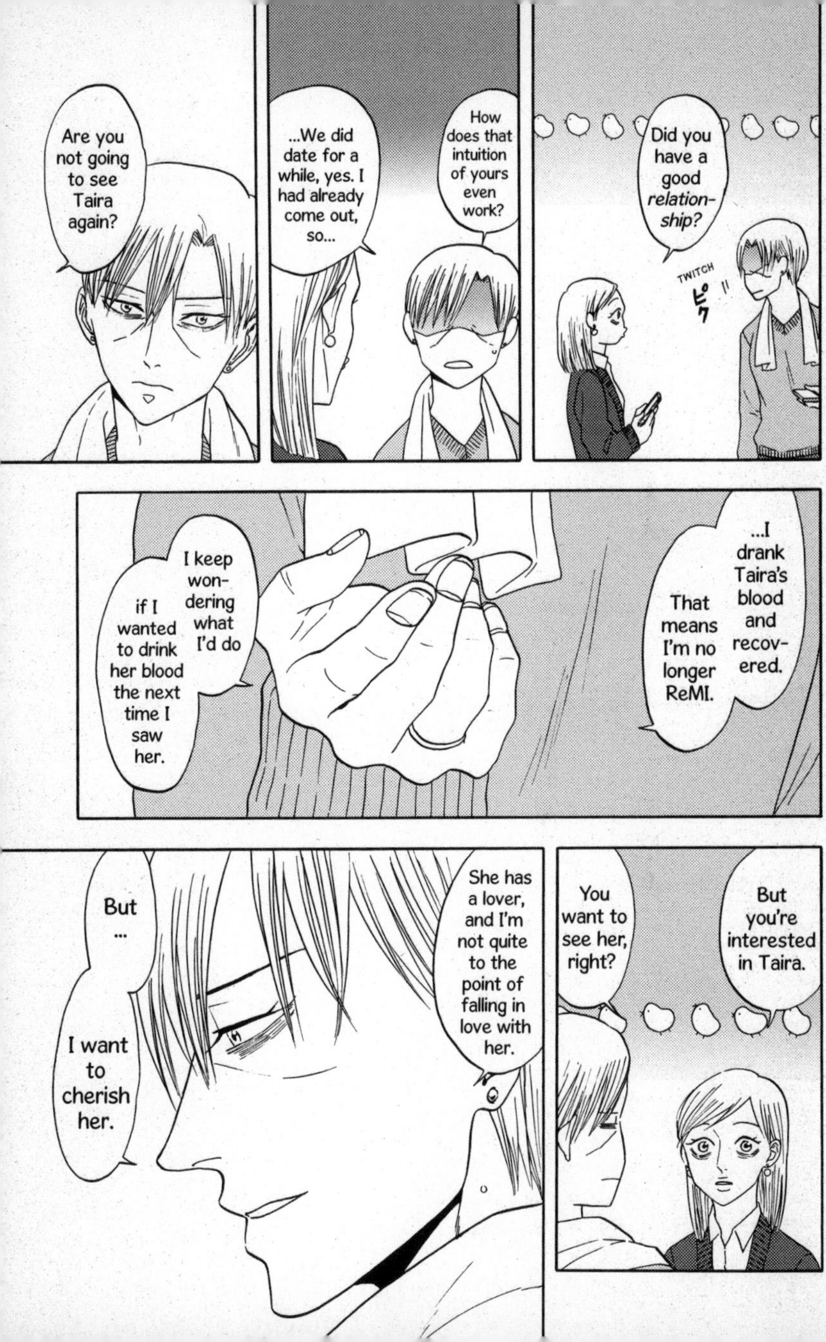
Did you have a good *relationship?*
TWITCH
ピク
How does that intuition of yours even work?
...We did date for a while, yes. I had already come out, so...
Are you not going to see Taira again?
...I drank Taira's blood and recovered.
That means I'm no longer ReMI.
I keep won-dering what I'd do
if I wanted to drink her blood the next time I saw her.
But you're interested in Taira.
You want to see her, right?
She has a lover, and I'm not quite to the point of falling in love with her.
But ...
I want to cherish her.

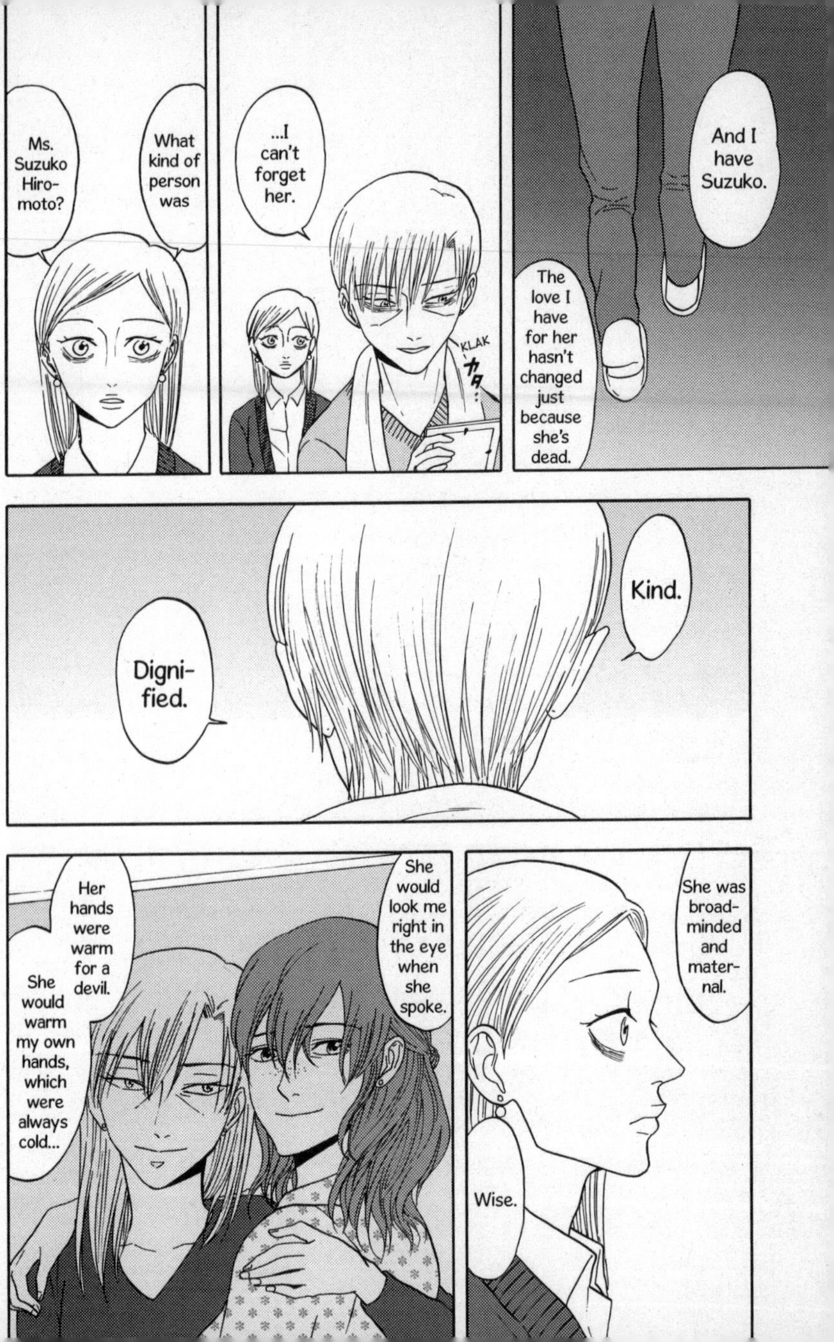
And I have Suzuko.
The love I have for her hasn't changed just because she's dead.
...I can't forget her.
KLAK
カタ
What kind of person was
Ms. Suzuko Hiromoto?
Kind.
Dignified.
She was broad-minded and maternal.
Wise.
She would look me right in the eye when she spoke.
Her hands were warm for a devil.
She would warm my own hands, which were always cold...

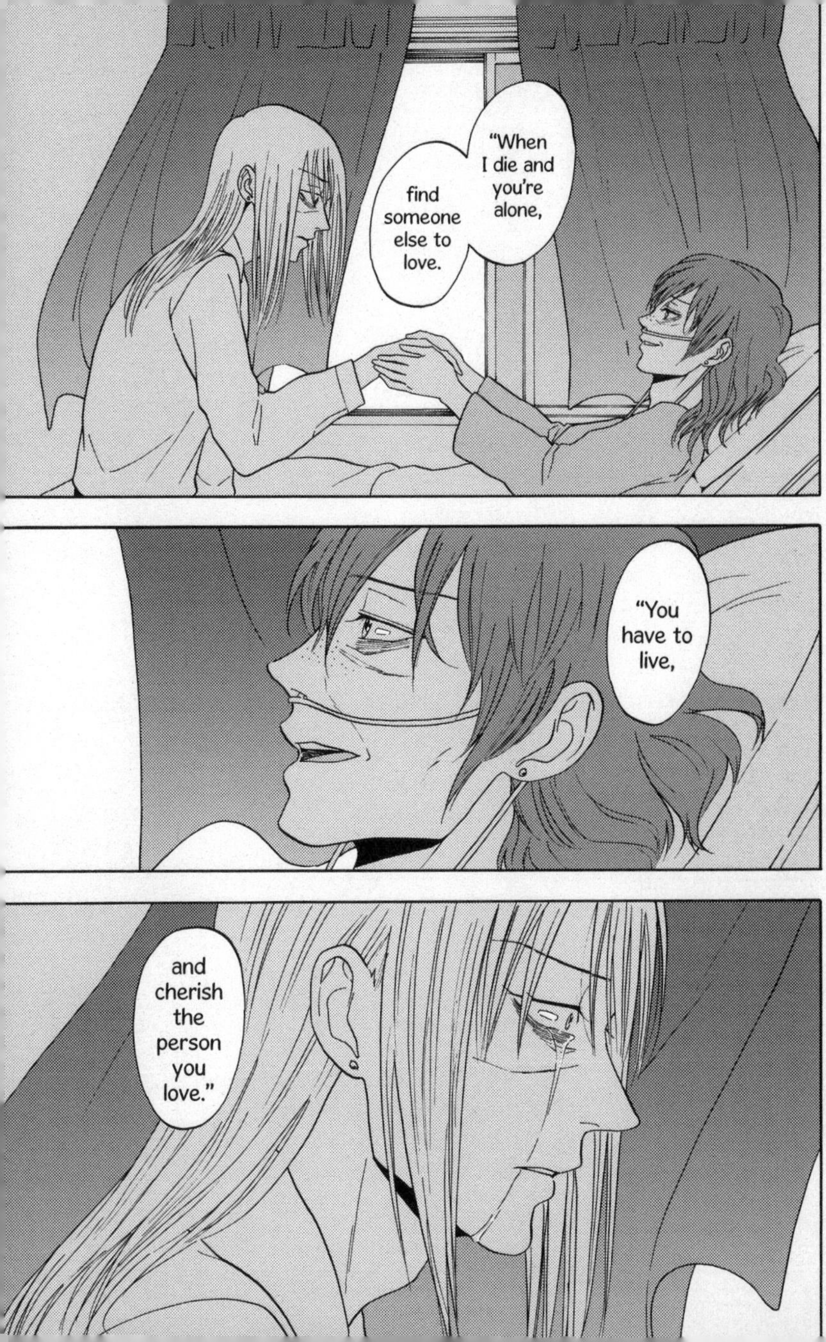
"When I die and you're alone,
find someone else to love.
"You have to live,
and cherish the person you love."

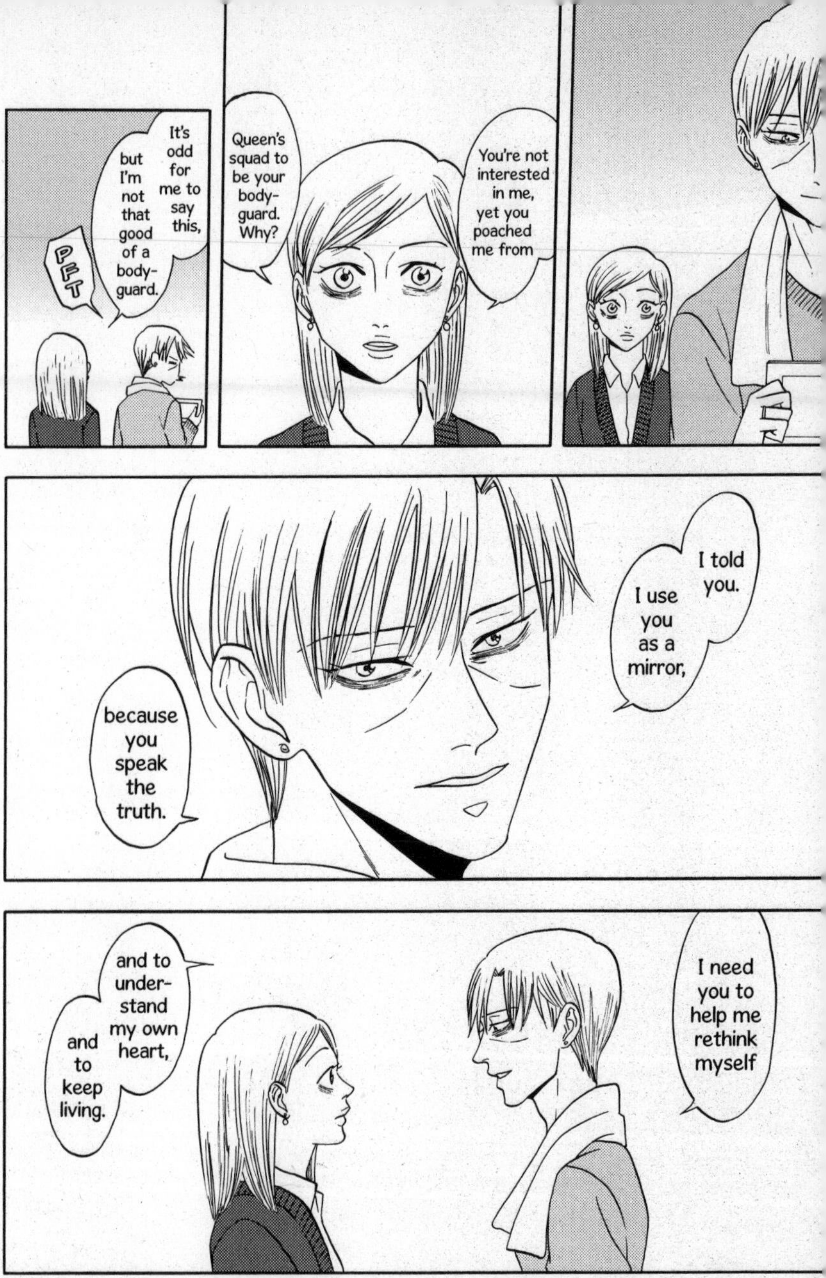
You're not interested in me, yet you poached me from
Queen's squad to be your body-guard. Why?
It's odd for me to say this,
but I'm not that good of a body-guard.
PFFT
I told you.
I use you as a mirror,
because you speak the truth.
I need you to help me rethink myself
and to under-stand my own heart,
and to keep living.

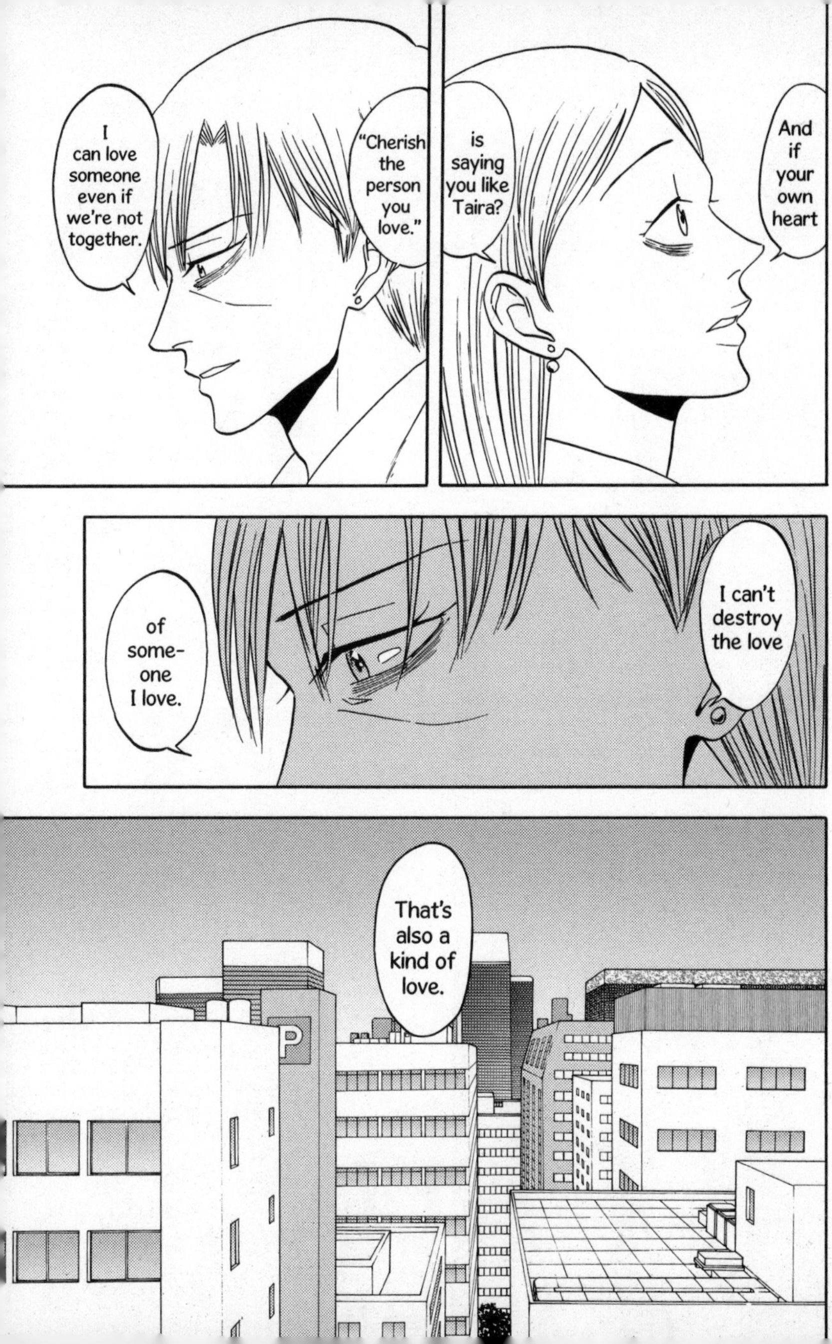
And if your own heart
is saying you like Taira?
“Cherish the person you love.”
I can love someone even if we’re not together.
I can’t destroy the love
of some-one I love.
That’s also a kind of love.

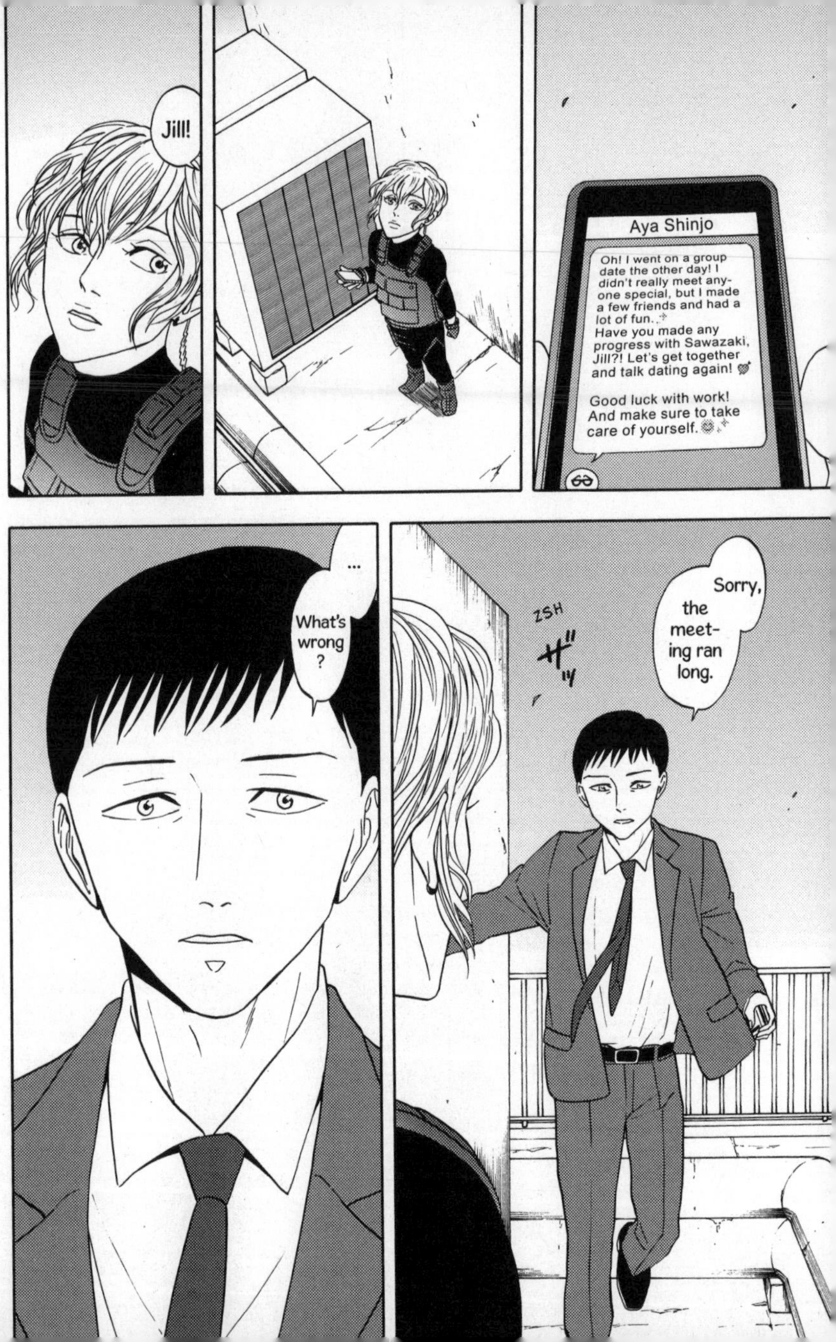
Aya Shinjo
Oh! I went on a group date the other day! I didn't really meet any-one special, but I made a few friends and had a lot of fun..
Have you made any progress with Sawazaki, Jill?! Let's get together and talk dating again!
Good luck with work! And make sure to take care of yourself.
Jill!
Sorry, the meet-ing ran long.
ZSH
...
What's wrong?

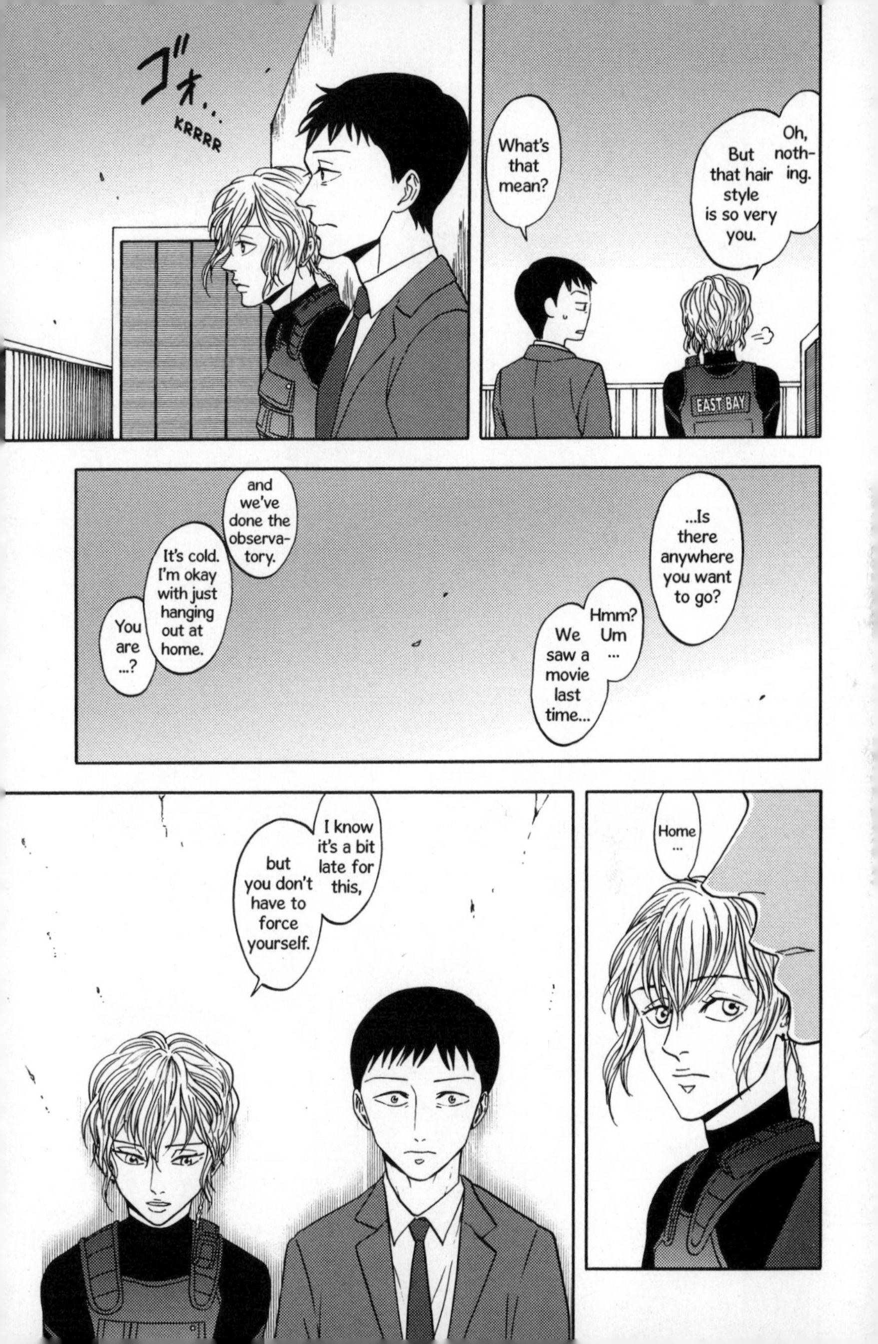
Oh, nothing.
But that hair style is so very you.
What's that mean?
ゴォ...
KRRRR
...Is there anywhere you want to go?
Hmm? Um ...
We saw a movie last time...
and we've done the observatory.
It's cold. I'm okay with just hanging out at home.
You are ...?
Home ...
I know it's a bit late for this,
but you don't have to force yourself.

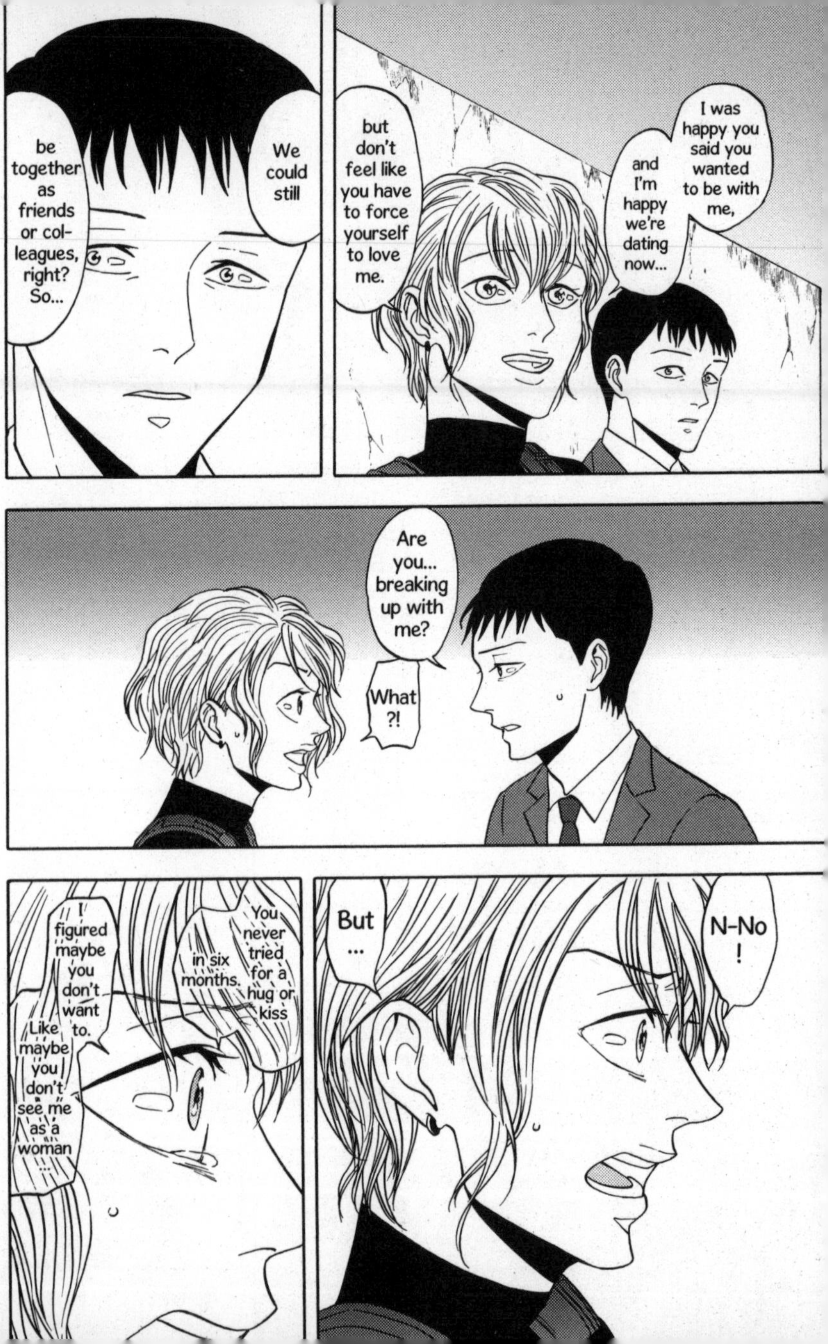
I was happy you said you wanted to be with me,
and I'm happy we're dating now...
but don't feel like you have to force yourself to love me.
We could still
be together as friends or col-leagues, right? So...
Are you... breaking up with me?
What?!
N-No!
But...
You never tried for a hug or kiss
in six months.
I figured maybe you don't want to.
Like maybe you don't see me as a woman...

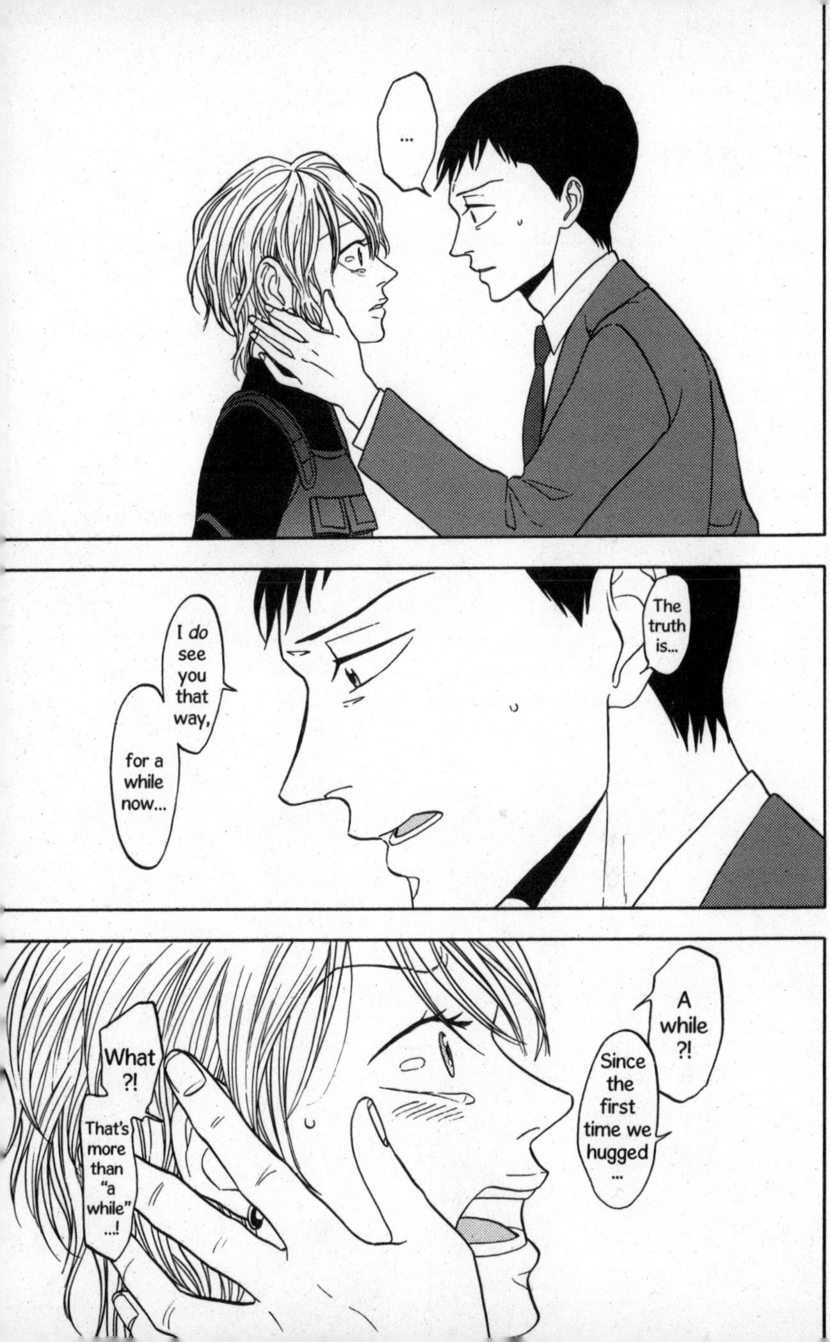
...
The truth is...
I do see you that way,
for a while now...
A while ?!
Since the first time we hugged ...
What ?!
That's more than "a while" ...!

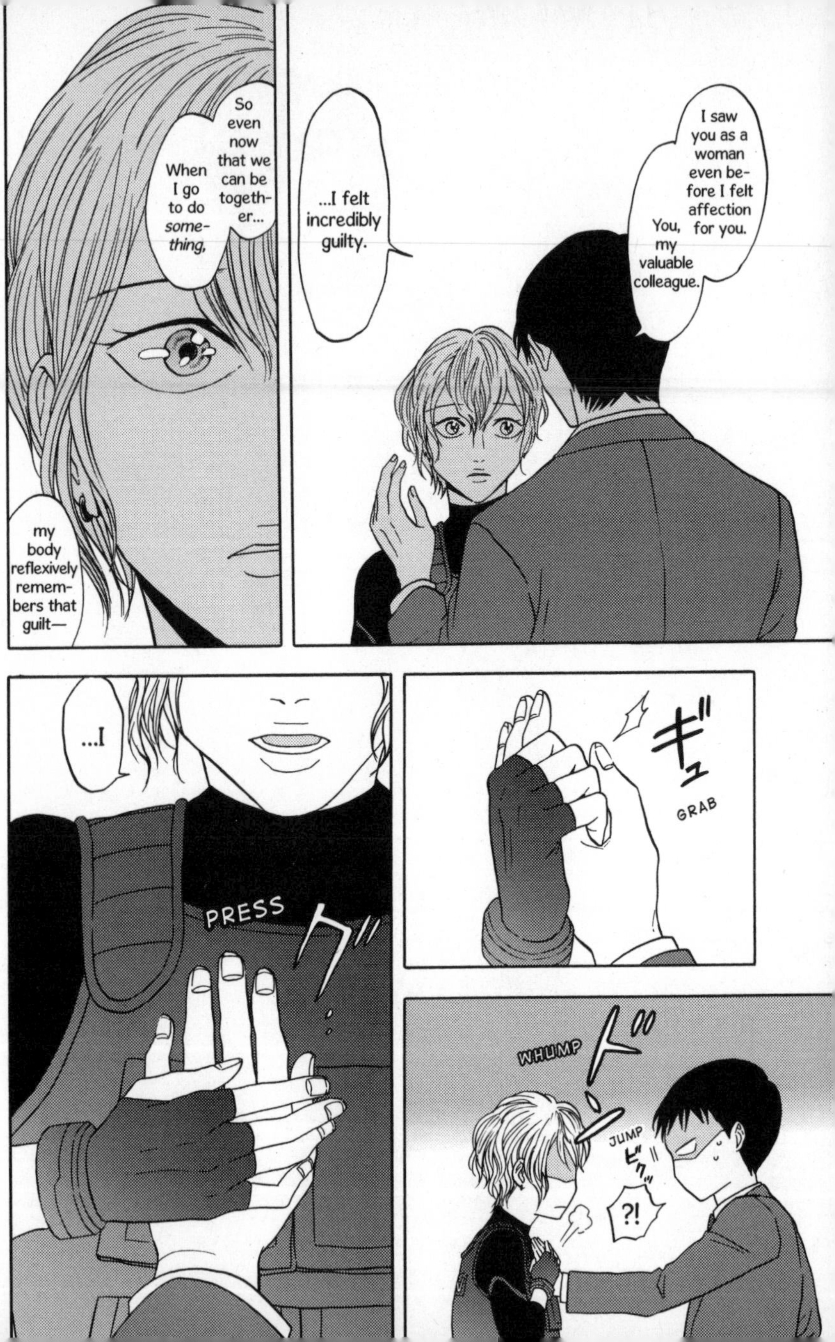
I saw you as a woman even before I felt affection for you.
You, my valuable colleague.
...I felt incredibly guilty.
So even now that we can be together...
When I go to do *something,*
my body reflexively remembers that guilt—
ギュ
GRAB
ドッ
WHUMP
ビクッ
JUMP
?!
...I
PRESS
グッ

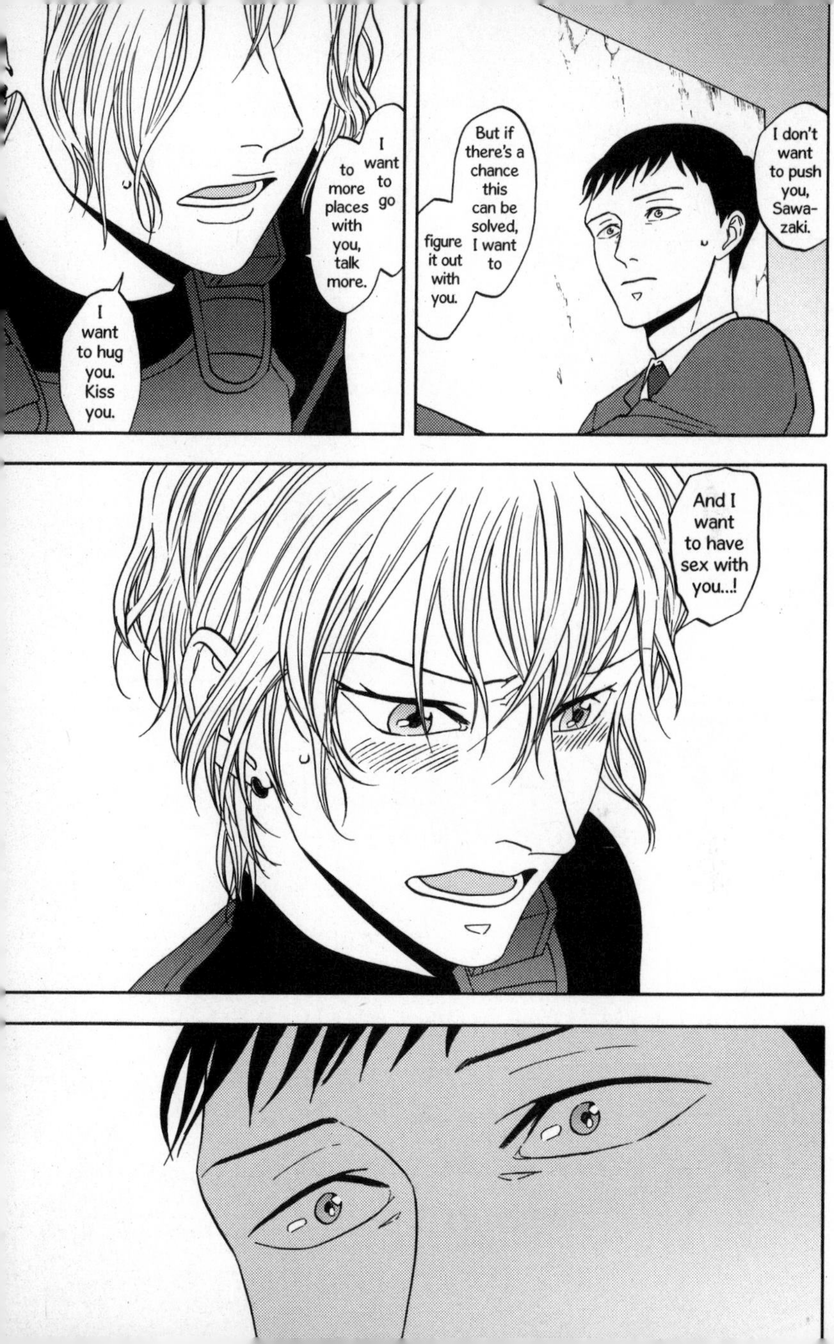
I don't want to push you, Sawazaki.
But if there's a chance this can be solved, I want to figure it out with you.
I want to go to more places with you, talk more.
I want to hug you. Kiss you.
And I want to have sex with you...!

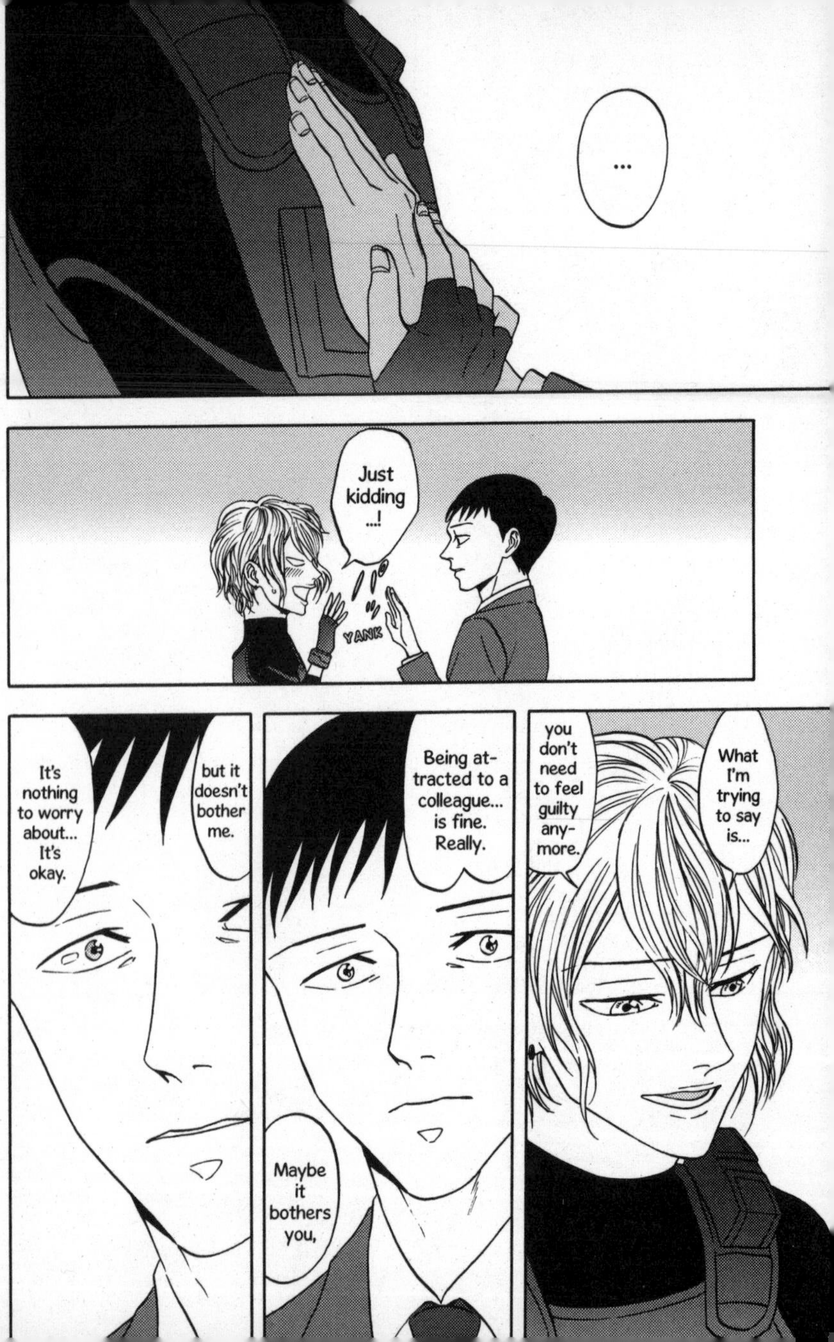
...
Just kidding ...!
YANK
What I'm trying to say is...
you don't need to feel guilty any-more.
Being at-tracted to a colleague... is fine. Really.
Maybe it bothers you,
but it doesn't bother me.
It's nothing to worry about... It's okay.

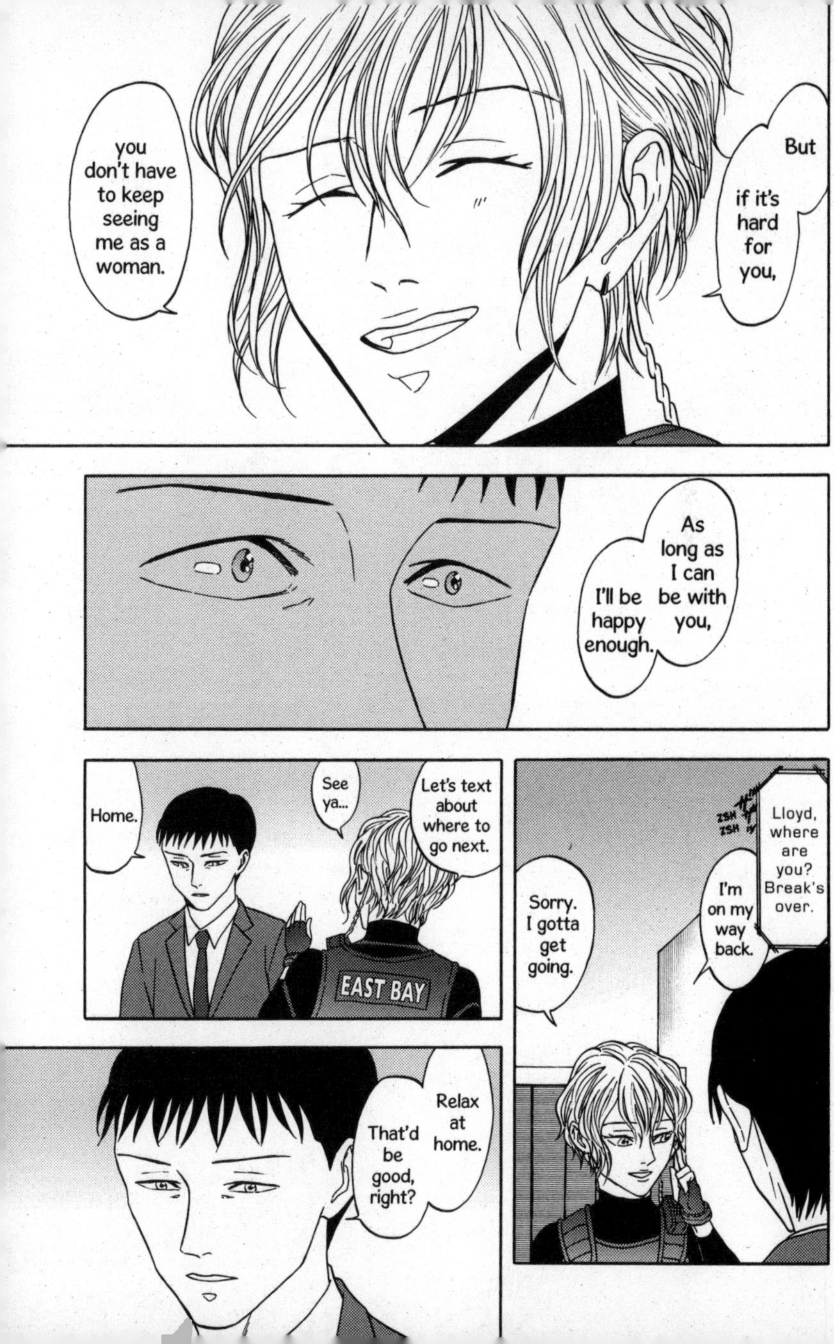
But
if it's hard for you,
you don't have to keep seeing me as a woman.
As long as I can be with you,
I'll be happy enough.
Lloyd, where are you? Break's over.
I'm on my way back.
Sorry. I gotta get going.
Let's text about where to go next.
See ya...
Home.
Relax at home.
That'd be good, right?

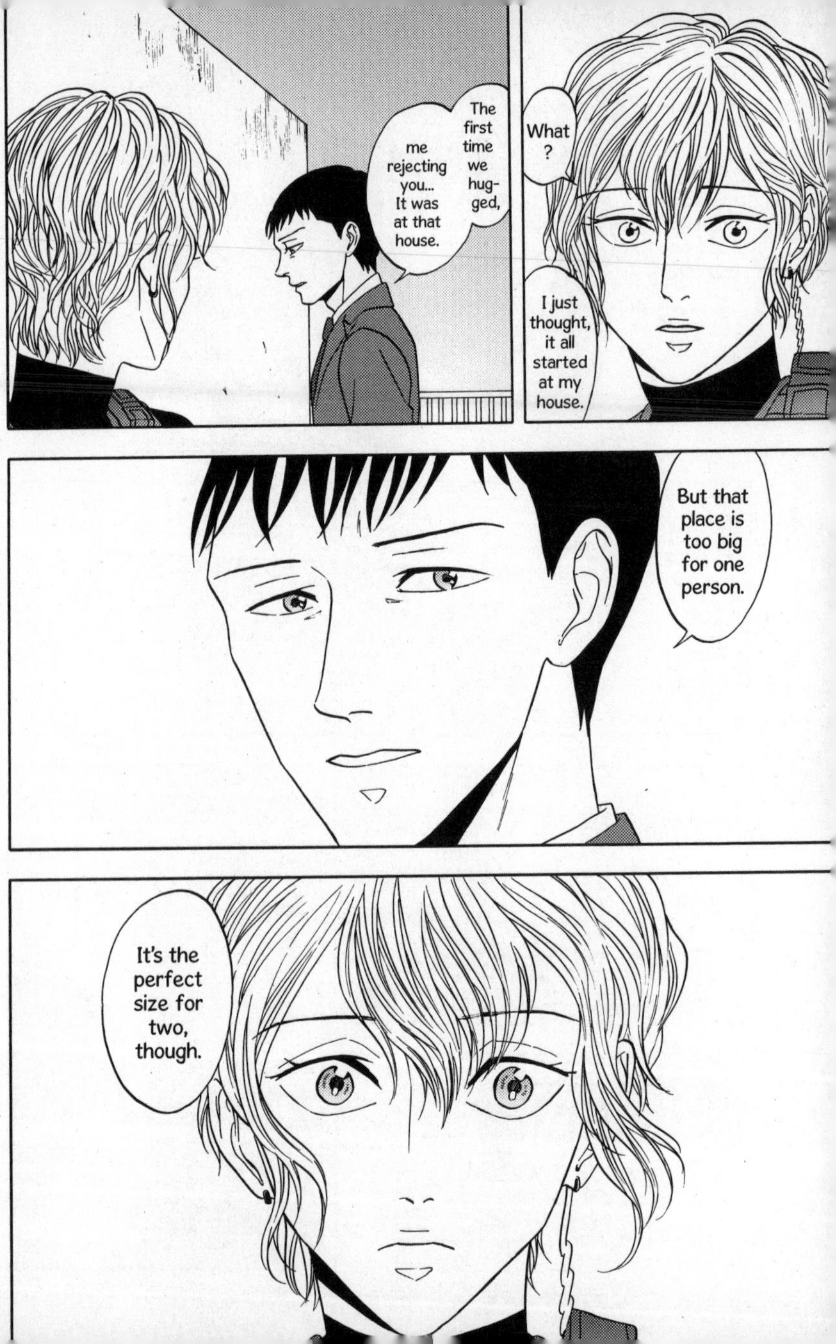
What?
I just thought, it all started at my house.
The first time we hug-ged,
me rejecting you... It was at that house.
But that place is too big for one person.
It's the perfect size for two, though.

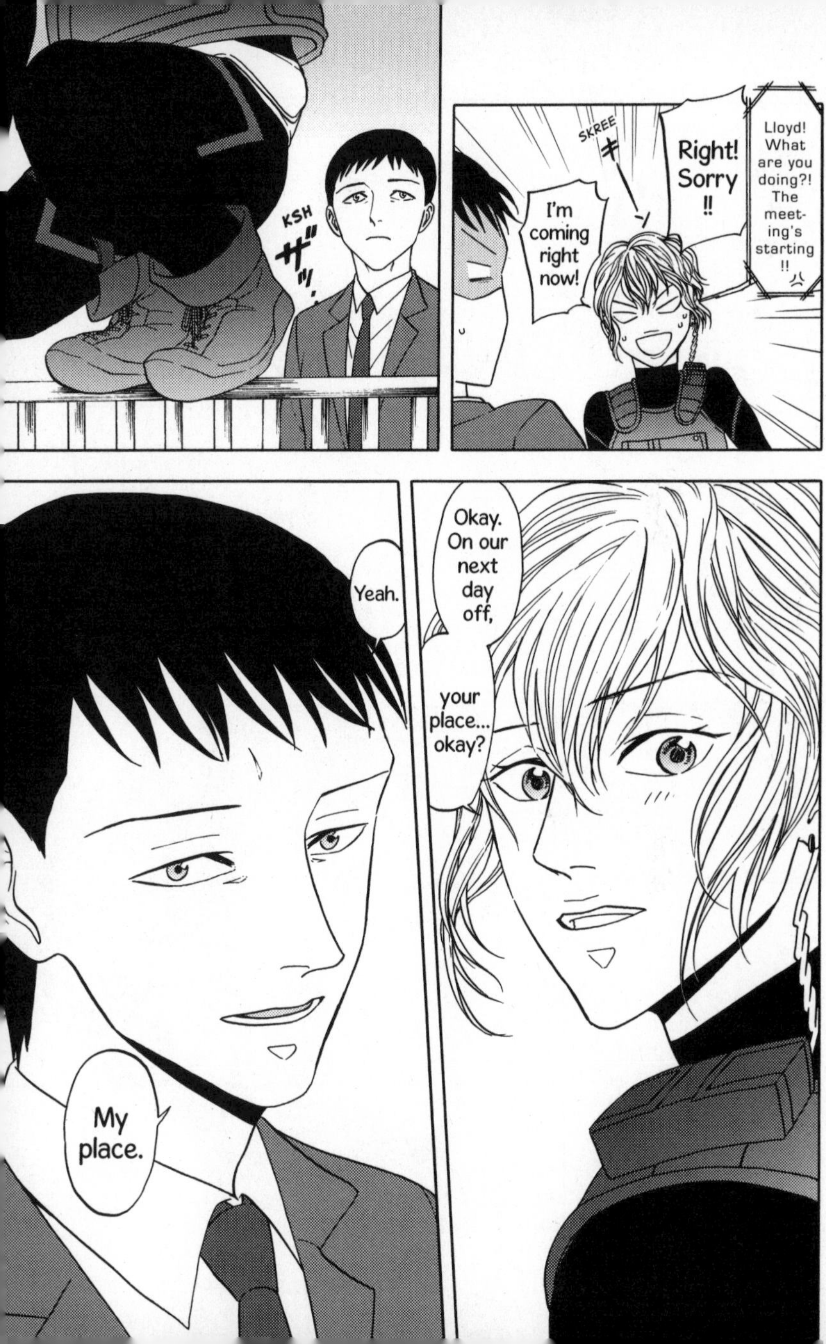
Lloyd! What are you doing?! The meet-ing's starting !!
Right! Sorry !!
SKREE
I'm coming right now!
KSH
Okay. On our next day off,
your place... okay?
Yeah.
My place.

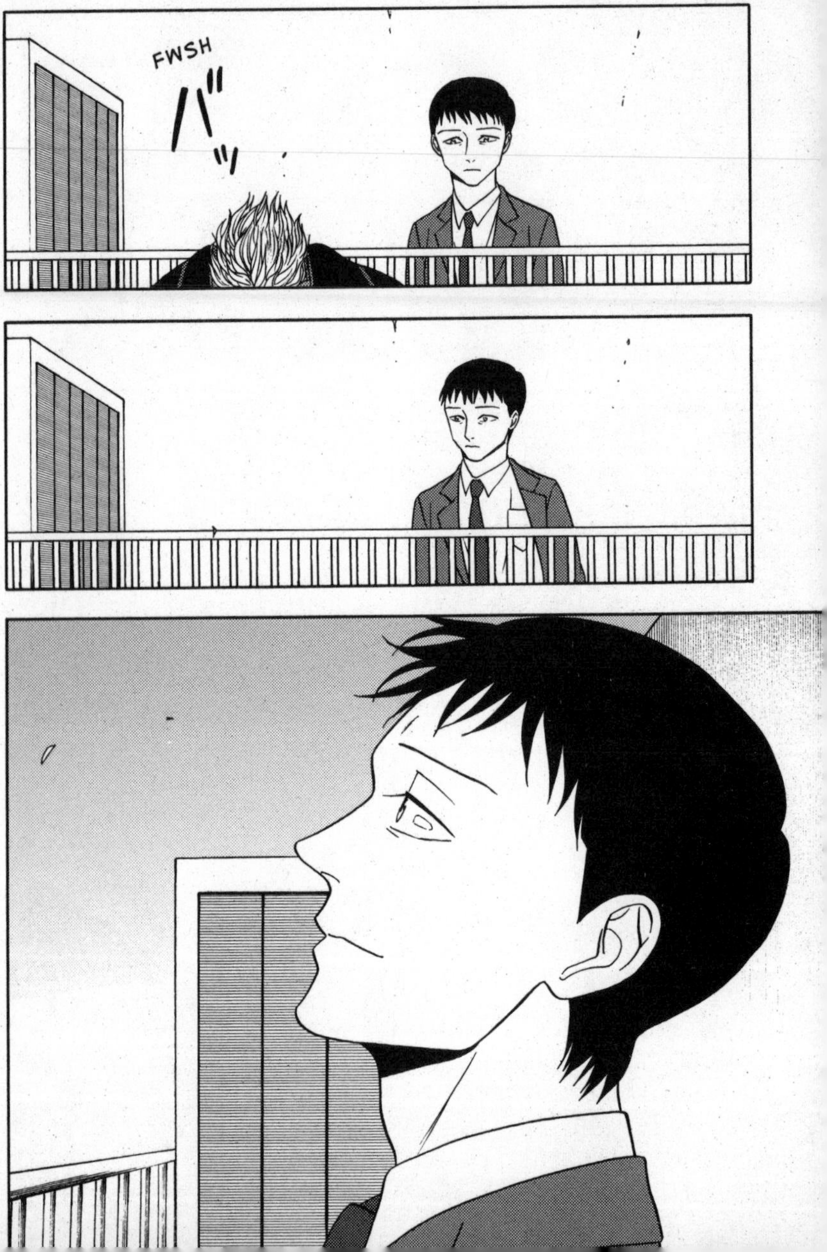
FWSH
バッ

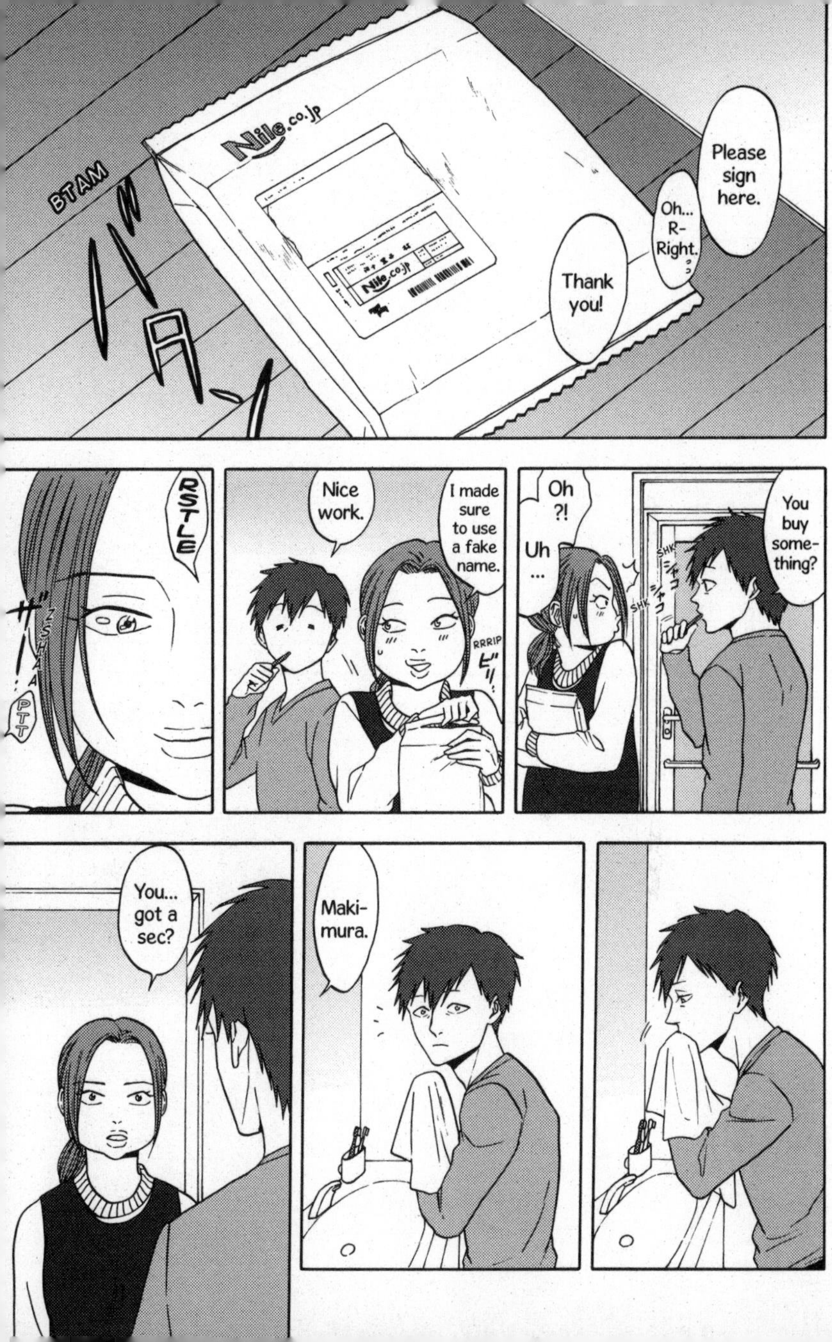
Please sign here.
Oh... R-Right.
Thank you!
BTAM
You buy some-thing?
SHK
SHK
Oh ?!
Uh ...
I made sure to use a fake name.
Nice work.
RRRIP
RSTLE
ZSHAA
PTT
Maki-mura.
You... got a sec?

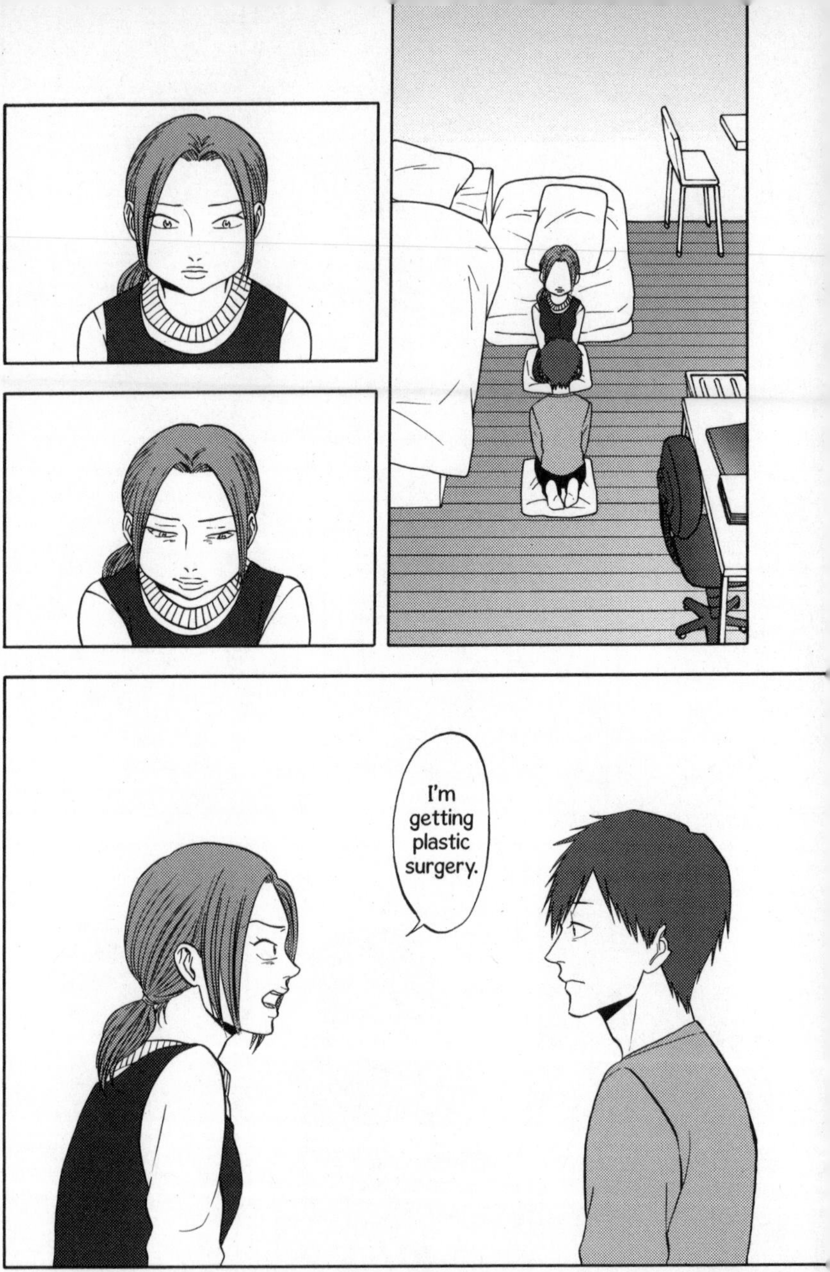
I'm getting plastic surgery.

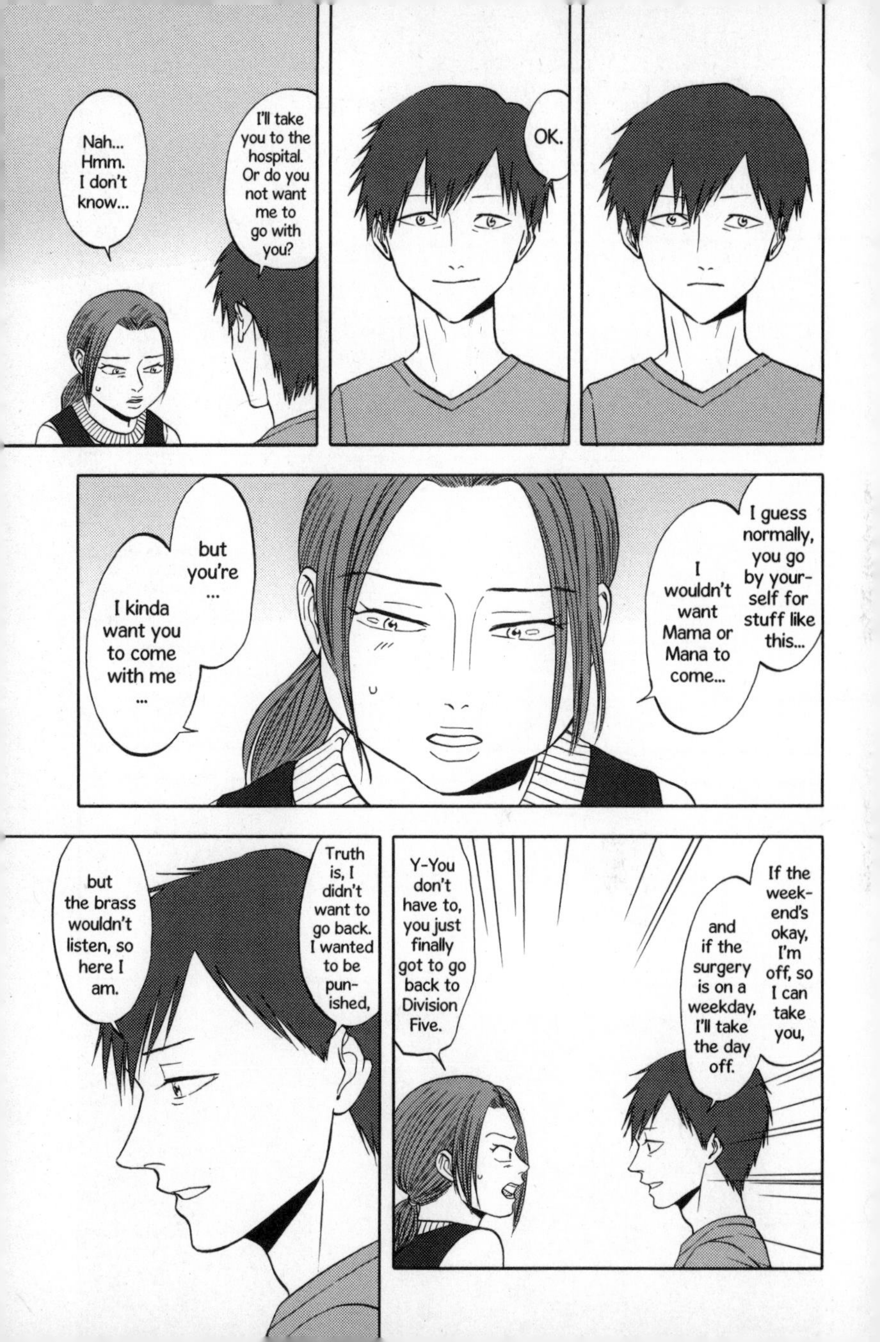
OK.
I'll take you to the hospital. Or do you not want me to go with you?
Nah... Hmm. I don't know...
I guess normally, you go by your-self for stuff like this...
I wouldn't want Mama or Mana to come...
but you're ...
I kinda want you to come with me ...
If the week-end's okay, I'm off, so I can take you,
and if the surgery is on a weekday, I'll take the day off.
Y-You don't have to, you just finally got to go back to Division Five.
Truth is, I didn't want to go back. I wanted to be pun-ished,
but the brass wouldn't listen, so here I am.

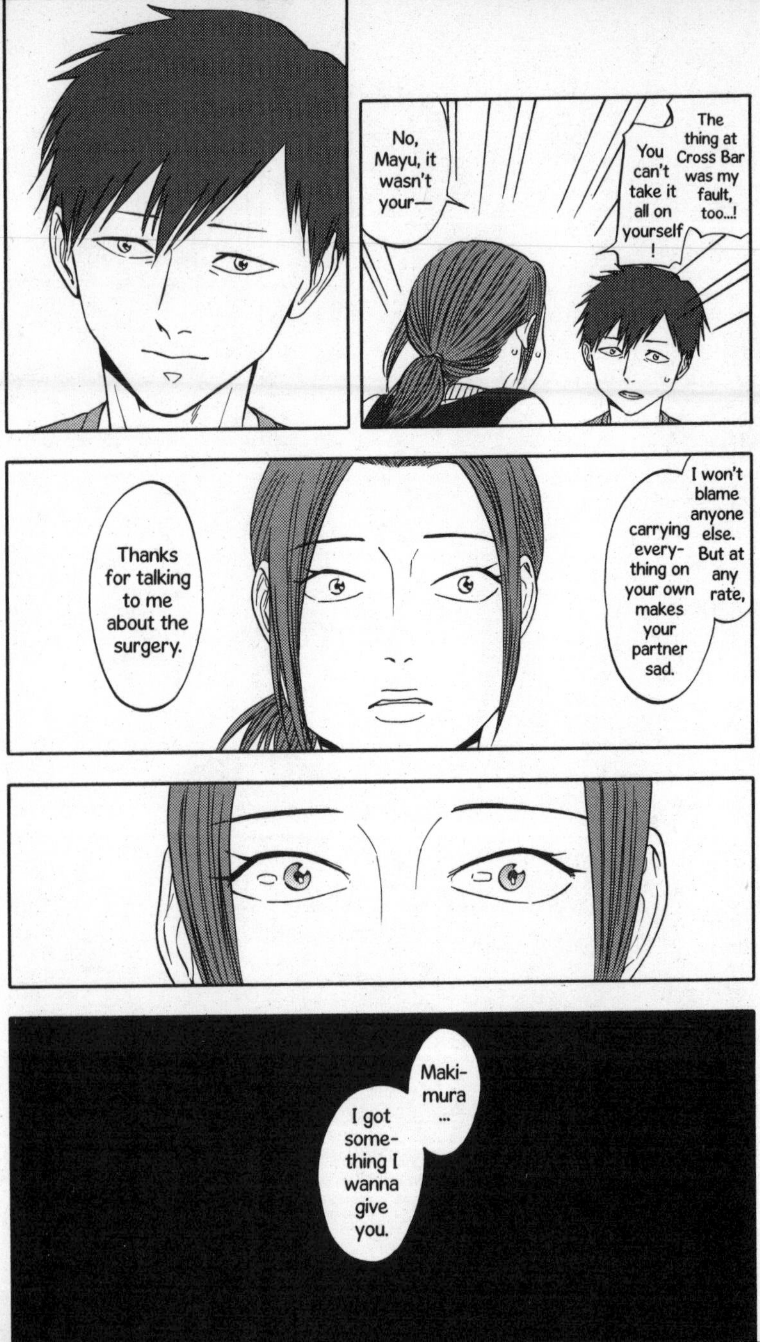
The thing at Cross Bar was my fault, too...!
You can't take it all on yourself!
No, Mayu, it wasn't your—
I won't blame anyone else. But at any rate,
carrying every-thing on your own makes your partner sad.
Thanks for talking to me about the surgery.
Maki-mura...
I got some-thing I wanna give you.

Well... open it up.

A present...?

For You

KRSH

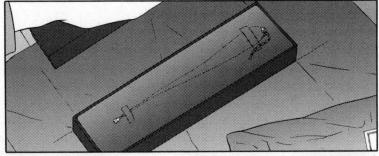

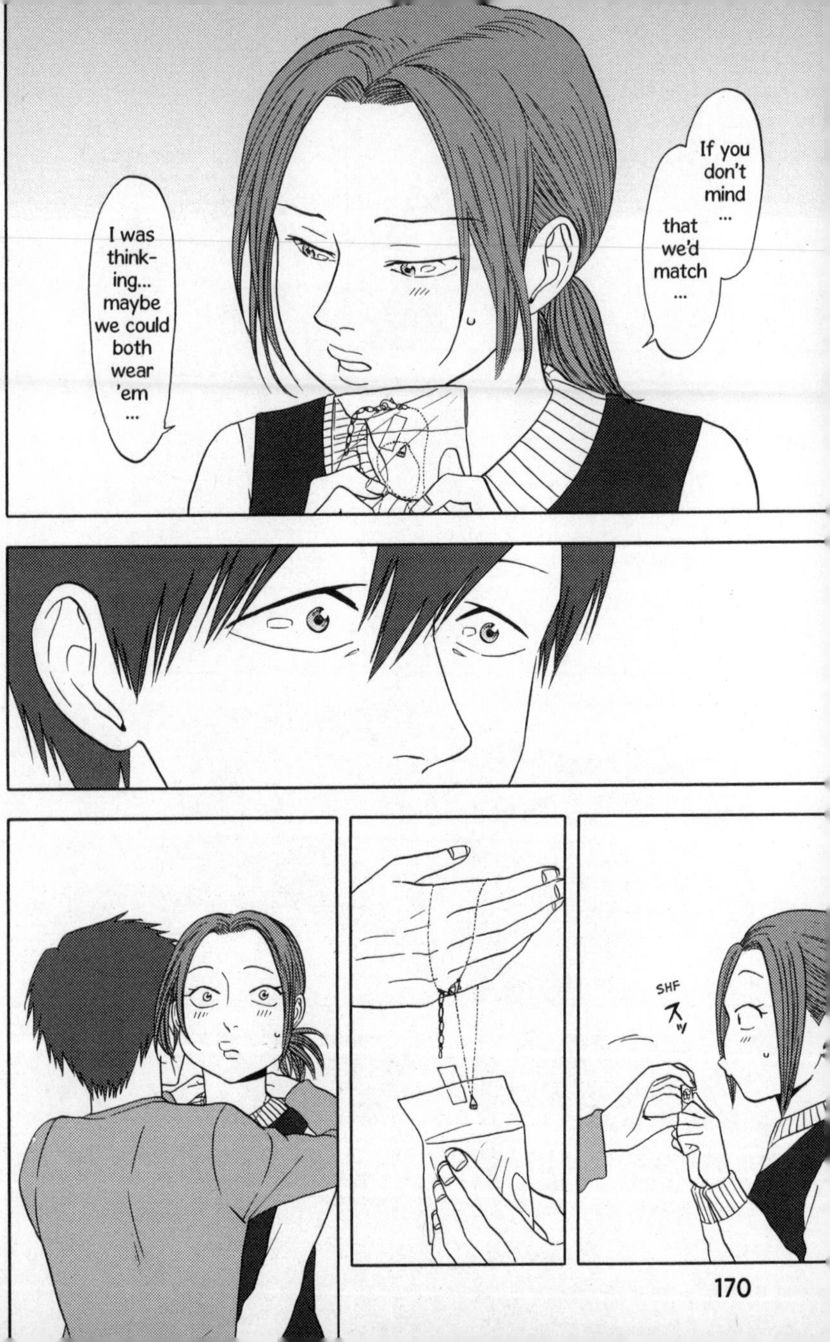
If you don't mind... that we'd match...
I was thinking... maybe we could both wear 'em...
SHF
スッ

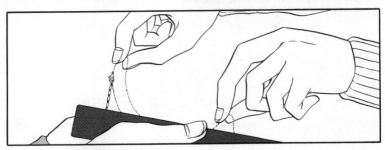

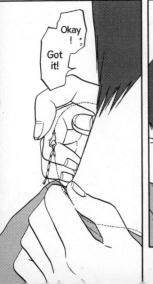

Okay
!?

Got
it!

Whoa
!
Stop it,
dummy
!!

FWOO

?
?
?

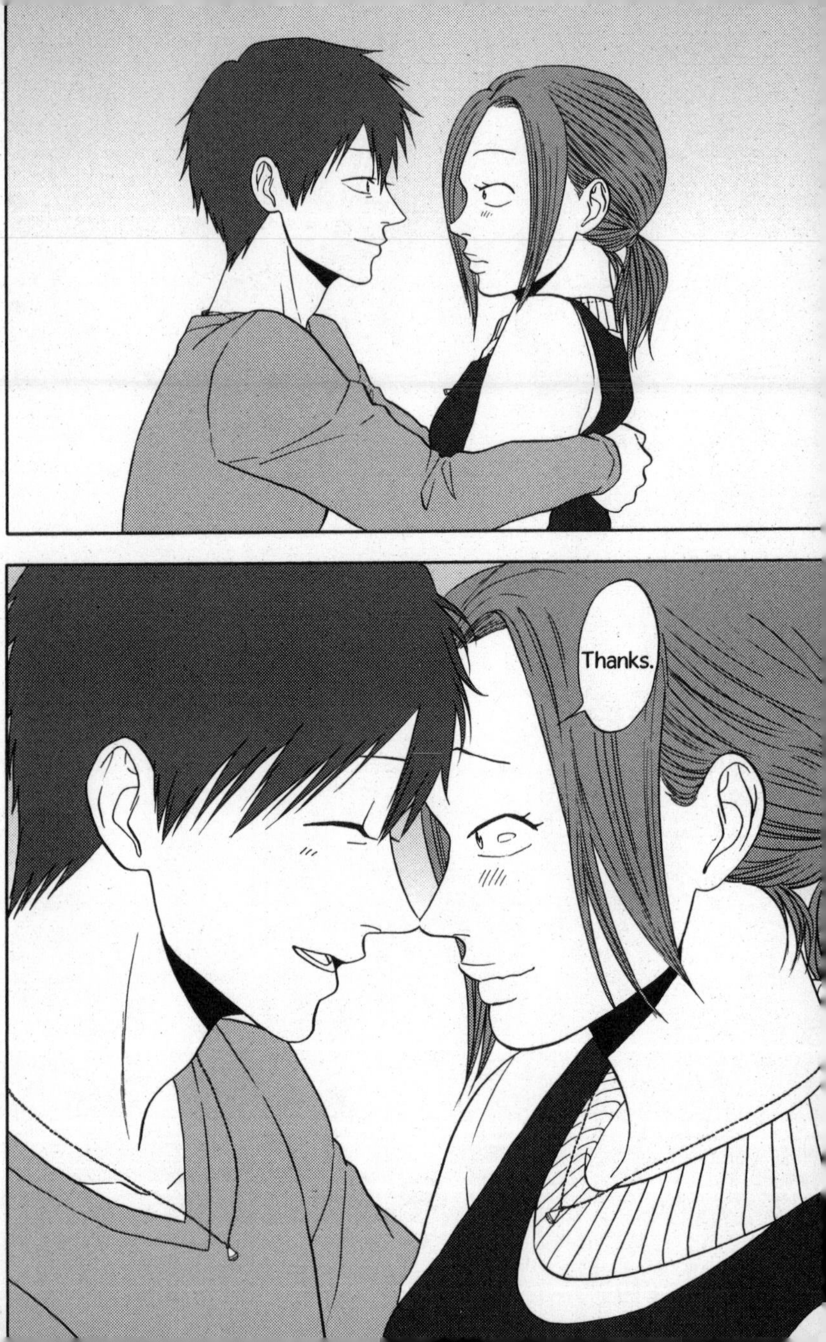

Thanks.

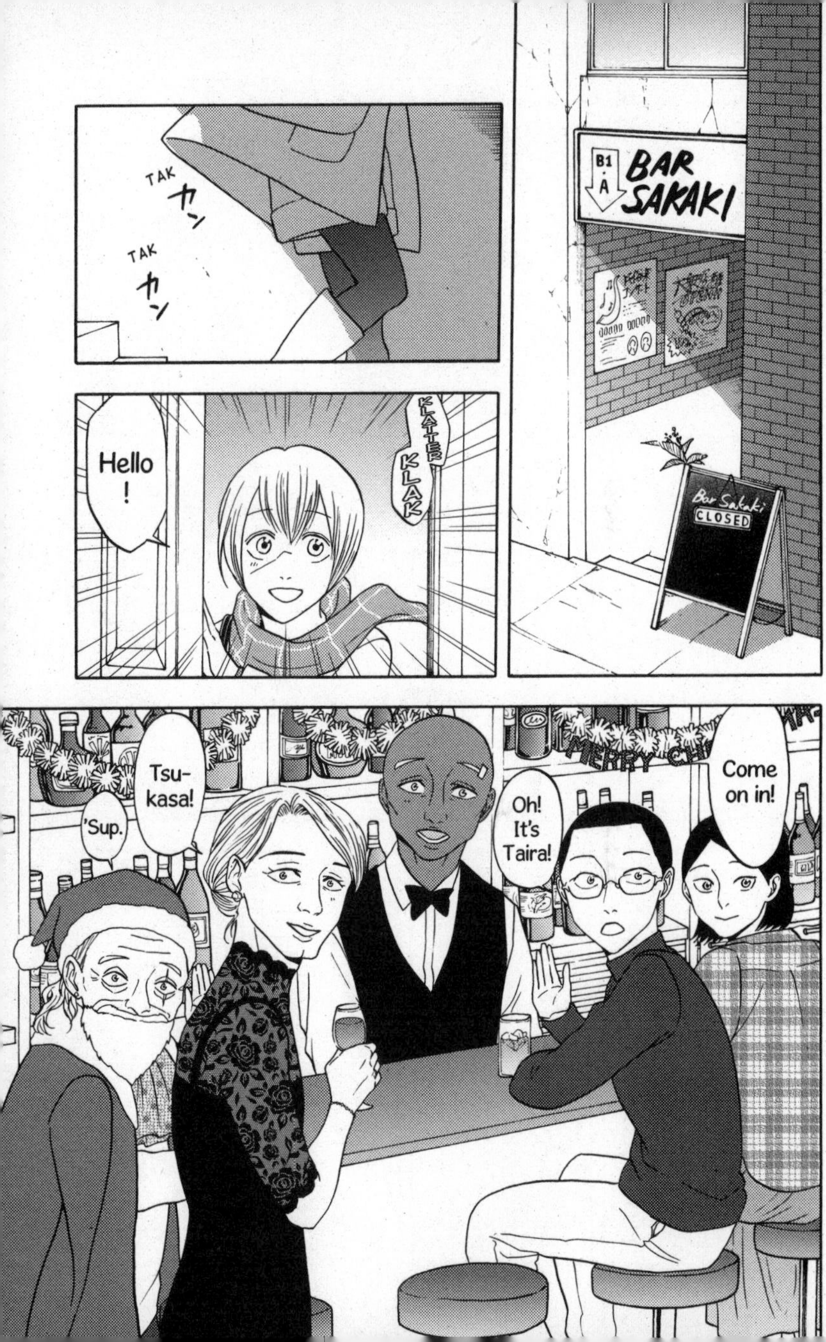

B1
BAR SAKAKI
Bar Sakaki
CLOSED
TAK
カン
TAK
カン
KLATTER KLAK
Hello!
Come on in!
Oh! It's Taira!
Tsu-kasa!
'Sup.

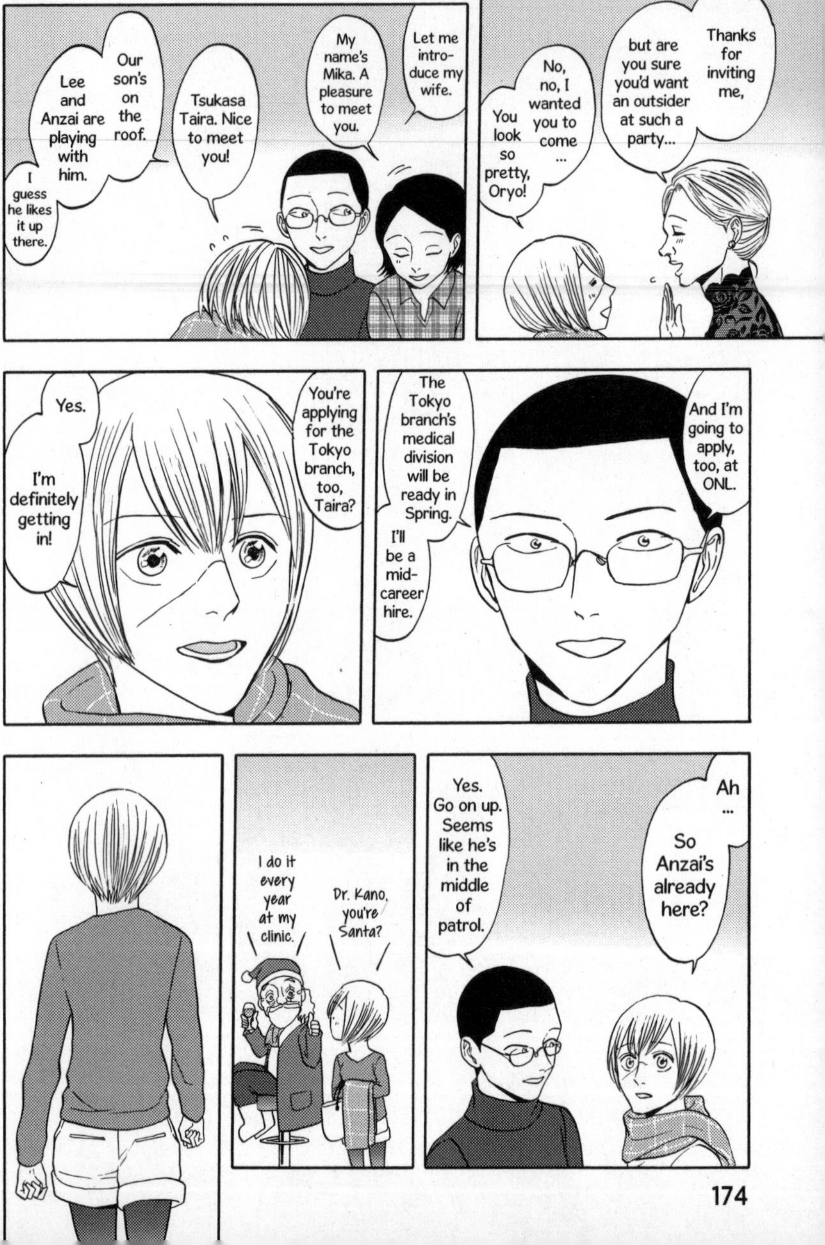
Thanks for inviting me,
but are you sure you'd want an outsider at such a party...
No, no, I wanted you to come ...
You look so pretty, Oryo!
Let me introduce my wife.
My name's Mika. A pleasure to meet you.
Tsukasa Taira. Nice to meet you!
Our son's on the roof.
Lee and Anzai are playing with him.
I guess he likes it up there.
And I'm going to apply, too, at ONL.
The Tokyo branch's medical division will be ready in Spring.
I'll be a mid-career hire.
You're applying for the Tokyo branch, too, Taira?
Yes.
I'm definitely getting in!
Ah ...
So Anzai's already here?
Yes. Go on up. Seems like he's in the middle of patrol.
Dr. Kano, you're Santa?
I do it every year at my clinic.

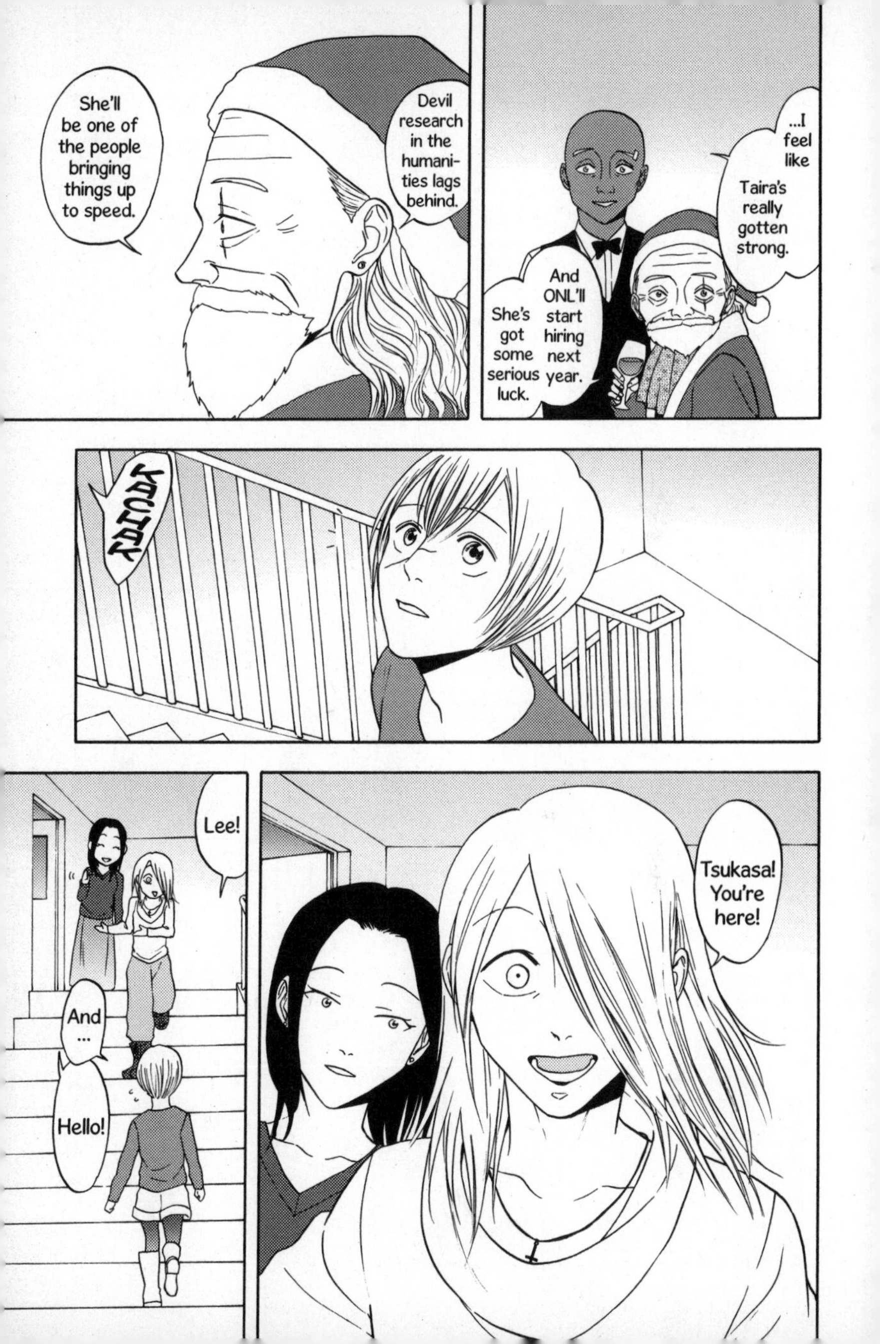
...I feel like Taira's really gotten strong.
And ONL'll start hiring next year.
She's got some serious luck.
Devil research in the humanities lags behind.
She'll be one of the people bringing things up to speed.
KACHAK
Tsukasa! You're here!
Lee!
And ...
Hello!

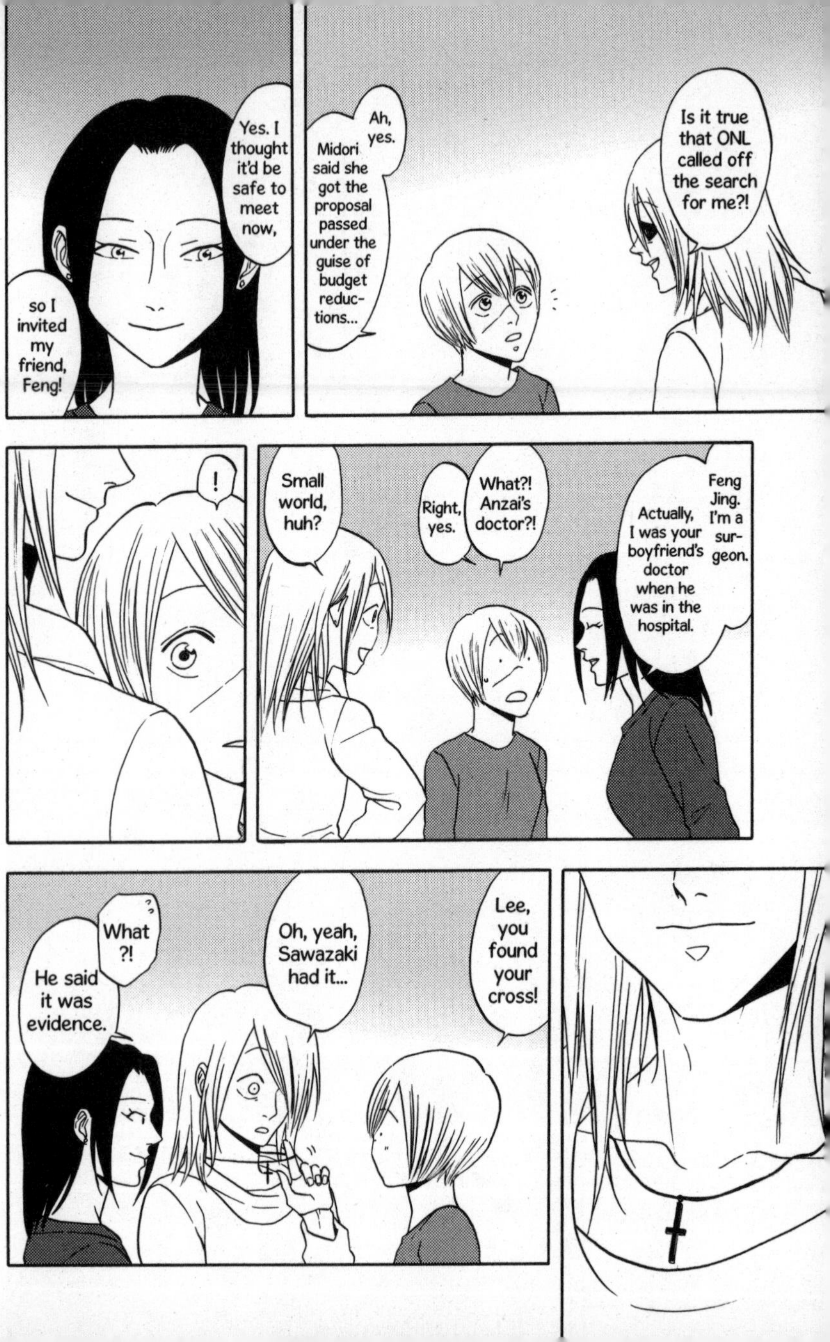
Is it true that ONL called off the search for me?!
Ah, yes.
Midori said she got the proposal passed under the guise of budget reduc-tions...
Yes. I thought it'd be safe to meet now,
so I invited my friend, Feng!
Feng Jing. I'm a sur-geon.
Actually, I was your boyfriend's doctor when he was in the hospital.
What?! Anzai's doctor?!
Right, yes.
Small world, huh?
!
Lee, you found your cross!
Oh, yeah, Sawazaki had it...
What ?!
He said it was evidence.

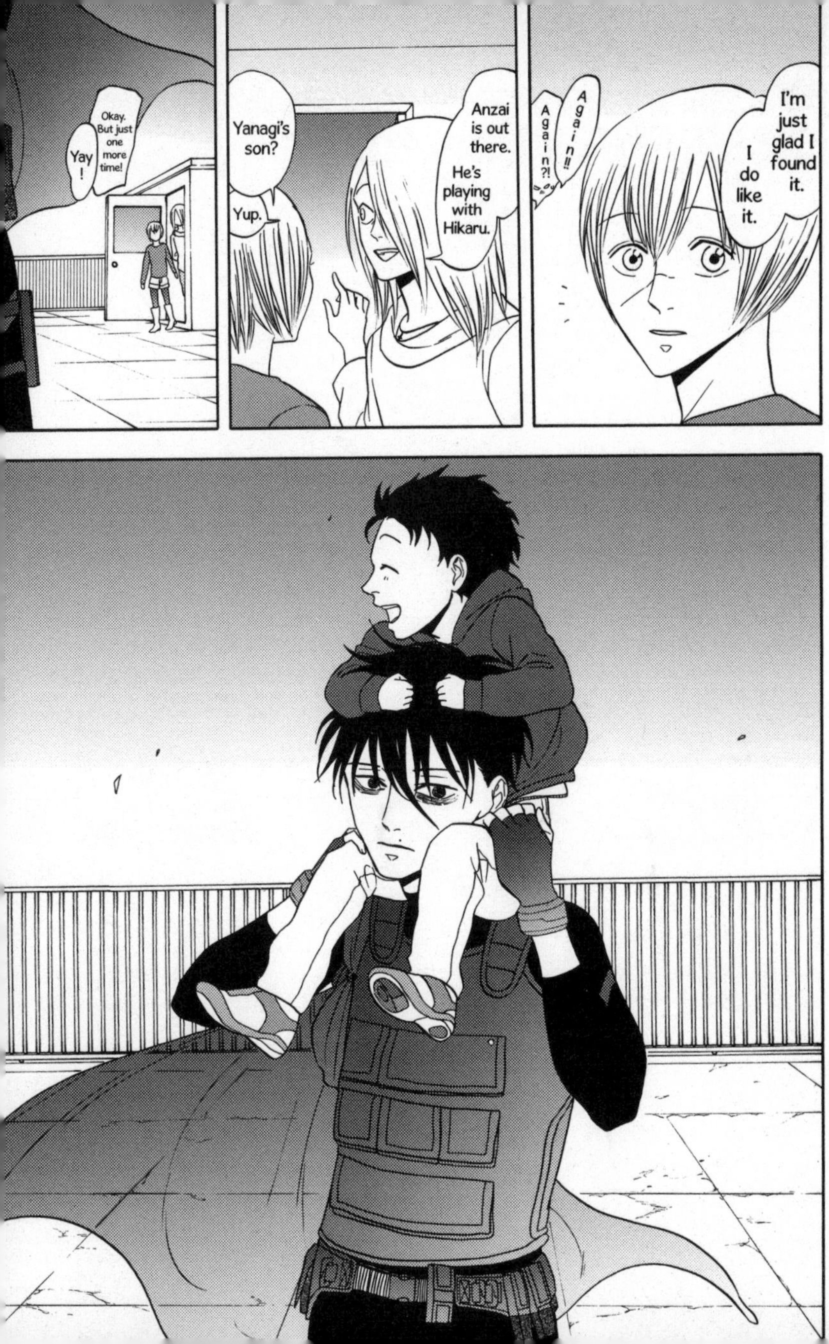

I'm just glad I found it.
I do like it.
Again!!
Again?!
Anzai is out there.
He's playing with Hikaru.
Yanagi's son?
Yup.
Okay. But just one more time!
Yay!

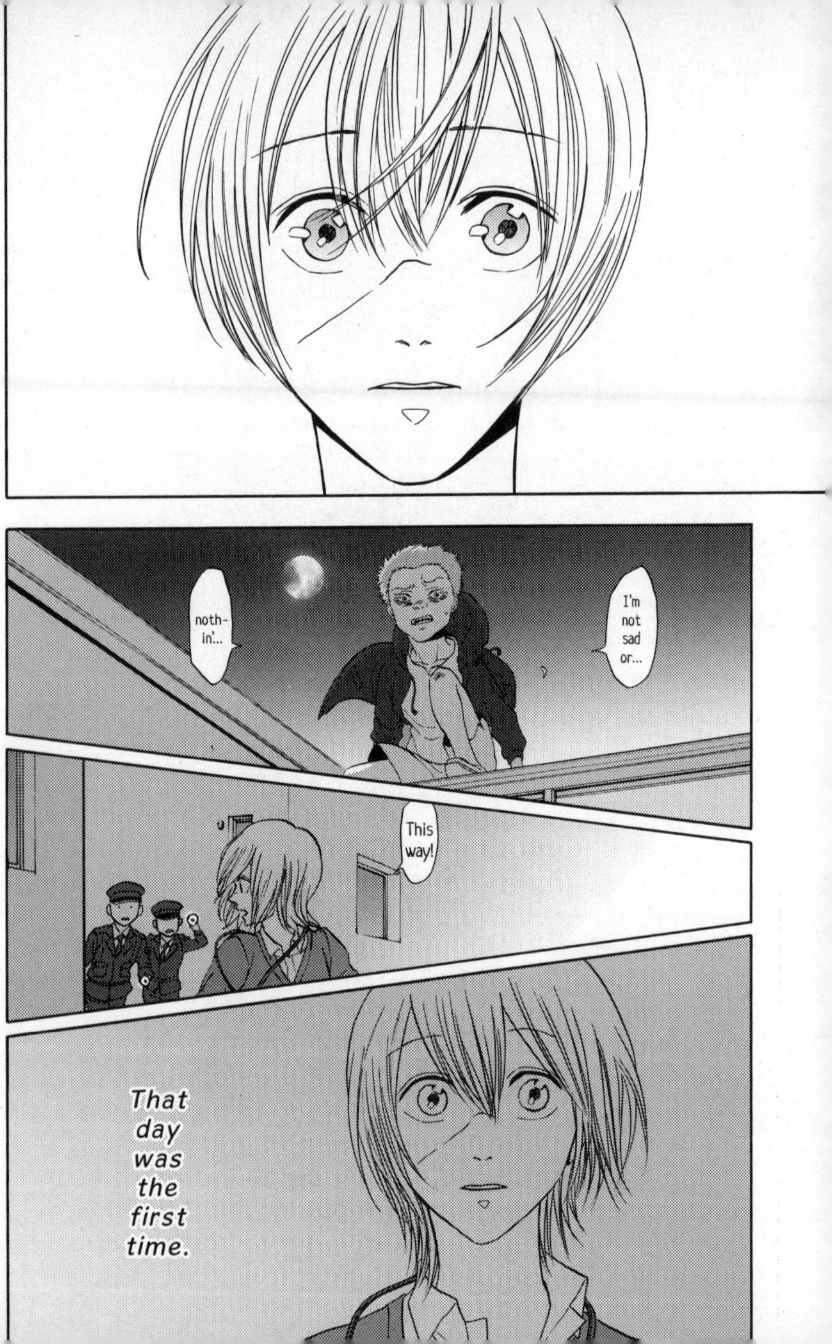
I'm not sad or...
noth-in'...
This way!
That day was the first time.

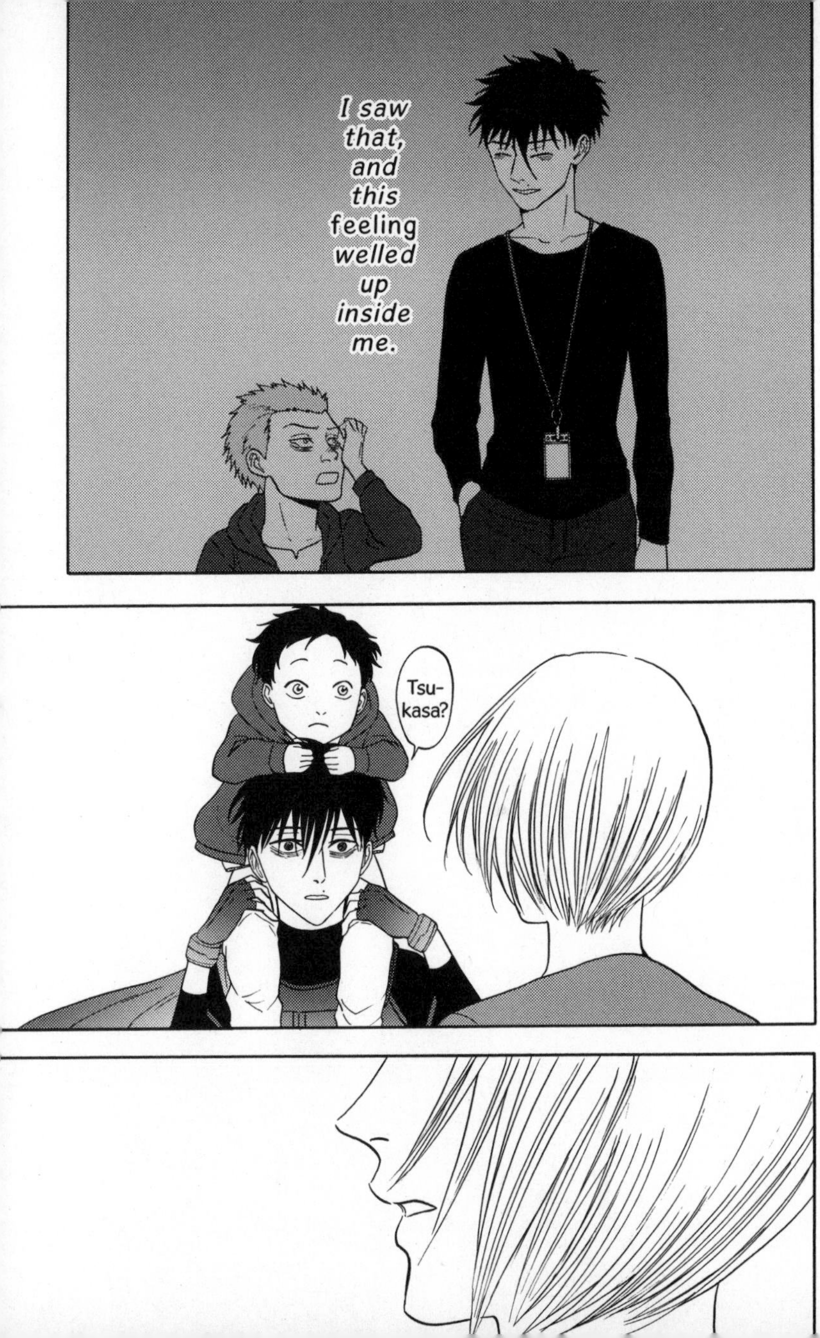
I saw that, and this feeling welled up inside me.
Tsu-kasa?

Will
you

come
to

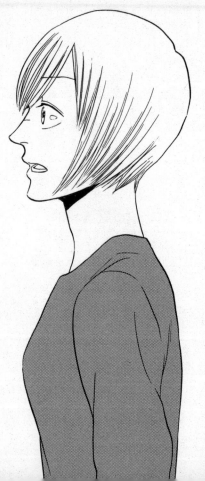

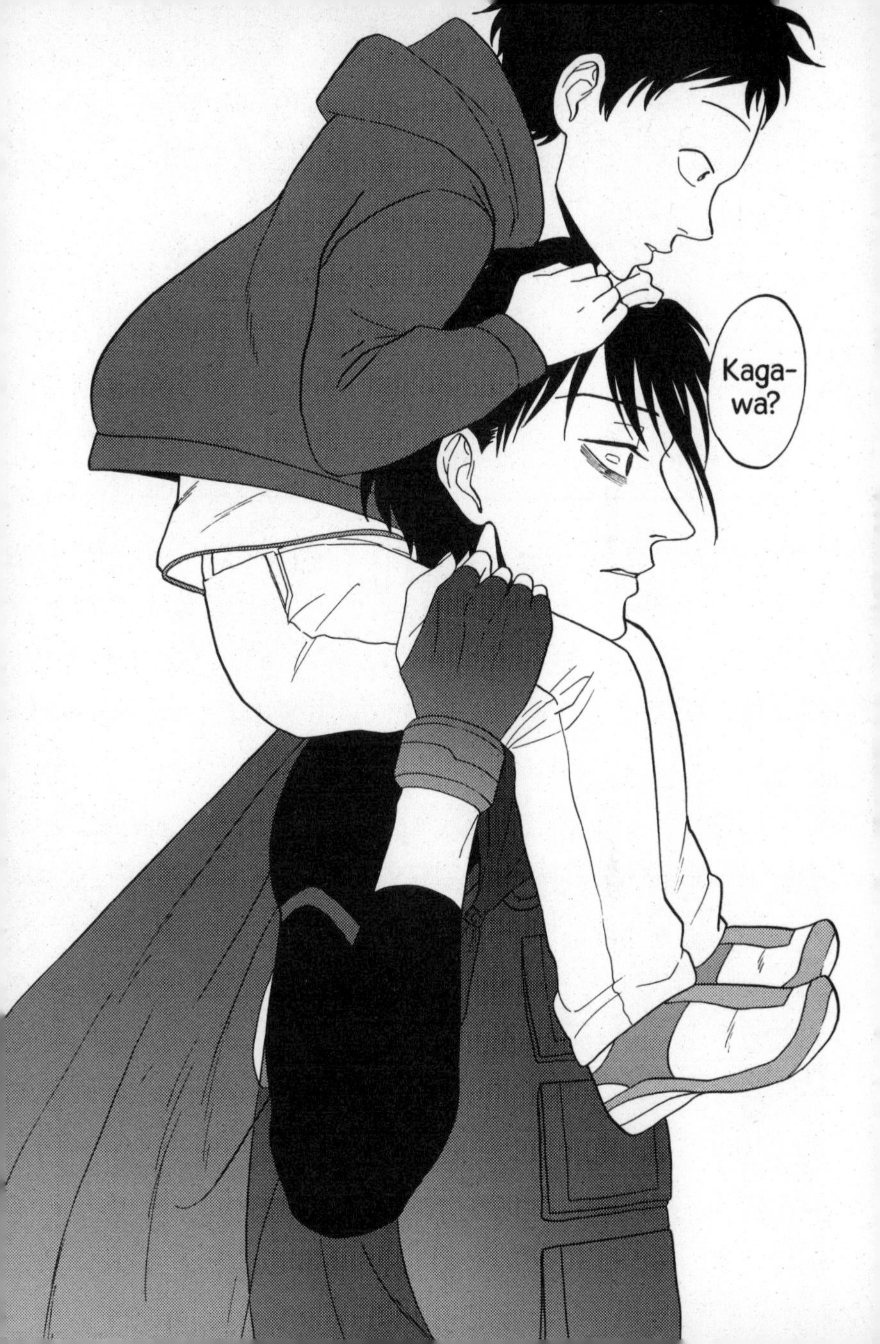
Kaga-
wa?

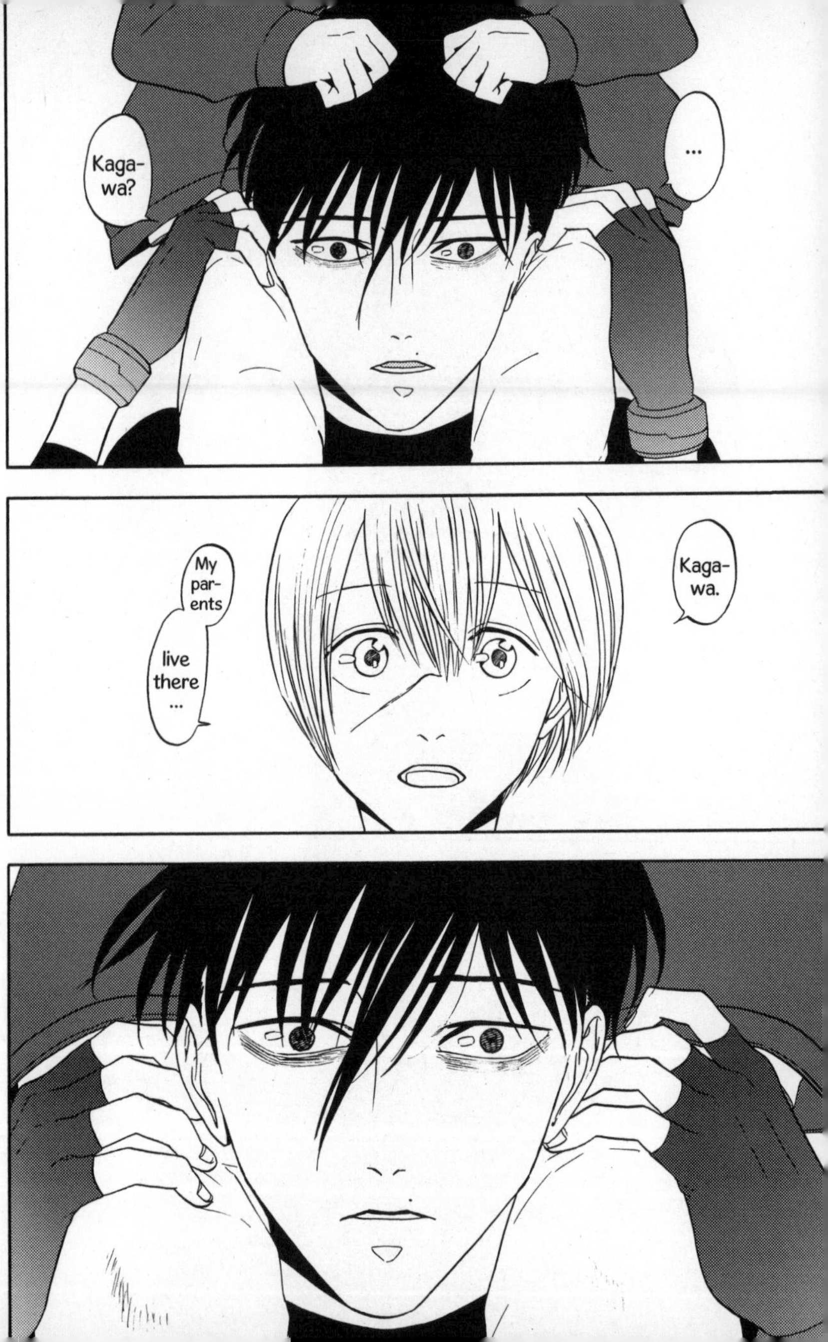
...
Kaga-wa?
Kaga-wa.
My par-ents
live there ...

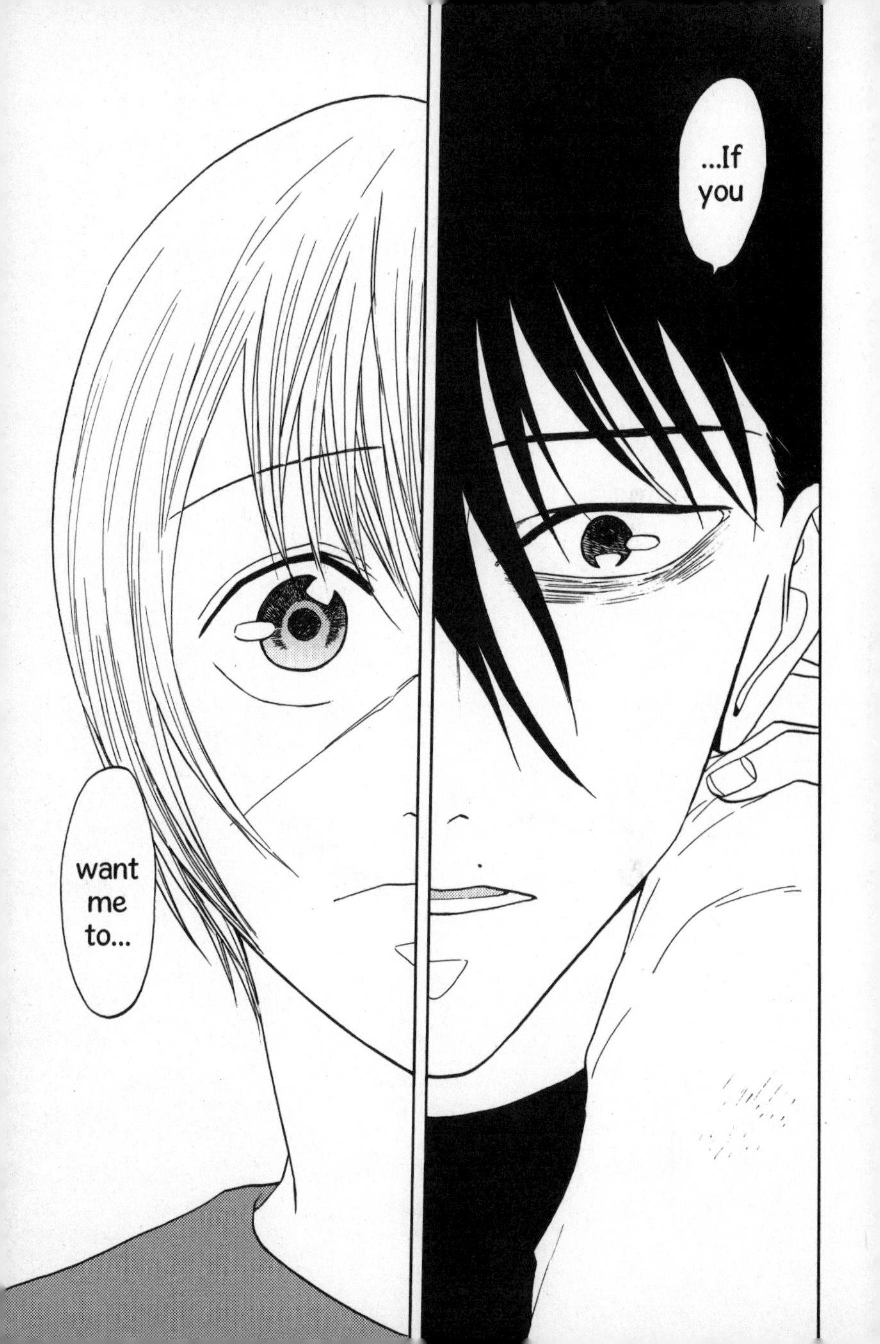
...If you
want me to...

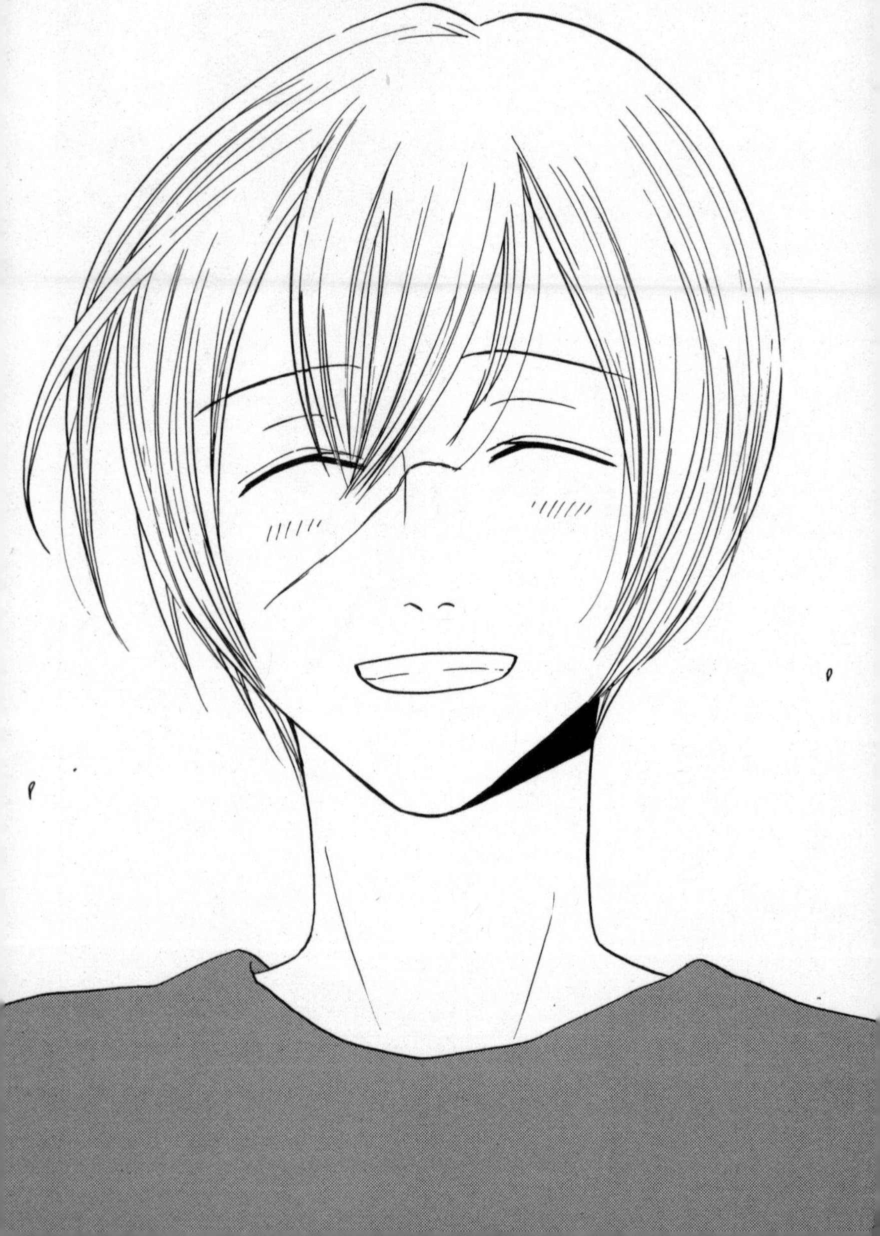

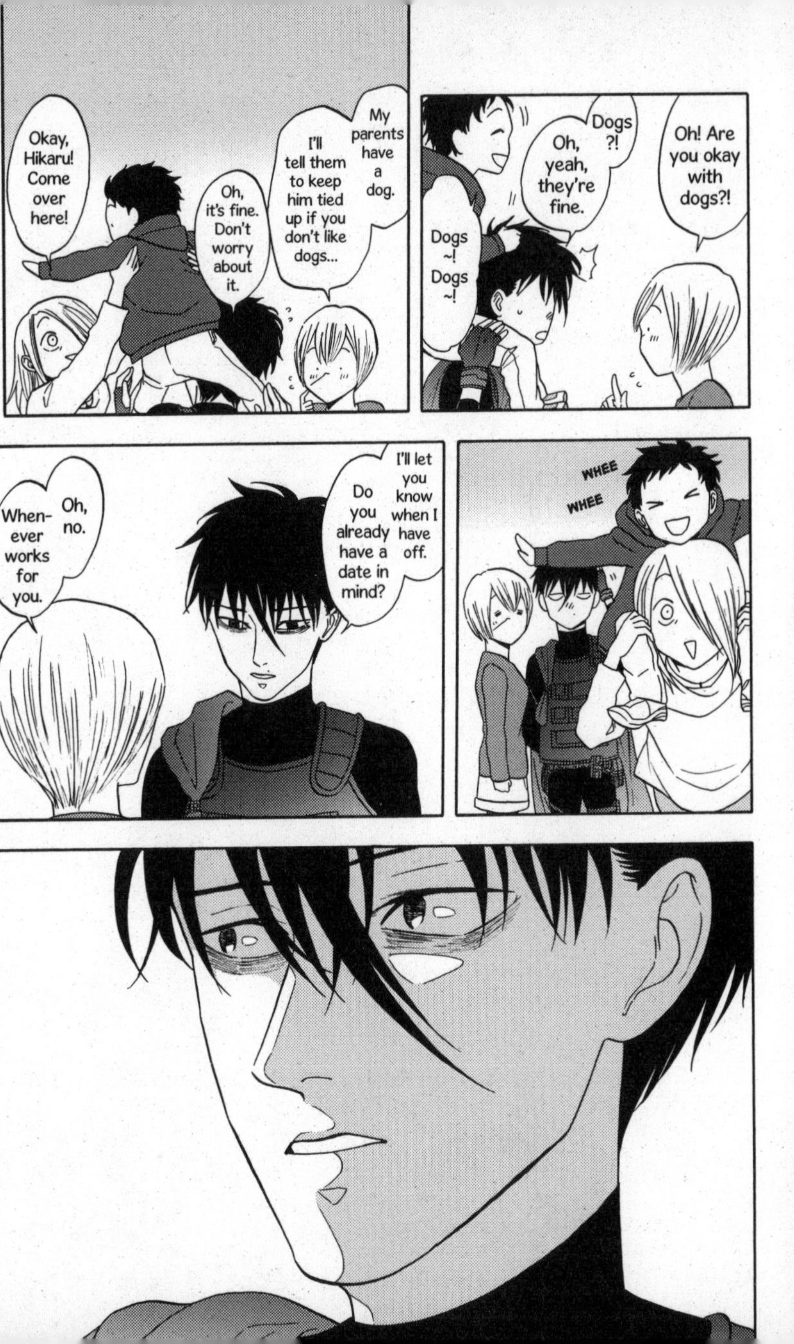
Oh! Are you okay with dogs?!
Dogs?!
Oh, yeah, they're fine.
Dogs~! Dogs~!
My parents have a dog.
I'll tell them to keep him tied up if you don't like dogs...
Oh, it's fine. Don't worry about it.
Okay, Hikaru! Come over here!
WHEE
WHEE
I'll let you know when I have off.
Do you already have a date in mind?
Oh, no.
When-ever works for you.

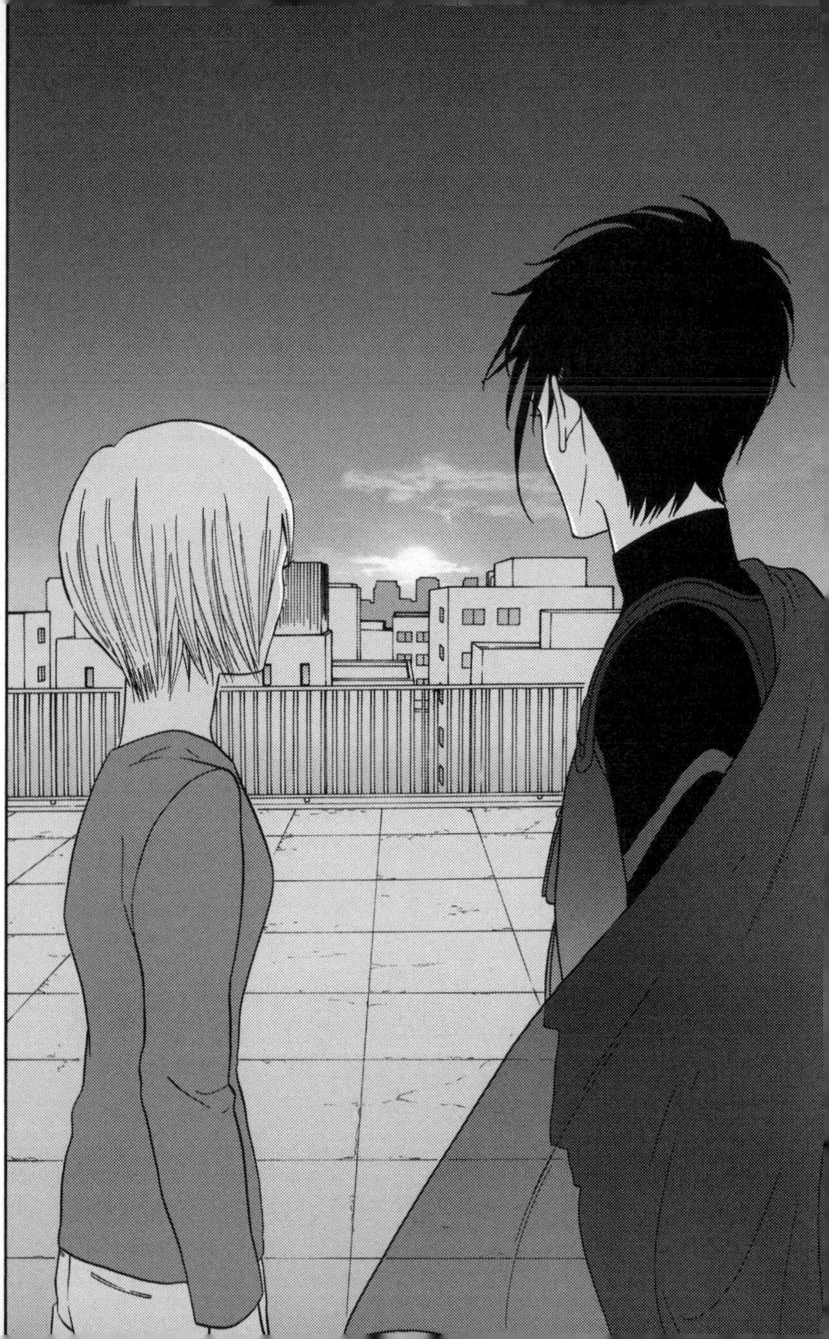

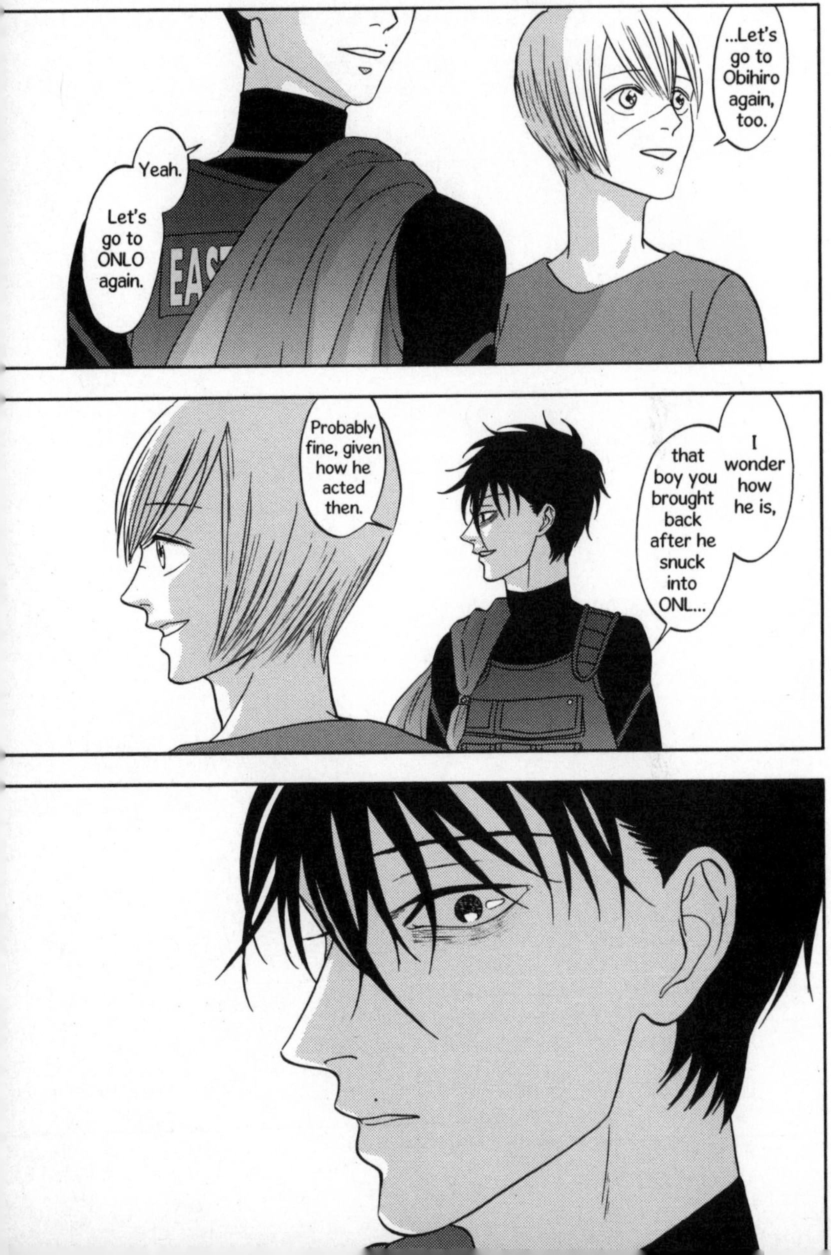
...Let's go to Obihiro again, too.
Yeah.
Let's go to ONLO again.
I wonder how he is,
that boy you brought back after he snuck into ONL...
Probably fine, given how he acted then.

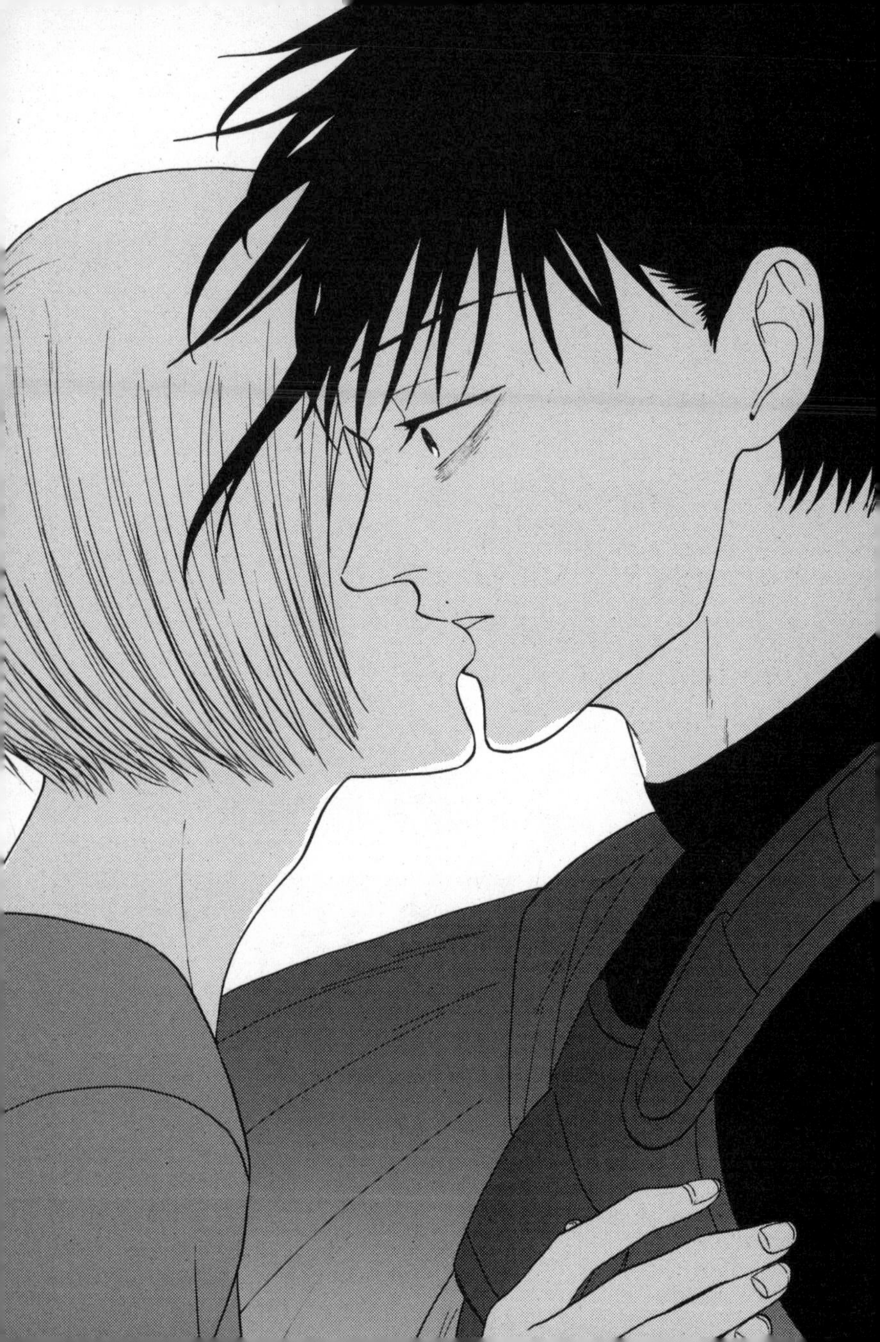

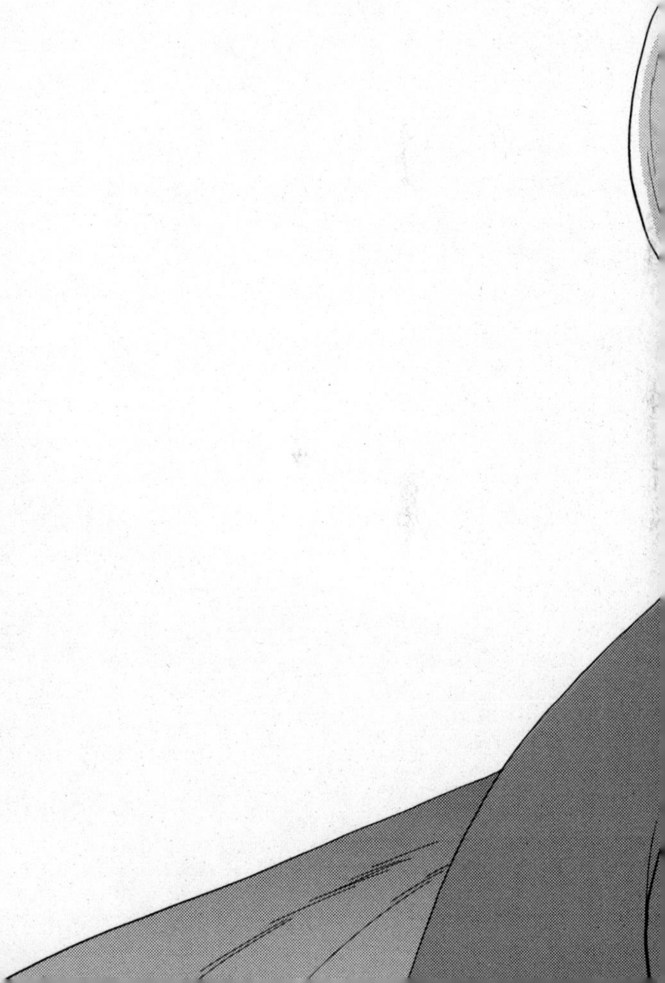

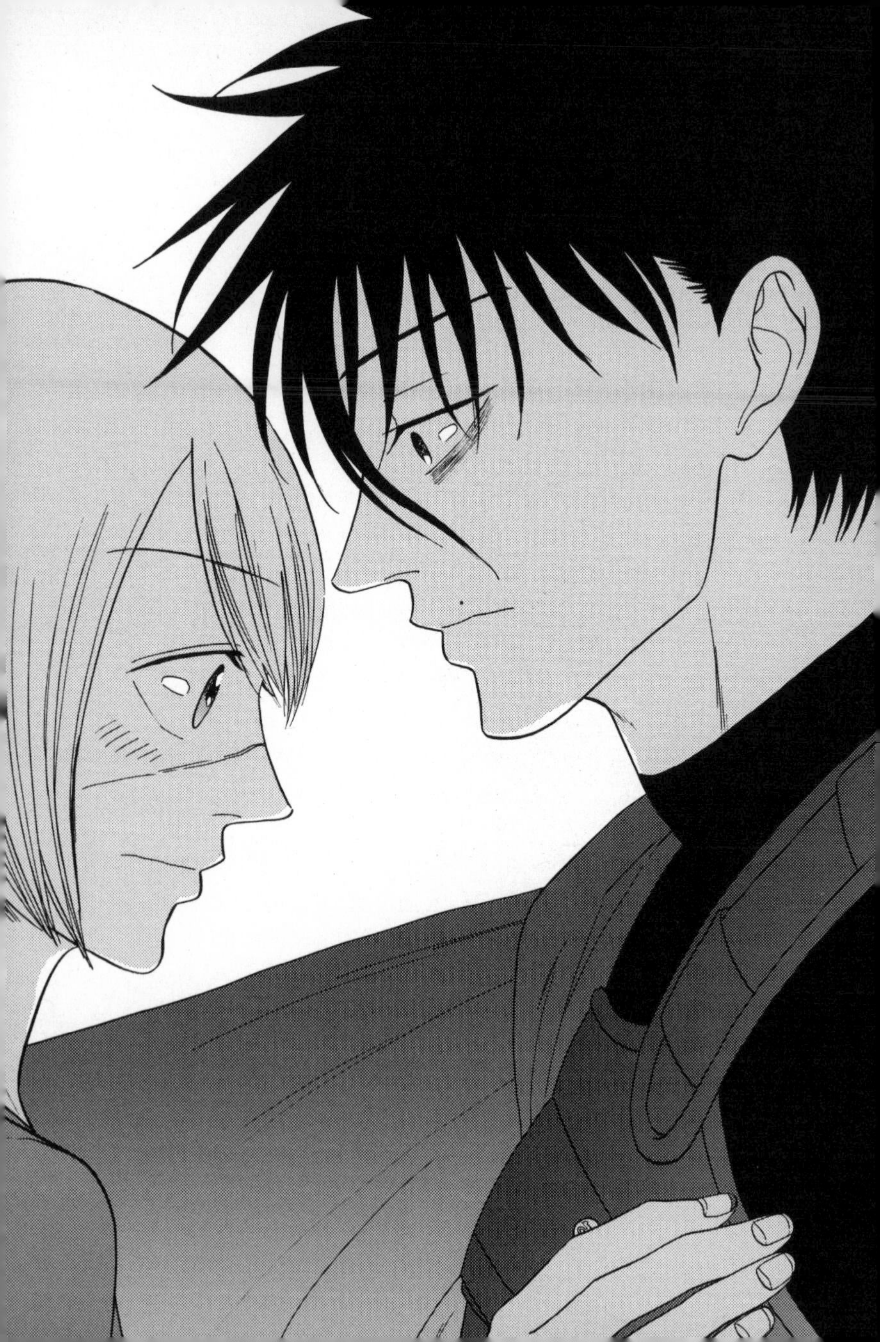

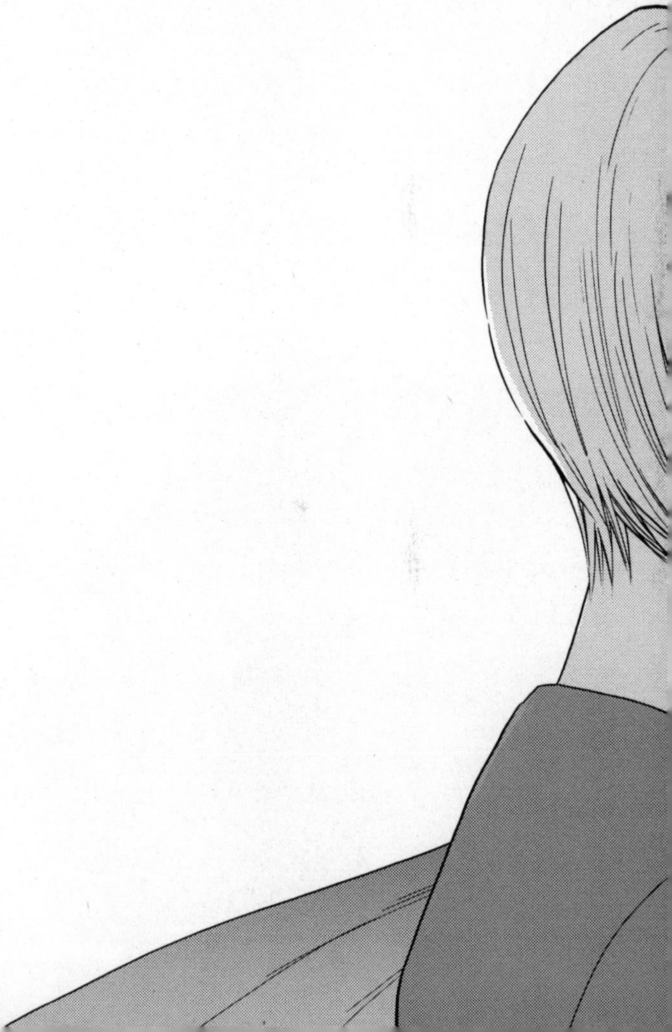

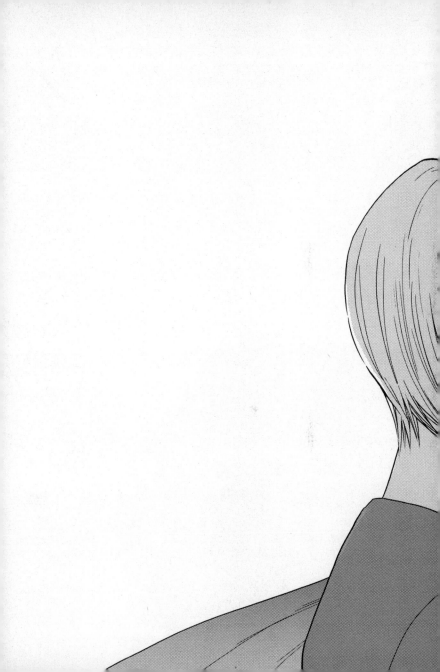

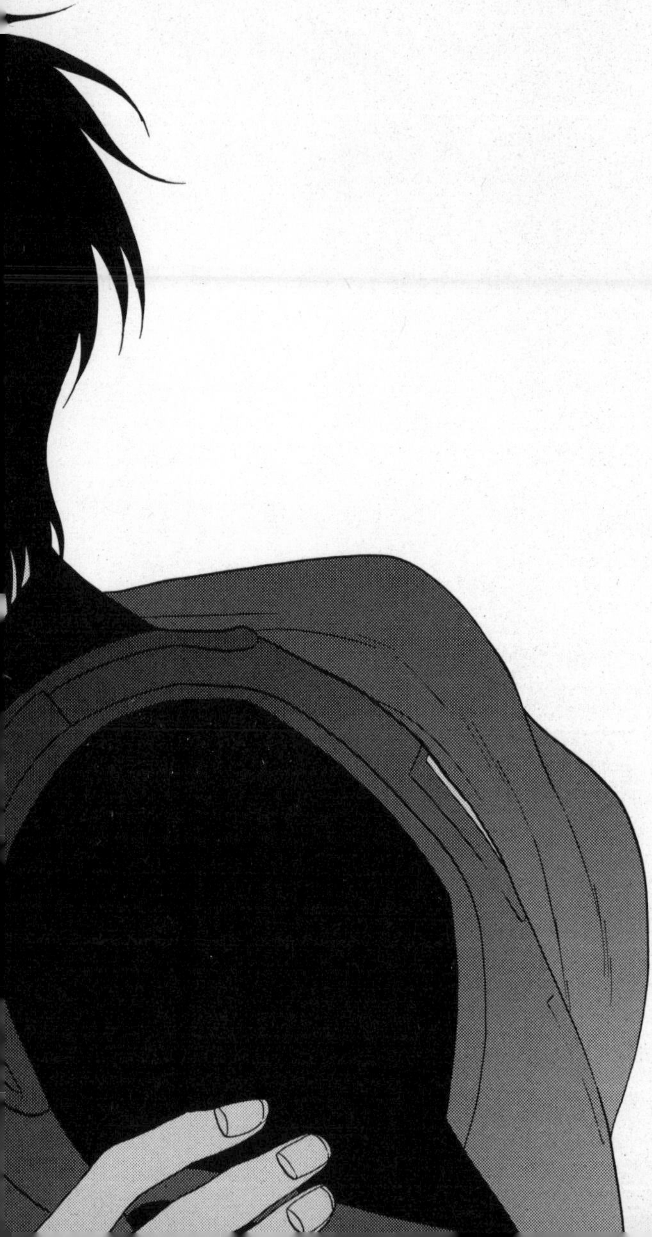

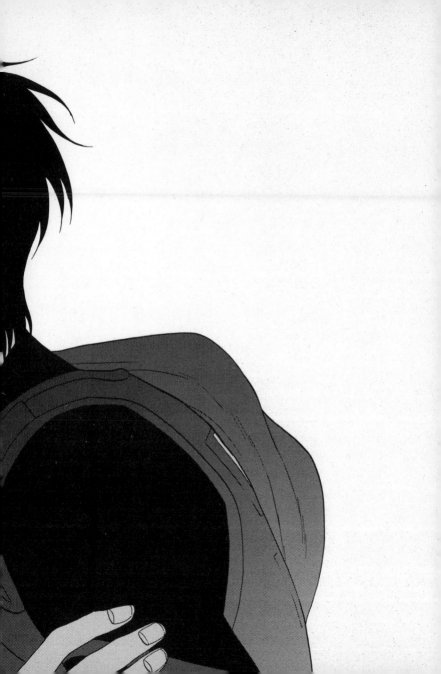

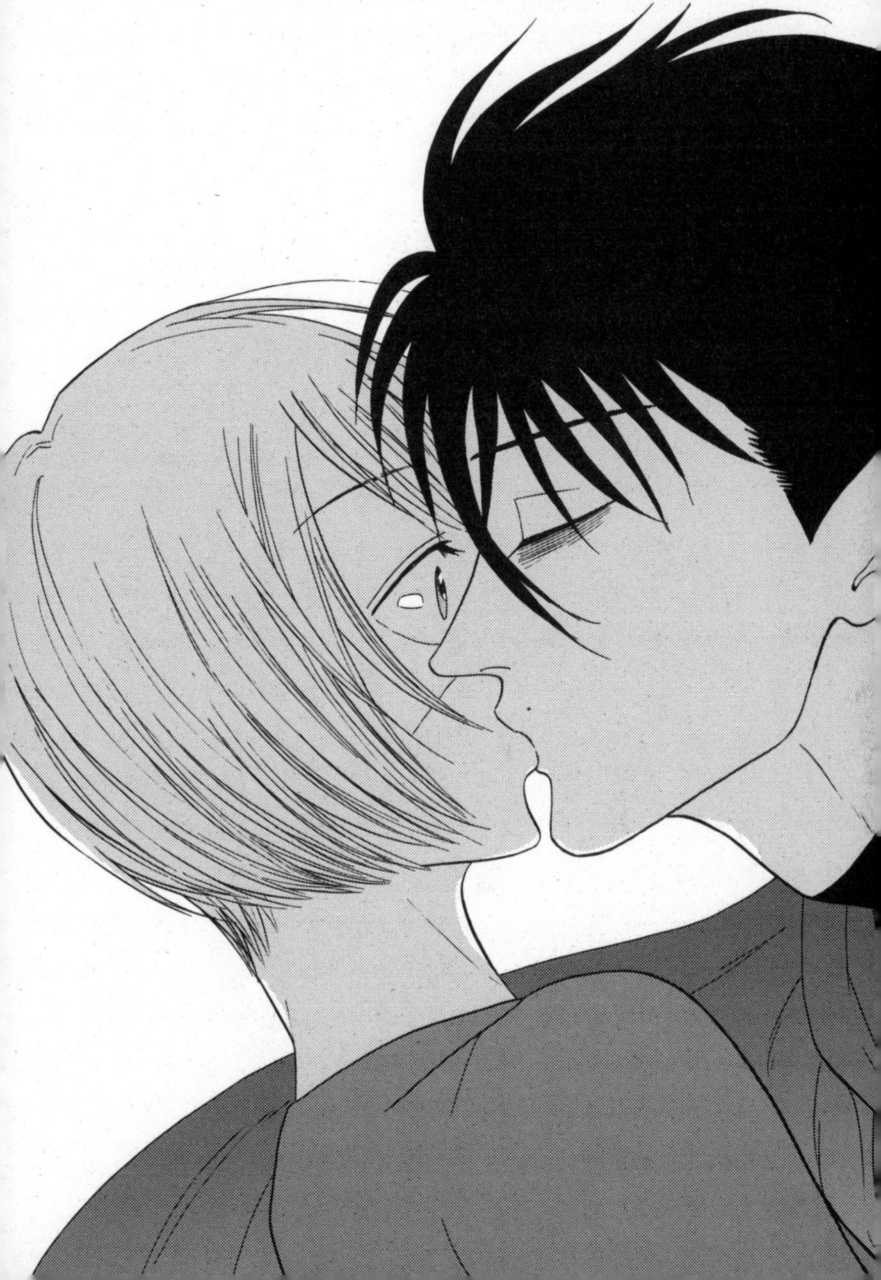

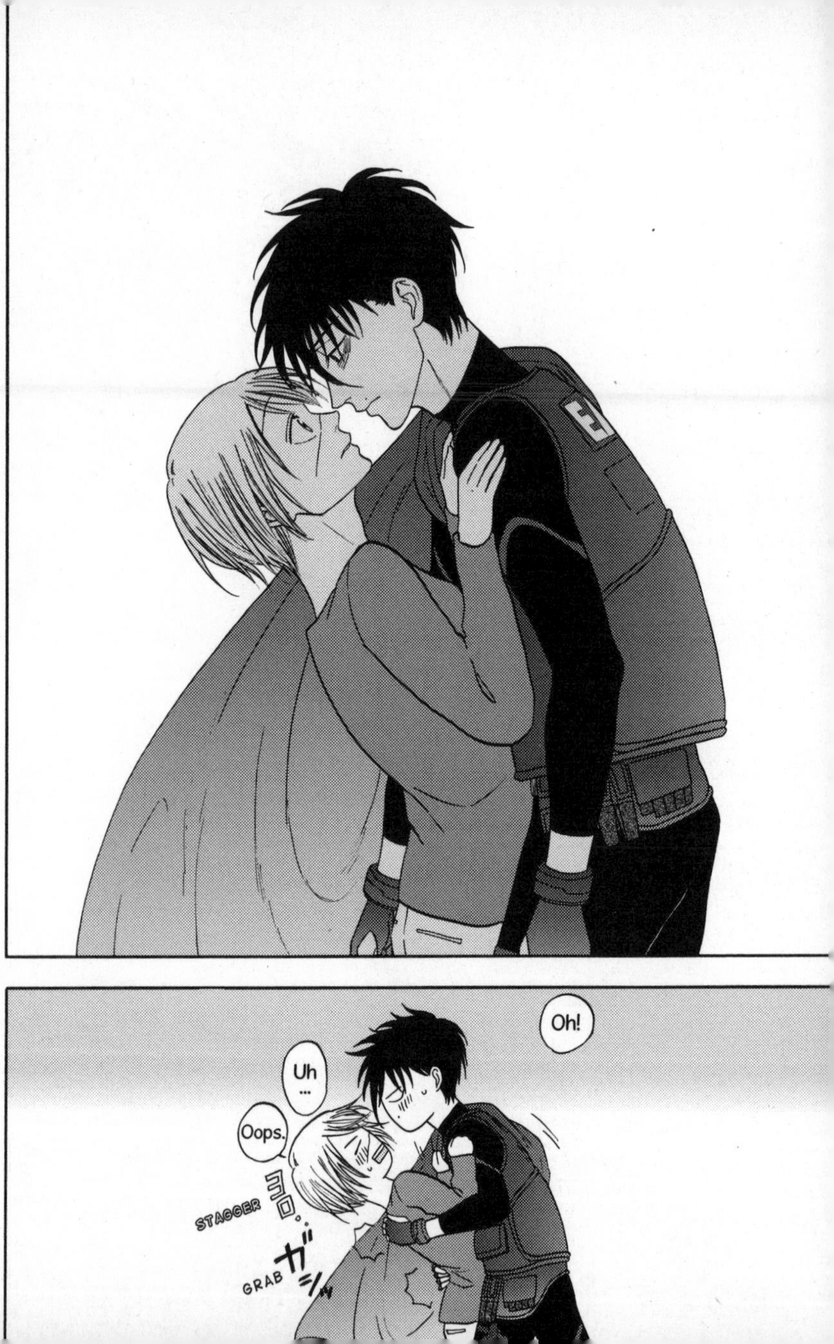
Oh!
Uh ...
Oops.
STAGGER
ヨロ
GRAB
ガシ

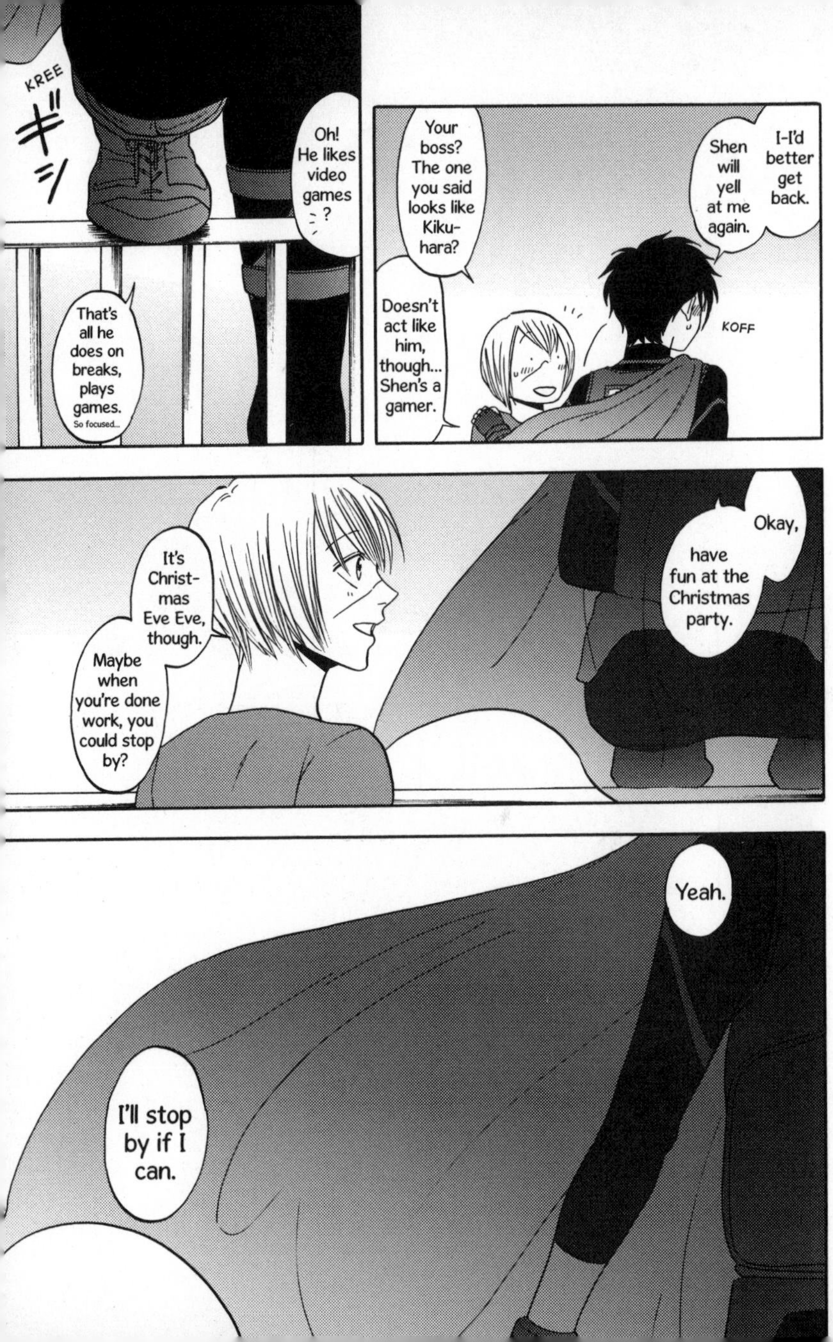
I-I'd better get back.
Shen will yell at me again.
KOFF
Your boss? The one you said looks like Kiku-hara?
Doesn't act like him, though... Shen's a gamer.
Oh! He likes video games ?
KREE
ギシ
That's all he does on breaks, plays games.
So focused...
Okay, have fun at the Christmas party.
It's Christmas Eve Eve, though.
Maybe when you're done work, you could stop by?
Yeah.
I'll stop by if I can.

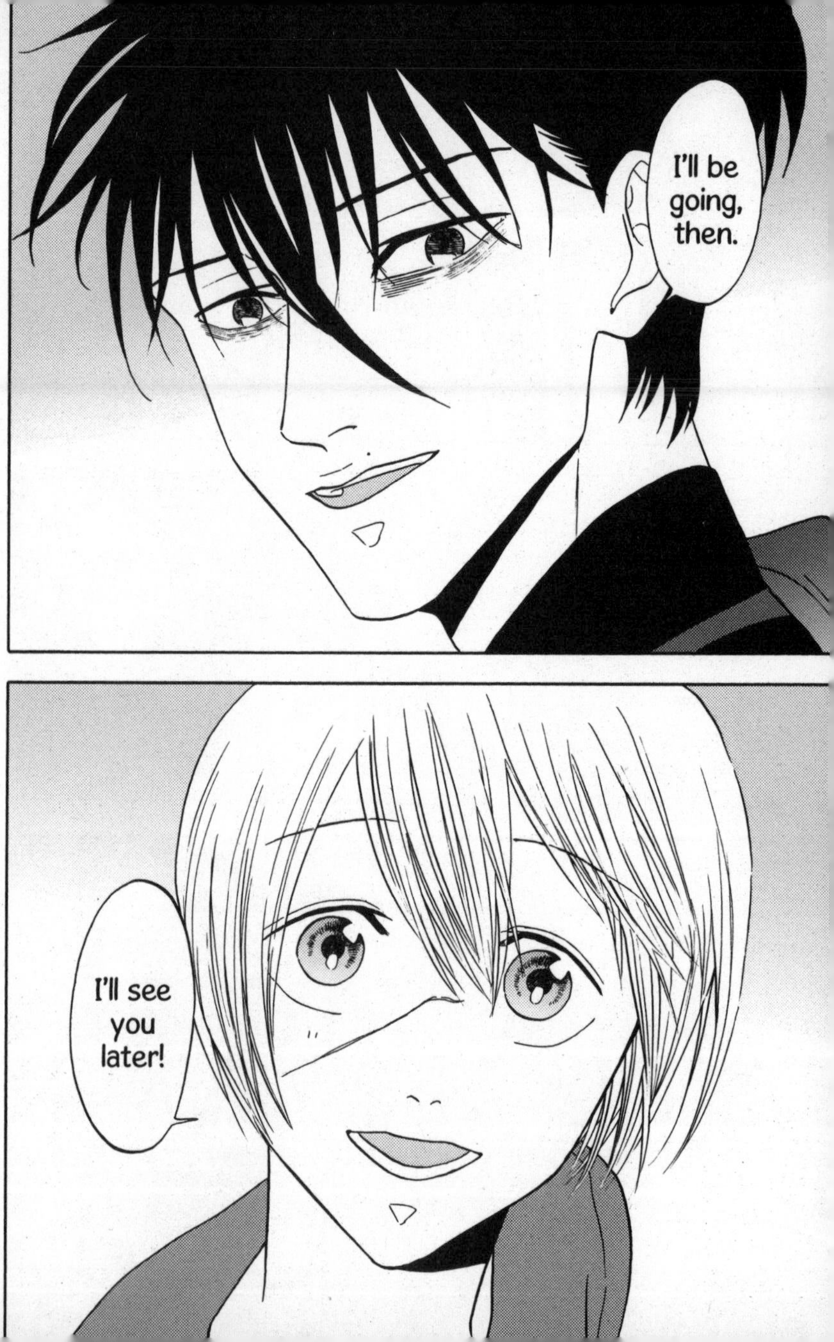
I'll be going, then.
I'll see you later!

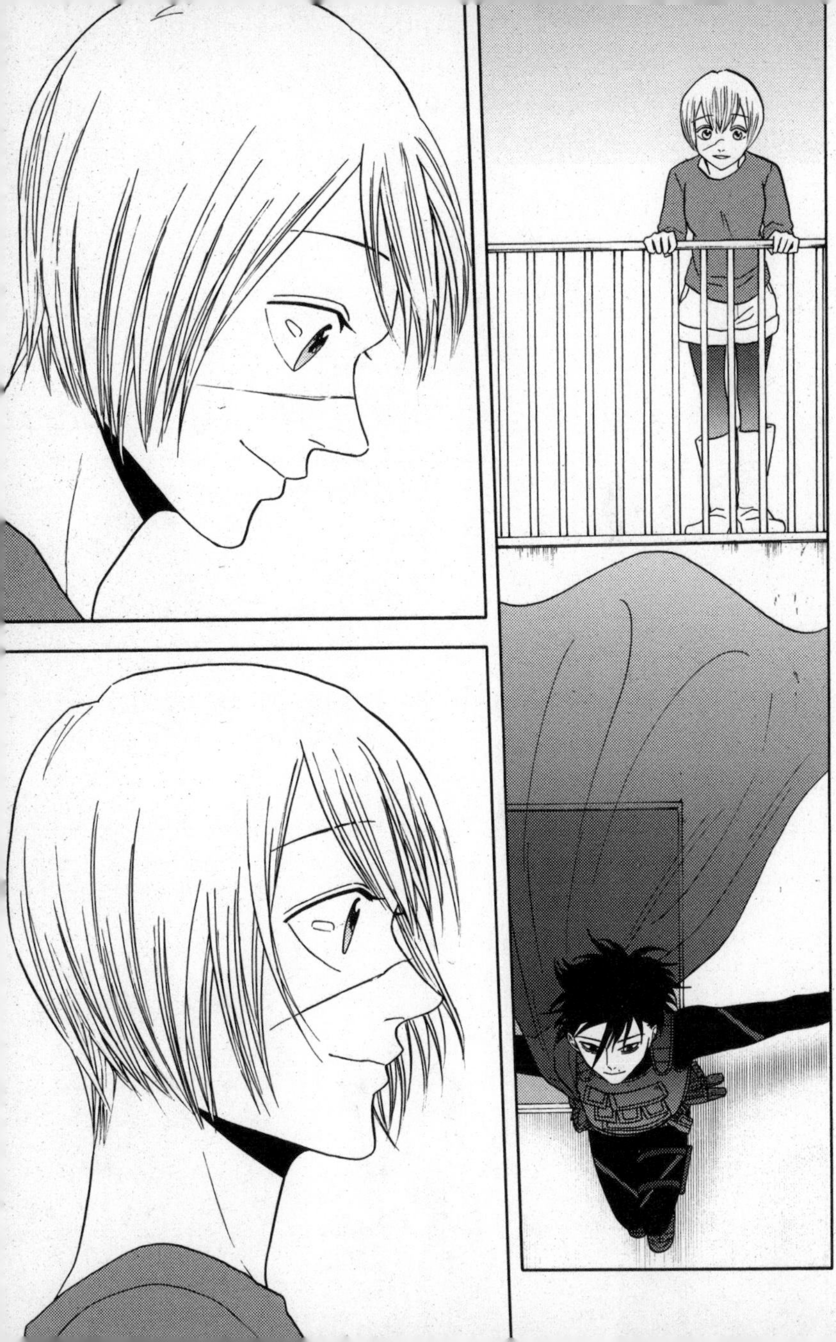

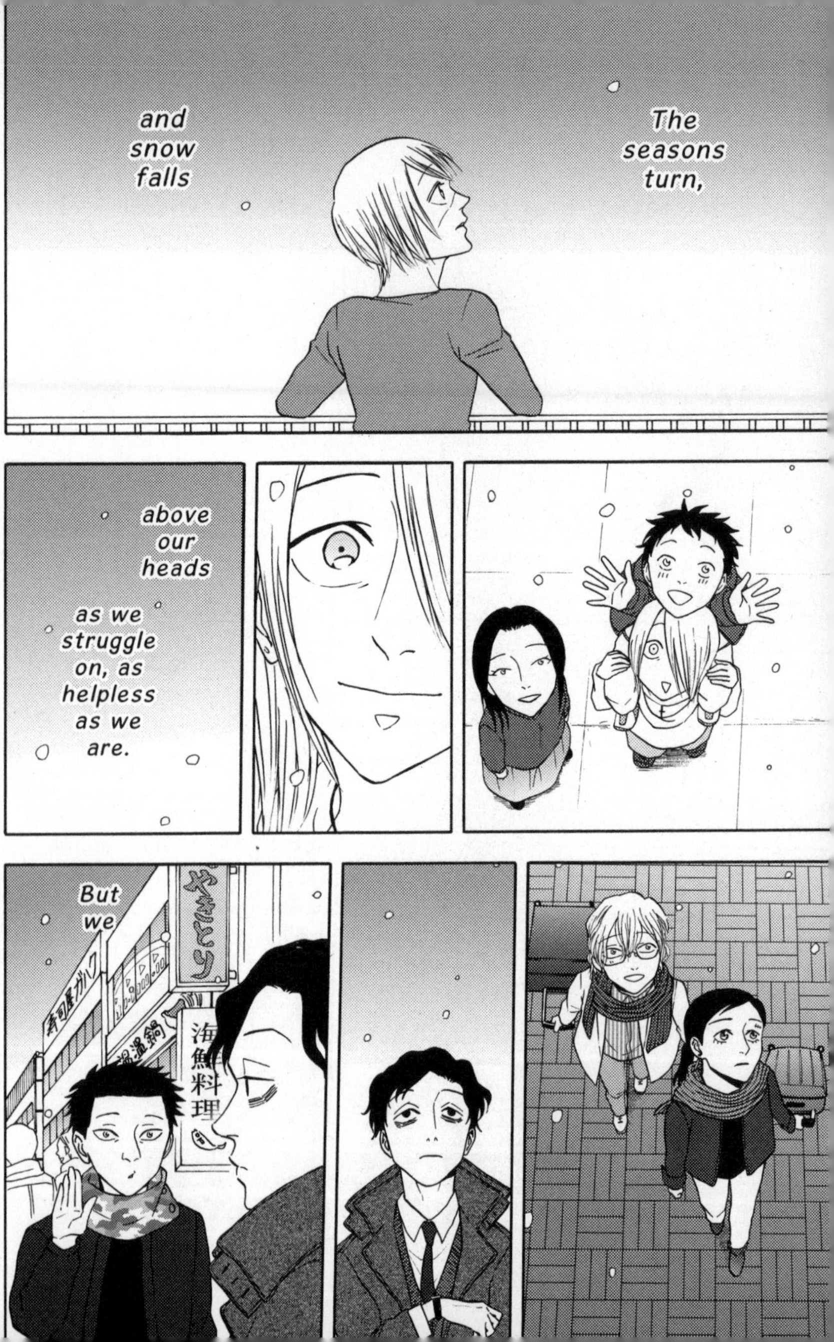

The seasons turn,
and snow falls
above our heads
as we struggle on, as helpless as we are.
やきとり
海鮮料理
But we

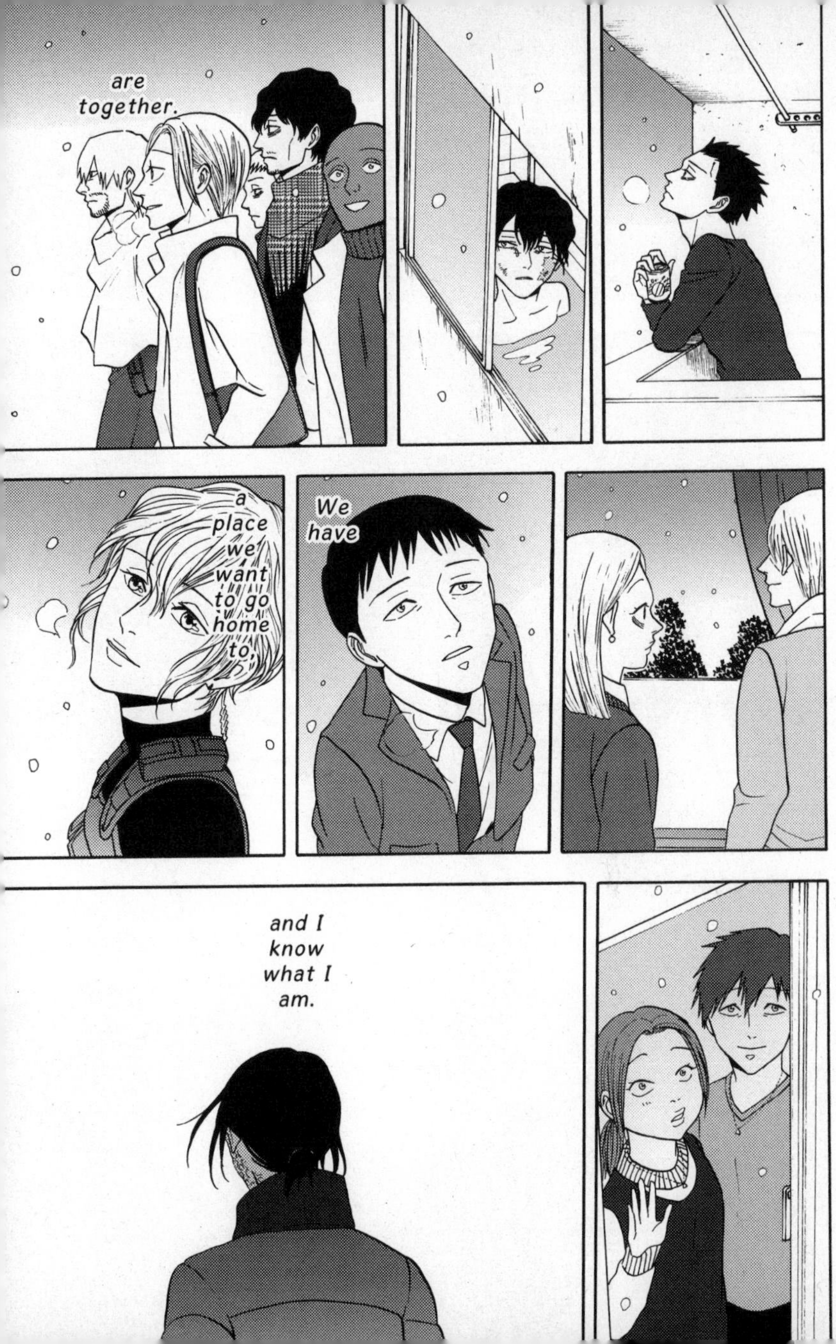
are together.
We have
a place we want to go home to,
and I know what I am.

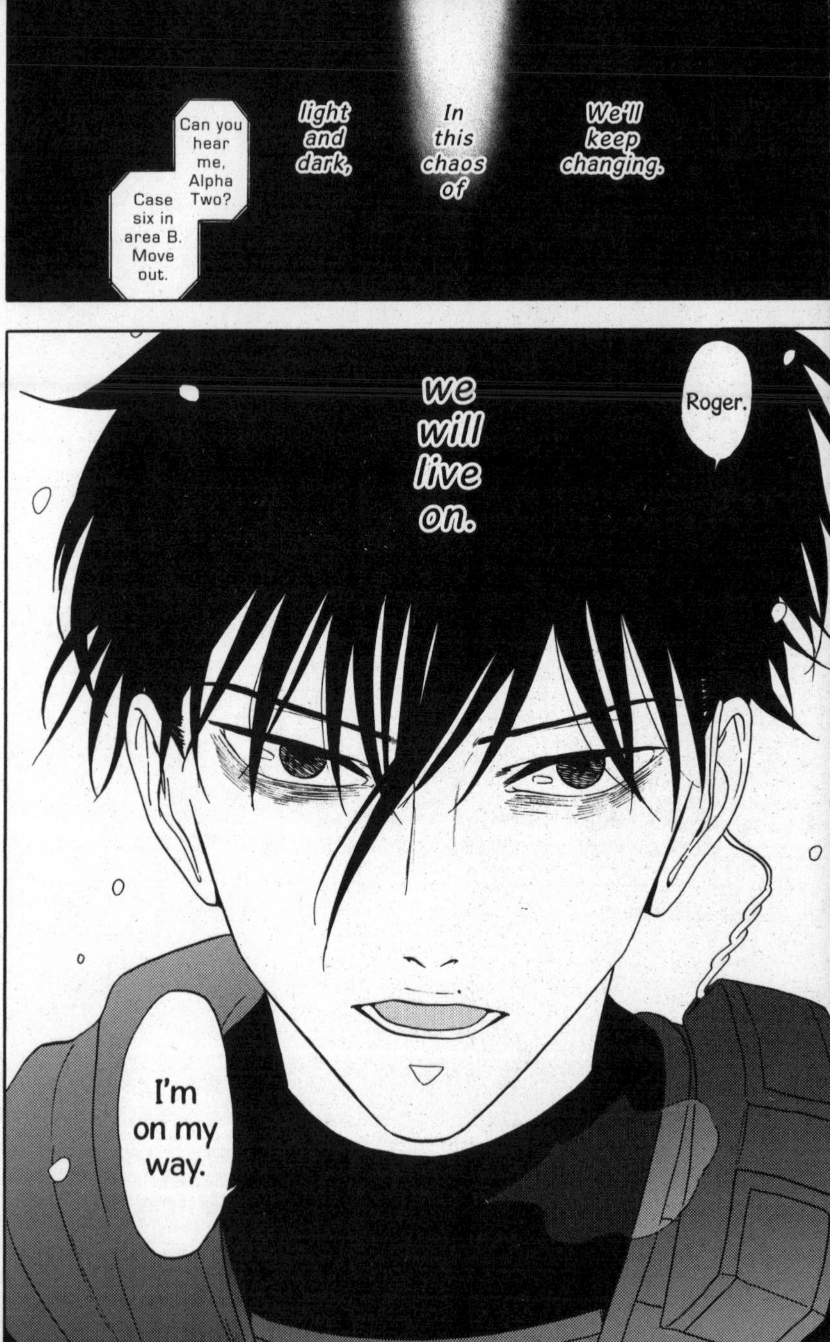

We'll keep changing.
In this chaos of
light and dark,
Can you hear me, Alpha Two?
Case six in area B. Move out.
Roger.
we will live on.
I'm on my way.

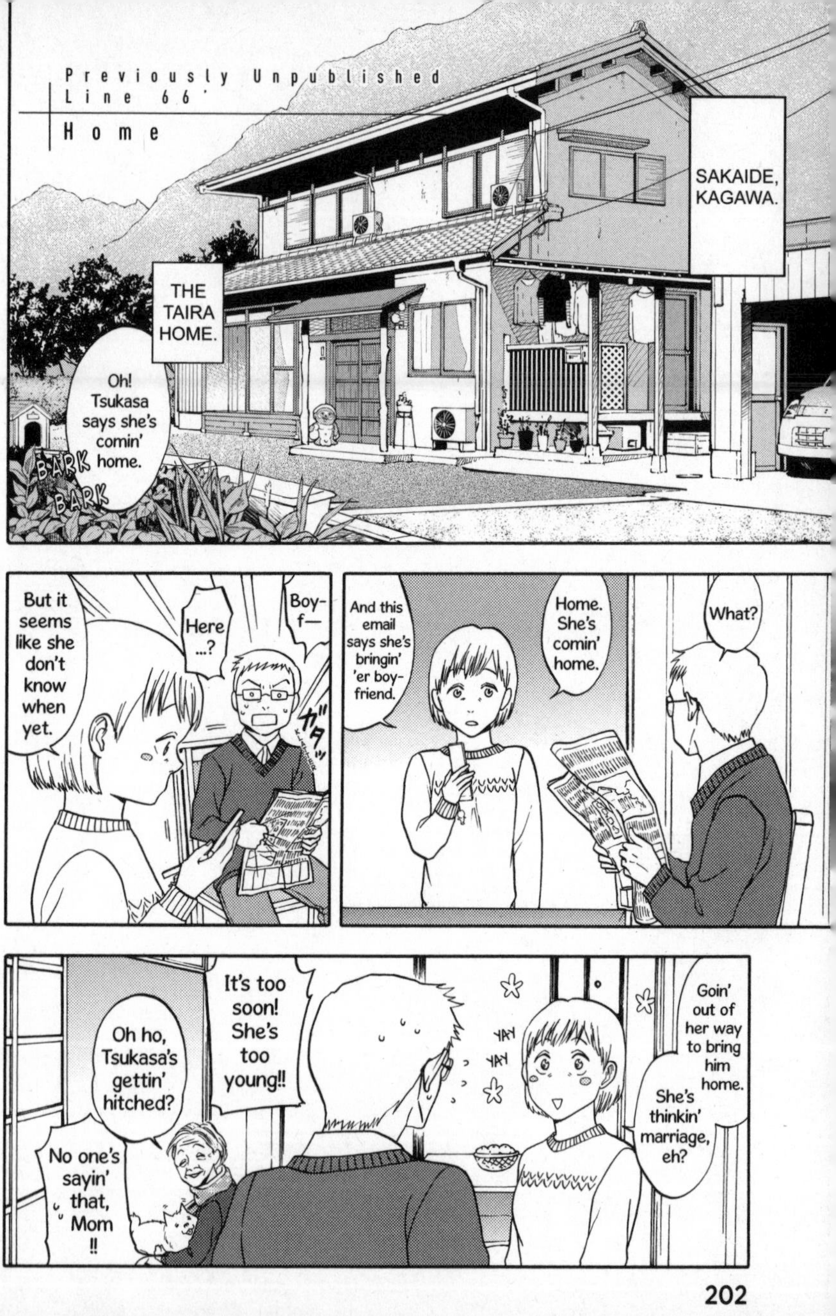
Previously Unpublished
Line 66
Home
SAKAIDE, KAGAWA.
THE TAIRA HOME.
Oh! Tsukasa says she's comin' home.
BARK BARK
What?
Home. She's comin' home.
And this email says she's bringin' 'er boyfriend.
Boy-f—
ガタッ
Here ...?
But it seems like she don't know when yet.
Goin' out of her way to bring him home.
She's thinkin' marriage, eh?
YAY YAY
It's too soon! She's too young!!
Oh ho, Tsukasa's gettin' hitched?
No one's sayin' that, Mom !!

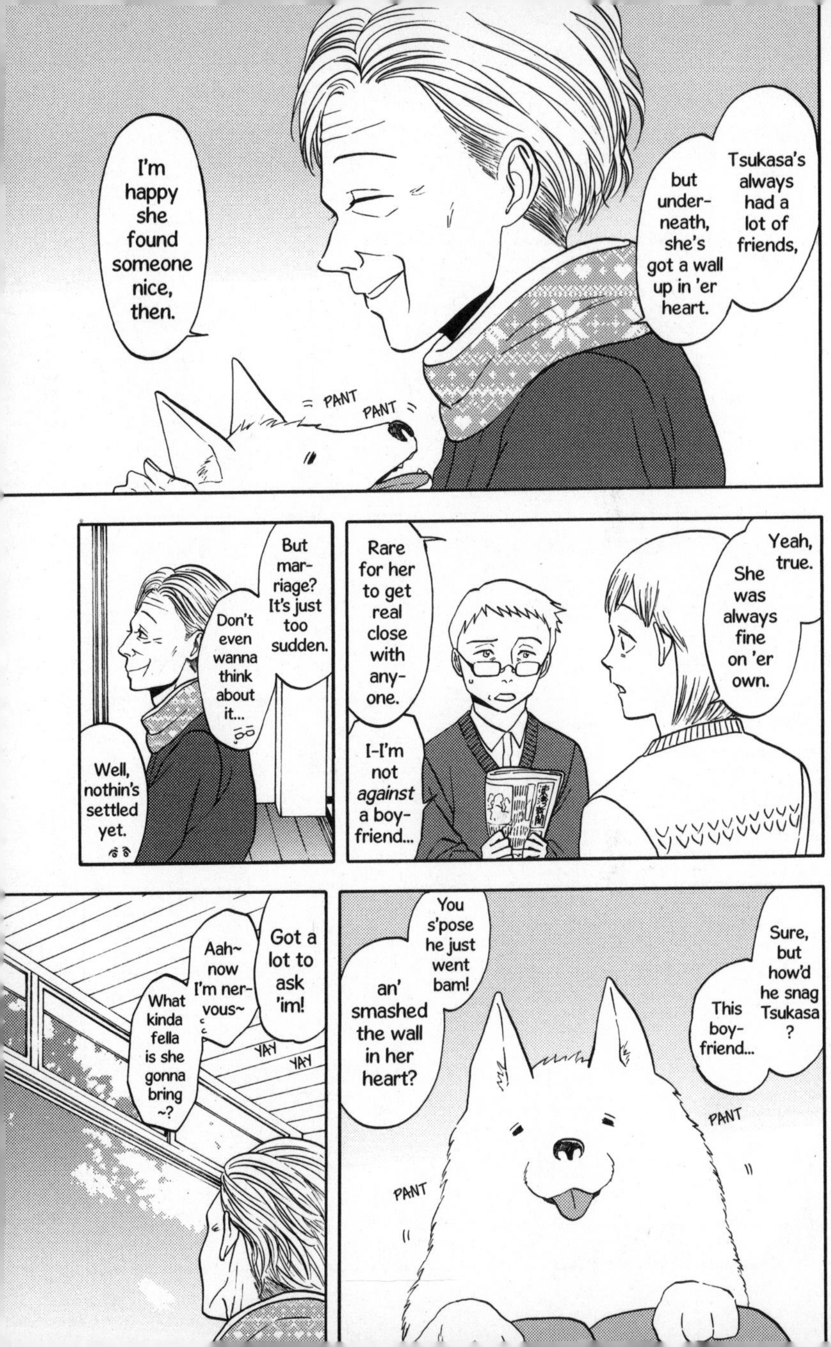
Tsukasa's always had a lot of friends,
but underneath, she's got a wall up in 'er heart.
I'm happy she found someone nice, then.
PANT
PANT
Yeah, true.
She was always fine on 'er own.
Rare for her to get real close with anyone.
I-I'm not *against* a boyfriend...
But marriage? It's just too sudden.
Don't even wanna think about it...
Well, nothin's settled yet.
Sure, but how'd he snag Tsukasa?
This boyfriend...
You s'pose he just went bam!
an' smashed the wall in her heart?
PANT
PANT
Got a lot to ask 'im!
Aah~ now I'm nervous~
What kinda fella is she gonna bring~?
YAY
YAY

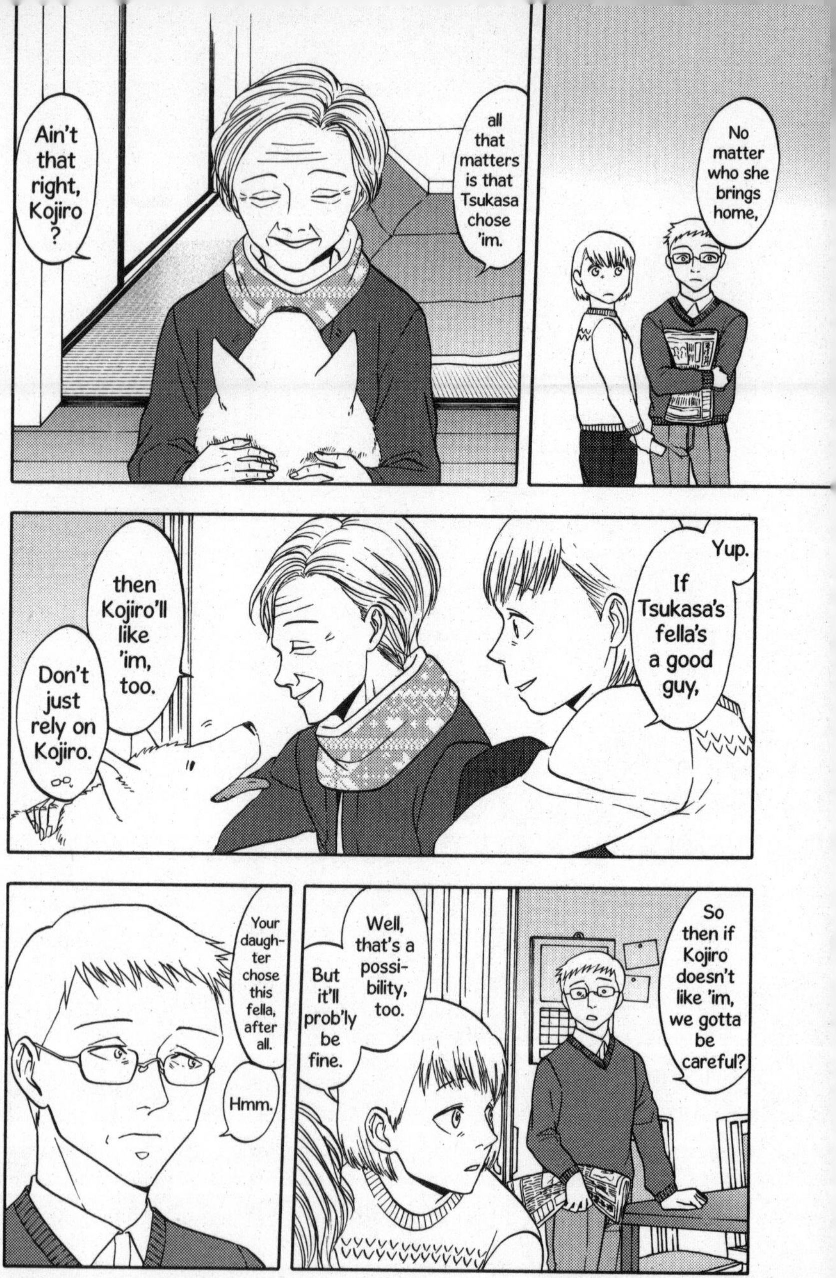
No matter who she brings home,
all that matters is that Tsukasa chose 'im.
Ain't that right, Kojiro?
Yup.
If Tsukasa's fella's a good guy,
then Kojiro'll like 'im, too.
Don't just rely on Kojiro.
So then if Kojiro doesn't like 'im, we gotta be careful?
Well, that's a possibility, too.
But it'll prob'ly be fine.
Your daugh-ter chose this fella, after all.
Hmm.

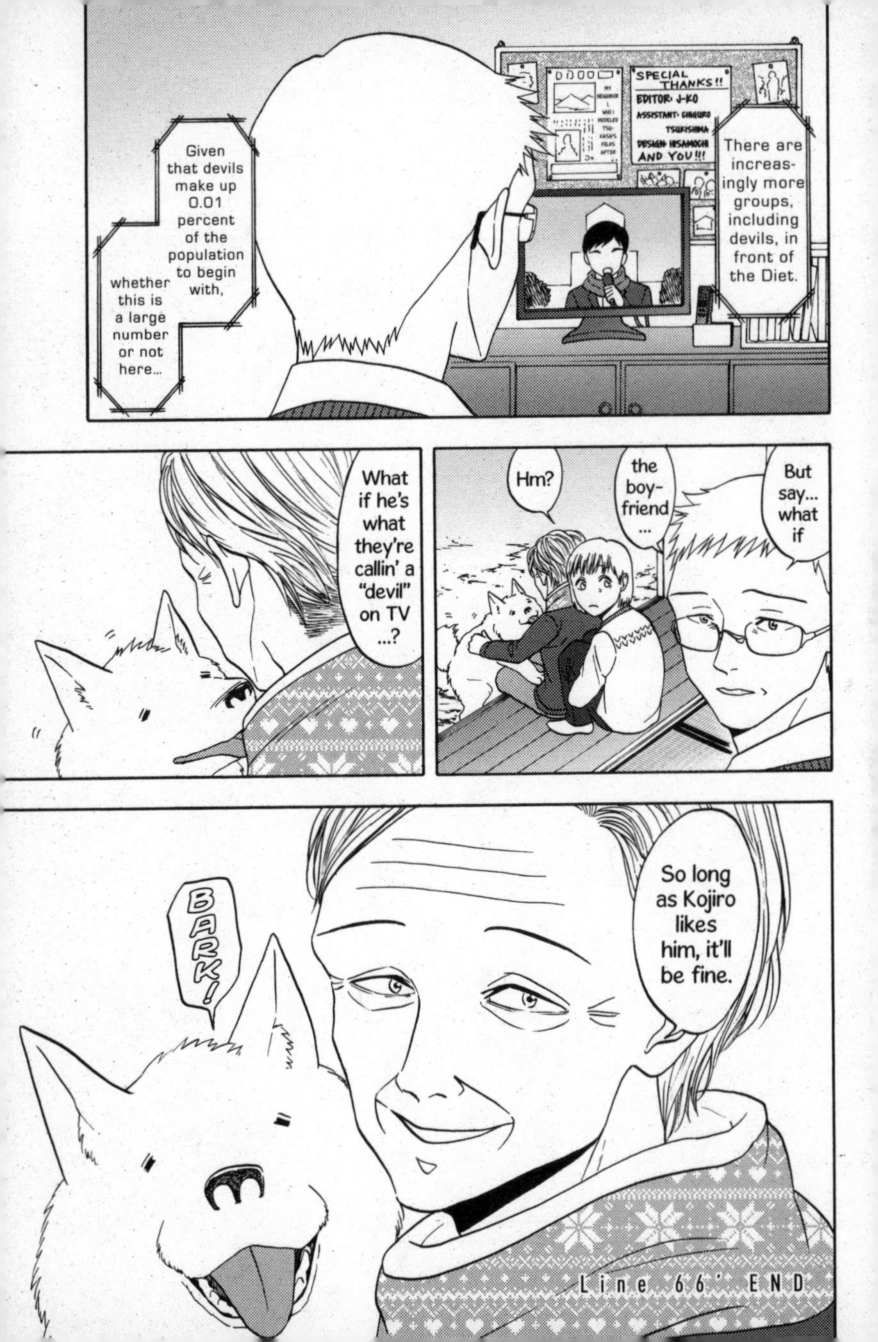
SPECIAL THANKS!!
EDITOR: J-KO
ASSISTANT: CHIGURO TSUKISHIMA
DESIGN: HISAMOCHI
AND YOU!!!
There are increasingly more groups, including devils, in front of the Diet.
Given that devils make up 0.01 percent of the population to begin with,
whether this is a large number or not here...
But say... what if
the boyfriend...
Hm?
What if he's what they're callin' a "devil" on TV ...?
So long as Kojiro likes him, it'll be fine.
BARK!
Line 66' END

QUESTIONS FOR EVERYONE

〈ANZAI〉

Q. What do you do on your days off?

A. I sleep or hang out with Tsukasa.

Q. What kind of books do you usually read?

A. I sometimes read new books Sawazaki lends me. Lots of non-fiction.

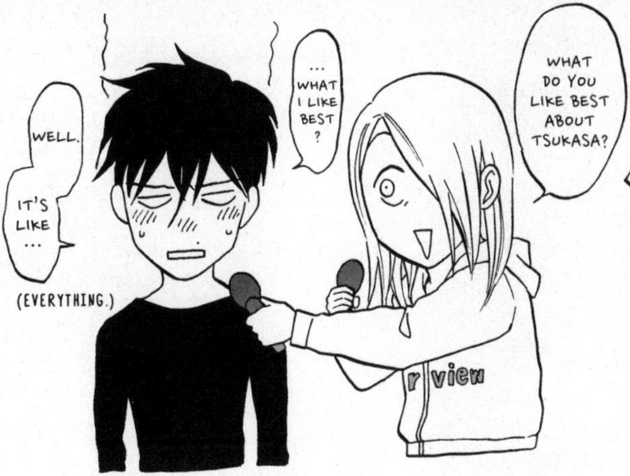
WHAT DO YOU LIKE BEST ABOUT TSUKASA?
... WHAT I LIKE BEST ?
WELL.
IT'S LIKE ...
(EVERYTHING.)
r view

〈TSUKASA〉

Q. What do you do for fun lately?

A. Seeing Anzai, research.

Q. What kind of music do you usually listen to?

A. I don't really listen to music, but I often end up liking the songs in commercials and things.

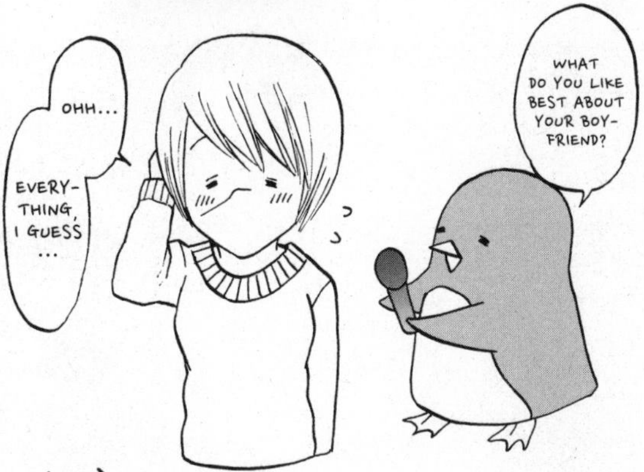
WHAT DO YOU LIKE BEST ABOUT YOUR BOY-FRIEND?
OHH...
EVERY-THING, I GUESS ...

〈MAYU〉

Q. What kind of person is Makimura?

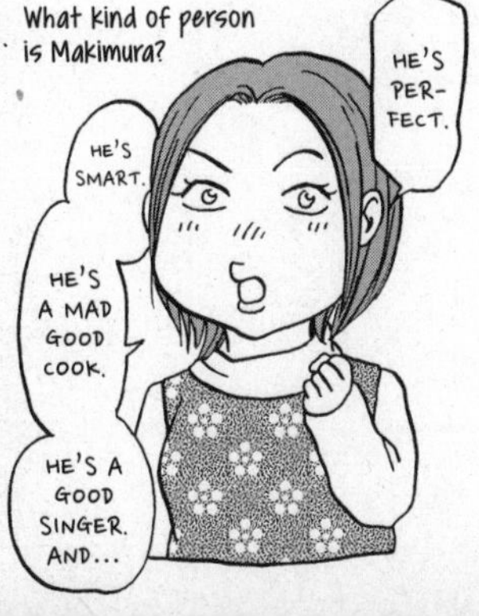
HE'S PER-FECT.
HE'S SMART.
HE'S A MAD GOOD COOK.
HE'S A GOOD SINGER. AND...

〈JILL〉

Q. Is there anything you'd like from Sawazaki?

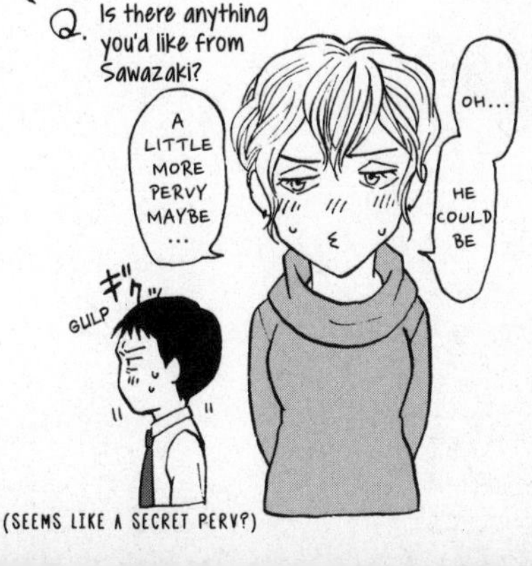
OH... HE COULD BE
A LITTLE MORE PERVY MAYBE ...
ギク
GULP
(SEEMS LIKE A SECRET PERV?)

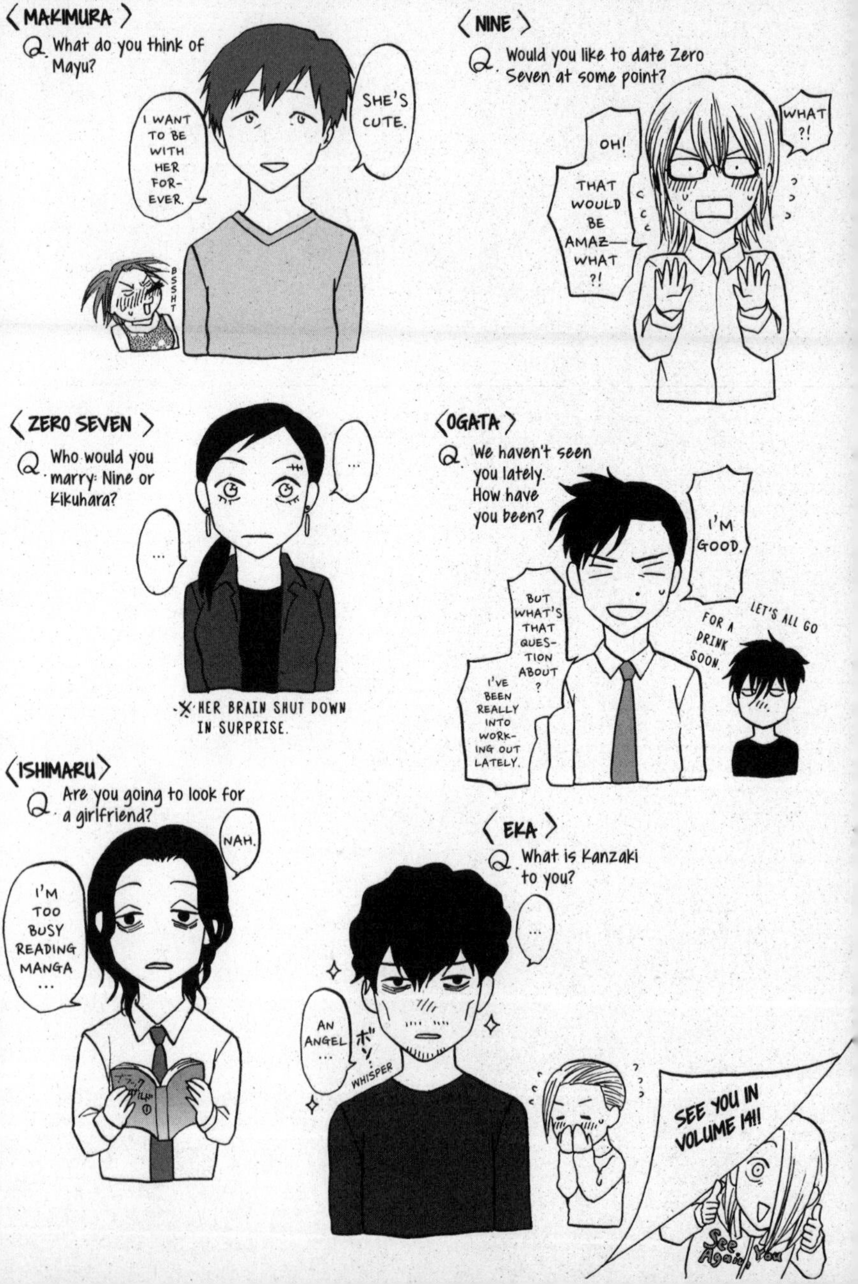

〈NINE〉
Q. Would you like to date Zero Seven at some point?
OH! THAT WOULD BE AMAZ—WHAT?!
WHAT?!
〈MAKIMURA〉
Q. What do you think of Mayu?
SHE'S CUTE.
I WANT TO BE WITH HER FOR-EVER.
BSSHT
〈OGATA〉
Q. We haven't seen you lately. How have you been?
I'M GOOD.
BUT WHAT'S THAT QUES-TION ABOUT?
I'VE BEEN REALLY INTO WORK-ING OUT LATELY.
LET'S ALL GO FOR A DRINK SOON.
〈ZERO SEVEN〉
Q. Who would you marry: Nine or Kikuhara?
...
...
※ HER BRAIN SHUT DOWN IN SURPRISE.
〈EKA〉
Q. What is Kanzaki to you?
...
AN ANGEL...
ボソ
WHISPER
SEE YOU IN VOLUME 14!!
See You Again
〈ISHIMARU〉
Q. Are you going to look for a girlfriend?
NAH.
I'M TOO BUSY READING MANGA...

NEXT VOLUME

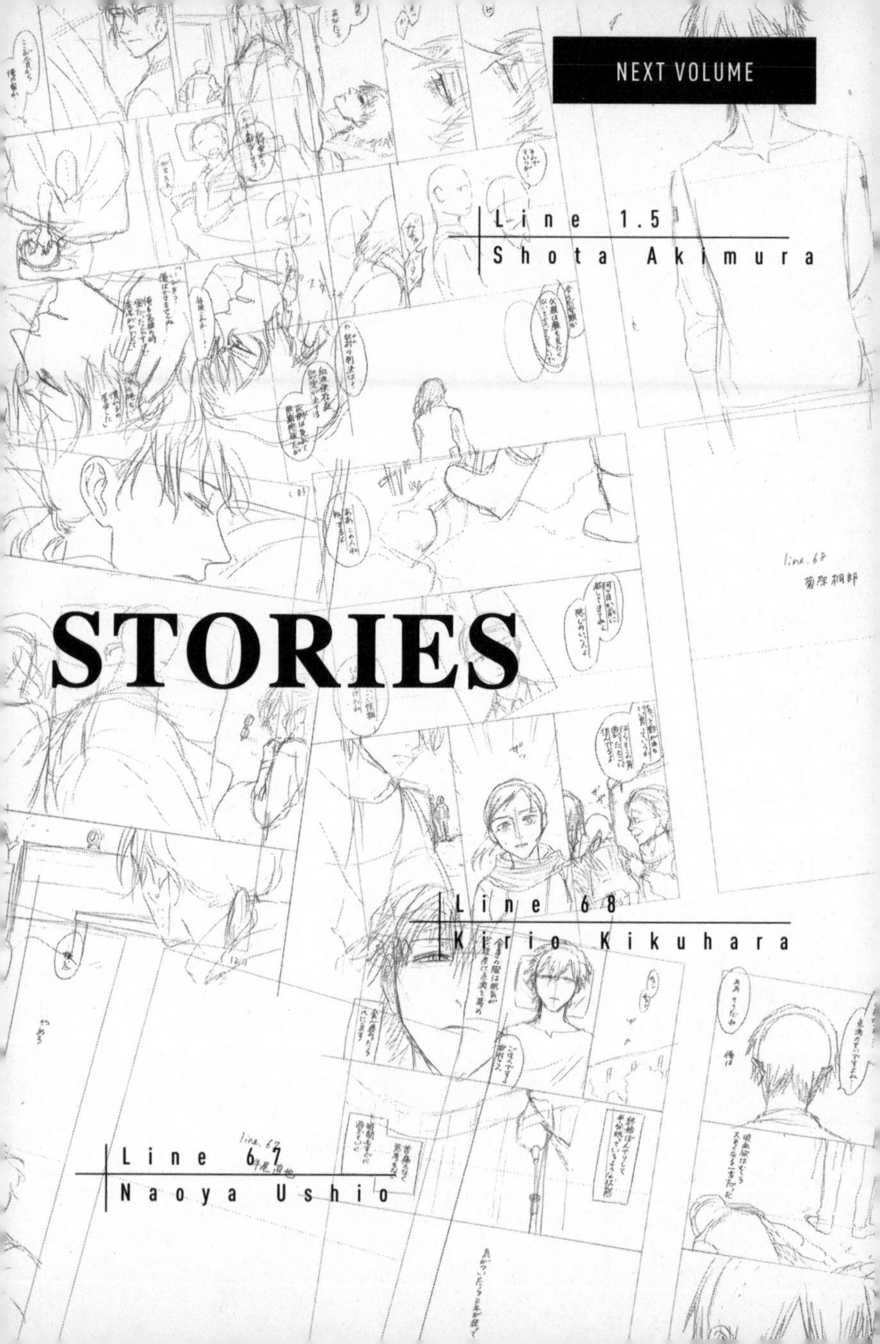

STORIES

Line 1.5
Shota Akimura

Line 68
Kirio Kikuhara

Line 67
Naoya Ushio

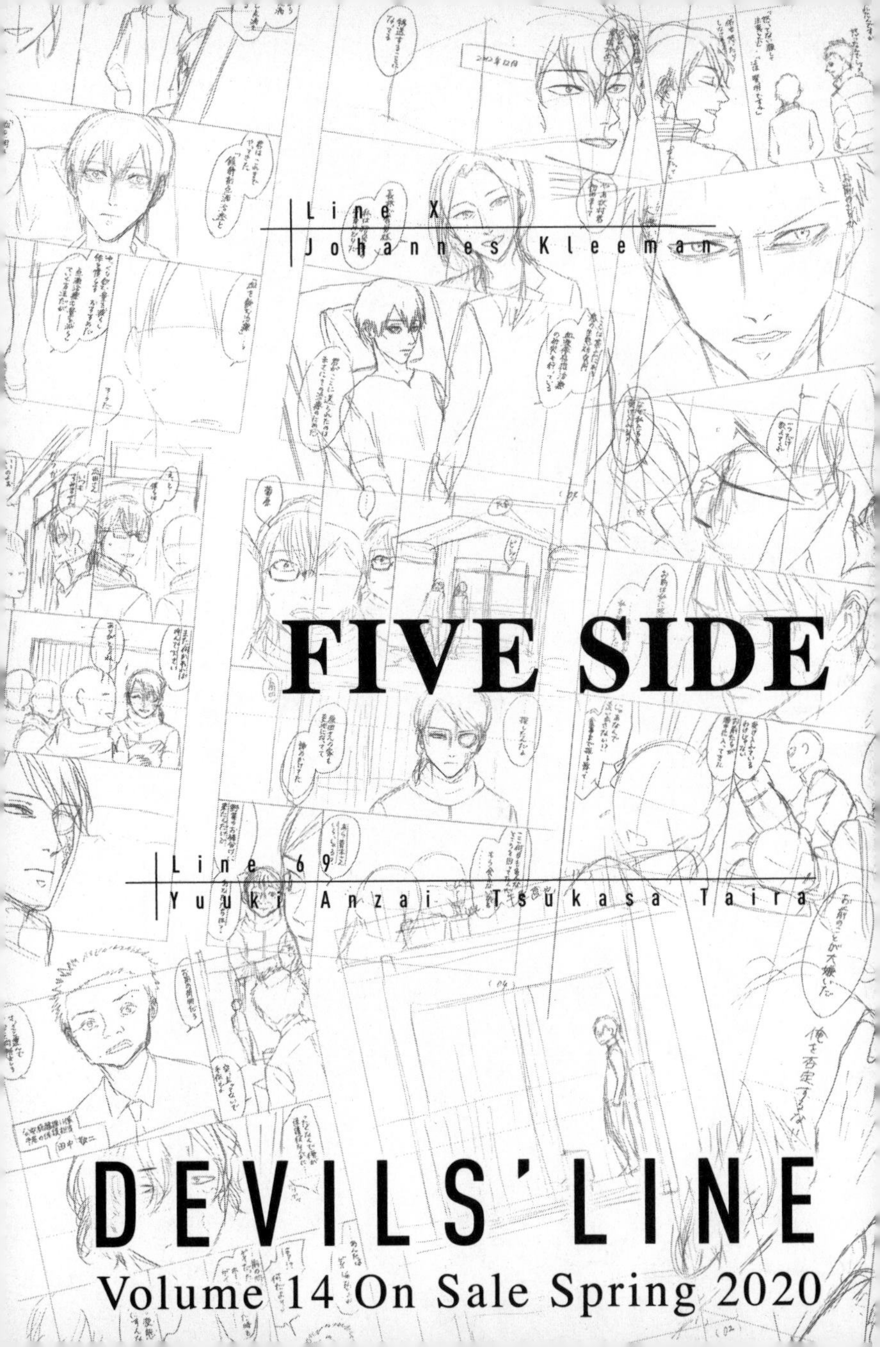

Line X
Johannes Kleeman

FIVE SIDE

Line 69
Yuuki Anzai Tsukasa Taira

DEVILS'LINE

Volume 14 On Sale Spring 2020

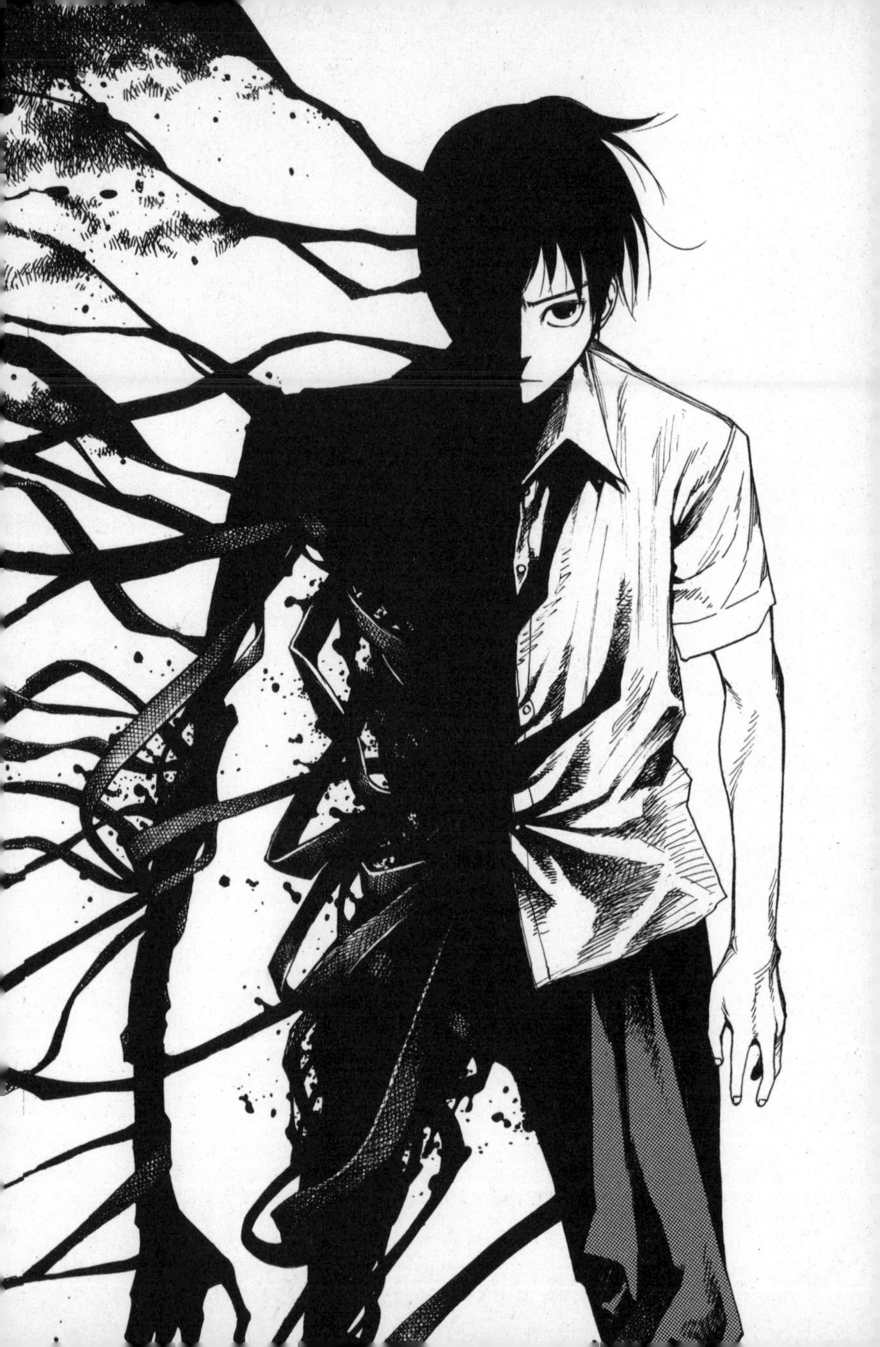

AJIN

DEMI-HUMAN

GAMON SAKURAI

SAY YOU GET HIT BY A TRUCK AND DIE.
YOU COME BACK TO LIFE. GOOD OR BAD?

FOR HIGH SCHOOLER KEI—AND FOR AT LEAST FORTY-SIX OTHERS—
IMMORTALITY COMES AS THE NASTIEST SURPRISE EVER.

SADLY FOR KEI, BUT REFRESHINGLY FOR THE READER, SUCH A FEAT
DOESN'T MAKE HIM A SUPERHERO. IN THE EYES OF BOTH THE GENERAL
PUBLIC AND GOVERNMENTS, HE'S A RARE SPECIMEN WHO NEEDS TO BE
HUNTED DOWN AND HANDED OVER TO SCIENTISTS TO BE EXPERIMENTED
ON FOR LIFE—A DEMI-HUMAN WHO MUST DIE A THOUSAND DEATHS
FOR THE BENEFIT OF HUMANITY.

VOLUMES 1-12 AVAILABLE NOW!

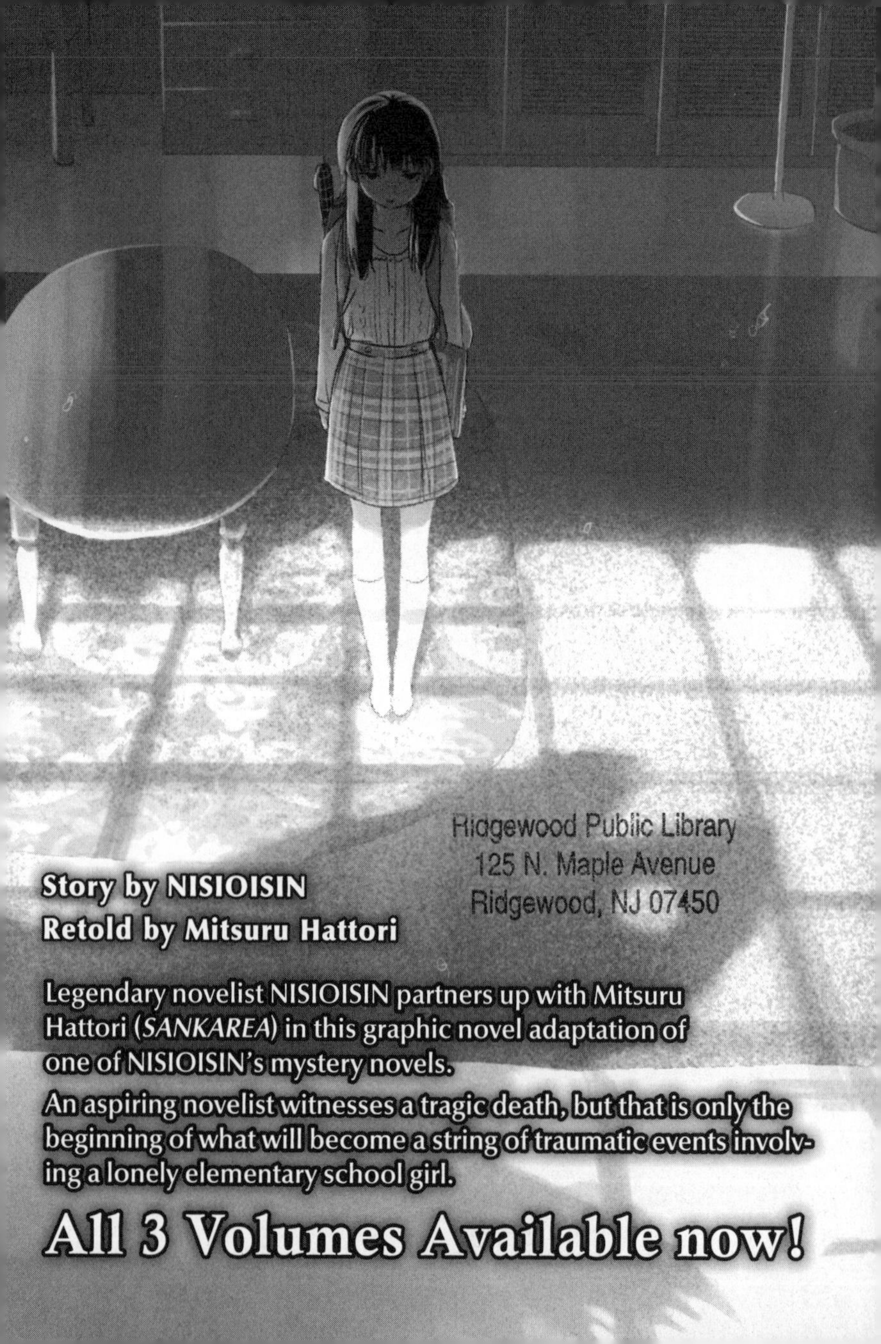
Story by NISIOISIN
Retold by Mitsuru Hattori
Legendary novelist NISIOISIN partners up with Mitsuru Hattori (*SANKAREA*) in this graphic novel adaptation of one of NISIOISIN's mystery novels.
An aspiring novelist witnesses a tragic death, but that is only the beginning of what will become a string of traumatic events involving a lonely elementary school girl.
All 3 Volumes Available now!

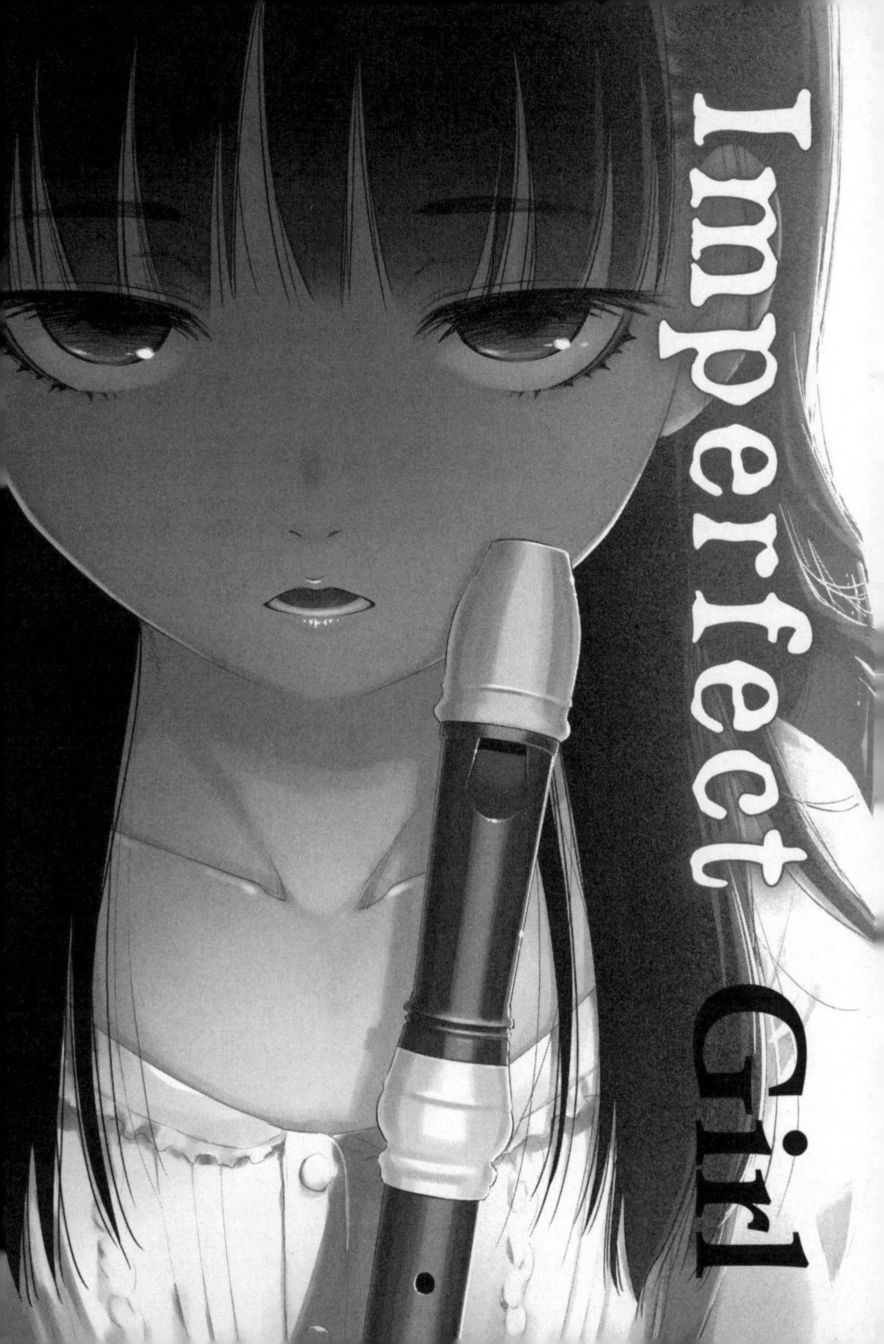
Imperfect Girl

DEVILS' LINE 13

A Vertical Comics Edition

Translation: Jocelyne Allen
Production: Risa Cho
Lorina Mapa

First published in Japan in 2019 by Kodansha, Ltd., Tokyo
Publication rights for this English edition arranged through Kodansha, Ltd., Tokyo
English language version produced by Vertical Comics, an imprint of Kodansha USA Publishing, LLC.

Translation provided by Vertical Comics, 2019
Published by Kodansha USA Publishing, LLC, New York

Originally published in Japanese as *Debiruzurain 13* by Kodansha, Ltd., 2019
Debiruzurain first serialized in *Morning two*, Kodansha, Ltd., 2013-2019

This is a work of fiction.

ISBN: 978-1-947194-63-2

Manufactured in the United States of America

First Edition

Kodansha USA Publishing, LLC.
451 Park Avenue South
7th Floor
New York, NY 10016
www.vertical-comics.com

Vertical books are distributed through Penguin-Random House Publisher Services.